Austronesian and Theoretical Linguistics

Linguistik Aktuell/Linguistics Today (LA)

Linguistik Aktuell/Linguistics Today (LA) provides a platform for original monograph studies into synchronic and diachronic linguistics. Studies in LA confront empirical and theoretical problems as these are currently discussed in syntax, semantics, morphology, phonology, and systematic pragmatics with the aim to establish robust empirical generalizations within a universalistic perspective.

General Editors

Werner Abraham
University of Vienna /
Rijksuniversiteit Groningen

Elly van Gelderen
Arizona State University

Advisory Editorial Board

Josef Bayer
University of Konstanz

Cedric Boeckx
ICREA/Universitat Autònoma de Barcelona

Guglielmo Cinque
University of Venice

Liliane Haegeman
University of Ghent

Hubert Haider
University of Salzburg

Terje Lohndal
University of Maryland

Christer Platzack
University of Lund

Ian Roberts
Cambridge University

Lisa deMena Travis
McGill University

Sten Vikner
University of Aarhus

C. Jan-Wouter Zwart
University of Groningen

Volume 167

Austronesian and Theoretical Linguistics
Edited by Raphael Mercado, Eric Potsdam and Lisa deMena Travis

Austronesian and Theoretical Linguistics

Edited by

Raphael Mercado
McGill University

Eric Potsdam
University of Florida

Lisa deMena Travis
McGill University

John Benjamins Publishing Company
Amsterdam / Philadelphia

The paper used in this publication meets the minimum requirements of American National Standard for Information Sciences – Permanence of Paper for Printed Library Materials, ANSI z39.48-1984.

Library of Congress Cataloging-in-Publication Data

Austronesian and theoretical linguistics / edited by Raphael Mercado, Eric Potsdam and Lisa deMena Travis.
     p.   cm. (Linguistik Aktuell/Linguistics Today, ISSN 0166-0829 ; v. 167)
"The papers presented within this volume were selected from the fourteenth meeting of the Austronesian Formal Linguistics Association (AFLA XIV), held May 4-6, 2007 at McGill University in Montreal, Quebec, Canada."
Includes bibliographical references and index.
     1. Austronesian languages--Congresses. I. Mercado, Raphael. II. Potsdam, Eric, 1964- III. Travis, Lisa deMena.
PL5022.A96   2010
499'.2--dc22   2010028219
ISBN 978 90 272 5550 1   (Hb ; alk. paper)
ISBN 978 90 272 8775 5   (Eb)

© 2010 – John Benjamins B.V.
No part of this book may be reproduced in any form, by print, photoprint, microfilm, or any other means, without written permission from the publisher.

John Benjamins Publishing Co. · P.O. Box 36224 · 1020 ME Amsterdam · The Netherlands
John Benjamins North America · P.O. Box 27519 · Philadelphia PA 19118-0519 · USA

Table of contents

Acknowledgements	VII
Introduction	1

Phonetics/Phonology/Morphology

The role of larynx height in the Javanese tense ~ lax stop contrast *Marc Brunelle*	7
Reduplication in Tanjung Raden Malay *Yanti and Eric Raimy*	25
Discontiguous reduplication in a local variety of Malay *Justin Nuger*	45
Phonological evidence for the structure of Javanese compounds *Katrina Schack Tang*	65
Intonation, information structure and the derivation of inverse VO languages *Mara Frascarelli*	81

Syntax

The case of possessors and 'subjects' *Cathryn Donohue and Mark Donohue*	103
Genitive relative constructions and agent incorporation in Tongan *Yuko Otsuka*	117
Possession syntax in Unua DPs *Elizabeth Pearce*	141
Seediq adverbial verbs: A review of the evidence *Arthur Holmer*	163
On the syntax of Formosan adverbial verb constructions *Henry Y. Chang*	183
Specification and inversion: Evidence from Malagasy *Ileana Paul*	213
VSO word order in Malagasy imperatives *Eric Potsdam*	231

A unified analysis of Niuean *Aki* Douglas Ball	249
Deriving inverse order: The issue of arguments Diane Massam	271
The impersonal construction in Tagalog Paul Law	297
Anaphora in traditional Jambi Malay Peter Cole, Gabriella Hermon and Yanti	327
On parameters of agreement in Austronesian languages Mark C. Baker	345
Index	375

Acknowledgements

In May of 2007 McGill University hosted the 14th Meeting of the Austronesian Formal Linguistics Association (AFLA). We would like to express our gratitude to all those who were involved in the conference and resulting selected proceedings. The conference was generously funded by the Social Sciences and Humanities Research Council of Canada, the Linguistics Department at McGill University, and the Taipei Economic and Cultural Office. We gratefully thank the students at McGill University, (Alyona Belikova, Gustavo Beritognolo, Jarren Bodily, Heather Burnett, Eva Dobler, Deena Fogle, Blakey Larsen, Luisa Meroni, Joey Sabbagh, Michelle St-Amour, Tobin Skinner, Naoko Tomioka, Athanasios Tsiamas and Jozina Vander Klok), Ezra Van Everbroek of Pasha, the abstract reviewers, and the conference participants, who all helped to make the conference such a success. We also wish to take this opportunity to thank the Theoretical and Applied Linguistics Laboratory at the University of Western Ontario, which hosts the permanent website for AFLA at http://westernlinguistics.ca/afla/index.html.

These papers represent the selected proceedings of AFLA XIV. The editors were helped in their jobs by Joey Sabbagh, Tobin Skinner, and Mona Luiza Ungureanu. We thank them for the excellent assistance they provided during various phases of the editing process, from review to final formatting. Each paper submitted to the proceedings was evaluated by at least two anonymous reviewers who were specialists in both Austronesian languages and formal linguistics. We thank them for their time and expertise in evaluating the papers. Finally, we thank Elly van Gelderen and Kees Vaes at John Benjamins for approaching us with the idea for this collection of papers.

Introduction

The papers presented within this volume were selected from the fourteenth meeting of the Austronesian Formal Linguistics Association (AFLA XIV), held May 4–6, 2007 at McGill University in Montreal, Quebec, Canada. AFLA was created in 1994 by five researchers who met for an informal workshop at the University of Toronto. The original objective was to provide a forum where researchers working on Austronesian languages within the context of generative linguistic theories could present and get feedback on their ideas.

Since 1994, AFLA has continued to meet annually and has been hosted by universities in Asia, Europe, and Australia as well as Canada and the United States. The size of the conference has grown considerably as has the range of topics. The first AFLA had five papers on the morpho-syntax of Malagasy, Tagalog, and Niuean. In more recent years, the scope of the papers has expanded to include semantics and phonology and other branches of the language family, notably the Formosan languages.

AFLA XIV had two specific goals. One was to continue the trend of broadening the scope of the papers by including more phonology papers and highlighting the contribution of research on the Formosan languages. The other goal was to encourage comparative research at two levels – within the language family (microvariation) and outside the language family (macrovariation). The papers in this volume reflect these goals.

The papers

The volume includes five phonology papers and twelve syntax papers. The five phonology papers present a range of topics from articulatory phonetics to syntactically informed prosody. **Brunelle's** paper describes how laryngoscopic information can provide insight into the articulation mechanisms of the tense/lax distinction in Javanese. He shows that there is relative lowering of the larynx in lax stops. Two of the phonology papers provide accounts for reduplication patterns. **Yanti and Raimy** show how Precedence Based Phonology can account for nine reduplication patterns found in Tanjung Raden Malay. **Nuger**, investigating discontiguous reduplication in Ulu Muar Malay, proposes that the patterns are best characterized not by edge anchoring but rather by a prosodic correspondence constraint. The last two phonology papers investigate problems of the syntax/phonology interface. **Tang** argues that the cyclic spell-out of syntactic domains that are input to the phonological component accounts for the pattern of vowel raising as it differs with compounds and phrases in Javanese. **Frascarelli** argues that intonational patterns in Malagasy and Tagalog support proposals that the V initial word order in these languages is derived by phrasal movement rather than by head movement.

Among the syntax papers, three discuss possessive constructions. **Donohue and Donohue** survey a range of Austronesian languages and argue that an analysis where possessors are treated as subjects of DPs cannot account for the variation found in these languages. **Otsuka** investigates a particular Tongan construction where the external argument of a relative clause is realized as a possessor on the head noun. She argues that this genitive is base-generated in the Spec, DP position and interpreted in the relative clause through pragmatics. **Pearce** discusses direct and indirect possession in Unua-Pangkumu and concludes that the indirect possessor is generated higher in the DP than the direct possessor.

Two syntax papers discuss the problem of adverbial predicates in Formosan languages. **Holmer** proposes that Seediq adverbial constructions are best captured as adverbial heads along the extended projection of the verb. **Chang**, surveying a range of Formosan languages, argues that the adverbial heads have both lexical and functional characteristics.

Two papers provide an in depth analysis of particular Malagasy constructions. **Paul** probes details of the *dia* specificational construction and argues that it is an inversion structure transposing the predicate and the topic. **Potsdam** investigates the imperative structure in Malagasy and argues that the unusual positioning of the apparent subject receives an explanation once one understands that this DP is a vocative rather than a subject.

Two papers discuss the realization of arguments in Niue. **Ball** focuses on the problem of instrumentals and *aki*, the predicate that introduces them in two different constructions. He uses the HPSG notion of 'argument composition' to account for the differences in these two *aki* constructions. **Massam** discusses the more general problem of accounting for the position of arguments in Niue. She observes that a roll-up analysis of phrase structure in Niue can account for the order of adverbial expressions but not arguments. As a solution, she suggests that arguments are merged outside of the VP and are introduced by higher functional heads.

Law examines the structure of impersonal constructions in Tagalog and proposes that these constructions are basically the same as existential constructions and possessive constructions in Tagalog. **Cole, Hermon, and Yanti** examine the binding facts of Jambi Malay and conclude that coreference is not determined by grammatical principles but rather by pragmatic considerations.

Finally, **Baker** investigates two macroparameters that account for agreement patterns crosslinguistically. In his study of these two parameters within the Austronesian language family, he observes that Austronesian languages show similar patterns of variation as Niger-Congo and Indo-European languages.

The papers presented here have an obvious common denominator – the language family under investigation. However, in terms of theoretical content, they represent a wide range of subjects that, nevertheless, contain recurring themes.

Themes

Conferences devoted to language families are expected to produce certain types of results. Often papers include new data, new analyses of old data, comparisons of closely related languages and speculations as to language change. Many of the papers of this volume have such contributions.

New data and new analyses

As is expected with papers devoted to an under-documented language family, many present new data. Cole, Hermon, and Yanti provide detailed data sets of binding facts in Jambi Malay. Pearce's paper introduces new data from possessive constructions in Unua-Pangkumu, Otsuka from Genitive Relative constructions in Tongan, Potsdam from imperative constructions in Malagasy, and Paul from specificational structures in Malagasy. Tang presents phonological data from compounds in Javanese, Yanti and Raimy give six additional reduplication patterns from Malay, and Frascarelli describes prosodic data from Malagasy and Tagalog.

Other papers provide new analyses for previously reported data. For example Nuger's paper proposes a different account of discontiguous reduplication in Ulu Muar Malay, Ball's paper offers an HPSG account for *aki* constructions in Niuean, and Brunelle reanalyzes a laryngoscopic video of Javanese stop articulation made in 1994.

Language variation and language change

A conference devoted to a language family is also expected to provide comparisons among related languages. Work of this type has become increasingly important as the interest in microvariation and microparameters has developed. Chang discusses the range of variation in adverbial constructions in Formosan languages. Otsuka shows how Genitive Relatives in Tongan differ from other Eastern Polynesian languages. Donohue and Donohue discuss differences in the realization of possessors across Austronesian languages.

The comparison of closely related language often leads to diachronic speculations and several papers have proposed possible paths of language development. Cole, Hermon, and Yanti suggest that the type of pragmatically controlled binding patterns that they find in Jambi Malay might lead to a grammaticalization of binding and a system of coreference similar to that found in languages like English. Holmer suggests that positioning of clitics following the first element of a sentence might lead to reanalyzing the clitic as verbal morphology and the first element as a verb. Yanti and Raimy, in the domain of phonology, point out that ambiguities in the structure of the reduplicating element could lead to innovative reduplication patterns.

Theories and theoretical constructs

As its name suggests, AFLA emphasizes not only data work but also theoretical work. The papers show a diversity of theories but also some common interest in particular theoretical constructs. While most of the syntax papers are written within the Minimalist program of Chomsky (1995), Ball works within the HPSG framework (Pollard & Sag 1994) and Donohue & Donohue use Lexical Decomposition Grammar (Wunderlich 1997, Kiparsky 2001). Within the Minimalist papers, several issues recur. Pearce and Massam both crucially use predicate fronting to account for word order while Frascarelli uses predicate fronting to account for prosody. Tang and Frascarelli both rely on cyclic spell-out of phases at the PF interface to account for phonological phenomena.

Looking inward and outward

Conferences and associations that are centered around a specific language family run the risk of become insular. While it is comfortable to present material to an audience that has a certain familiarity with the data and the issues, it is crucial that the results of this research eventually reach a wider audience.

One step in the direction of communication beyond the boundaries is to relate the discoveries within the language family to similar facts in unrelated languages. Many of the papers in this volume do exactly this. Cole, Hermon, and Yanti compare the binding facts of Jambi Malay, Tuvaluan, and Madurese to the binding facts of languages such as English. Frascarelli contrasts the intonation in inverse (predicate fronting) VO languages like Malagasy and Tagalog with a direct (V-movement) VO language like Italian. Holmer discusses languages as diverse as Hebrew, Scottish Gaelic, Nootka, Car Nicobarese, Choapan Zapotec, Finnish and Estonian. Baker brings to his work on Austronesian, a macroparameter devised for Indo-European languages and Niger-Congo languages. Discussing a wide variety of languages outside of the Austronesian language family (Kilega, Zulu, Swahili, Kinande, Spanish, Welsh, Icelandic, Hindi, Burushanski, Georgian), he shows that the parameters that are relevant for these languages also predict a clustering of characteristics in Austronesian languages.

The other step is to bring the findings of the conference to the attention of the larger linguistics community. It is with this goal in mind that we have gathered these papers and created this volume.

References

Chomsky, N. 1995. *The Minimalist Program*. Cambridge MA: The MIT Press.
Kiparsky, P. 2001. Structural Case in Finnish. *Lingua* 111: 315–376.
Pollard, C.J. & Sag, I.A. 1994. *Head-Driven Phrase Structure Grammar*. Chicago IL: University of Chicago Press.
Wunderlich, D. 1997. Cause and the structure of verbs. *Linguistic Inquiry* 28: 27–68.

PHONETICS/PHONOLOGY/MORPHOLOGY

The role of larynx height in the Javanese tense ~ lax stop contrast*

Marc Brunelle
University of Ottawa

> Javanese has a phonemic contrast between two series of stops. Tense stops are modern reflexes of Proto-Austronesian voiceless stops while lax stops correspond to former voiced stops. This complex contrast includes acoustic properties such as pitch, voice quality, vowel quality and VOT. Although different acoustic studies have yielded similar results, there is still disagreement over the type of articulatory mechanism(s) responsible for the tense~lax opposition. In this study, a laryngoscopic video of two Javanese speakers recorded by Katrina Hayward in 1994 is reanalyzed to determine if vertical laryngeal position is playing a role in the Javanese stop contrast. Results reveal a consistent lowering of the larynx during lax stops, suggesting similarities with Mainland Southeast Asian register.

In Javanese, stop voicing was lost in all positions, except after nasals. It was replaced by a contrast between plain voiceless stops and a series of voiceless stops associated with a low pitch, a long voice onset time (VOT), a breathy voice quality and relatively high vowels. A few minimal pairs are given in (1), where reflexes of original voiced stops are marked with a subscript dot.

(1) /paku/ 'nail' /p̣aku/ 'standard'
    /pipi/ 'cheek' /p̣ipi/ 'aunt'
    /kali/ 'river' /ḳali/ 'to dig'

Since this opposition is acoustically subtle, it has been successively described as a contrast between unaspirated and aspirated stops (Samsuri 1958), voiceless unaspirated and voiced aspirated stops (Poedjosoedarmo 1974), light and heavy stops (Horne 1974; Fagan 1988), tense and lax stops (Hayward 1993; 1995), clear vs. breathy stops (Adisasmito-Smith 2004) and stiff vs. slack stops (Ladefoged & Maddieson 1996).

---

* Many thanks to Reza Falahati for processing the data and to Ricardo Tabone for preparing the MATLAB scripts used in this experiment.

Thanks to experimental work conducted since the late 1980s, the acoustic properties that make up the contrast have now been established more objectively. They are reviewed in Section 1, together with the articulatory mechanisms that may be responsible for their production. A study of one of these articulatory mechanisms – the vertical position of the larynx – is then presented in Sections 2 and 3, showing that this articulatory dimension can play an important role in the production of the contrast. Finally, similarities between the tense~lax contrast and Southeast Asian register and their implication for phonological theory is discussed in Section 4. Note that we arbitrarily use the labels tense and lax to designate the two series of Javanese stops. The tense stops are the modern reflexes of proto-Austronesian voiceless stops while the lax stops are the reflexes of former voiced stops.

1. Previous phonetic studies of the tense ~ lax contrast

Overall, acoustic investigations of the tense~lax contrast yield similar results, despite small idiosyncratic differences among subjects. It is now well established that the contrast is realized through a set of pitch, voice quality and vowel quality distinctions that are reviewed in Section 1.1. What is less well understood is how these acoustic properties are articulated. The most common hypotheses are discussed in Section 1.2.

1.1 Acoustic properties

Acoustic studies of the Javanese tense~lax stop contrast consistently show that it is realized through minor differences in pitch, voice quality, VOT and vowel quality, with a certain amount of variation among speakers. Pitch tends to be higher after tense than lax stops (Fagan 1988; Hayward 1993; 1995; Adisasmito-Smith 2004; Thurgood 2004), but this difference is not found in all speakers (Adisasmito-Smith 2004; Thurgood 2004). Voice quality differences, on the other hand, are more systematic. All studies looking into this question find a steeper spectral slope (i.e. a breathier voice quality) after lax stops than tense stops (Hayward 1993; 1995; Adisasmito-Smith 2004). Fagan (1988) also finds a systematically longer VOT after lax stops, which is likely caused by the same articulatory mechanisms as voice quality (other studies do not investigate this question). Finally, vowel quality is also a correlate of the contrast, although this needs to be qualified. While F1 is systematically lower after lax stops than after tense stops (Fagan 1988; Hayward 1993; 1995; Thurgood 2004), F2 differences seem more variable and depend on the vowel under investigation. In short, the tense~lax contrast seems to be systematically realized through minor voice quality and VOT distinctions, accompanied by more variable pitch and vowel quality differences.

(2) Summary of the acoustic properties of the tense~lax stop contrast

Tense stops	Lax stops
Short VOT	Long VOT
Higher pitch on foll. vowel	*Lower pitch on foll. vowel*
Following vowel is modal	Following vowel is breathy
Foll. vowel has a higher F1	Foll. vowel has a lower F1

1.2 Possible articulatory mechanisms

Three types of articulatory mechanisms have been proposed to account for these acoustic properties: The position of the tongue-root, the opening of the glottis and the vertical position of the larynx. Poedjosoedarmo (1986) first suggests that the contrast could be caused by the position of the tongue-root, following a proposal developed by Gregerson (1973) for acoustically similar types of oppositions in Mainland Southeast Asian languages. Her claim is that the tongue-root is fronted during the production of lax stops (Poedjosoedarmo 1986). However, this hypothesis has proven to be too restrictive: While the position of the tongue-root explains the differences in vowel quality (as the tongue tip moves along with the tongue root), it fails to account for differences in voice quality, VOT and pitch.

Other authors have therefore proposed that Javanese lax stops are produced with a relatively open glottis (Hayward 1995; Ladefoged & Maddieson 1996; Adisasmito-Smith 2004; Dresser 2005). This approach is more fruitful because it can account for pitch, voice quality and VOT differences. Glottal opening is not only generally involved in the production of breathiness and VOT, but it also accounts for the low pitch associated with the lax stops because the vocal folds vibrate more slowly when the glottis is open. However, it cannot by itself account for the F1 differences in the vowels following the two series of stops as it has no known relationship to formant frequencies.

For this reason, a third articulatory mechanism, larynx height, has been proposed to account for the tense~lax contrast (Catford 1964, Fagan 1988, Hayward 1993). Larynx height can produce by itself most of the acoustic properties of the tense~lax stop contrast, even if other mechanisms may also be involved. Since this articulation is discussed in detail in Sections 2 and 3, we now review its acoustic effects.

The first acoustic property that can be attributed to differences in larynx height is a change in formant frequencies (vowel quality). The effect of vertical laryngeal position on formant frequencies is often overlooked because tongue position is typically the main predictor of vowel quality differences. However, vertical laryngeal position affects the length of the vocal tract, a dimension that has long been recognized as a central factor in determining formant frequencies (Crandall 1925; Chiba & Kajiyama 1941). Since lengthening the vocal tract tends to lower formants, a low larynx is associated with lower formants. This effect is especially pronounced for F1, which is largely dependent on the size of the cavity between the glottis and the point of maximum constriction between the tongue and the palate. The relatively low F1 of the vowels following lax stops, which makes these vowels sound more closed than their tense stop counterparts, may thus be attributed to a low larynx. In fact, this mechanism has already been proposed to explain the minor vowel quality differences found in vowels following tense and lax stops in Javanese (Fagan 1988; Ladefoged & Maddieson 1996; Thurgood 2004).

Another acoustic property of the Javanese stop contrast that can be accounted for by larynx height movement is pitch. The association between raised larynx and high pitch and lowered larynx and low pitch has been discussed by many authors as early as the first half of the 20th century (see Honda, Hirai et al. 1999 for a discussion of early research), but the effect of the action of the extrinsic laryngeals muscles, which raise and lower the larynx, on the vocal folds is difficult to model in the absence of good imaging techniques. Fortunately, a recent MRI study by a team of Japanese researchers sheds light on the biomechanical underpinnings of the correlation between pitch and larynx height (Honda, Hirai et al. 1999). The effect of the vertical position of the larynx on pitch seems to be largely due to the anterior convexity of the spine at the level of the larynx. As the larynx moves up and down, it also rotates on the front-back axis, which has the effect of modifying the angle between the cricoid and thyroid cartilages. Since the extremities of the vocal folds are attached to these two cartilages, any change in their relative position has an effect on the degree of stretching of the vocal folds. This is illustrated in Figure 1, where we can clearly see that the vocal folds are shorter when the larynx is low than when it is raised (all other things being equal). A low larynx indirectly results in slack vocal folds, which vibrate more slowly and yield a lower pitch than more stretched vocal folds.

The breathy voice quality and the longer VOT that are usually found after lax stops are more difficult to explain through larynx height. The only explanation proposed so far in the literature is a speculative relaxation of the suprahyoid muscles during larynx lowering (Laver 1980). However, there may be a more mechanical explanation: First,

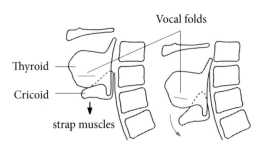

Figure 1. The effect of vertical laryngeal position on vocal fold length (reproduced from Honda, Hirai et al. 1999)

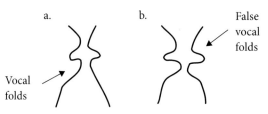

Figure 2. Effect of larynx height on the vertical tension of the vocal folds (reproduced from Arnold 1961)

a lowering of the larynx results in increased subglottal pressure. Second, larynx lowering also has a direct effect on the setting of the vocal folds, as shown in Figure 2. While the vocal folds are almost touching when the larynx is in default position (2b), they stretch vertically when the larynx is pulled down (2a), which reduces the degree of contact between them. Together, these two mechanisms can facilitate a leakage of the air contained in the subglottal cavity through the glottis. Since the glottis is opened during the production of voiceless stops (recall that lax stops are normally voiceless), this high transglottal airflow does not affect lax stops themselves, but rather, it delays the onset of voicing and drags on onto the beginning of the following vowel, resulting in breathiness.

Larynx height is therefore a good candidate to explain the main three acoustic properties of the Javanese tense~lax stop contrast, even if it is not the only articulatory mechanism involved in it. It is also a plausible articulatory mechanism from a diachronic perspective. We know that a low larynx position favours stop voicing by increasing transglottal pressure (Westbury & Keating 1986)[1]. Since Javanese lax stops are the modern reflexes of Proto-Malayo-Polynesian voiced stops, it is possible that a lowering of the larynx originally meant to favour voicing has been preserved in lax stops after the loss of the voicing contrast.

However, at this point, the role of larynx height is still speculative. In the next two sections, we present an experiment, based on a laryngoscopic video made by Katrina Hayward et al. (1994), which shows that there is indeed a difference in larynx height between the two series of Javanese stops.

2. Methods

A laryngoscopic movie made by a team led by Katrina Hayward in 1994 (Hayward, Grafield-Davies et al. 1994) has been processed and measured to quantify larynx height during the production of tense and lax stops. In this section, we describe the

---

1. However, a lowered larynx does not automatically result in voicing. An abduction of the glottis or a stiffening of the vocal folds can prevent vocal fold vibrations, even if the larynx is low.

laryngoscopic video (2.1), present the assumptions and techniques used to make the measurements and underline their potential limits (2.2) and review the data processing procedure (2.3).

2.1 The video

The experiment consists of a reanalysis of a laryngoscopic movie made in Java by Katrina Hayward and her team in 1994 (Hayward, Grafield-Davies et al. 1994). The speakers whose larynges had been filmed in the movie are a male subject and a female subject from the Yogyakarta area. In order to make the video, a beam of fiberoptic had been inserted through their nasal cavities, as shown in Figure 3. One end of the beam was positioned in the pharynx, while the other end was attached to a camera located outside the vocal tract. Hayward's video was shot at a rate of 25 images per second.

Hayward's subjects were asked to read successively six repetitions of 20 near-minimal pairs contrasting in the presence of tense and lax stops. These minimal pairs included at least two instances of words with each stop preceding the vowel /i/ (see the wordlist in the Appendix). The words were not read in a frame sentence, but were occasionally preceded by a function word to facilitate fluency. In the current experiment, only the first 10 minimal pairs, in which the stops are not prenasalized, are analyzed.

2.2 Measurements made on the video

The only established technique for measuring vertical laryngeal displacement is the thyroumbrometer (Ewan and Krones 1974; Ewan 1979), but this instrument is unfortunately no longer available. A four-electrode electroglottograph, like the model

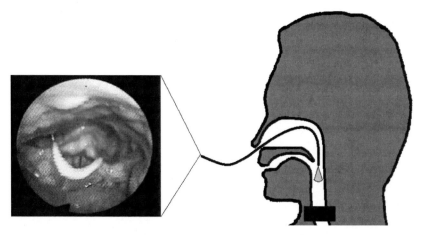

Figure 3. Position of beam of fiberoptic for soft laryngoscopy

EG2-PC commercialized by Glottal Enterprises may potentially be used for measuring larynx height, but this technique has not yet been tested and refined. A quantification of the laryngoscopic movie has thus seemed to be a more reliable way of making a first assessment of larynx height because it is possible to visualize the articulatory mechanisms under study. To our knowledge, no attempt has ever been made to quantify the vertical displacement of the larynx in such a way, but after doing an exploratory laryngoscopy[2], we have come to the conclusion that a relatively accurate assessment of the vertical position of the larynx can be achieved by measuring the width of the epiglottis, which is the only hard tissue (cartilage) that can be used as a reference point on laryngoscopic videos. Since the epiglottis is attached to the front pharyngeal wall, which is pulled downwards when the larynx is lowered, a lowering of the larynx is accompanied by a corresponding lowering of the epiglottis (although these two indicators are probably not perfectly correlated). This is illustrated in Figure 4.

In order to quantify the displacement of the epiglottis, its width has been measured on image frames extracted from the video, as illustrated in Figure 5 (as shown in the figure, a low larynx position results in a narrower epiglottis on the laryngoscopic image). After extracting the available 25 image frames per seconds from the movie, the width of the epiglottis on each of these frames has been marked manually and measured automatically, in pixels, using the basic functionalities of the EdgeTrak software (http://vims.cis.udel.edu/EdgeTrak/). This method does not allow a quantification of larynx height in absolute units, but it does yield the relative vertical position of the epiglottis during the production of sentences, for individual speakers.

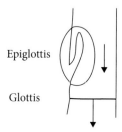

Figure 4. Schematic view of the vertical displacement of the epiglottis accompanying larynx lowering

---

2. Special thanks to Norman Hogikyan, Department of Otolaryngology, and Marci Rosenberg, Department of Speech-Language Pathology, University of Michigan, Ann Arbor, for their help and advice. All errors and misinterpretations are ours.

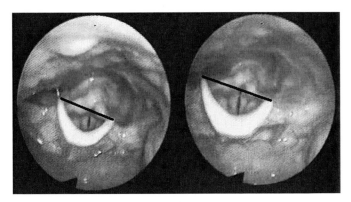

Figure 5. Epiglottal width as measured with a low (left) and a high (right) larynx, male subject

This method has four types of limitations:

1. Apart from larynx height, the position of the tongue can also affect the pharyngeal wall, potentially resulting in vertical and horizontal displacement of the epiglottis. To avoid this pitfall, only the vowel /i/ has been measured (/i/ is the control vowel in Hayward's wordlist). The choice of a constant vowel allows us to assume that changes in epiglottal position are attributable to vertical laryngeal movement.
2. The angle of the epiglottis on the front-back axis changes depending on its vertical position. The epiglottis tends to be kept closer to the pharyngeal wall when the larynx is high and to be slightly pulled backwards when the larynx is low. The amplitude of this effect largely depends on the anatomical idiosyncrasies of the subjects, but it does not affect epiglottal width per se. However, it can make the manual marking of the edges of the epiglottis less accurate as they are viewed from a different angle.
3. Epiglottal width measurements are reliable only if we assume that the beam of fiberoptic placed in the pharynx remains in a constant position. While any horizontal displacement of the beam is visible and can be controlled for, it is possible that the beam slightly moves in or out of the nasal cavity during the recording session. This is important, since a change in the distance between the extremity of the fiberoptic beam and the default larynx position would obviously affect measurements and distort the results. Hayward gives no indication of such changes as her movie was not designed to measure larynx height, but even if they were to have taken place, there is no reason to believe that one group of stops would be more affected than the other.
4. The last potential problem affects only the female subject. Because the amplitude of the vertical displacement of her larynx is quite large, her epiglottis is sometimes so high that it spans out of the video frame, as shown in Figure 6. No attempt has been made at inferring epiglottal width on these images, which have simply been excluded.

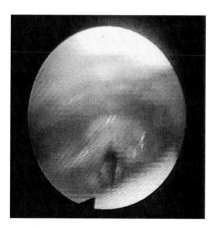

Figure 6. Example of image where the epiglottis is outside the scope of the video

2.3 Data processing

The sound tracks and the image frames have been extracted from the laryngoscopic video with a specially designed MATLAB script and the edges of the epiglottis have been marked manually on each image frame as described in the previous section. The sound and images have then been processed as illustrated schematically in Figure 7. The beginning and end points of each segment have been determined visually from spectrograms created in Praat. Since the quality of the sound tracks extracted from the video is far from excellent, no attempt has been made at determining more than these basic reference points (vowel onset and offset, stop onset and offset). Each image frame has then been automatically assigned to a specific segment by comparing its time with the reference points measured from the corresponding sound file. The epiglottis has been measured in each image frame using the technique described in the previous section and the epiglottal width values of all the frames falling during each segment have been averaged. Finally, the mean epiglottal width of each type of segment has been calculated (tense and lax stops at each place of articulation and vowel /i/ following them).

Because of the low time resolution of the video (only 25 images per second), it is impossible to compare the width of the epiglottis during the various phases of production of stops and vowels. It would be interesting, for example, to know if the point of maximum lowering of the larynx is associated with the closure or the release of a stop or with the transitions or steady-state portion of a vowel. Unfortunately, the image frames fall at regular intervals (each 40 msecs), independently of speech events. The linguistic units that are used as a basis for the measurements must therefore be long enough (more than 40 msec) to insure that they contain at least one image frame. This is another reason why a single average epiglottal width value has been obtained for each segment.

16   Marc Brunelle

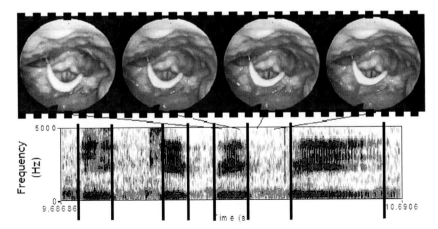

Figure 7. Schematic representation of the association of image frames with specific segments

3. Results

Results show that, for both speakers, epiglottal width is greater during and after the production of tense stops than during and after the production of lax stops. Figures 8–11 show the difference in epiglottal width between the two registers. The number of stars above each place of articulation indicates the statistical significance threshold of the difference in epiglottal width, as obtained from a two-tailed Student t-test. Three stars mean that $p < 0.001$, two stars, $p < 0.01$, one star, $p < 0.1$ and no star means that the difference is not significant.

Figures 8 and 9 illustrate mean epiglottal width during the entire duration of the stops (from beginning of closure to onset of voicing) followed by the vowel /i/. For the

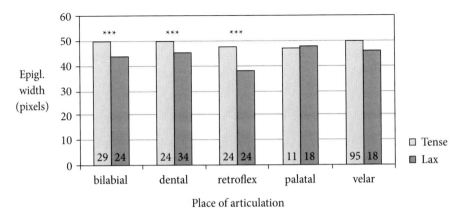

Figure 8. Mean epiglottal width during stops, male subject (n at the bottom of columns)

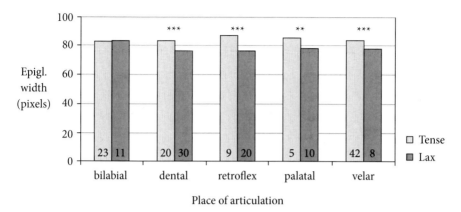

Figure 9. Mean epiglottal width during stops, female subject (n at the bottom of columns)

male subject (Figure 8), a t-test shows that the epiglottal width is significantly greater in tense stops for the bilabial, dental and retroflex places of articulation. The difference between tense and lax stops is not significant for palatals and velars, although the difference is in the expected direction in the case of velars. Results are even more robust in the case of the female subject. In Figure 9, her tense stops have a significantly larger epiglottal width for all places of articulation, except bilabial. This suggests that the epiglottis, and by extension the larynx, is higher during the production of tense stops.

The epiglottis is also higher during the production of the vowel /i/ after tense stops than after lax stops. For the male subject, in Figure 10, this is true of all places of articulation, except palatal, while the female speaker conforms to the pattern for all places of articulation except bilabial, as shown in Figure 11.

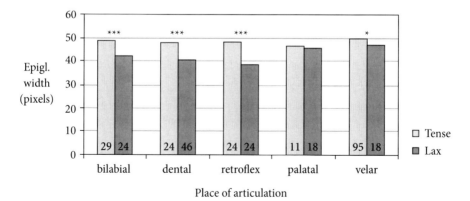

Figure 10. Mean epiglottal width during the vowel /i/ after stops, male subject (n at the bottom of columns)

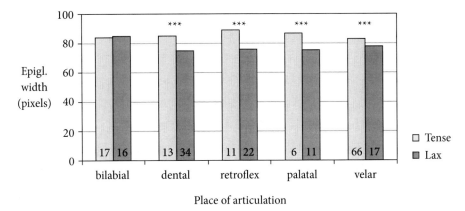

Figure 11. Mean epiglottal width during the vowel /i/ after stops, female subject (n at the bottom of columns)

It is important to note that even if some combinations of subject and place of articulation are short of statistical significance, no place of articulation has a statistically greater epiglottal width for lax stops than tense stops. It seems that the gaps in statistical significance are due to the relatively small number of measured tokens combined with extreme outliers rather than to an absence of contrast in epiglottal width. Therefore, if our assumption that epiglottal width is correlated with larynx height is valid (as illustrated in Figure 4), we can claim that (1) the larynx is generally higher during tense stops than during lax stops; and (2) the larynx is also higher during the vowels following tense stops than during the vowels following lax stops. Unfortunately, the results are not fine-grained enough to indicate whether the difference between the two series is greater during the stops or during the vowels.

4. Discussion

The acoustic correlates of the Javanese tense~lax contrast are reminiscent of the acoustic properties found in a type of contrast that is common in Mainland Southeast Asian languages (Gregerson 1973; Huffman 1976; Ferlus 1979 for an overview). In many Mon-Khmer, Sino-Tibetan and Austronesian languages of the area, voicing had been lost in onset stops and replaced by a bundle of pitch, voice quality, vowel quality and aspiration features realized on the vowel following the stops. A number of languages further extended the contrast to syllable-initial sonorants. These properties are collectively referred to as *register*. The relative importance of the acoustic cues of register varies considerably from language to language, but there is a clear tendency for the low register, which is the modern reflex of voiced stops, to have a lower pitch, a breathier voice quality, higher vowels and slightly more aspirated stops. This is exactly what is found in Javanese, as had been casually noted by James Matisoff in the early 1970s: "While we're at it, we should also account for the fact that many Western Austronesian languages (like Javanese) have acquired register systems." (Matisoff 1973: 87). Acoustic properties therefore suggest parallels between the Javanese tense~lax contrast and Mainland Southeast Asian register and there are reasons to believe that there are also articulatory similarities between the two phenomena. The differences in larynx height observed in the Javanese tense~lax contrast have also been noted impressionistically and inferred acoustically in a number of Mainland Southeast Asian register languages (Hari 1970; Gregerson 1973; Ferlus 1979; L-Thongkum 1987; Meechan 1992; Edmondson, Esling et al. 2000; Brunelle 2005; 2006) and in Madurese (Trigo 1991; Cohn 1993).

Obviously, it would be much too simplistic to claim that larynx lowering is the only articulatory mechanism responsible for either Southeast Asian register or the Javanese tense~lax contrast[3]. As will be discussed below, other mechanisms could play a role in these contrasts, to varying degrees depending on language and speaker. Nonetheless, the articulatory evidence that we have supports the view that the Javanese tense~lax contrast is not a unique phenomenon. Like register, it stems from the loss of a voicing contrast in stops and, from a phonetic point of view, it has the same acoustic properties as register and seems to share at least one articulatory mechanism with it, namely larynx lowering. The Javanese tense~lax contrast should therefore be treated as a variant of the register contrast.

Since register is shared by Javanese and Mainland Southeast Asian languages, a few words about the possibility of language contact in the development of the Javanese stop contrast are in order. While similarities between the Madurese and Javanese stop contrasts are likely to be due to either contact or shared innovation, there is no historical evidence of intensive contact between Java and Mainland Southeast Asia (at least not the kind of contact that could trigger structural changes at the phonological or phonetic levels). Thus, the most careful position is that the development of register on Java and on the Mainland are independent phenomena that have similar phonetic motivations. The fact that some Nilotic languages have phonological contrasts that are also diachronically and phonetically very similar to register (Denning 1989) further supports the possibility of its independent development. Since we lack data on the vertical position of the larynx in Mainland Southeast Asian register languages, we leave the question open and turn to the issue of the fine-grained articulatory realization of Javanese register.

Is the contrast between the tense and lax series a property of the stops, of the vowels that follow them or of the entire syllable? In the absence of independent phonological evidence, finding the point of maximal difference in epiglottal width (i.e. larynx

---

3. Moreover, some articulatory gestures can interfere with larynx lowering. For example, implosives usually cause a high pitch because they are realized with tense vocal folds and an adducted glottis.

height) between the lax and tense series could shed light on the issue. Unfortunately, as mentioned at the end of the previous section, the low time resolution of Hayward's video does not allow conclusions about the timing of the maximal difference in epiglottal width. However, we can speculate that as long as speakers produce phonetic outputs that are similar to those of other members of their speech community, variation in phonetic realization is likely, if not to be expected. Some speakers could phase the point of maximal lowering of the larynx with the lax stop itself, while other speakers could time it with the beginning of the following vowel or the entire syllable. Provided that the movement of the larynx is not too rapid, its acoustic consequences would be easily identifiable for listeners in spite of phasing variations. One could even suppose that different groups of speakers produce the acoustic contrast in qualitatively different ways. Because of the differences in the shapes of their vocal tracts, of articulatory movements reinforcing or replacing larynx lowering (such as a direct control of vocal fold tension and glottal opening) or of socio-phonetic motivations, some speakers or groups of speakers could be contrasting the lax and tense series through a subset of the available acoustic properties, while others could be relying on another. As long as listeners know how to decode these acoustic cues and learn to associate them with the proper phonological categories, intelligibility is not hindered. This scenario is more than speculative since variation across speakers is attested: Some speakers show a contrast in pitch and F2 while others only use voice quality and F1 (Fagan 1988; Hayward 1993; 1995; Adisasmito-Smith 2004; Thurgood 2004).

This takes us to the issue of the nature of the phonological representation of the register contrast, more specifically under its Javanese guise, the tense~lax stop contrast. Should the register contrast be represented with a well-established articulatory feature? The only feature that has been explicitly proposed to capture Southeast Asian register is [Lowered Larynx] (Meechan 1992; Cohn 1993; Brunelle 2005). While the present study suggests that a lowering of the larynx indeed occurs during the production of the low register (i.e. the lax stops), other articulatory mechanisms may be involved, such as a direct control of vocal fold tension, glottal opening and tongue position. A possible account for these potentially complex interactions of articulatory strategies is that there is a simple articulatory feature, like [Lowered Larynx], combined with various phonetic enhancement strategies, be they universal (Stevens, Keyser et al. 1986; Keyser & Stevens 2001; 2006) or language specific. However, unless we rigidly adhere to universalist assumptions, there is no reason to believe that all learners develop an identical phonological representation for the register contrast. As long as all speakers 1) have cognitive categories that correspond to the high register (tense stops) and the low register (lax stops); and 2) acoustically produce the contrast in a way that is similar to the way that the rest of their speech community (or of one well-established dialectal or social subgroup) produces it, the way in which the contrast is represented in individual grammars and articulated by different speakers can vary widely. Therefore, instead of proposing that the Javanese stop contrast is captured by a single articulatory feature, it seems more economical to propose that speakers have a contrast between two relatively abstract categories (tense and lax) and that they learn the phonetic properties that are associated to them through exposure and through trial and error.

5. Conclusion

This reanalysis of Hayward's laryngoscopic video provides the first direct quantitative evidence supporting the claim made by other researchers that the vertical position of the larynx plays a role in the Javanese tense~lax stop contrast (Catford 1964; Fagan 1988; Hayward 1993; Ladefoged & Maddieson 1996). The position of the larynx is lower during the production of lax stops than during their tense counterparts. Further, as discussed in Section 1.2, larynx height could be partly responsible for most of the acoustic correlates of the contrast. Unfortunately, because of the low time resolution of the video, the technique developed here is not sophisticated enough to determine the phasing of the precise larynx height targets with the syllable. Further studies using other techniques are therefore needed.

While larynx height differences are found in both of Hayward's subjects, results obtained by previous researchers show that there are important acoustic differences across speakers and that the realization of the Javanese stop contrast is unlikely to be entirely attributable to the vertical position of the larynx (Fagan 1988; Hayward 1993; 1995; Adisasmito-Smith 2004; Thurgood 2004). Rather than adopting a phonological representation in which a feature directly referring to larynx height, such as [Lowered Larynx], captures the tense~lax contrast, we thus argue for a more abstract type of contrast that can vary quantitatively and representationally across speakers.

Finally, the phonetic and diachronic similarities between the Javanese tense~lax contrast and Mainland Southeast Asian register support Matisoff's view that Javanese is a register language (Matisoff 1973). It is improbable that the development of the Javanese tense~lax contrast is due to contact with Mainland Southeast Asia, but from diachronic and typological perspectives, much is to be gained in a systematic comparison of the two phenomena.

References

Adisasmito-Smith, N. 2004. *Phonetic Influences of Javanese on Indonesian*. PhD dissertation, Cornell University.
Arnold, G.E. 1961. Physiology and pathology of the cricothyroid muscle. *Laryngoscope* 71: 687–753.
Brunelle, M. 2005. Register in Eastern Cham: Phonological, Phonetic and Sociolinguistic approaches. PhD dissertation, Cornell University.

Brunelle, M. 2006. A phonetic study of Eastern Cham register. In *Chamic and Beyond*, P. Sidwell & A. Grant (eds), 1–36. Sidney: Pacific Linguistics.
Catford, I. 1964. Phonation types: The classification of some laryngeal components of speech production. In *In Honor of Daniel Jones*, D. Abercrombie, D. Fry, P. MacCarthy, N. Scott & J. Trim (eds), 26–37. London: Longmans.
Chiba, T. & Kajiyama, M. 1941. *The Vowel: Its nature and structure*. Tokyo: Kaisekan.
Cohn, A.C. 1993. Consonant-vowel interactions in Madurese: The feature lowered larynx. *Papers from the regional meeting of the Chicago Linguistic Society* 29: 105–119.
Crandall, I. 1925. The sounds of speech. *Bell System Technical Journal* 4: 586–625.
Denning, K. 1989. The Diachronic Development of Phonological Voice Quality, with Special Reference to Dinka and the other Nilotic Languages. PhD dissertation, Stanford University.
Dresser, C. 2005. *A Phonological Account of Javanese Stops*. Midcontinental Workshop on Phonology (MCWOP11), Ann Arbor MI.
Edmondson, J., Esling, J., Harris, J., Shaoni, L. & Ziwo, L. 2000. The aryepiglottic folds and voice quality in the Yi and Bai language: laryngoscopic case studies. *Mon Khmer Studies* 31: 83–100.
Ewan, W. 1979. Laryngeal Behavior in Speech. *Report of the Phonology Laboratory, Berkeley* 3.
Ewan, W. & Krones, R. 1974. Measuring larynx movement using the thyroumbrometer. *Journal of Phonetics* 2: 327–335.
Fagan, J. L. 1988. Javanese Intervocalic Stop Phonemes. *Studies in Austronesian Linguistics* 76: 173–202.
Ferlus, M. 1979. Formation des registres et mutations consonantiques dans les langues Mon-Khmer. *Mon Khmer Studies* VIII: 1–76.
Gregerson, K. 1973. Tongue-root and Register in Mon-Khmer. In *Austroasiatic Studies*, P. N. Jenner, L. Thompson & S. Starosta (eds), 323–369. Honolulu HI: University Press of Hawaii.
Hari, M. 1970. Thakali Tone and Higher Levels. In *Occasional Papers of the Wolfenden Society on Tibeto-Burman Linguistics*. A. Hale & K. Pike (eds), 125–142. Urbana IL: University of Illinois.
Hayward, K. 1993. /p/ vs. /b/ in Javanese: Some Preliminary Data. *Working Papers in Linguistics and Phonetics* 3: 1–33.
Hayward, K. 1995. /p/ vs. /b/ in Javanese: The Role of the Vocal Folds. *Working Papers in Linguistics and Phonetics* 5: 1–11.
Hayward, K., Grafield-Davies, D., Howard, B. J., Latif, J. & Allen, R. 1994. *Javanese Stop Consonants: The Role of the Vocal Folds*. London: School of Oriental and African Studies. (Video).
Honda, K., Hirai, H., Masaki, S. & Shimada, Y. 1999. Role of vertical larynx movement and cervical lordosis in F0 control. *Language and Speech* 42(4): 401–411.
Horne, E. 1974. *Javanese-English dictionary*. New Haven CT: Yale University Press.
Huffman, F. 1976. The register problem in fifteen Mon-Khmer languages. *Oceanic Linguistics special publication* Austroasiatic Studies, Part 1, 13: 575–589.
Keyser, S.J. & Stevens, K.N. 2001. Enhancement revisited. In *Ken Hale: A Life in Language*, M. Kenstowitz (ed), 271–291. Cambridge: The MIT Press.
Keyser, S.J. & Stevens, K.N. 2006. Enhancement and overlap in the speech chain. *Language* 82: 33–63.
L-Thongkum, T. 1987. Phonation types in Mon-Khmer languages. *UCLA Working Papers in Phonetics* 67: 29–48.
Ladefoged, P. & Maddieson, I. 1996. *The Sounds of the World's Languages*. Oxford: Blackwell.
Laver, J. 1980. *The Phonetic Description of Voice Quality*. Cambridge: CUP.
Matisoff, J. 1973. Tonogenesis in Southeast Asia. In *Consonant Types and Tone*, L. Hyman (ed.), 71–96. Los Angeles CA: USC.

Meechan, M. 1992. Register in Khmer: The Laryngeal Specification of Pharyngeal Expansion. MA thesis, University of Ottawa.
Poedjosoedarmo, G. 1974. Role Structure in Javanese. PhD dissertation, Cornell University.
Poedjosoedarmo, G. 1986. The symbolic significance of pharyngeal configuration in Javanese speech: Some preliminary notes. *Nusa* 25: 31–37.
Samsuri 1958. Javanese Phonology. MA thesis, University of Indiana.
Stevens, K., Keyser, S.J. & Kawasaki, H. 1986. Toward a phonetic and phonological theory of redundant features. In *Invariance and Variability in Speech Processes*, J. Perkell & D.H. Klatt (eds), 426–447. Hillsdale NJ: Lawrence Erlbaum Associates.
Thurgood, E. 2004. Phonation Types in Javanese. *Oceanic Linguistics* 43(2): 277–295.
Trigo, L. 1991. On pharynx-larynx interactions. *Phonology* 8: 113–136.
Westbury, J.R. & Keating, P.A. 1986. On the naturalness of stop consonant voicing. *Journal of Linguistics* 22: 145–166.

Appendix

Wordlist used in the movie "Javanese Stop Consonants: The Role of the Vocal Folds" (Hayward, Grafield-Davies et al. 1994). (*b, d, dh, j* and *g* are lax stops. *th* and *dh* represent tense and lax retroflex stops, respectively). All stops, regardless of their position in the syllable, and all instances of the vowel /i/ following a stop were measured. A second wordlist in which stops are preceded by nasals is not investigated in this paper.

Tense	English Gloss	Lax	English Gloss
iki pipi	this is a cheek	iki bibi	this is aunt
iki pitik	this is a chicken	iki bibit	this is a seed
iki tipis	this is thin	iki dimar	this is a lamp
iki titik	this is a full stop	didilat	is licked
iki thinthil	this is a chicken liver	didhidhis	is removed from hair (lice)
iki thiwul	this is thiwul (type of porridge)	didhidhik	is educated
iki cilik	this is small	umi jijik	Umi is disgusted
iki cipir	this is cipir (type of vegetable)	lagi jibeg	is (still) overburdened
iki kikil	this is a leg (e.g. of lamb, served as food)	iki gilep	this is shining
dikinthil	is followed	digiling	is ground

Reduplication in Tanjung Raden Malay*

Yanti and Eric Raimy
University of Delaware, Atma Jaya Catholic University
and University of Wisconsin-Madison

In this article, we present novel reduplication data from Tanjung Raden Malay (henceforth TR Malay) and provide a formal analysis of all reduplication patterns in TR Malay within Precedence Based Phonology (Raimy 2000, 2009). TR Malay exhibits three patterns of reduplication previously documented in other Malay dialects, such as Standard Indonesian and Riau Indonesian: full reduplication, CV reduplication, and C[ə] reduplication. However, Tanjung Raden Malay exhibits six additional patterns. We claim that TR Malay has innovated the additional six patterns, and the three reduplication patterns attested in all varieties of Malay discussed here are the basic patterns. Our analysis puts forth a theory that explains the connections between the six innovated and three common reduplication patterns in Tanjung Raden Malay.

1. Introduction

This paper has three purposes. The first is to document reduplication patterns found in Tanjung Raden Malay (henceforth TR Malay), which is a Malay dialect spoken in the village of Tanjung Raden (literally means 'Prince Cape') in the Jambi Province of Southern Sumatra, Indonesia. The TR Malay data presented in this paper were gathered from naturalistic recordings of various speakers and elicitation from 3 consultants of different ages (16, 23, 50 years old). Naturalistic recordings consisted of conversations, personal narratives and stories. For the elicited data, consultants were required to confirm or refute the existence of certain forms and to further illustrate the

---

* This research is made possible by funding from the National Science Foundation (grant number BCS-0444649, awarded to Peter Cole, Gabriella Hermon and Uri Tadmor). We would like to express our gratefulness to our consultants from Tanjung Raden, especially Ibu Mariana, Sudirman, Raden Endang, and many others. We would also like thank the attendees at AFLA XIV who contributed many useful comments, the two anonymous reviewers who provided extremely constructive criticism and especially to Uri Tadmor for his valuable comments on this paper.

use of those forms in sentences. Some of the reduplication types in this paper did not occur very frequently in the naturalistic data; consequently, we made use of previously elicited data.

The second aim of this study is to provide a formal analysis for these reduplication patterns based on Precedence Based Phonology (PBP), as proposed by Raimy (2000, 2009). Thirdly, we show that the PBP model provides an insightful account of how the innovations in TR Malay reduplication came to be.

The paper is organized as follows. Section 2 presents background information on reduplication in other Malay dialects. Section 3 displays the reduplication patterns attested in TR Malay. Section 4 provides an analysis of TR reduplication using the PBP model. Section 5 presents an account of how language learners' ambiguities in the analysis of reduplication have led to language change. Section 6 concludes the paper.

2. Reduplication in other Malay dialects

Previous studies on different Malay varieties show that Malay exhibits both partial and full reduplication (Sneddon 1996, Gil 2005). Sneddon (1996) points out that Standard Indonesian (SI) exhibits three types of reduplication: full reduplication, partial reduplication and imitative reduplication, as shown in (1–3) (Sneddon 1996: 16–22).

(1) Full reduplication
   a. gula   'sugar'   gula-gula   'sweets'
   b. duduk   'sit'   duduk-duduk   'sit about'

(2) Partial reduplication
   a. tangga 'ladder'   tetangga   'neighbor'
   b. laki   'husband' lelaki   'man'

(3) Imitative reduplication
   a. sayur   'vegetable' sayur-mayur   'vegetables'
   b. warna   'color'   warna-warni   'all kinds of colors'

Similarly, Gil (2005) shows that Riau Indonesian (RI) uses both full and partial reduplication. In addition, RI also exhibits multiple reduplication. An example of each reduplication type found in RI is presented in (4–6).

(4) Full reduplication (Gil 2005: 50)
   Suara kau putus-putus kenapa?
   voice 2   RED-cut.off why
   'Why does your voice keep getting cut off?'

(5) Partial reduplication (Gil 2005: 58)
    Baju-nya   ko-koyak itu.
    clothes-ASSOC RED-tear DEM-DEM:DIST
    'Your shirt's all frayed.'

(6) Multiple reduplication (Gil 2005: 58)
    Udah   si-si-siap?
    PFCT   RED-ready
    'Is everything ready?'

Due to space limitations, we leave a review of the semantic functions of reduplication in Malay dialects aside and refer the reader to Sneddon (1996) for more information.

3. Reduplication types in Tanjung Raden Malay

Like other varieties of Malay, TR Malay exhibits both full and partial reduplication. In contrast to SI, partial reduplication in TR Malay is still very productive.

(7) Full reduplication
    a. /saŋko/ 'think' /saŋko-saŋko/ 'think'
    b. /baɲaʔ/ 'a lot' /baɲaʔ-baɲaʔ/ 'too much'

(8) Partial reduplication
    a. /kawan/ 'friend' /ka-kawan/ 'friends'
    b. /main/ 'play' /ma-main/ 'play about'

Similarly to SI, TR Malay also has imitative reduplication as shown in (9).

(9) Imitative reduplication
    a. /lauʔ/ 'side dish' /lauʔ-pauʔ/ 'side dishes'
    b. /asal/ 'origin' /asal-usul/ 'origin'

The semantic functions of reduplication are similar to those in SI. The reduplication of nouns, for instance, forms the meaning of a group of the noun being reduplicated (the exact number is unspecified). Reduplicated adjectives may function as adverbs and adverbial intensifiers. Reduplication of verbs shows that the action is not done seriously. Some examples of these functions are shown in (10).

(10) a. /budaʔ/ 'kid'   /budaʔ-budaʔ/ 'kids'
     b. /baju/ 'shirt'   /baju-baju/   'shirts'
     c. /eloʔ/ '(is) nice' /eloʔ-eloʔ/   '(are) nice'
     d. /main/ 'play'   /main-main/   'play about'

The semantic functions of reduplication in TR Malay need further research; however, in this paper, we only focus on the phonological properties of reduplication. For an overview of TR Malay phonology see Tadmor & Yanti (2005) and Yanti (2010).

3.1 Full reduplication

Full reduplication occurs when the reduplicant copies all segments of the base. This type of reduplication can apply to any base and is widely accepted among speakers. Some examples are presented in (11).

(11) a /kiro/ 'think' /kiro-kiro/ 'average'
 b. /dulu/ 'before' /dulu-dulu/ 'long time ago'
 c. /main/ 'play' /main-main/ 'play about'
 d. /siaŋ/ 'daytime' /siaŋ-siaŋ/ 'during the day'
 e. /ʊbat/ 'medicine' /ʊbat-ʊbat/ 'medicines'
 f. /enaʔ/ 'delicious' /enaʔ-enaʔ/ 'very delicious'
 g. /dʊlʊr/ 'relative' /dʊlʊr-dʊlʊr/ 'relatives'
 h. /tabok/ 'slap' /tabok-tabok/ 'slap repeatedly'
 i. /mᵇoʔ/ 'older sister' /mᵇoʔ-mᵇoʔ/ 'older sisters'
 j. /lap/ 'rag' /lap-lap/ 'rags'
 k. /ban/ 'tire' /ban-ban/ 'tires'
 l. /jaramᵇa/ 'bridge' /jaramᵇa-jaramᵇa/ 'bridges'
 m. /pariyʊʔ/ 'pot' /pariyʊʔ-pariyʊʔ/ 'pots'
 n. /batrʊŋ/ 'k.o.fish' /batrʊŋ-batrʊŋ/ 'a group of *batruŋ*'

3.2 Full reduplication with glottal stop

This reduplication pattern occurs when the reduplicant is a complete copy of the base except for a word final consonant which is replaced by a glottal stop [ʔ]. Speaker's intuitions vary with respect to this type of reduplication. As described here, one of our three consultants (the eldest one) accepts this type of reduplication in elicitation, while the other two speakers only accept it if the base is /k/-final.

(12) a. /ɪkʊt/ 'follow' /ɪkʊʔ-ɪkʊt/ 'imitate'
 b. /alat/ 'tool' /alaʔ-alat/ 'tools'
 c. /dikit/ 'a little' /dikiʔ-dikit/ 'little by little'
 d. /rampok/ 'rob' /rampoʔ-rampok/ 'rob'
 e. /ləmᵇap/ '(is) damp' /ləmᵇaʔ-ləmᵇap/ '(are) damp'
 f. /raʊp/ 'scoop' /raʊʔ-raʊp/ 'scoop repeatedly'

3.3 Full reduplication without final consonant

This pattern occurs when the reduplicant consists of the entire base except for a word final consonant. Examples follow.

(13) a. /sopan/ 'polite' /sopa-sopan/ 'very polite'
 b. /cabaŋ/ 'branch' /caba-cabaŋ/ 'branches'

c.	/dikit/	'a little'	/diki-dikit/	'little by little'
d.	/cakap/	'say'	/caka-cakap/	'chitchat'
e.	/gamal/	'gong'	/gama-gamal/	'gongs'
f.	/sʊbʊr/	'fertile'	/sʊbʊ-sʊbʊr/	'very fertile'
g.	/catar/	'rent'	/cata-catar/	'rent'
h.	/sekoʔ/	'one'	/seko-sekoʔ/	'one by one'
i.	/ancʊr/	'destroyed'	/ancʊ-ancʊr/	'destroyed'
j.	/alat/	'tool'	/ala-alat/	'tools'

3.4 CV reduplication

CV reduplication occurs when a reduplicant is the copy of the first consonant vowel sequence of the base (14a–g), not the first syllable, (14h–j).

(14) a. /dulu/ 'before' /du-dulu/ 'long time ago'
      b. /kiro/ 'think' /ki-kiro/ 'average'
      c. /cubo/ 'try' /cu-cubo/ 'try about'
      d. /budaʔ/ 'kid' /bu-budaʔ/ 'kids'
      e. /lebar/ 'wide' /le-lebar/ 'very wide'
      f. /koyaʔ/ 'torn' /ko-koyaʔ/ 'torn'
      g. /makan/ 'eat' /ma-makan/ 'eat'
      h. /ɟantan/ 'male' /ɟa-ɟantan/ 'male'   *ɟan-ɟantan
      i. /rampok/ 'rob' /ra-rampok/ 'rob'   *ram-rampok
      j. /teŋkat/ 'level' /te-teŋkat/ 'levels'   *teŋ-teŋkat

3.5 C[a] reduplication

C[a] reduplication occurs when the first consonant of the base and the pre-specified vowel [a] form a reduplicant, as illustrated in (15). Speakers also vary in the extent to which they accept this form. Younger speakers show arbitrary lexical variation as to whether a root can undergo this reduplication pattern.

(15) a. /kiro/ 'think' /ka-kiro/ 'average'
      b. /koyaʔ/ 'torn' /ka-koyaʔ/ 'torn'
      c. /buwat/ 'make' /ba-buwat/ 'make'
      d. /rugaw/ 'tangle' /ra-rugaw/ 'tangle'
      e. /potoŋ/ 'cut' /pa-potoŋ/ 'cut repeatedly'
      f. /makan/ 'eat' /ma-makan/ 'eat'
      g. /kawan/ 'friend' /ka-kawan/ 'friends'
      h. /ɟarambа/ 'bridge' /ɟa-ɟarambа/ 'bridges'
      i. /ɟalan/ 'walk/street' /ɟa-ɟalan/ 'walk around/streets'

3.6 C[ə] reduplication

C[ə] reduplication occurs when the first consonant of the base is followed by a pre-specified schwa to form the reduplicant, as shown below.

(16) a. /pagi/ 'morning' /pə-pagi/ 'early morning'
 b. /sopan/ 'polite' /sə-sopan/ 'more polite'
 c. /kitar/ 'about' /kə-kitar/ 'about'
 d. /subʊr/ 'fertile' /sə-subʊr/ 'fertile'
 e. /kanaʔ/ 'young child' /kə-kanaʔ/ 'young child'
 f. /pasat/ 'pay attention' /pə-pasat/ 'pay attention'

3.7 CV[ʔ] reduplication

CV[ʔ] reduplication occurs when the first consonant vowel sequence of the base is followed by a glottal stop to form the reduplicant. Younger speakers do not favor this reduplication pattern and only accept half or fewer of the reduplicated forms accepted by the older generation.

(17) a. /lasaʔ/ 'restless' /laʔ-lasaʔ/ 'very restless'
 b. /lambat/ 'slow' /laʔ-lambat/ 'slowly'
 c. /buwat/ 'make' /buʔ-buwat/ 'make something up'
 d. /boŋkot/ 'root' /boʔ-boŋkot/ 'roots'
 e. /teŋoʔ/ 'look' /teʔ-teŋoʔ/ 'look/observe'
 f. /pondoʔ/ 'hut' /poʔ-pondoʔ/ 'huts'

3.8 C[aʔ] reduplication

C[aʔ] reduplication occurs when the reduplicant is a copy of the first consonant of the base followed by a pre-specified vowel [a] and a glottal stop [ʔ]. Like CV[ʔ] reduplication, younger speakers do not prefer this pattern. They accept fewer than half of the reduplicated forms accepted by speakers from the other generation.

(18) a. /piɟat/ 'massage' /paʔ-piɟat/ 'give massage repeatedly'
 b. /lasaʔ/ 'restless' /laʔ-lasaʔ/ 'very restless'
 c. /lambat/ 'slow' /laʔ-lambat/ 'slowly'
 d. /teŋoʔ/ 'look' /taʔ-teŋoʔ/ 'look/observe'

3.9 C[əʔ] reduplication

The last reduplication type found in TR Malay is when the reduplicant is a copy of the first consonant of the base followed by a pre-specified schwa [ə] and the glottal stop [ʔ]. Some examples are shown in (19).

(19) a. /kilat/ 'shinning' /kəʔ-kilat/ 'very shinning'
    b. /sɪbʊʔ/ 'busy' /səʔ-sɪbʊʔ/ 'very busy'
    c. /kəciʔ/ 'small' /kəʔ-kəciʔ/ 'very small'
    d. /dikit/ 'a little' /dəʔ-dikit/ 'a little'
    e. /deweʔ/ 'alone' /dəʔ-deweʔ/ 'alone'

It should be pointed out that, if a word can undergo CV[ʔ] reduplication, it can also undergo C[aʔ] and C[əʔ] reduplication; however, two exceptions have been found, as illustrated in (20).

(20) a. /boŋkot/ 'root' /boʔ-boŋkot/ *baʔ-boŋkot *bəʔ-boŋkot
    b. /teŋkat/ 'level' /teʔ-teŋkat/ *taʔ-teŋkat *təʔ-teŋkat

This concludes our description of the nine reduplication patterns observed in Tanjung Raden Malay.

4. Precedence based phonology

In this section, we provide a formal analysis of the reduplication patterns of TR Malay presented in Section 3. Our analysis is couched within Precedence Based Phonology (Raimy 1999, 2000, 2005, 2009).

Precedence Based Phonology (PBP) proposes that phonological representations consist of both segments (bundles of distinctive features) and precedence relations (which order the segments) in addition to other aspects of 3-D phonological representations (Halle 2002). Both segments and precedence relations can be manipulated by the morphology and phonology. Raimy (1999, 2000) proposes that precedence relations are represented by an arrow, →, where 'X → Y' indicates that 'X precedes Y'. Furthermore, the beginning and end of a phonological representation are indicated by begin, '#', and end, '%', symbols.

To fully explain PBP and how reduplication is accounted for in this model, we begin by showing how the total reduplication pattern in (11) is derived. Non-reduplicated forms are represented in the traditional way except for the addition of the '#' and '%' symbols along with the precedence relation indicators as in (21) below.

(21)   base   reduplicated   PBP representation
    a. kiro   kiro-kiro $\# \to k \to i \to r \to o \to \%$
    b. dʊlʊr   dʊlʊr-dʊlʊr $\# \to d \to \upsilon \to l \to \upsilon \to r \to \%$

Reduplication is a form of affixation (Marantz 1982) in that phonological material is added to a stem due to the spell-out of some morpho-syntactic feature. Reduplication without pre-specified material demonstrates that the phonological exponent of a morpho-syntactic feature can consist solely of a precedence relation. The surface effect of reduplication results from the concatenation of a precedence relation (or path of precedence relations and segments) which creates a 'loop' in a phonological representation.

A 'loop' is nothing more and nothing less than a precedence relation (or path of precedence relations and segments) that causes a symmetrical and transitive reflexive precedence relationship between segments. (22) presents the reduplicated forms of the examples in (21).

(22) a. # → k → i → r → o → %
       (loop from o back to k)

 b. # → d → ʊ → l → ʊ → r → %
       (loop from r back to ʊ)

If we follow the precedence links in both representations in (22), we see that we can return to any segment we start from, which indicates that the overall precedence structures in these forms are symmetric and reflexive. Visually, there is a 'loop' in the representation, but there is no special formal status to this aspect of the representation.

Phonology contains a linearization process that resolves any reflexive and symmetrical attributes through the copying and repetition of segments. For the purposes of this paper, we only need to recognize that linearization causes the single repetition of all segments 'within a loop'. Consequently, the representations in (22) will be linearized as in (23). For detailed discussion of linearization see Raimy (1999, 2000, 2003).

(23) a. # → k → i → r → o → k → i → r → o → %
     b. # → d → ʊ → l → ʊ → r → d → ʊ → l → ʊ → r → %

Both forms in (23) show total reduplication because all of the segments in each stem are contained in the 'loop'. Distinctions in patterns of reduplication are accounted for by altering the description of how the precedence link is concatenated to the base. Anchor Point Theory (Raimy 2005, 2009) provides a constrained formalism of possible precedence links that accounts for all reduplication patterns. Each precedence link (or path of precedence links and segments) that represents a reduplication pattern is defined by two points: its 'begin' (what the link follows, foot of arrow) and 'end' (what the link precedes, head of arrow) and they must be legitimate Anchor Points.

4.1 Full reduplication

The total reduplication pattern in TR Malay described in (11) has the formal description based on the anchor points in (24).

(24) a. 'begin anchor point' → 'end anchor point'
       Begin anchor point   = 'last segment'
       End anchor point   = 'first segment'
   b. Stems
     (i) # → s → a → ŋ → k → o → %
     (ii) # → b → a → ɲ → a → ʔ → %

c. Reduplicated forms
   (i) # → s → a → ŋ → k → o → %
   (ii) # → b → a → ɲ → a → ʔ → %

d. Linearization
   (i) # → s → a → ŋ → k → o → s → a → ŋ → k → o → %
   (ii) # → b → a → ɲ → a → ʔ → b → a → ɲ → a → ʔ → %

(24a) presents the description of the precedence relation which is the phonological exponent of the total reduplication pattern. Total reduplication is defined as a precedence relation that connects the 'last segment' to the 'first segment'. Because of the generalness of this description, whether the stem begins or ends with a vowel or a consonant is irrelevant. Whatever the first and last segments are, they are now in a precedence relationship which creates a 'loop' which contains the whole stem as shown in (24c). Finally, when linearization occurs, as in (24d), we achieve the surface effect of repeating the entire stem that we recognize as total reduplication.

4.2 Full reduplication without final consonant

The difference between the full reduplication pattern described above, in (24), and the full reduplication without consonant pattern presented in (13) can be produced by simply altering the begin anchor point in (24a). Below, in (25), we present the analysis of the full reduplication with no consonant pattern (e.g. a 'no coda' effect).

(25) a. 'begin anchor point' → 'end anchor point'
     Begin anchor point = 'last vowel'
     End anchor point   = 'first segment'

   b. Stem
      # → g → a → m → a → l → %

   c. Reduplicated form
      # → g → a → m → a → l → %

   d. Linearization
      # → g → a → m → a → g → a → m → a → l → %

By simply making the description of the Begin anchor point in (25a) 'last vowel' we achieve the effect of the full reduplication with no consonant pattern. There will be total repetition of the form but a word final consonant will not be repeated. This is the result of the particular anchor points in (25a) when we consider the form in (25c). The 'loop' created in the form in (25c) does not contain the final consonant of the stem in (25b); consequently, this consonant is not repeated when linearization occurs. Also note that the anchor points directly encode the prefixing nature of this pattern (e.g. the word final consonant is omitted in the first repetition and retained in the second repetition). The way in which linearization treats representations like that in (25c) creates the prefixing aspect of this pattern.

4.3 CV reduplication

The CV reduplication pattern showed in (14) can be formalized as in (26).

(26) a. 'begin anchor point' → 'end anchor point'
Begin anchor point = 'first vowel'
End anchor point = 'first segment'

b. Stem
\# → k → i → r → o → %

c. Reduplicated form
\# → k → i → r → o → %

d. Linearization
\# → k → i → k → i → r → o → %

In (26), the minimal alteration of the Begin anchor point produces a distinct reduplication pattern. In (26a), we have altered the Begin anchor point to 'first vowel'. This causes the 'loop' in the reduplicated form in (26c) to only contain the first consonant and vowel sequence. When linearized, this produces the surface pattern of CV reduplication as in (26d).

At this point, we have demonstrated the full variation of anchor points utilized by all of the reduplication patterns documented in TR Malay. All reduplication patterns attested in TR Malay use as an End anchor point 'first segment' and then we can produce three distinct reduplication patterns by altering the Begin Anchor Point among 'last segment', 'last vowel' and 'first vowel'. The next question is how the remaining six reduplication patterns can be accounted for. The answer to this question is based on taking Marantz's (1982) position that reduplication is affixation to its logical conclusion. To do this, we only need to allow segmental material to occur as part of the phonological exponence associated with a 'reduplication pattern'.

4.4 Full reduplication with glottal stop

The most straightforward demonstration of reduplication as affixation is shown by the full reduplication with a glottal stop pattern in (12). This pattern can be obtained by simply adding [ʔ] to the analysis of the full reduplication without final consonant in (25), as shown in (27).

(27) a. 'begin anchor point' → ʔ → 'end anchor point'
    Begin anchor point   = 'last vowel'
    End anchor point   = 'first segment'

  b. Stem
     # → ɪ → k → ʊ → t → %

  c. Reduplicated form
     # → ɪ → k → ʊ → t → %
           ↑   ↓
           ⎣ ʔ ⎦

  d. Linearization
     # → ɪ → k → ʊ → ʔ → ɪ → k → ʊ → t → %

The only difference between the full reduplication without final consonant pattern in (25) and the full reduplication with glottal stop pattern is the addition of a [ʔ] to the phonological exponence of this pattern in (27a). The anchor point settings for both patterns are identical. With the pre-specified [ʔ] as a part in this reduplication pattern, we produce the correct surface forms with no other modifications, as illustrated in (27d).

4.5 CV[ʔ] reduplication

To account for the CV[ʔ] reduplication pattern presented in (17), we can modify our analysis of CV reduplication in (26) along the same lines we did above for the full reduplication with no consonant pattern. (28) demonstrates the analogous modification and how it produces the CV[ʔ] reduplication pattern.

(28) a. 'begin anchor point' → ʔ → 'end anchor point'
    Begin anchor point   = 'first vowel'
    End anchor point   = 'first segment'

  b. Stem
     # → l → a → s → a → ʔ → %

  c. Reduplicated form
     # → l → a → s → a → ʔ → %
              ↖↓
               ʔ

  d. Linearization
     # → l → a → ʔ → l → a → s → a → ʔ → %

As with our approach to the full reduplication with a glottal stop pattern, the simple addition of a pre-specified glottal stop to the CV reduplication pattern in (26a) produces the correct analysis of the CV[ʔ] reduplication pattern, as shown in (28a).

The ability to add segmental material to the 'reduplicative morphemes' continues to be useful when we turn our attention to the C[a], C[ə], C[aʔ] and C[əʔ] reduplication patterns. In addition to the appropriate segmental material for each of these reduplication patterns, we must modify the settings of the Anchor Points to properly describe the reduplication patterns. The commonality across these four reduplication patterns is that only the stem initial consonant is being repeated. One way to limit reduplication to a single segment is to specify both Anchor Points in an identical manner. This produces the effect that the 'loop' will begin and end on the same segment.

4.6 C[a] reduplication

(29) demonstrates the utility of specifying the Anchor Points for an affix in an identical manner. We further add the pre-specified vowel [a] in order to account for the C[a] reduplication pattern from (15).

(29) C[a] reduplication
    a. 'begin anchor point' → a → 'end anchor point'
        Begin anchor point   = 'first segment'
        End anchor point   = 'first segment'
    b. Stem
        # → k → i → r → o → %
    c. Reduplicated form
        # → k → i → r → o → %
            ↺ a
    d. Linearization
        # → k → a → k → i → r → o → %

By setting both the Begin and End anchor points in (29a) to 'first segment', we create a loop with the pre-specified segment /a/ on it around the first segment of this form (shown in (29c)). (29d) demonstrates that the form linearizes to the correct surface form.

It should be noted that it is very likely that patterns which only reduplicate the word initial consonant and some pre-specified material will actually require the Begin anchor point to be set to 'first consonant' and limited to word initial position. We leave this complexity aside in this paper, but developing it would explain the restriction of these patterns to consonant initial forms. The CV pattern would also benefit from this refinement and an alternative analysis of the pre-specification of schwa in the C[ə] and C[əʔ] patterns as being epenthetic could also be developed. We leave these issues for future research.

4.7 Remaining reduplication patterns

The remaining three reduplication patterns, C[ə], C[aʔ], and C[əʔ], are now simply accounted for by appropriately specifying the segmental material for each pattern. By simply replacing the pre-specified /a/ in (29a) with [ə], [aʔ] and [əʔ] in an appropriate manner, we derive these three reduplication patterns. (30) summarizes these substitutions.

(30) Remaining reduplication patterns
    a. C[ə] reduplication
        'begin anchor point' → ə → 'end anchor point'
        Begin anchor point   = 'first segment'
        End anchor point   = 'first segment'
    b. C[aʔ] reduplication
        'begin anchor point' → a → ʔ → 'end anchor point'
        Begin anchor point   = 'first segment'
        End anchor point   = 'first segment'
    c. C[əʔ] reduplication
        'begin anchor point' → ə → ʔ → 'end anchor point'
        Begin anchor point   = 'first segment'
        End anchor point   = 'first segment'

We now have a descriptively adequate formal analysis of the nine reduplication patterns in TR Malay. The following section will elucidate how these nine reduplication patterns arose.

5. Language acquisition and change

Three reduplication patterns are common to Standard Indonesian (SI), Riau Indonesian (RI) and Tanjung Raden (TR) Malay.

(31) Reduplication patterns common to SI, RI, and TR Malay.
    a. Full reduplication
    b. CV reduplication
    c. C[ə] reduplication

In addition to these three reduplication patterns, TR Malay has six further reduplication patterns that are not found in either SI or RI. We assume that these six reduplication patterns are innovations in TR Malay and believe that these innovations are connected to the three common patterns of reduplication in some manner. At the present time, we do not know when these innovations occurred. Moreover, it appears that some of them are being lost again, as evidenced by the fact that our younger speakers reject some patterns that the older speaker accepts.

One interesting aspect of the PBP approach to reduplication is that, for many reduplicated forms, there are multiple settings of anchor points that will produce the correct surface forms. These analytic ambiguities are generally ignored or even considered an embarrassment. However, we would like to suggest that these analytic ambiguities actually provide an insight into language change. Specifically, we argue that the six innovative reduplication patterns in TR Malay result from analytical ambiguity of surface reduplicated forms.

Learners make decisions about how to analyze the ambient language, which results in their particular grammar. Although simplicity of analysis has been a guide to linguistic analysis and provides insights into language acquisition, it is not entirely clear that all learners choose the same analysis for ambiguous surface forms. Yang (2002) argues that a selectionist learner maintains multiple grammars through the acquisition process. The presence of multiple grammars can also be used to account for language variation. Ambiguities in the analysis of surface forms will support multiple distinct analyses, and, when these distinct analyses are applied to new forms, language change can occur. Lightner (1972) recognizes this possibility and Fitzpatrick & Nevins (2004) argue that this situation is the origin of and explains dialectal variation in Tigrinya (Rose 2003). Furthermore, Nevins & Vaux (2003) and Idsardi & Raimy (2005) demonstrate the robustness of ambiguity leading to distinct analyses in ludlings. We follow this line of inquiry and demonstrate how each of the innovative reduplication patterns can be derived from ambiguities in surface forms of the reduplication patterns in (31).

5.1 Full reduplication without final consonant

The innovative reduplication pattern that we will derive first is the full reduplication without final consonant pattern presented in (13) and analyzed in (25). The key insight to understanding the genesis of this pattern is that any surface reduplication pattern that is full reduplication of a vowel final base is ambiguous between the description of full reduplication in (24) and full reduplication without final consonant in (25). To see this consider the data in (32) which is drawn from (7), (10) and (11) used to demonstrate full reduplication in TR Malay.

(32) Ambiguous full reduplication
      base   reduplicated form
a. saŋko   saŋko-saŋko
b. baɟu   baɟu-baɟu
c. kiro   kiro-kiro
d. dulu   dulu-dulu

All bases of reduplication that end in a vowel and show total reduplication are ambiguous about whether the 'loop' is defined from the 'last segment' (as in (24) for total reduplication) or from the 'last vowel' (as in (25) for full reduplication without final consonant). In previous sections we made the traditional assumption that forms like those in (32) were clearly cases of full reduplication but we must recognize that these types of forms also satisfy the description of full reduplication without final consonant. If learners are faced with a similar ambiguity, we can then infer that the innovation of the full reduplication without consonant pattern results from a two part acquisition process. First, the learner analyzes reduplicated forms such as those in (32) with the full reduplication without final consonant analysis of (25). Second, the learner uses this generalization on a form that ends in a consonant to create a reduplicated form. This chain of events is presented in (33).

(33) Ambiguity of some full reduplication forms

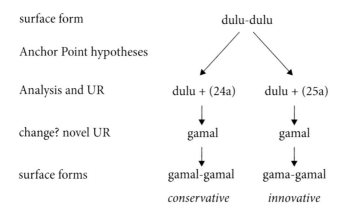

The general approach to innovation we are developing here takes advantage of ambiguity of analysis in surface forms to explain how a learner can make generalizations that lead to language change. In (33), we see that either the generalization in (24) or the one in (25) will correctly account for the surface form *dulu-dulu*. Depending on whether a learner analyzes this form according to (24) or (25) either a 'conservative' or an 'innovative' grammar will emerge. The 'conservative' grammar will produce a surface total reduplication pattern for the consonant final form *gamal* because it adopts the full reduplication analysis of (24). The 'innovative' grammar on the other hand would produce the novel surface form *gama-gamal* if the generalization in (25) is adopted instead. This grammar is 'innovative' because novel reduplication patterns can be produced via the surface ambiguity of vowel final bases, even if the learner never hears an example of the novel pattern.

In the above example, the ambiguity in how to analyze a reduplication pattern is based on Anchor Points. In the next section, ambiguities based on whether a phonological rule applied or whether something is pre-specified explain the other innovations in TR Malay.

5.2 C[ə] reduplication

The C[ə] reduplication pattern presented previously in (15) demonstrates a different type of ambiguity that can give rise to language change. In TR Malay, a rule that shows variable application reduces an [a] to [ə] when [a] precedes the penultimate vowel. This process is particularly common in quick speech. The presence of this rule creates an ambiguity for C[ə] reduplicated forms based around what the underlying identity of the prespecified vowel is. The pre-specified vowel in this reduplication pattern could be either [ə] with no application of the 'schwa rule' or it could be [a] with the application of the schwa rule.

(34) Ambiguity of C[ə] forms

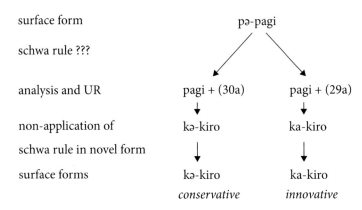

The presence of the 'schwa rule' creates an ambiguity in the analysis of the C[ə] reduplication pattern. The learner will recognize that the vowel in this pattern must be pre-specified but is then faced with the question as to whether to take a concrete or abstract approach to this particular affix. A concrete analysis, where the learner assumes that the surface schwa is not the result of the 'schwa rule', will produce the 'conservative' grammar, where the analysis of (30a) is adopted. An abstract analysis of this reduplication pattern, where the learner posits an /a/ as the memorized pre-specified vowel and derives the surface schwa from the application of the 'schwa rule', can produce the novel C[a] pattern, in cases where the 'schwa rule' does not apply. Given this analysis of the C[ə] pattern, the C[a] pattern can emerge as an innovative reduplication pattern.

Another factor that should be considered in the innovation of the pre-specified [a] is the presence of bases which show CV reduplication and have [a] as the first vowel of the base. When these forms are considered, there is the ambiguity of whether the [a] in the reduplicant is being copied or is pre-specified.

(35) CV or C[a] reduplication

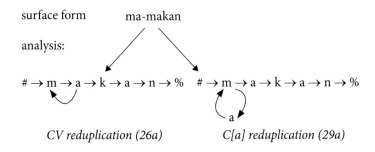

In (35), both CV and C[a] reduplication analyses are congruent with a form like *mamakan*. This ambiguity will further support the ambiguity of URs for the C[ə] pattern providing further evidence to posit an underlying /a/ as part of a reduplication pattern. Ambiguity based on whether segmental material is pre-specified or not also helps us understand the development of the pre-specified [ʔ] in TR Malay reduplication patterns.

5.3 Full reduplication with glottal stop

The final type of ambiguity that needs to be identified to explain the innovative reduplication patterns in TR Malay is whether a particular repeated phoneme is a copy or pre-specified. For this question, we focus on forms that end in a glottal stop which are quite common in TR Malay. Bases ending in a glottal stop that show the surface pattern of full reduplication are ambiguous between an analysis whereby the glottal stop is a copy, as in a full reduplication pattern in (24) versus an analysis whereby the glottal stop is pre-specified, as in the innovated full reduplication with glottal stop pattern, (27).

(36) Pre-specification ambiguity

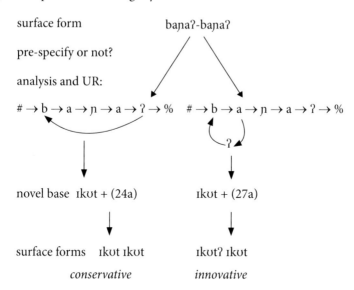

(36) illustrates the ambiguity of glottal stop final bases when they show surface full reduplication. If bases of this type are high enough in frequency, a learner may transfer the base final [ʔ] to be part of the reduplication pattern as a pre-specified segment. If this generalization is made, as in the 'innovative' path in (36), then, when it is applied to a base which does not end in a [ʔ], a novel surface reduplicated form will be generated.

This type of ambiguity is analogous to the one suggested for bases with /a/ as the first vowel and CV reduplication, which further supported the ambiguity of underlying vowels affected by the application of the 'schwa rule'. The possible presence of a rule that creates an alternation between [k] and [ʔ] (McDonald 1976: 8) in different forms of Indonesian would produce a similar type of pressure to support the pre-specified approach to the glottal stop. A sensitivity to the presence of this rule may also explain why two of the consultants restrict the reduplication of the full reduplication with glottal stop pattern to only bases that end in /k/.

5.4 Combinations of innovations

Sections 5.1–5.3 demonstrated three types of ambiguities in reduplicated forms that constitute the core of the innovations in TR Malay reduplication patterns. The most important aspect of the analysis presented here is that, at this point, we have demonstrated how all of the primitives required for our analysis of TR Malay in Section 4 can arise from ambiguities of analysis. (37) presents the primitive pieces necessary to account for the reduplication patterns in Standard Indonesian (SI) and Riau Indonesian (RI).

(37) Primitives of reduplication in SI and RI

Pattern		Begin AP	Vowel	Consonant	End AP
a.	Full	last segment	Ø	Ø	first segment
b.	CV	first vowel	Ø	Ø	first segment
c.	C[ə]	first segment	ə	Ø	first segment

In (37), the three reduplication patterns can be accounted for by using three distinct Anchor Points, 'first segment', 'last segment' and 'first vowel' and a pre-specified schwa. The immediately preceding sections demonstrated how the surface forms that give rise to the reduplication patterns and specific pieces of phonological material in (37) are actually ambiguous and support the surface patterns and phonological material in (38) below.

(38) Ambiguous primitives and novel surface patterns in TR Malay

Pattern		Begin AP	Vowel	Consonant	End AP
a.	Full	last segment	Ø	Ø	first segment
b.	Full w/o cons	last vowel	Ø	Ø	first segment
c.	Full w/ʔ	last vowel	Ø	ʔ	first segment
d.	CV	first vowel	Ø	Ø	first segment
e.	C[ə]	first segment	ə	Ø	first segment
f.	C[a]	first segment	a	Ø	first segment

The general theme that developed the novel patterns in (38) was noting how ambiguities in the surface forms of full reduplicated forms can support the novel generalizations in (38b–c) and how ambiguities in CV and C[ə] reduplication patterns can support (38f).

To complete the explanation for the origin of the reduplication patterns in TR Malay, we must understand where the remaining reduplication patterns, CV[ʔ], C[aʔ] and C[əʔ], come from. We suggest that these three remaining patterns are to be expected, provided that there is any sort of economization or pressure for symmetry in grammatical systems.

(39) Symmetry of reduplication in TR Malay

	Pattern	Begin AP	Vowel	Consonant	End AP
a.	Full	last segment	Ø	Ø	first segment
b.	Full w/o cons	last vowel	Ø	Ø	first segment
c.	Full w/ʔ	last vowel	Ø	ʔ	first segment
d.	CV	first vowel	Ø	Ø	first segment
e.	CV[ʔ]	first vowel	Ø	ʔ	first segment
f.	C[ə]	first segment	ə	Ø	first segment
g.	C[a]	first segment	a	Ø	first segment
h.	C[əʔ]	first vowel	ə	ʔ	first segment
i.	C[aʔ]	first vowel	a	ʔ	first segment

(39) demonstrates that no new phonological material, either as a pre-specified segment or as an Anchor Point, is needed to derive the analyses for all the reduplication patterns in TR Malay. The only provision is for grammar to allow the pre-specified glottal stop to occur with the CV, C[a] and C[ə] reduplication patterns, thus deriving the final three TR Malay reduplication patterns (39e, h and i).

These final three patterns must be accounted for in this grammatical way, instead of invoking ambiguity, primarily because they are not ambiguous with other attested reduplication patterns in Malay dialects. Invoking symmetry or economy in grammar has provided many striking results in previous analyses of language (Chomsky 1975, Chomsky & Halle 1968, Lightner 1972, to name a few), so, we should not be surprised to see its utility here. For a more recent discussion of symmetry and economy in phonology see Clements (2009).

6. Conclusion

In the present paper, we have introduced novel data documenting the reduplication patterns in TR Malay and provided a formal analysis of these patterns based on PBP. One advantage of adopting the PBP analysis is that it captures quite directly the similarities among the different reduplication patterns in TR Malay. The formal analysis provides a connection between the reduplication patterns in different dialects of Malay and a method of determining how reduplication patterns are related. We do recognize that a formal morpho-phonological analysis is but one facet of understanding the reduplication patterns attested in TR Malay. Further developments in our knowledge of social factors in language acquisition, statistical aspects of language acquisition, frequency aspects of language acquisition, exceptions to generalizations and restrictions on patterns and incorporating these advancements into the present analysis will improve our ability to capture the characteristics of TR Malay specifically and of human language in general.

References

Chomsky, N. 1975. *The Logical Structure of Linguistic Theory*. New York NY: Plenum Press.
Chomsky, N. & Halle, M. 1968. *The Sound Pattern of English*. Cambridge MA: The MIT Press.
Clements, G N. 2009. The role of features in phonological inventories. In *Contemporary views on architecture and representations in phonology*, E. Raimy & C. Cairns (eds), 19–68. Cambridge MA: The MIT Press.
Fitzpatrick, J. & Nevins, A. 2004. Linearizing nested and overlapping precedence in multiple reduplication. In *The Proceedings of the 27th Penn Linguistics Colloquium*, S. Arunachalam & T. Scheffler (eds), 75–88. Philadelphia PA: University of Pennsylvania.
Gil, D. 2005. From repetition to reduplication in the Riau Indonesian. In *Studies on Reduplication*, B. Hurch (ed.), 31–64. Berlin: Mouton de Gruyter.
Halle, M. 2002. Speculations about the representations of words in memory. In *From memory to speech and back: Papers on phonetics and phonology 1954-2002*, 122–136. Berlin: Mouton de Gruyter.
Idsardi, William & Raimy, E. 2005. Remarks on language play. Ms, University of Maryland and University of Wisconsin. <http://www.ling.umd.edu/~idsardi/work/2005lgplay.pdf>.
Lightner, T. 1972. *Problems in the Theory of Phonology*. Edmonton: Linguistic Research.
Macdonald, R.R. 1976. *Indonesian Reference Grammar*. Washington DC: Georgetown University Press.
Marantz, A. 1982. Re reduplication. *Linguistic Inquiry* 13:435–482.
Nevins, A. & Vaux, B. 2003. Metalinguistic, shmetalinguistic: The phonology of shm-reduplication. In *The Proceedings of the 39th Chicago Linguistics Society*. <http://ling.auf.net/lingBuzz/000319>.
Raimy, E. 1999. Representing Reduplication. PhD dissertation, University of Delaware.
Raimy, E. 2000. *The Phonology and Morphology of Reduplication*. Berlin: Mouton de Gruyter.
Raimy, E. 2003. Asymmetry and linearization in phonology. In *Asymmetry in Grammar*, Vol. 2: *Morphology, Phonology, Acquisition* [Linguistik Aktuell/Linguistics Today 58], A.M. Di Sciullo (ed.), 129–146. Amsterdam: John Benjamins.
Raimy, E. 2005. Prosodic residue in an A-templatic world. Paper presented at Linguistics Colloquium Series, University of Delaware.
Raimy, E. 2009. Deriving reduplicative templates. In *Contemporary Views on Architecture and Representations in Phonology*, E. Raimy & C. Cairns (eds), 383–404. Cambridge MA: The MIT Press.
Rose, S. 2003. Triple take: Tigre and the case of internal reduplication. *San Diego Linguistic Papers* 1:109–128.
Sneddon, J.N. 1996. *Indonesian Reference Grammar*. Sydney: Allen & Unwin.
Tadmor, U. & Yanti. 2005. Complex oral-nasal as boundary markers in traditional Jambi Malay. Paper presented at ISMIL 9, July 27-29, in Maninjau, Indonesia.
Yang, C. 2002. *Knowledge and Learning in Natural Language*. Oxford: OUP.
Yanti, 2010. A Reference Grammar of Jambi Malay. PhD dissertation, University of Delaware.

Discontiguous reduplication in a local variety of Malay[*]

Justin Nuger
University of Maryland

Discontiguous partial reduplication patterns, in which a string of segments in the reduplicant corresponds with a discontiguous string of segments in the base, have been observed in various languages in the Austronesian and Austro-Asiatic families. Several such patterns show a preference for the anchoring of the segments at both edges of the base. I propose that edge-anchoring reduplication, though typologically rare, is the result of natural interaction between fundamental phonological constraints, specifically when CONTIG-BR is ranked below constraints on reduplicant size. Support for my proposal is offered from Ulu Muar Malay, whose edge-anchoring reduplication pattern is, I argue, the result of prosodic correspondence requirements, and not the result of segmental prominence at both edges (contra Nelson 2003).

1. Introduction

Discontiguous reduplication patterns have been attested in a variety of languages, most notably from the Austronesian and Austro-Asiatic families. Patterns of discontiguous reduplication arise when the string of segments that form a reduplicant morpheme stands in correspondence with a discontiguous string of segments from the reduplicative base. These patterns are relatively uncommon in the languages of the world, but when they are attested, the resulting reduplicants have a tendency to stand in correspondence with segmental material clustering around the edges of the reduplicative base. In recent work in Optimality Theory (Prince and Smolensky 2004), Hendricks

---

[*] I am indebted to Calixto Aguero-Bautista, Arto Anttila, Lev Blumenfeld, Sandy Chung, Mark Donohue, Heather Goad, Rufus Hendon, Sharon Inkelas, Junko Ito, Mike Kenstowicz, Paul Kroeger, Raph Mercado, Armin Mester, Jaye Padgett, Glyne Piggott, and Kie Zuraw for their valuable discussion of this material. I also owe thanks to a lot of the graduate students in the UCSC linguistics department – in particular Pete Alrenga, Noah Constant, Jesse Saba Kirchner, and Dave Teeple, who should be blamed for some of the nicer elements in this work.

(2001) and Nelson (2003) have analyzed these "edge-anchoring" discontiguous reduplication patterns using constraints that stipulate anchoring of both edge segments.

Here, I consider a pattern of apparent "edge-anchoring" discontiguous reduplication in the Ulu Muar dialect of Malay. An example of this pattern is shown below in (1).

(1) Ulu Muar Malay Discontiguous Reduplication (Hendon 1966)[1]
tarɪʔ ⇒ **taʔ**-tarɪʔ "accordion"

The [ta] in the reduplicant prefix corresponds with the initial consonant and vowel in the stem, while the [ʔ] corresponds with the rightmost segment in the stem. The medial segments [rɪ] in the stem have no corresponding segments in the reduplicant. Foreshadowing the analysis to come, I argue that base-reduplicant discontiguity of the type exemplified in (1) does not result from faithfulness to both the left and right edges. Instead, anchoring is limited to the edge with which the reduplicant morpheme is aligned (or, on a different view, the edge to which it attaches).[2] In Ulu Muar Malay, the reduplicant morpheme is a prefix, so anchoring is established only at the left edge. The preservation of the rightmost segment is not due to anchoring but is instead a necessary side-effect of reduplicant maximality and prosodic correspondence. Evidence against right-edge anchoring is presented, providing further empirical support for this analysis.

2. Ulu Muar Malay reduplication

Ulu Muar Malay is a dialect of vernacular Malay, which is in the Malayo-Polynesian subgroup of Austronesian languages and is spoken on the Malay Peninsula in the Negeri Sembilan region. It is unknown how many remaining speakers are left today: as of 1966, when the major fieldwork on this language was conducted, it was already a low-prestige dialect faced with extinction (Rufus Hendon, p.c.).

The discontiguous pattern of reduplication in Ulu Muar Malay, an example of which has been given in (1), yields a CVC syllable prefix. Further examples of this pattern are given in (2), illustrating the effects of reduplication of stems ending with segments of different types.

(2) Ulu Muar Malay Type III Reduplication (Hendon 1966: 58–59)
    a. Stop-final stems:
        i. tarɪʔ ⇒ **taʔ**-tarɪʔ "accordion"
        ii. budaʔ ⇒ **buʔ**-budaʔ "children"

---

[1]. Where it aids expositional clarity, reduplicated segments have been printed in **boldface**. Numerical indices indicate what I analyze as corresponding segments.

[2]. See Lunden 2004 for an Optimality-Theoretic treatment of Marantz's Generalization (Marantz 1982) and motivation for the connection between ANCHOR and ALIGN constraints.

  iii. sikɪt ⇒ **sɪʔ**-sikɪt "various small quantities"
  iv. gɑlap ⇒ **gɑʔ**-gɑlap "is repeatedly dark"
 b. Nasal-final stems:
  i. siaŋ ⇒ **sɪɲ**-siaŋ "during the daytime on various days"[3]
  ii. dajaŋ ⇒ **dan**-dajaŋ "handmaidens"
  iii. diam ⇒ **dɪn**-diam "remains silent"
 c. [h]-final stems:
  i. pueh ⇒ so-**pʊh**-pueh "to their complete satisfaction"

The Type III pattern shown above is one of several patterns of reduplication in Ulu Muar Malay. Each pattern is conditioned by the phonological shape of the stem. According to Hendon (1966), the discontiguous pattern of reduplication is found only with stems which either: (i) begin with [s] and end in a stop or nasal, or (ii) begin with a consonant (other than [s]) and end in a stop, nasal, or [h]. Because the shape of the reduplicant depends purely on the phonological shape of the stem, the various reduplication patterns do not bear a one-to-one correspondence with a semantic function. That is to say, the same pattern of reduplication may be used to form plural nominals from singular nominals, to intensify adjectives, to form iterative predicates from semelfactive predicates, etc.

 A few descriptive generalizations can be drawn from the data in (2). First, it has already been observed that reduplicant morphemes are monosyllabic and of the form CVC: the derivation of reduplicant size is discussed in § 2.1. Second, the onset consonant in the reduplicant syllable corresponds with the initial consonant in the base, while the coda consonant in the reduplicant syllable corresponds with the final consonant in the base: this apparent edge anchoring is discussed in § 2.2. Third, the nucleus vowel in the reduplicant corresponds with the leftmost vowel in the base: vowel selection is discussed in § 2.3. Finally, there are some feature mismatches between BR-corresponding coda segments, as well as between BR-corresponding high vowels, neither of which bear directly on the present analysis of the BR-correspondence relation itself (but are nevertheless discussed briefly in the Appendix).

 The discontiguous reduplication analysis I advance here is laid out in parts. Since discontiguous reduplication is necessarily partial reduplication (total reduplication is naturally contiguous) the reduction of the reduplicative base can be analyzed in Optimality Theory by isolating a set of constraints that dominate MAX-BR. Once the size of the reduplicant is established, it must be populated with segments corresponding to segments in the base. In most languages, the prototypical situation involves contiguous reduplication, where CONTIG-BR is ranked relatively highly. By contrast, languages containing patterns of discontiguous reduplication must rank CONTIG-BR lower. The task, then, is to identify the crucial set of constraints that must dominate CONTIG-BR to yield the attested pattern. Ultimately, a ranking of both sets of

---

3. [s] is treated here as post-alveolar.

constraints – those that dominate MAX-BR and those that dominate CONTIG-BR – must be (and are) established.

2.1 Maximal syllable reduplicants

The reduplicant morpheme has the shape of a CVC syllable. In Ulu Muar Malay, complex onsets are attested, but long vowels, diphthongs, and complex codas are not attested. Setting aside the issue of complex onsets for the time being, I tentatively treat CVC syllables as maximal.

One long-standing technique used to derive maximal syllable reduplicants in Optimality Theory has been to invoke Generalized Alignment constraints such as ALL-σ-LEFT (McCarthy and Prince 1993a, Mester and Padgett 1994) defined below in (3).

(3) ALIGN(σ, L, PWd, L) (henceforth ALL-σ-LEFT): Align the left edge of each syllable to the left edge of the prosodic word in which it is contained.
(gradiently assessed; each intervening syllable incurs one violation)

By appealing to the TETU[4] ranking of ALL-σ-LEFT below MAX-IO but above MAX-BR, stems are permitted to contain as many syllables in the output as can be formed from the segments remaining from the input, while reduplicants are optimally monosyllabic.[5] Any reduplicant containing more than a single syllable incurs unnecessary extra violations of ALL-σ-LEFT. Segments must then be deleted until just one syllable remains, while obeying the phonotactics of the language; the fewest possible segments are deleted to minimize violations of the lower ranked MAX-BR. Tableau 1 illustrates the way in which Ulu Muar Malay discontiguous reduplicants fill the maximal syllable "template."

In Tableau 1 and throughout this paper, I use both the symbols ☞ and ☜ to indicate the winners calculated in the tableau, but only ☞ indicates the candidate that is the attested output in Ulu Muar Malay.

Candidate 1:a is ruled out because it is too large and incurs unnecessary violations of ALL-σ-LEFT. While candidate 1:b is monosyllabic, more segments have been deleted than is necessary. The remaining candidates contain CVC reduplicant syllables: this is the optimal syllable size for reduplicants.[6] The fact that there are, at present,

---

4. TETU refers to the OT phenomenon known as "The Emergence of The Unmarked;" see McCarthy and Prince 1994.

5. This is not strictly true. I must crucially assume a high ranking constraint guaranteeing realization of the reduplicant; this could be formalized as some version of REALIZEMORPHEME (Kurisu 2001). Obviously the null reduplicant would best satisfy ALL-σ-LEFT, but REALIZEMORPHEME would militate against this result by requiring that a reduplicant be realized overtly.

6. I have mentioned that Ulu Muar Malay phonotactics occasionally permit complex onsets. It might therefore be predicted that a candidate like glaʔ-galap may emerge. That this prediction is not borne out may be attributed to violations of LINEARITY-BR, an issue that I leave aside.

Tableau 1. Reduplicant size restricted by ALL-σ-LEFT

	RED-/gɑlap/	MAX-IO	ALL-σ-L	MAX-BR
a.	g₁a₂.l₃a₄p₅-g₁a₂.l₃a₄p₅		****!**	
b.	g₁a₂-g₁a₂.lap		***	***!
c. ☞	g₁a₂l₃-g₁a₂.l₃ap		***	**
d. ☞	g₁a₂p₅-g₁a₂.lap₅		***	**
e. ☞	g₁a₂ʔ₅-g₁a₂.lap₅		***	**

three winners simply means that more constraints are necessary to select the actual output. The identification of these constraints is the primary objective of the immediately following sections.

2.2 "Anchoring" the edges

The most striking question arising from the Ulu Muar Malay discontiguous reduplication pattern in (2) is why the reduplicant syllable corresponds with both edges of the base, at the expense of contiguity violations. Such a scenario is typologically rare but nonetheless predicted given the flexibility of constraint ranking in Optimality Theory.

Beginning with the left edge, I assert that Positional Faithfulness (Beckman 1999) plays a decisive role in this phenomenon in the form of an anchoring constraint that targets the edge of the stem to which the reduplicant affix attaches, which is the left edge in the Ulu Muar Malay pattern. With respect to the preservation of the right-edge segment, I do not assume that there is any such edge anchoring. Instead, I argue that this phenomenon is the result of Prosodic Correspondence (McCarthy and Prince 1993b, Benua 1995, Ito et al. 1996).

2.2.1 *Anchoring the left edge*

Marantz (1982) observes that there is a general tendency for reduplicative prefixes to correspond with the left edge of the reduplicative base. Though he does not discuss patterns of discontiguous reduplication, I temporarily assume (and later argue) that this correlation holds in the pattern examined here, expressed formally via the Positional Faithfulness constraint L-ANCHOR-BR (Beckman 1999). This constraint is violated whenever the leftmost segment of the reduplicative base does not have a correspondent in the reduplicant. Consider Tableau 2, for instance.

The relevant candidate is 2:a, which exhibits an instance of "wrong-edge reduplication." That this output is not attested provides evidence for some constraint on left-edge faithfulness: if no such constraint were present in the grammar of Ulu Muar Malay, it might be expected that CONTIG-BR would create a preference for a contiguous reduplicant like that in 2:a or 2:c (2:b contains a contiguous reduplicant as

Tableau 2. Left-edge segment preserved from the stem

RED-/galap/		L-ANCH-BR	ALL-σ-L	MAX-BR
a.	$l_3a_4p_5$-ga.$l_3a_4p_5$	*!	***	**
b.	g_1a_2-g_1a_2.lap		***	***!
c. ☟	$g_1a_2l_3$-$g_1a_2.l_3$ap		***	**
d. ☟	$g_1a_2p_5$-$g_1a_2.$lap$_5$		***	**
e. ☞	$g_1a_2ʔ_5$-$g_1a_2.$lap$_5$		***	**

well, but it is too small). Candidates 2:a and 2:c are immediately given further consideration below.

2.2.2 Finding a coda, or, "not anchoring the right edge"

Prosodic correspondence refers to the idea that corresponding segments should share the same syllabic role.[7] With respect to reduplication, prosodic correspondence tries to ensure that the onset of a reduplicant syllable corresponds with an onset in the base, and likewise for nuclei and codas. The concept of prosodic correspondence has been motivated by constraints on several different output-output correspondence relations, such as base-reduplicant correspondence (McCarthy & Prince 1993b), base-truncatum correspondence (Benua 1995), and base-argot correspondence (Ito et al. 1996).

Contra previous accounts of Ulu Muar Malay discontiguous reduplication (e.g. Kroeger 1989, Nelson 2003), I argue that prosodic correspondence is responsible for picking out the segment at the right edge of the base for preservation in the reduplicant as a coda, due to its status as the only coda in the syllabified stem. Put another way, the leftmost CVC sequence of segments in the base is unable to fill the CVC reduplicant template because it does not contain a coda. It is exactly this problem that rules out candidate 2:c above.

The attested correspondence relation is illustrated schematically in (4).

(4) Reduplicant coda corresponds with nearest stem coda:

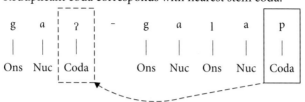

The Optimality-Theoretic constraint responsible for the prosodic correspondence relation in (4) is formalized below as CORR-Σ-ROLE-BR (Aguero-Bautista 1998, Kenstowicz

---

7. I thank Armin Mester for originally suggesting that I pursue a prosodic correspondence analysis.

2005; cf. McCarthy & Prince 1993b), which can be thought of as a quasi generalized anchoring constraint. Rather than anchoring PWd or MWd positions (i.e., left edge/ right edge), for example, this constraint induces an anchoring of syllabic positions.

(5) CORR-Σ-ROLE-BR: Let ℜ be a base-reduplicant correspondence relation. ∀x and ∀y such that x and y are segments and xℜy, assess a violation if x and y do not have the same syllabic role (onset, nucleus, or coda).
(Informal definition: BR-Corresponding segments should match in syllabic role.)

CORR-Σ-ROLE-BR must outrank CONTIG-BR to allow skipping of medial onset consonants in favor of codas in the base. If CONTIG-BR » CORR-Σ-ROLE-BR, an onset consonant nearer to the other reduplicated segments in the stem would be resyllabified as a coda in the reduplicant so as to minimize CONTIG-BR violations, contrary to what is attested. In effect, candidate 2:c would be predicted to win, given this incorrect ranking. Instead, the stem-final coda is selected to serve as the reduplicant syllable's coda (and thereby incurring CONTIG-BR violations), indicating that CORR-Σ-ROLE-BR crucially outranks CONTIG-BR.

In Tableau 3, candidate 3:a (= candidate 2:c) is ruled out by CORR-Σ-ROLE-BR. Even though the reduplicant in 3:a is a maximal syllable, its [l] is syllabified as a coda while the correspondent [l] in the base is syllabified as an onset. The candidate with a core syllable reduplicant (candidate 3:b) loses because its reduplicant syllable is not maximal. This result has been established previously via ALL-σ-LEFT » MAX-BR, but 3:b in this tableau now provides evidence for the ranking of MAX-BR » CONTIG-BR.

Tableau 3. CORR-Σ-ROLE-BR preserves the only available coda[8]

	RED-/galap/	CORR-Σ-ROLE-BR	ALL-σ-LEFT	MAX-BR	CONTIG-BR
a.	$g_1a_2l_3$-$g_1a_2.l_3$ap	*!	***	**	
b.	g_1a_2-g_1a_2.lap		***	***!	
c. ☜	$g_1a_4?_5$-$g_1a.la_4p_5$		***	**	**
d. ☞	$g_1a_2?_5$-$g_1a_2.lap_5$		***	**	**

---

8. Syllable boundaries are indicated with periods. For the purposes of assessing violations of CORR-Σ-ROLE-BR in each tableau, an onset is any consonant that is either (i) word-initial, or (ii) immediately following a morpheme boundary (-) or syllable boundary (.). All other consonants are codas. Contrary to appearance, we have not yet seen evidence for a crucial ranking between CORR-Σ-ROLE-BR and MAX-BR. For present purposes, the placement of CORR-Σ-ROLE-BR is arbitrary as long as it dominates CONTIG-BR. But see Tableau 6 in § 3.3 for evidence that CORR-Σ-ROLE-BR » MAX-BR.

As the only coda consonant in the base is [p], it is this consonant that is selected by CORR-Σ-ROLE-BR to correspond with the coda in the reduplicant, which is neutralized to [ʔ] – see candidates 3:c and 3:d. The key difference between the winning candidates 3:c and 3:d lies in the selection of the preserved vowel, which is explored further in the following section.

The prosodic correspondence analysis of what looks like "right-edge anchoring" makes a clear prediction: if there were any medial coda in the stem, this coda would be selected to stand in correspondence with the reduplicant's coda rather than any stem-final coda. I have not found an attested Ulu Muar Malay stem containing a medial cluster that has successfully undergone the discontiguous reduplication pattern described by Hendon (1966); indeed, the phonotactics of Ulu Muar Malay generally prohibit medial consonant clusters in native words. However, a few borrowings with medial clusters exist in the language. These borrowings, examples of which are given below in (6), could provide the relevant testing ground for this prediction. At this point in time, I have no idea whether it is borne out.

(6) Ulu Muar Malay words containing medial clusters (Hendon 1966: 25)
    a lintah "water leech"
    b caklat "chocolate"
    c paspʊt "passport"
    d kastam "customs service"

2.2.3 Initial syllable prominence

Now, the edge consonants in the reduplicant have correspondents in the base, established via positional faithfulness and prosodic correspondence. A new question arises, however. If both consonantal edges of a polysyllabic base are anchored in a monosyllabic reduplicant, which vowel in the base should correspond with the vowel in the reduplicant? Put differently, which edge should be considered "dominant" when segments from the middle of the base must be selected to stand in correspondence with the reduplicant? CONTIG-BR is already maximally violated, so it can serve no function in singling out a vowel among the remaining medial segments for preservation in the reduplicant.[9]

In patterns of contiguous reduplication, Marantz's Generalization states that BR-correspondence strings should have a left-to-right directionality or a right-to-left directionality. The paradox in the present case is that both directionalities manifest themselves simultaneously, resulting in partial reduplicants that correspond with both the leftmost and the rightmost consonant in the base. Nevertheless, Ulu Muar Malay discontiguous reduplicants show preservation of the vowel nucleus in the stem-initial syllable, which lends further support for the idea that Positional Faithfulness is functioning to preserve material from the left edge when all else is equal. Nelson (2003)

---

9. Even so, it may be the case that CONTIG-BR violations are in some sense "postponed" as long as possible. Thanks are due to Kie Zuraw for this idea.

accounts for this fact with the constraint FAITH-V_1, which requires faithfulness to the leftmost vowel, citing evidence from both Parisian and Québec French (Charette 1991: 203).[10] Beckman (1999: Ch. 2) also provides phonological evidence for faithfulness to the root-initial vowel in patterns of Shona vowel neutralization showing that initial vowels remain unneutralized, as well as phonological evidence for a constraint on faithfulness to the initial syllable in general.

Given that MAX is a Correspondence-Theoretic faithfulness constraint on deletion, I propose the constraint MAX-INITIAL-σ-BR as the relevant Positional Faithfulness constraint preventing deletion of segments in the initial syllable. This constraint subsumes the utility of the aforementioned left-edge-targeting constraints L-ANCHOR-BR and FAITH-V_1, but it makes a different theoretical claim and a different empirical prediction. MAX-INITIAL-σ-BR assures that the initial vowel is preserved whenever the initial consonant is preserved by virtue of the fact that they occur in the same initial syllable, which Beckman (1999) argues to be a prominent position. In contrast, there is no such intrinsic connection between L-ANCHOR-BR and FAITH-V_1. Furthermore, MAX-INITIAL-σ-BR predicts that any and all additional segmental material in the initial syllable would be preserved as well, whether this be a coda or another consonant in a complex onset; the combination of L-ANCHOR-BR and FAITH-V_1 makes no such prediction.

I adopt the MAX-INITIAL-σ-BR analysis and argue for its superiority in § 3.3. The diagram in (7) illustrates schematically the way in which MAX-INITIAL-σ-BR works.

(7) All segments in the initial syllable of the base are preserved:

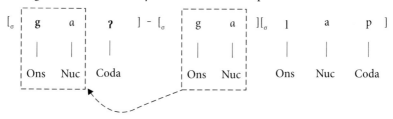

Tableau 4 shows how it interacts with the other constraints under discussion. The crucial distinction in Tableau 4 is between candidates 4:d and 4:e.

The reduplicant's vowel in candidate 4:d corresponds with the vowel in the final syllable rather than the vowel in the initial syllable. Candidate 4:e, on the other hand, contains a reduplicant whose vowel corresponds with the vowel in the stem-initial syllable, as required by MAX-INITIAL-σ-BR, and is thus selected as the winner. Of

---

10. Deletion of [ə] is allowed in medial syllables in both Parisian and Québec French, e.g., *matelas* "mattress." Compare this to the *pas de rôle* "no role" example, where [pa.də.ʁol] ⇒ [pa.dʁol] (Rialland 1986, Raffelsiefen 2005). However, [ə] is not deleted in initial syllable position in a disyllabic word in Parisian French (*cheval*, vs. Québec French *cheval* "horse"). Deletion is not allowed in polysyllabic words like *cependant* "however" in either dialect of French.

Tableau 4. MAX-INITIAL-σ-BR ensures that initial vowel is preserved

RED-/galap/		MAX-INIT-σ-BR	CORR-Σ-ROLE-BR	MAX-BR	CONTIG-BR
a.	l₃a₄p₅-ga.l₃a₄p₅	*!*		**	
b.	g₁a₂l₃-g₁a₂.l₃ap		*!	**	
c.	g₁a₂-g₁a₂.lap			***!	
d.	g₁a₄ʔ₅-g₁a.la₄p₅	*!		**	**
e. ☞	g₁a₂ʔ₅-g₁a₂.lap₅			**	**

course, CONTIG-BR must be lowly ranked so as to prevent contiguous reduplicants, as in 4:a, 4:b, and 4:c, from emerging in the output.

I now summarize the ranking arguments necessary to yield the discontiguous reduplication pattern seen in (2). In order to derive the size of Ulu Muar Malay discontiguous reduplicants – i.e., a CVC maximal syllable – the TETU ranking of MAX-IO » ALL-σ-LEFT » MAX-BR restricts reduplicants to a single syllable. Furthermore, ranking {MAX-INITIAL-σ-BR, CORR-Σ-ROLE-BR, MAX-BR} » CONTIG-BR yields the discontiguous shape of the reduplicant, given the type of stems that Hendon (1966) claims trigger this pattern of reduplication. MAX-INITIAL-σ-BR ensures that the initial CV from the stem is preserved in the reduplicant, and the combination of CORR-Σ-ROLE-BR and MAX-BR ensure that a coda consonant from elsewhere in the word is preserved as well, if one is available.

3. Previous analyses and theoretical implications

3.1 Kroeger 1989: Pre-OT

Many aspects of the OT analysis I propose in § 2 are directly inspired by those of the analysis advanced by Kroeger (1989). To foster a greater understanding for the motivation behind the OT analysis in § 2, it is worthwhile to review Kroeger's analysis briefly.

For Kroeger, the discontiguous partial reduplication process in Ulu Muar Malay is full reduplication followed by a truncation process, which proceeds via a three-step operation.

(8) Kroeger's Three-Step Operation
1. Parse a light (CV) syllable from the left edge (one mora).
2. Parse a single consonant on the right edge.[11]
3. Apply a deletion operation to the residue.

---

11. This targeting of a single consonant is permitted because Kroeger views the rightmost consonant as an extraprosodic appendix.

The operation imposes licensing conditions on particular syllables and segments and then deletes any syllables or segments that are not licensed. An example derivation of **gaʔ**-gɑlap from gɑlap is illustrated below, in (9).

(9) Example derivation of **gaʔ**-gɑlap (Kroeger 1989: 201)
 1. gɑlap (base)
 2. **gɑlap**-gɑlap (full reduplication)
 3. [gɑ]la[p]-gɑlap (parsing: one left-edge mora, one right-edge consonant)
 4. [gɑ][p]-gɑlap (deletion of residue in copy)
 5. gaʔ-gɑlap (syllabification, neutralization, assimilation)

Kroger's analysis argues that the initial vowel is preserved because of its position in the initial CV syllable: its preservation necessarily entails preservation of the initial consonant as well. This observation is similarly encoded in the OT analysis in § 2 via the constraint MAX-INITIAL-σ-BR, which militates against deletion of any segment in the initial syllable.

While Kroeger analyzes the right-edge segment as an appendix, I treat it as a lone coda – i.e., as syllabified along with the rest of the word. My analysis therefore permits its preservation because there is a coda position available in the reduplicant for it, and its preservation satisfies CORR-Σ-ROLE-BR since it bears the same prosodic role in the reduplicant. Both the analysis in § 2 and the analysis advocated by Kroeger (1989) argue that right-edge copying is the result of some special property of the rightmost consonant arising from language-specific phonotactics, independent from any theory-driven particularities of consonants occurring at an edge.

Furthermore, both analyses predict that no right-edge copying occurs with stems that are vowel-final. This prediction is examined in detail in § 3.3.

3.2 Recent work in OT

There are a few recent analyses of discontiguous reduplication in OT, including Nelson's (2003) Asymmetric Anchoring Theory, which specifically considers the Ulu Muar Malay reduplication phenomenon under discussion here.[12]

Nelson accounts for edge-anchoring reduplication patterns by deriving minimal reduplicants with both edges anchored. Rather than treating the minimality of the reduplicant as an effect of ALL-σ-LEFT, Nelson derives reduplicant minimality via place markedness. Her meta-constraint PLACEMARKEDNESS favors small reduplicants since they ban any segment linked to place features.[13] To allow the edges to be

---

12. Cf. Hendricks' (2001) Compression Model, which treats a similar phenomenon in Semai, an Austro-Asiatic language spoken in Papua New Guinea.

13. None of the candidates in Tableau 5 contain reduplicants with only placeless segments. I assume that in adopting an analysis where PLACEMARKEDNESS acts as a size restrictor, higher ranked IDENT-F constraints would be necessary to preserve place features.

Tableau 5. Nelson's Asymmetric Anchoring analysis[14]

RED-/buda?/		E-ANCH-BR	FAITH-V_1	*PLACE
a.	$b_1u_2.d_3a_4?_5$-$b_1u_2.d_3a_4?_5$			********!
b.	b_1u_2-b_1u_2.da?	*!		******
c.	$b_1\upsilon_2d_3$-$b_1u_2.d_3$a?	*!		*******
d.	$d_3a_4?_5$-bu.$d_3a_4?_5$	*!	*!	******
e.	$b_1a_4?_5$-b_1u.da$_4?_5$		*!	******
f. ☞	$b_1\upsilon_2?_5$-b_1u_2.da$?_5$			******

preserved, Nelson ranks EDGE-ANCHOR-BR[15] above PLACEMARKEDNESS. The initial vowel is preserved by FAITH-V_1, as discussed in § 2.3.

In Tableau 5, MAX-BR and CONTIG-BR (omitted for space) have to be ranked below PLACEMARKEDNESS (*PLACE), and they function in the same way as in my analysis, presented in § 2. Candidate 5:a is ruled out by virtue of its size: containing a full reduplicant, it incurs more violations of PLACEMARKEDNESS than is necessary. Candidates 5:b–c are ruled out because the rightmost segment in the base is not preserved in the reduplicant, violating EDGE-ANCHOR-BR. The candidate with a "wrong-edge" reduplicant, candidate 5:d, violates EDGE-ANCHOR-BR as well, since the leftmost segment in the base is not preserved in the reduplicant. Furthermore, it violates FAITH-V_1 because the initial vowel is not preserved. Candidate 5:e violates FAITH-V_1, as the wrong vowel is preserved, even though both edge consonants are anchored. Candidate 5:f remains as the winner.

The analysis presented in Tableau 5 works elegantly, and it is very interesting. The PLACEMARKEDNESS component ensures that reduplicants be as small as possible, without referring to the fact that reduplicants are optimally monosyllabic. The segments that remain are all treated as prominent: the edges and the initial vowel need to be preserved, so EDGE-ANCHOR-BR and FAITH-V_1 guarantee this preservation.

Despite their possible superficial similarity, there are several theoretical differences between Nelson's analysis and the one advanced here. First, if the right edge is preserved because of a constraint that guarantees preservation of both edges – EDGE-ANCHOR-BR – the correlation between right-edge anchoring and the fact that codas occur only at the right edge is treated as accidental. Furthermore, the anchoring of the onset and the anchoring of the nucleus from the initial syllable are guaranteed by two different constraints on Nelson's analysis, but only one constraint on the present analysis.

---

14. The high vowels in the reduplicants in Tableau 5 are represented as tense in open syllables and lax in closed syllables. See the Appendix for details and rationale.

15. Nelson (2003) argues against right-anchoring, but if one recognizes right-anchoring as valid, then Nelson's EDGE-ANCHOR-BR is theoretically equivalent to a PWd-level constraint disjunction of LEFT-ANCHOR-BR and RIGHT-ANCHOR-BR, as discussed below in § 4.

Let us imagine for a moment that the basic insight behind Marantz's Generalization can be expressed in OT as a correlation (as Lunden 2004 suggests). If the ranking of alignment constraints parallels the ranking of prominence constraints, Marantz's Generalization holds. In other words, if the left edge is treated as more prominent than the right edge (FAITH-LEFT » FAITH-RIGHT), then the reduplicant should align to the most prominent edge (ALIGN-LEFT » ALIGN-RIGHT). The analysis presented in Tableau 5 is incompatible with such a characterization, leaving reduplicant placement unexplained. In other words, it is unclear why the reduplicant is prefixed under Nelson's analysis since she treats both edges as simultaneously prominent.

The brief study of vowel-final stems below sheds more light on the key differences between the two analyses.

3.3 Treatment of vowel-final stems: Evidence for prosodic correspondence

As in other Austronesian languages, Ulu Muar Malay unsurprisingly contains plenty of vowel-final words that are permitted to undergo reduplication as well. In fact, there are two different reduplication processes that Ulu Muar Malay vowel-final stems may undergo. They may be fully reduplicated, or alternatively, they may undergo partial reduplication, which yields a CV reduplicant prefix corresponding with the initial CV syllable of the base.[16] Hendon (1966) refers to the total reduplication pattern as Type I and the CV partial reduplication pattern as Type IV. (Recall that Hendon calls the discontiguous pattern under discussion Type III.) In this section, I show that the "Type IV" CV pattern can actually be reduced to a special subtype of the "Type III" CVC pattern, compatible with vowel-final stems.

(10) Type I Reduplication of vowel-final stem
    rajo ⇒ **rajo**-rajo "persons of royal descent"
(11) Type IV Reduplication of vowel-final stem (Kroeger 1989: 59)
    suko ⇒ bo-**su**-suko ati- e "are enjoying themselves"

Setting the total reduplication pattern in (10) aside, consider example (11). The reduplicant prefix in (11) is **su-**, which corresponds to the initial syllable in the base [suko]. This phenomenon is compatible with the analysis that I have proposed for discontiguous reduplicants in § 2 because of the conditional nature of prosodic correspondence. The coda in the reduplicant is licensed by virtue of the presence of a coda in the base.

Vowel-final stems provide evidence for the biconditionality of prosodic correspondence in Ulu Muar Malay. That is, a coda surfaces in the reduplicant if and only if there is a coda in the base. If there are no medial codas in native Ulu Muar Malay words, then vowel-final words in Ulu Muar Malay cannot contain any codas at all. As

---

16. The issue of why and how a particular stem may undergo multiple patterns of reduplication is beyond the scope of this chapter, but see Spaelti 1997 for a treatment of multipattern reduplication in Nakanai.

such, my analysis predicts that there cannot be a coda in the reduplicant (even a placeless one), since resyllabifying an onset in the stem as a coda in the reduplicant is prohibited by CORR-Σ-ROLE-BR.

Thus, the same analysis proposed for the discontiguous cases also predicts the contiguity and the size of CV reduplicants resulting from vowel-final stems, as shown in Tableau 6.

Candidate 6:a contains another "wrong-edge" reduplicant. It incurs two violations of MAX-INITIAL-σ-BR since neither the initial consonant nor the initial vowel from the stem is preserved in the reduplicant. Candidate 6:b contains a CVC reduplicant but is ruled out by CORR-Σ-ROLE-BR because [k] is an onset in the base but a coda in the reduplicant. The candidate with the wrong vowel preserved, candidate 6:c, is likewise ruled out by MAX-INITIAL-σ-BR. The initial vowel must be preserved, not the final vowel. And the preservation of both vowels in candidate 6:e comes at the expense of additional ALL-σ-LEFT violations because Ulu Muar Malay does not permit tautosyllabic vowel clusters (Hendon 1966), which is possibly guaranteed by a highly ranked constraint like $*[_\sigma...VV...]$.

Tableau 6 shows that the presence of a coda in the base is necessary to license a coda in the reduplicant. Thus the CV pattern of reduplication reduces to a variant of the discontiguous CVC pattern. On the other hand, Nelson's (2003) analysis of discontiguous reduplication in Ulu Muar Malay is only formulated to explain the Type III pattern and does not extend to cover the vowel-final cases, even with a crucial unranking of constraints. Tableau 7 illustrates the problem.

Now, if Ulu Muar Malay did permit syllable-internal vowel clusters, such as *[suo], then the predicted output on Nelson's analysis would be ***suo**-suko, contrary to fact. As it stands, treating the initial vowel as well as the edge segments as prominent makes the wrong prediction for vowel-final stems. One is forced to copy an additional consonant to break up the resulting vowel cluster to satisfy both EDGE-ANCHOR-BR and FAITH-V_1 at the expense of a PLACEMARKEDNESS violation, resulting in what resembles full reduplication for sufficiently short stems, like [suko].

Tableau 6. Type IV Reduplication gets the same analysis as Type III

	RED-/suko/	MAX-INIT-σ-BR	CORR-Σ-ROLE-BR	ALL-σ-L	MAX-BR	CONT-BR
a.	k_3o_4-su.k_3o_4	*!		***	**	
b.	$s_1u_2k_3$-$s_1u_2.k_3$o		*!	***	*	
c.	s_1o_4-s_1u.ko_4	*!		***	***	**
d. ☞	s_1u_2-s_1u_2.ko			***	**	
e.	$s_1u_2k_3o_4$-$s_1u_2.k_3o_4$			****!**		

Tableau 7. Type IV Reduplication cannot get the same analysis as Type III (Nelson 2003)

	RED-/suko/	E-ANCH-BR	FAITH-V_1	*PLACE	CONTIG-BR
a.	k_3o_4-su.k_3o_4	*!	*	******	
b.	$s_1u_2k_3$-$s_1u_2.k_3$o	*!		*******	
c.	s_1o_4-s_1u.ko_4		*!	******	**
d. ☹	s_1u_2-s_1u_2.ko	*!		******	
e. ☞	$s_1u_2k_3o_4$-$s_1u_2.k_3o_4$			********	

All of the remaining candidates in Tableau 7 with monosyllabic reduplicants incur at least one violation of either EDGE-ANCHOR-BR or FAITH-V_1. Candidate 7:a violates both of these constraints: there is one violation of EDGE-ANCHOR-BR since the left-edge consonant is not anchored, and one violation of FAITH-V_1 since the initial vowel is not preserved in the reduplicant. Candidate 7:b incurs a violation of EDGE-ANCHOR-BR since the rightmost vowel [o] is not preserved. Note that, in contrast to the analysis presented in Tableau 6, the preservation of [k] in candidate 7:b does not violate any constraint except for PLACEMARKEDNESS (*PLACE), the size restrictor. The [k] in the analogous candidate 6:c from Tableau 6 has incurred a violation of CORR-Σ-ROLE-BR since the copy in the reduplicant is syllabified as a coda, whereas its correspondent in the base is an onset.

At this point, candidates 7:c and 7:d each violate either EDGE-ANCHOR-BR or FAITH-V_1, leaving candidate 7:e as the unlikely winner. The fact that candidate 7:e resembles the Type I total reduplication pattern (Hendon 1966) is furthermore entirely accidental and due to the shape of the particular base [suko]. If the base were to contain an extra syllable (like the hypothetical *[sukola]), even total reduplication would be impossible on Nelson's analysis due to her PLACEMARKEDNESS constraint.

The core issue in the extension of Nelson's analysis to vowel-final stems amounts to a competition among the vowels [u] (the vowel in the initial syllable) and [o] (the vowel at the right edge). This competition is only brought about because of the constraint EDGE-ANCHOR-BR, which prefers discontiguity in any partial reduplicant. In contrast, the extension of my analysis to vowel-final stems is straightforward: no prominence is placed on the right edge whatsoever, and the choice of vowel proceeds without a problem. The initial CV syllable is preserved exactly as it is in the discontiguous cases above, and prosodic correspondence is satisfied since there is no viable coda in the base – at the right edge, or otherwise – to serve as a correspondent for a coda in the reduplicant.

4. In conclusion

I have shown that explanation of the apparent "both-edge anchoring" phenomenon in (2) does not necessitate constraints like EDGE-ANCHOR-BR. The alternative analysis proposed in § 2 is based on conditional licensing of codas: if there is a coda at the right edge of a stem, then a coda is licensed at the right edge of the reduplicant. The prosodic correspondence constraint CORR-Σ-ROLE-BR prohibits any non-coda in the base from standing in correspondence with a coda in the reduplicant. The imposition of conditions on the licensing of reduplicant codas allows for simple extension of the same analysis to stems that do not contain codas.

The problem with relying on EDGE-ANCHOR-BR to preserve right-edge codas, as Nelson (2003) does, is that this constraint attempts to preserve segments at the right edge, regardless of whether or not they are codas, contrary to the attested facts. Since it has been shown that such reliance on EDGE-ANCHOR-BR to preserve right-edge coda consonants is not necessary, questions arise regarding the status of constraints like EDGE-ANCHOR in Universal Grammar.

Consider Beckman's (1999) Positional Faithfulness Theory, which designates the left edge as a prominent position, but not the right edge.[17] Positional Faithfulness Theory is founded on the idea that faithfulness constraints can be formulated either as general or positional. General constraints apply to all positions within a domain, while positional constraints only apply to prominent positions. Nelson (2003) argues that EDGE-ANCHOR should be treated as a general constraint on anchoring, while LEFT-ANCHOR should be treated as a positional constraint on the leftmost segment. The ultimate goal of Nelson's formulation of the anchoring constraints in this way is to do away with RIGHT-ANCHOR (which is in line with Beckman's proposal).

While I support the goal, I take issue with the means of achieving it. In my view, ANCHOR constraints are already positional versions of MAX constraints. If one adopts this view, the formulation of a constraint EDGE-ANCHOR, then, treats both edges as prominent positions. EDGE-ANCHOR itself is functionally equivalent to a local constraint disjunction of LEFT-ANCHOR$\vee_{Dom}$RIGHT-ANCHOR.

(12) Comparison of EDGE-ANCHOR with LEFT-ANCHOR ∨ RIGHT-ANCHOR

RED-CVC	E-ANCH-BR		RED-CVC	L-ANCH-BR $\vee_{PWd}$R-ANCH-BR
$C_1V_2C_3$- $C_1V_2C_3$		vs.	$C_1V_2C_3$- $C_1V_2C_3$	
C_1V_2- C_1V_2C	*		C_1V_2- C_1V_2C	*
V_2C_3- CV_2C_3	*		V_2C_3- CV_2C_3	*
V_2-CV_2C	**		V_2-CV_2C	**

---

17. Beckman cites phonetic and psycholinguistic evidence, *e.g.*, Hawkins and Cutler 1988, as the basis for this claim.

It thus makes sense to consider EDGE-ANCHOR a notational variant of LEFT-ANCHOR $\vee_{\text{Dom}}$ RIGHT-ANCHOR. EDGE-ANCHOR-BR then, by definition, refers to the right edge as a target for preservation in the reduplicant.[18] Although it has been shown that the right edge may be targeted as prominent in some instances (e.g. tone distribution; see Zhang 2004), there is no prima facie evidence for right-edge prominence in the Ulu Muar Malay discontiguous reduplication pattern presented in (2), as the reduplication of vowel-final stems indicates.

In contrast, the analysis I advance in § 2 does not refer to the right edge in any constraint definition, but instead derives right-edge preservation via constraint interaction – as a language-specific accident, basically. The main theoretical difference between the analysis described here and the EDGE-ANCHOR analysis in Nelson 2003 is that only the former is directly compatible with Positional Faithfulness Theory, as formulated by Beckman.

Nevertheless, my analysis may not be correct. Both Nelson's and my analyses make very clear and very strong empirical predictions. If there is a medial coda in the base, my analysis predicts that this coda would be selected to correspond with a coda consonant in the reduplicant, whether or not a stem-final coda is present as well. In contrast, Nelson's analysis predicts that the stem-final coda would be selected to correspond with a coda in the reduplicant even if there were a medial coda present in the base. While societal and geographical circumstances make it difficult to test these predictions in Ulu Muar Malay, the analyses might be tested on other languages with edge-anchoring reduplication patterns: either on other dialects of Malay or on Austro-Asiatic languages that show the same kind of patterns. A crosslinguistic study of this magnitude is unfortunately beyond the scope of the present work. However, I have shown in this chapter that it is possible for patterns of discontiguous reduplication to be analyzed without constraints that stipulate discontiguity, like EDGE-ANCHOR. The type of crosslinguistic study described above would be extremely valuable in determining the validity of such an analysis, as well as the practicality of positing constraints like EDGE-ANCHOR in Universal Grammar.

References

Aguero-Bautista, C. 1998. Cyclic and identity effects in Spanish diminutives and augmentatives. Generals Paper, Massachusetts Institute of Technology.

Beckman, J. 1999. *Positional Faithfulness: An Optimality Theoretic Treatment of Phonological Asymmetries*. New York NY: Garland.

Benua, L. 1995. Identity effects in morphological truncation. In *Papers in Optimality Theory* [University of Massachusetts Occasional Papers in Linguistics 18], J. Beckman, L. Walsh Dickey & S. Urbanczyk (eds), 77–136. Amherst MA: GLSA.

---

18. This claim obviously extends to Hendricks' (2001) use of RIGHT-ANCHOR-BR in his Compression Model treatment of Semai discontiguous reduplicants.

Charette, M. 1991. *Conditions on Phonological Government*. Cambridge: CUP.

Dumas, D. 1978. Phonologie des réductions vocaliques en français québécois. PhD dissertation, Université de Montréal.

Hawkins, J.A. & Cutler, A. 1988. Psycholinguistic factors in morphological asymmetry. In *Explaining Language Universals*, J.A. Hawkins (ed.), 280–317. Oxford: Blackwell.

Hendon, R. 1966. *The Phonology and Morphology of Ulu Muar Malay* [Yale University Publications in Anthropology 70]. New Haven CT: Yale University.

Hendricks, S. 2001. Bare-consonant reduplication without prosodic templates: Expressive reduplication in Semai. *Journal of East Asian Linguistics* 10: 287–306.

Ito, J., Kitagawa, Y. & Mester, A. 1996. Prosodic faithfulness and correspondence: Evidence from a Japanese argot. *Journal of East Asian Linguistics* 5: 217–294.

Ito, J. & Mester, A. 2003. *Japanese Morphophonemics: Markedness and Word Structure* [Linguistic Inquiry Monograph 41]. Cambridge MA: The MIT Press.

Kenstowicz, M. 2005. Paradigmatic uniformity and contrast. In *Paradigms in Phonological Theory*, L.J. Downing, T.A. Hall & R. Raffelsiefen (eds), 145–169. Oxford: OUP.

Kroeger, P. 1989. Discontinuous reduplication in vernacular Malay. *Berkeley Linguistics Society* 15: 193–202.

Kurisu, K. 2001. The Phonology of Morpheme Realization. PhD dissertation, University of California, Santa Cruz.

Légaré, L. 1978. Deux règles d'accentuation dans les voyelles hautes du dialecte québécois. MA thesis, Université de Montréal.

Lunden, A. 2004. Reduplicant placement, anchoring, and locality. Ms, College of William and Mary. (Available on the Rutgers Optimality Archive: ROA-885).

Marantz, A. 1982. Re reduplication. *Linguistic Inquiry* 13: 434–482.

McCarthy, J. & Prince, A. 1993a. Generalized alignment. In *Yearbook of Morphology*, G. Booij & J. van Marle (eds), 79–153. Dordrecht: Kluwer.

McCarthy, J. & Prince, A. 1993b. Prosodic morphology I: Constraint interaction and satisfaction. Technical Report RuCCS-TR-2, Rutgers University. (Available on the Rutgers Optimality Archive: ROA-537).

McCarthy, J. & Prince, A. 1994. The emergence of the unmarked: Optimality in prosodic morphology. In *Proceedings of NELS 24*, Mercè Gonzàlez (ed.), 333–379. Amherst MA: GLSA.

McLaughlin, A. 1986. Une (autre) analyse de la distribution des variants des voyelles hautes en français montréalais. *Revue québécoise de linguistique théorique et appliquée* 5: 179–214.

Mester, A. & Padgett, J. 1994. Directional syllabification in generalized alignment. In *Phonology at Santa Cruz 3*, J. Merchant, J. Padgett & R. Walker (eds), 79–85. Santa Cruz CA: UCSC Linguistics Research Center. (Available on the Rutgers Optimality Archive: ROA-1).

Nelson, N. 2003. Asymmetric Anchoring. PhD dissertation, Rutgers University. (Available on the Rutgers Optimality Archive: ROA-604).

Prince, A. & Smolensky, P. 2004. *Optimality Theory: Constraint Interaction in Generative Grammar*. Malden MA: Blackwell.

Raffelsiefen, R. 2005. Paradigm uniformity effects vs. boundary effects. In *Paradigms in Phonological Theory*, L.J. Downing, T.A. Hall & R. Raffelsiefen (eds), 211–262. Oxford: OUP.

Rialland, A. 1986. Schwa et syllabes en français. In *Studies in Compensatory Lengthening*, L. Wetzels & E. Sezer (eds), 187–226. Dordrecht: Foris.

Spaelti, P. 1997. Dimensions of Variation in Multi-Pattern Reduplication. PhD dissertation, University of California, Santa Cruz.

Zhang, J. 2004. The role of contrast-specific and language-specific phonetics in contour tone distribution. In *Phonetically Based Phonology*, B. Hayes, R. Kirchner & D. Steriade (eds), 157–190. Cambridge: CUP.

Appendix: Featural mismatches

As mentioned in § 2, there are at least two other phonological processes that apply to Type III reduplicants, namely high vowel laxing and coda placelessness. Specifically, high vowel laxing refers to the fact that the correspondents of [u] and [i] surface as [ʊ] and [ɪ] in a CVC reduplicant. Additionally, stops serving as reduplicant codas must appear as [ʔ], while a nasal coda in a reduplicant prefix must assimilate to the place of the following onset in the base. The only other consonant licensed in the coda position in reduplicants is [h]. This restriction is what I am referring to as coda placelessness.

While these processes do not bear directly on the previous discussion of reduplicant discontiguity (or the Correspondence-Theoretic representation thereof), they are explored briefly here. Local constraint conjunction can be applied to account for both of these patterns straightforwardly.[19] I begin by examining the descriptive generalizations that require explanation.

First, high vowel laxing occurs only in closed syllables (i.e., syllables with a coda). In Optimality-Theoretic terminology, this generalization can be captured by the constraint NO-CODA$\wedge_\sigma$*[+HIGH, +ATR].[20] Second, coda placelessness can be analyzed as place feature deletion occurring only on codas. Another conjoined constraint can capture this generalization in OT: NO-CODA$\wedge_{seg}$*PLACE, where *PLACE can be thought of as a *STRUC constraint against association of segments to place features (like Nelson's PLACEMARKEDNESS).

These two phenomena have different scopes of application, as well. High vowel laxing occurs across the board in all closed syllables (i.e. in both the base and the reduplicant), but conditioned coda placelessness is a phenomenon observed in reduplicants only. The TETU ranking schema applied earlier to account for reduplicant size can also cover the distribution of these two featural mismatches as well, illustrating the utility of an OT analysis to explain these facts.

Recall that the TETU ranking of MAX-IO » ALL-σ-LEFT » MAX-BR is invoked to reduce reduplicant size to a single syllable without affecting the shape or size of the base. Similarly, ranking IDENT-IO » NO-CODA$\wedge_{seg}$*PLACE » IDENT-BR permits

---

19. There are some technical issues surrounding the minimal domain in which these constraints apply; further explication lies beyond the scope of this chapter. See Ito and Mester 2003 for a recent discussion of local constraint conjunction.

20. I am treating [ATR] as the relevant feature that distinguishes [i] from [ɪ] and [u] from [ʊ]; cf. discussions of Québec French high vowel laxing in closed syllables in Dumas 1978, Légaré 1978, and McLaughlin 1986.

placeless codas in reduplicants but not in stems. Tableau A clearly illustrates how coda placelessness is restricted to reduplicant codas.

What about high vowel laxing? Since high vowel laxing occurs in closed syllables in both reduplicants and stems, the constraint against tense high vowels in closed syllables can simply be ranked over both IDENT-IO and IDENT-BR.

Tableaus A and B show how an OT analysis can simultaneously account for the distribution of placeless codas and high, lax vowels via constraint interaction. This account could easily be integrated into the analysis presented in § 2 for greater precision.

Tableau A. Coda placelessness in reduplicants only

RED-/galap/		IDENT-IO	NO-CODA∧$_{seg}$*PLACE	IDENT-BR
a.	g$_1$a$_2$p$_5$-g$_1$a$_2$.laʔ$_5$	*! (ʔ)	* (p)	* (p)
b.	g$_1$a$_2$ʔ$_5$-g$_1$a$_2$.laʔ$_5$	*! (ʔ)		
c.	g$_1$a$_2$p$_5$-g$_1$a$_2$.lap$_5$		**! (p, p)	
d. ☞	g$_1$a$_2$ʔ$_5$-g$_1$a$_2$.lap$_5$		* (p)	* (ʔ)

Tableau B. High vowel laxing in all closed syllables

RED-/sikit/		NO-CODA∧$_σ$ *[+HIGH, +ATR]	IDENT-IO	IDENT-BR
a.	s$_1$i$_2$ʔ$_5$-s$_1$i$_2$.kit$_5$	*!* (iʔ, it)		* (ɪ)
b.	s$_1$i$_2$ʔ$_5$-s$_1$i$_2$.kɪt$_5$	*! (iʔ)	* (ɪ)	* (ʔ)
c.	s$_1$ɪ$_2$ʔ$_5$-s$_1$i$_2$.kit$_5$	*! (it)		** (ɪ, ʔ)
d.	s$_1$ɪ$_2$ʔ$_5$-s$_1$ɪ$_2$.kɪt$_5$		**! (ɪ, ɪ)	* (ʔ)
e. ☞	s$_1$ɪ$_2$ʔ$_5$-s$_1$i$_2$.kɪt$_5$		* (ɪ)	** (ɪ, ʔ)

Phonological evidence for the structure of Javanese compounds

Katrina Schack Tang
University of California, Los Angeles

This paper presents field data from Javanese showing that Noun-Noun and Noun-Adjective compounds in Javanese are phonologically distinct from both non-compound words and phrases. I explore the idea that this behavior can be explained by a syntactic approach in which this difference arises from a distinction between early and late spell-out (Chomsky 1999). I further argue that various phonological approaches to the same data are unable to produce the desired surface forms.

1. Javanese compounds[1]

Javanese compound phonology shows unique behavior within the language, in that it is distinct from both the phonology of non-compound words and the phonology of phrases. Specifically, both parts of a compound behave as if they are at the end of a prosodic word, even when a clitic follows the compound. However, a non-compound word followed by a clitic does not show this behavior.

In this paper, I will explore the proposal that this phenomenon arises as an effect of the interface between syntax and phonology; the phonological pattern provides evidence for the syntactic derivation. I compare a syntactic account of these data to several purely phonological or morphophonological approaches and argue that these data result from a difference in syntactic derivation between compound words and phrases. Specifically, a distinction between early and late spell-out (Chomsky 1999) can account for the fact that the behavior of a compound word is distinct from that of a phrase. The analysis presented here is also in keeping with Marantz's (to appear) distinction between inner and outer word formation in Distributed Morphology.

---

1. Thanks to Rachmi Diyah Larasati for her patience as a language consultant, to Hilda Koopman, Kie Zuraw, and Tomoko Ishizuka, and two anonymous reviewers for their feedback assisting in refining the arguments in this paper, and to Hilda, Kie, Tomoko, Asia Furmanska, Chacha Mwita, and Briana Bejarano for participating in the data collection.

1.1 Data

The data in this paper were all collected through field work with one female speaker at UCLA. The consultant has lived in both Central Javanese (Jogjakarta) and East Javanese (Malang) dialect areas. Indeed, the patterns described here are generally similar to other descriptions of Central Javanese, e.g. Hayward (1999). All data are in Ngoko, or informal, register. The consultant also speaks Indonesian, English, and Arabic.

The compound-specific patterns presented here have not been described previously, though Horne (1974) and Hayward (1999) imply that the first member of a compound has unexpected pronunciation by pointing out several compound words as phonologically exceptional forms.

1.2 Outline of paper

In the following section, I compare the phonology of compounds to that of words and of phrases and show that it is distinct from both. I also provide non-phonological diagnostics for compounds. I then outline a syntactic explanation for this distinction in Section 3 and follow this with a sketch of several phonological approaches which, I argue, are incapable of accounting for these data. In Section 4, I discuss several pieces of data that do not fall into the pattern discussed here and consider a possible account for them. Section 5 provides the conclusions of the present work.

2. Phonology and compounds

In this section, I describe the basic distribution of [a] and [ɔ] in this dialect of Javanese. Throughout this paper, I treat /a/ as underlying since [ɔ] alternates with both [a] and [o] (see Tang 2006). However, as far as compounds are concerned, the same facts must be explained no matter which sound is considered basic.

2.1 The [a]/[ɔ] alternation in Javanese

The sounds [a] and [ɔ] are in complementary distribution in non-cliticized words in Javanese. The basic pattern is as follows: [a] occurs word-internally and before suffixes, and [ɔ] occurs word-finally. However, before the definite clitic -ne, both [a] and [ɔ] are acceptable pronunciations. Examples are given in (1).[2]

---

2. The data are provided in roughly phonetic transcription, except that the distinction indicated by [p,b], [k,g], etc., is one of phonation rather than voicing.

(1) a. [a] word-internally   luwaʔ³   'palm civet'
    b. [ɔ] word-finally   gulɔ, *gula   'sugar'
    c. [a] before suffixes⁴   ḍoŋa-ʔne, *ḍoŋɔ-ʔne 'pray (for s.o.)'
    d. [a] and [ɔ] before clitics gula-ne, gulɔ-ne   'the sugar'

Exceptions to this pattern arise from vowel harmony, since a preceding /a/ harmonizes with the following /a/. Thus, when [bɔsɔ] 'language' is followed by the clitic -ne, it may be pronounced [basane] 'the language'. *[basɔ] and *[bɔsane] are impossible pronunciations since harmony does not occur.⁵

There are two restrictions on this harmony system. First, it does not apply to syllables earlier than the stem's penult; for example, in [acɔrɔ] 'event', the first /a/ fails to harmonize, and this word cannot be pronounced *[ɔcɔrɔ]. Second, harmony applies only to open syllables; the /a/ in [ɟalmɔ] 'human being' fails to harmonize since it occurs in a closed syllable, and *[ɟɔlmɔ] is not an acceptable variant.

This paper is unable to fully address the variability that does occur in the [a]/[ɔ] alternation before -ne since, with only one speaker, the motivation is difficult to determine. However, the variability is not idiosyncratic since Hayward (1999) also reports variability between [a] and [ɔ] before clitics. The consultant's self-reported differences between *Xa-ne* and *Xɔ-ne* pronunciations are variously attributed to dialect, emotion, intention, semantics, and social or economic class, and other potential factors include education, frequency, a language change in process, and homophony avoidance. This bears further investigation.

Since the causes of this variation are poorly understood, this paper does not attempt to deal with it systematically. Rather, in the remainder of the paper I will focus on the fact that, in non-compounds, /a/ *can* surface as [a] before the clitic -ne.

2.2 No [a]/[ɔ] alternation in nominal compounds

Compound phonology deviates from this pattern, however. In nominal compounds, /a/ still surfaces as [ɔ] in word final position, as is shown in (2).

(2) /kəmbaŋ/ 'flower' + /gula/ 'sugar' → [kəmbaŋgulɔ] 'candy'

However, in a compound, /a/ also surfaces as [ɔ] before the clitic -ne, and [a] is never permitted as a variant form. Thus, the definite form of (3) still contains [ɔ], as shown in (3).

(3) kəmbaŋ + gula + -ne → [kəmbaŋgulɔne], *[kəmbaŋgulane]   'the candy'

---

3. While [ɔ] can also occur in this position, such an [ɔ] would alternate with [o] rather than with [a].
4. Variation may be permitted before certain suffixes, but data on this topic are limited.
5. The clitic -ne has two forms, [ne], which follows vowels, and [e], which follows consonants.

The final /a/ of the first part of a compound also surfaces as [ɔ], and again, [a] is never permitted as a variant form, as is shown in (4):

(4) anḍa *'ladder'* + wiḍoḍari *'goddess'* → [ɔndɔwiḍoḍari],
                                          *[anḍawiḍoḍari] *'rainbow'*

The obligatory pronunciation of /a/ as [ɔ] indicates that each part of a compound behaves like it is at the end of a phonological word (p-word), even when it is not. This freezing effect is not merely a metrical phenomenon since other four-syllable words do not show this behavior.

(5) /kapulaga -ne/ → [kapulɔgɔne], [kapulagane]
    cardamom D
    'the cardamom'

As shown in (5), the final /a/ of a four syllable non-compound can be pronounced as either [a] or [ɔ] before -*ne*.

2.3 Phrasal phonology

Compound phonology differs not only from word phonology but also from phrasal phonology. In a noun-adjective phrase, an /a/-final noun and adjective both surface with final [ɔ], as expected. Examples are provided in (6):

(6) a. wɔŋ   ṭuwɔ
       person old
       'old person'

    b. kɔncɔ lanaŋ
       friend male
       'male friend'

The definite clitic -*ne* may follow a noun-adjective AP in Javanese (see Ishizuka 2008). In such a DP, -*ne* forms a phonological unit with the adjective. The adjective, however, behaves just like a noun which is followed by -*ne*, in that the /a/-final adjective is permitted to surface with either final [a] or final [ɔ], as shown in (7).

(7) /wɔŋ   ṭuwa -ne/ → [wɔŋ ṭuwɔne], [wɔŋ ṭuwane]
    person old   D
    'the old person'

This contrasts with the otherwise homophonous compound of the same noun and adjective, which does not permit this variation, as shown in (8).

(8) /wɔŋ- ṭuwa   -ne/ → [wɔŋṭuwɔne], *[wɔŋṭuwane]
    person- old>parents D
    'the parents'

Thus, phonological behavior is one diagnostic for a compound in Javanese, since the behavior of compounds is distinct from both that of words and that of phrases.

2.4 Extent of the phenomenon

This unique phonology applies to all examples of Noun-Noun and Noun-Adjective compounds that were tested and were familiar to the consultant. In Javanese, these compounds are left-headed or have an external head. Other types of left headed compounds (NV, N(VN)) do not seem to show this behavior. The data are limited, but I will comment on these compounds in Section 4.1. Although reduplicated nouns have sometimes been treated as compounds, they also do not share the phonology of N-N and N-A compounds in Javanese, a fact which I discuss in Section 4.2.

2.5 Non-phonological diagnostics for compounds

The phonological diagnostics for compounds introduced in the previous section are supported by more traditional diagnostics for compounds. First, Javanese compounds exhibit contiguity; they cannot be interrupted by a clitic or an adjective. For example, in isolation, (9a) is ambiguous; it can have either the compound meaning, 'rainbow', or the non-compound meaning, 'goddess's ladder'. However, if the clitic -*ne* is added, here acting as a genitive, the ambiguity is resolved by the position of the clitic. In (9b), where the clitic occurs between the two nouns, only the non-compound meaning is possible, whereas in (9c), where the clitic follows the second noun, only the compound meaning is possible.

(9) a. ɔndɔ̙ wiḑoḑari   'rainbow' or 'goddess's ladder'
       ladder goddess
    b. anḑa -ne wiḑoḑari   'the goddess's ladder'
       ladder D goddess
    c. ɔndɔ̙ wiḑoḑari -ne   'the rainbow'
       ladder goddess D

Likewise, the examples in (10) show that an adjective cannot interrupt a compound. (10a) and (10c) both consist of a noun followed by the adjective meaning 'male'; (10a) is a phrase, while (10c) is interpreted here as a compound. This is made clear when a nationality adjective such as 'Javanese' is inserted between the noun and the adjective, as in (10b) and (10d). This is the usual position for nationality adjectives in Javanese (see Ishizuka 2008), and, so, the phrase in (10b) receives its expected phrasal interpretation. However, when the adjective is inserted between the two parts of a compound, as in (10d), the result cannot be interpreted while retaining the meaning given in (10c).

(10) a. wɔŋ lanaŋ
person male
'man' (phrase in Javanese)

b. wɔŋ jɔwɔ lanaŋ
person Javanese male
'Javanese man'

c. kɔncɔ-lanaŋ
friend male
'boyfriend' (compound)

d. ?*kɔncɔ jɔwɔ lanaŋ
friend Javanese male
?*meaning: 'Javanese boyfriend'

Finally, compounds in Javanese typically show some degree of semantic drift. For example, the compound provided in (11) combines 'flower' and 'sugar' to mean 'candy'. While candy is usually sweetened with sugar and may bear a resemblance to a flower, there is a clear abstraction away from the literal meaning of these two morphemes.

(11) kəmbaŋ- gulɔ 'candy'
flower sugar

Thus, Javanese compounds are distinguished from phrases by the fact that they are non-interruptable and by their semantic drift, and when either part of the compound ends in /a/, they are further distinguished by their phonology. In the remainder of the paper, I focus specifically on this unique phonological aspect.

3. Phonology in the syntax

I argue that the unique phonology of Javanese compounds can be best analyzed under an approach where compounds are syntactically derived. The phonological difference between compounds and phrases, then, rests on compounds reaching spell-out earlier in the derivation than phrases.

The syntax works roughly as follows (details are given in the following section). In the DPs under consideration here, the surface order is Noun-Adjective-Determiner. However, the surface order is the opposite order of these elements when they are merged; N is merged first, then A, and then D. These are rolled up in order to derive the correct surface order: the NP first raises to Spec-AP, and the [NP A] constituent then raises to Spec-DP, resulting in the surface constituency [[N A] D] (Cinque 2005; for Javanese, Ishizuka 2008).

The crux of this approach is the claim that compounds differ from phrases in that, in a N-A compound, N and A are both merged below a phase head, whereas in a [N A] phrase, the A is merged above this head. Since phase-internal material is spelled out at the end of a phase, this results in a difference in the spell-out of A (Chomsky 1999). The phonological pattern resulting in this difference is as follows: A word-final /a/ at spell-out is raised to [ɔ], but a non-final /a/ at spell-out remains [a].

I illustrate this by comparing the derivation of the compound [wɔŋ-tuwɔ] 'parents' to the phrase [wɔŋ tuwa] 'old person'. I then compare these forms with the addition of the clitic -ne (cf. examples 7 and 8 in Section 2.3).

3.1 Derivation of compounds

I first consider the derivation of the compound [wɔŋ-tuwɔ] 'parents'. The tree in (12) illustrates the minimum process needed to derive the correct phonology for the compound; the noun *wɔŋ* merges with the adjective *tuwa*, forming an AP. This AP, in turn, merges with a higher phrase, which I refer to as XP; the phonology indicates that X must be a phase head.[6]

(12)

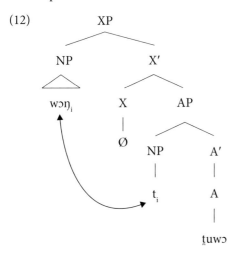

The NP *wɔŋ* then raises to the specifier of XP, presumably to fulfill its edge feature (cf. Kayne 2005), yielding the correct surface order *wɔŋ tuwa*. Since X is a phase head, spell-out then occurs for any material remaining below X; specifically *tuwa* is spelled out at this stage in the derivation. Since the /a/ in *tuwa* is word-final, it is now spelled out as [tuwɔ].

However, I assume that, parallel to the phrase formation, the noun in the compound actually originates below the adjective, thus permitting the correct scopal relationships. The surface word order results from N raising around A; the movement is illustrated in the context of a DP in (13).

In order to derive [wɔŋ -tuwɔ-ne], a DP with -ne as its head is eventually merged with this XP. The entire XP then moves to Spec-DP, as illustrated in (13), resulting in the correct linear order.

---

6. The exact labels of the constituents here are unimportant; of key importance is the relative position of the phase head within the derivation.

(13)

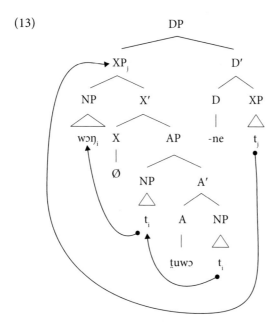

The morpheme ṭuwa is no longer p-word final when the derivation reaches the point where the DP is spelled out. However, since ṭuwa has already been spelled out as [ṭuwɔ], the phrase is pronounced [wɔŋ-ṭuwɔ-ne].

This analysis does, however, raise the question of what this phase head X might be. The data currently available do not provide a definitive answer to this question. However, one strong possibility is that X is a functional head such as n (see Embick & Noyer, 2006; Marantz, to appear) that assigns this compound nominal status. If this is the case, then the root adjective /ṭuwa/ first merges with the root noun /wɔŋ/, and this noun in turn raises to Spec-nP.[7]

3.2 Adjective phrases and non-compound nouns

The derivation of the compound above contrasts with that of the phrase [wɔŋ ṭuwɔ] 'old person', as shown in (14).

---

7. A reviewer suggests that these compounds might actually have the structure [[n a]$_n$] -ne]$_{DP}$. The difference in phonology between compounds and phrases could then be explained by an optional restructuring rule that allows a bracket to be erased only if it is derived in the same syntactic cycle. From a purely phonological perspective, this idea is problematic for the reasons outlined in Section 3.3.3. From a syntactic perspective, there is currently no additional evidence to suggest that an optional restructuring rule of this sort should exist. While greater relative depth of compounds is achieved in either analysis, a hierarchical structure permits semantic scope. Hierarchical structures are commonly assumed in analyzing other types of compounds (cf. Bok-Bennema and Kampers-Mahne 2006, among many others). Barring further evidence then, I have taken the viewpoint here that the morphology has the same basic structure as the syntax.

(14)

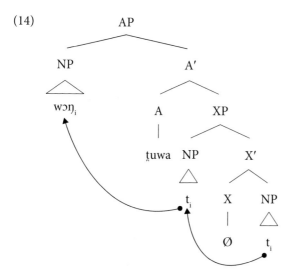

Here, only the noun *wɔŋ* is merged below the head X, and the NP containing it moves to Spec-XP as above. Spell-out occurs after this move, but there is no material remaining below X to be spelled out. NP then raises again to Spec-AP, yielding the correct surface order. When this AP is spelled out, both *wɔŋ* and *tuwa* are p-word final since both meet the minimal word requirements in Javanese and no clitic is present. This results in the pronunciation [wɔŋ tuwɔ].

However, if the determiner *-ne* is added to this phrase, *tuwa* is no longer p-word final at spell-out, as shown in 15.

(15)

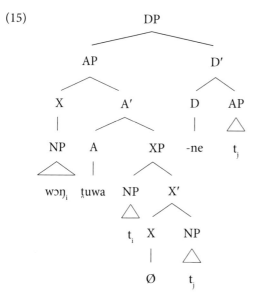

To derive [wɔŋ ṭuwane] 'the old person', the determiner -*ne* is merged above the AP *wɔŋ ṭuwa*, and the AP then raises to the specifier position of the resulting DP. At spell-out, ṭuwa is no longer p-word final since -*ne* is a clitic, nor has ṭuwa previously been spelled out. Consequently, the phrase is pronounced [wɔŋ ṭuwa-ne], at least in the variant under discussion here.

A bare noun ending in /a/ will behave the same way as the adjective ṭuwa does in this phrase since the noun will move out from under XP before the spell-out of XP occurs. Since the spell-out of this noun then occurs when the DP is spelled out, the noun will end in [ɔ] if no clitic is present and [a] if a clitic is present.

Thus, the difference between the pronunciation of the compound and the phrase can be derived as a consequence of their syntactic derivation.

3.3 Problems with phonological approaches

Phonology is often times considered as unable to access syntactic derivation directly. However, as I will show in this section, a phonological or morphophonological account that cannot refer to the syntactic derivation also fails to account for the data at hand. Due to space restrictions, the discussion is limited to basic versions of the theories under consideration.

3.3.1 *Lexical phonology*

Lexical phonology (Kiparsky 1982) has been employed to explain the phonology of compounds in English (Halle & Mohanan 1985) and Malayalam (Mohanan 1986). Because lexical phonology divides phonological derivation into levels, it is able to treat derived words differently from non-derived words. However, this approach cannot account for the Javanese data because there is no way to appropriately distinguish between roots and compounds.

A lexical phonology approach might be set up with four levels at which phonological changes can occur: (1) Roots, (2) Compounding, (3) Affixation, and (4) Cliticization. If /a/-raising occurs at the root level, the derivation is as below.

	/aṇḍa/	/aṇḍa/
	/lanaŋ/	
Root	ɔṇḍɔ, lanaŋ	ɔṇḍɔ
Compound	ɔṇḍɔlanaŋ	ɔṇḍɔ
Clitic	ɔṇḍɔlanaŋe	ɔṇḍɔne

The goal is to derive the output [aṇḍa-ne] 'the ladder' from the input /aṇḍa/ 'ladder' and to derive [ɔṇḍɔ-lanaŋ-e] 'the ladder (specific kind)' from the inputs /aṇḍa/ 'ladder' and /lanaŋ/ 'male'. However, if vowel raising applies at the root level, /aṇḍa/ becomes [ɔṇḍɔ] for both the compound and the non-compound form. This cannot be undone at the final cliticization level. While [ɔṇḍɔne] is a grammatical output in Javanese, it is impossible to also derive [aṇḍane] under this analysis: if /a/-raising is obligatory, then [anḍane] fails to be derived, but if /a/-raising is optional, then it should be optional for /anḍa-lanaŋ/ as well, predicting that *[anḍa-lanaŋ] is a possible output. Finally, if /a/-raising follows compounding, it is impossible to derive [ɔnḍɔ-lanan] since the final /a/ would no longer be final once compounding occurs and, consequently, it would not be subject to /a/-raising.

3.3.2 *Paradigm uniformity*
A second approach used to account for morphophonological variation is that of paradigm uniformity (Steriade 2000). Using this approach, it is possible to assume that the bare form of a word is the base and, further, that a compounded stem must match the base. However, this is unmotivated, especially since there is no principled reason, at least in current versions of the theory, that the compound should be required to match the base while an affixed or cliticized stem is not required to do so.

This is not to say that paradigm uniformity plays no role in Javanese phonology. This pressure does seem to exist and may account for the alternate pronunciation of cliticized non-compounds as *X*[ɔ]-*ne*.

3.3.3 *Prosodic structure*
Finally, prosodic structure has been used to explain Rendaku in Japanese compounds (Ito & Mester 2003). However, this approach is also problematic for Javanese. If a Javanese compound consists of two p-words, for example, then /a/-raising must apply at the p-word boundary. Thus, the nouns /upa/ 'rice grain' and /ɹiwa/ 'soul' combine to form a compound with both /a/'s raised [upɔ]$_\omega$ [ɹiwɔ]$_\omega$.

However, cliticization becomes problematic. If, as is typically assumed, the clitic is a part of another p-word, then this predicts the correct result for the non-compound noun /ɹiwa/, which forms a single p-word with the clitic *-ne*. Since the /a/ is not at a p-word boundary, /a/-raising fails to apply, and the resulting form is [ɹiwane]$_\omega$. On the other hand, though several possibilities exist for parsing the five syllable form /upa-ɹiwa-ne/, none of them result in the correct pronunciation. If *-ne* forms a p-word with the second half of the stem, the result is *[upɔ]$_\omega$ [ɹiwane]$_\omega$, with the second /a/ failing to undergo raising. If the entire compound forms a single p-word, the result is *[up-aɹiwane]$_\omega$, with no raising at all. Finally, if *-ne* is not permitted to form a prosodic constituent on its own, the structure *[upɔ]$_\omega$ [ɹiwɔ]$_\omega$ [ne]$_\omega$ is banned even though the pronunciation would be correct. Permitting *-ne* to be an independent p-word is problematic for several reasons. First, Javanese has a rarely broken minimal word requirement of two moras. Second, although *-ne* can attach phonologically to both nouns and adjectives, it can never stand on its own.

Even if the prosodic hierarchy approach is further refined, permitting a clitic and a prosodic word to combine to form a larger constituent such as a clitic group (Hayes 1989), this approach still presents problems. For example, if /ɹiwa-ne/ is parsed as [[ɹiwa]$_\omega$[ne]]$_{CG}$, then /a/-raising must apply at a higher level than the p-word since /a/ is permitted to surface as [a] here. Since /a/-raising does apply in compounds followed by -*ne*, this boundary must be intermediate between the prosodic word and the clitic group, forming a structure such as [[[upɔ]_ω[ɹiwɔ]_ω]_X[ne]]_CG. However, not only is such a structure otherwise unmotivated, but it still predicts the wrong result. If /a/-raising takes place at the intermediate level X, not at the lower p-word level, then this should actually be pronounced *[[[upa]_ω[ɹiwɔ]_ω]_X[ne]]_CG since the first p-word is not followed by an X-level boundary. Thus, prosodic structure seems unpromising as an explanation for this phenomenon.

3.4 Local summary

To summarize, a syntactic account is better equipped to explain the Javanese phonological alternation under discussion than a phonological account is. This implies that the phonology-syntax interface is more direct than many phonologists assume it to be.

4. Remaining puzzles

This paper has primarily addressed the syntax and phonology of a specific type of compound in Javanese. However, this has implications for the rest of the grammar. In this section, I address several apparent compounds that do not conform to the phonological pattern established above. I also address reduplicated forms, showing them to be different from compounds. Finally, I consider whether the pattern discussed in this paper is present in other areas of Javanese grammar.

4.1 Compounds with phrasal phonology

In the data collected thus far, there are two apparent compounds that do not show the freezing effect established in the examples above. Both of these appear to be left headed nominal compounds that differ from the ones discussed above in that they contain a verb.

The first is a noun-verb compound, shown in (16).

16. /raɟa/ + /kaya/ → [rɔɟɔ-kɔyɔ-ne], [rɔɟɔ-kaya-ne]
    king   resemble   *raɟa-kaya-ne
    'person who owns a lot of (stolen) livestock'

The freezing in [rɔɟɔ] is predicted, considering the compound forms above; however, the variability in /kaya/ is puzzling. The order of the morphemes is also unexpected; Javanese has VO instead of the OV order present in this compound. This contrasts with the noun-noun and noun-adjective compounds presented above, where the morphemes have the same order that they would in a phrase. Thus, this compound must be derived differently than those presented above. The simplest approach is that the NP/

raja/ 'king' merges with the V /kaya/ 'resemble'. The entire VP then raises to the specifier position of XP to acquire nominal status and thereby avoids being spelled out under XP. At spell-out, then, /raja/ is p-word final but /kaya/ is not when followed by -ne.

In the second example, shown in (17), a verb combines with a noun, and a second noun is added to this combination.

(17) /ṭukaŋ/ + (/rasa/ + /səga/) → [ṭukaŋ-rɔsɔ-səgɔ-ne],
worker taste rice   [ṭukaŋ-rɔsɔ-səga-ne]
'taster (by profession)'

Again, the final noun fails to show the phonological freezing that is expected in a compound. However, this form was checked only phonologically. It is possible that -ne may be compound-internal; for example, (17) could have the structure (ṭukaŋ + (rasa + (səga-ne))). If -ne is added before compounding takes place, then, even if /rasa-ne/ is spelled out early in the derivation, it is predicted to show the same variability /rasa-ne/ does in isolation.

4.2 Reduplication

Nominal reduplication is also phonologically distinct from noun-noun compounding in Javanese. Reduplication is sometimes thought to be a form of compounding (e.g. McCarthy & Prince 1988); however, the data here imply that, if reduplication does produce compounds, they have a different structure from other noun-noun compounds in Javanese. An example of reduplication is given in (18).

(18) RED + /anḍa/ 'ladder' + -ne → [ɔnḍɔ-ɔnḍɔ-ne],   'the ladders'
                              [ɔnḍɔ-anḍa-ne],
                              [anḍa-anḍa-ne][8]

Thus, the second copy can be pronounced as [anḍa] or [ɔnḍɔ] before -ne, just as the non-reduplicated noun can. The first copy can be pronounced as [ɔnḍɔ] before either pronunciation of the second; harmony is not obligatory. However, if the second copy is pronounced with [a], the first is required to be so as well.

The forms where the reduplicant matches the base are not surprising, given that this pressure exists cross-linguistically (McCarthy & Prince, 1995) and that Javanese has vowel harmony. What is surprising is that [ɔnḍɔ-anḍa-ne] is also an accepted pronunciation. There are several possible explanations here. One is that the input form actually has /ɔ/ instead of /a/, though this raises further difficulties in the grammar (see Tang 2006). Another is that /a/-raising, like harmony, is foot based in Javanese, in that a foot boundary can serve as the proper environment for /a/-raising. This is difficult to test, however, since four-syllable monomorphemic words are uncommon.

---

8. I abstract away from issues of initial glottal stop insertion.

4.3 Beyond compounds

Finally, given that a syntactic mechanism has been proposed to account for the phonological freezing shown in compounds, the grammar should be explored more carefully to determine whether this freezing is actually more widespread. The data collected so far are quite limited, but there are several points that are suggestive.

First, the phrase /wɔŋ ɟawa-ne/, shown in (19), can only be pronounced [wɔŋ ɟɔwɔne].

(19) wɔŋ   ɟɔwɔ   -ne
      person Javanese D
      'the Javanese person'

That is, even though most adjectives ending in /a/ can be pronounced with either [a] or [ɔ] before -ne, /ɟawa/ does not show this flexibility. Since nationality adjectives are low, there is a possibility that this effect results from the same syntax that produces the freezing effect in compounds. If this is the case, however, the XP referred to in (12) must be something other than nP.

Second, /a/ is pronounced as [a] before most verbal suffixes. However, variation is allowed before the imperative suffixes -nɔnɔ and -nən. This has not been tested extensively; however, if this difference proves to be systematic, this could be taken as indication that a similar effect is present in the verbal syntax. This would be the expected direction of the effect since the imperative suffixes are assumed to be quite high, merged after vP, while other suffixes in Javanese correspond to voice or theme, suggesting that they are merged below vP.

5. Conclusion

In this paper, I have addressed the phonology-syntax interface in Javanese. I argue that the unique phonology of Javanese compounds provides evidence that these compounds are derived by raising a noun across a silent phase head, forcing spell-out of part of the compound. The analysis presented here, then, implies that certain phonological processes are able to apply iteratively at certain stages of the syntactic derivation; this is similar to the idea of cyclic rule application in Lexical Phonology (Kiparsky 1982) and elsewhere, where phonological rules are interleaved with morphological operations. I argue that in Javanese, they are interleaved with a syntactic operation instead, in keeping with the idea of cyclic spell-out.

References

Bok-Bennema, R. & Kampers-Mahne, B. 2006. Taking a closer look at Romance compounds. In *New Perspective on Romance Linguistics*, Vol. 1: *Morphology, Syntax, Semantics, and*

Pragmatics [Current Issues in Linguistic Theory 275], C. Nishida & J.-P. Monteruil (eds), 13-26. Amsterdam: John Benjamins.
Chomsky, N. 1999. Derivation by phase. *MIT Occasional Papers in Linguistics* 18.
Cinque, G. 2005. Deriving Greenberg's Universal 20 and its exceptions. *Linguistic Inquiry* 36: 315-32.
Embick, D. & Noyer, R. 2007. Distributed morphology and the syntax/morphology interface. In *Oxford Handbook of Linguistics Interfaces,* G. Ramchand & C. Reiss, (eds), 289-324. Oxford: OUP.
Halle, M. & Mohanan, K.P. 1985. Segmental phonology of Modern English. *Linguistic Inquiry* 16: 57-116.
Hayes, B. 1989. The prosodic hierarchy in meter. In *Rhythm and Meter*, P. Kiparsky & G. Youmans (eds), 201-260. Orlando FL: Academic Press.
Hayward, K. 1999. Lexical phonology and the Javanese vowel system. *SOAS Working Papers in Linguistics* 9: 191-225.
Horne, E.C. 1974. *Javanese-English Dictionary*. New Haven CT: Yale University Press.
Ito, J. & Mester, A. 1999. *Japanese Morphophonemics: Markedness and Word Structure.* Cambridge MA: The MIT Press.
Ishizuka, T. 2008. Deriving the order of constituents in the Javanese DP. Ms, UCLA.
Kayne, R. 2005. Some notes on comparative syntax: With special reference to English and French. In *Movement and Silence,* R. Kayne (ed.), 277-333. Oxford: OUP.
Kiparsky, P. 1982. Lexical phonology and morphology. In *Linguistics in the Morning Calm,* Seok Yang (ed.), 3-91. Seoul: Hanshin.
McCarthy, J. & Prince, A. 1988. Quantitative transfer in reduplicative and templatic morphology. In *Linguistics in the Morning Calm 2,* Linguistic Society of Korea (ed.), 3-35. Seoul: Hanshin.
McCarthy, J. & Prince, A. 1995. Faithfulness and reduplicative identity. In *University of Massachusetts Occasional Papers in Linguistics* 18: *Papers in Optimality Theory*, J. Beckman, S. Urbanczyk & L.W. Dickey (eds), 249–384. Amherst MA: GLSA.
Marantz, A. To appear. Phases and words. Ms, MIT.
Mohanan, K.P. 1986. *The Theory of Lexical Phonology*. Dordrecht: Reidel.
Steriade, D. 2000. Paradigm uniformity and the phonetics-phonology boundary. In *Papers in Laboratory Phonology 5: Acquisition and the lexicon*, M. Broe & J. Pierrrehumbert (eds), 313-334. Oxford: OUP.
Tang, K.S. 2006. On [ɔ] in Javanese: Harmony, opacity, and variability. Ms, UCLA.

Appendix: Javanese compounds

1. N-N and N-A Compounds (+ -*ne*, where relevant)
   a. /anḍa/ 'ladder' + /wiḍoḍari/ 'goddess' →
      [ɔnḍɔ-wiḍoḍari-ne], *[anḍa-wiḍoḍari-ne]   '*the rainbow*'
   b. /kəmbaŋ/ 'flower' + /gula/ 'sugar' →
      [kəmbaŋ-gulɔ-ne], *[kəmbaŋ-gula-ne]   '*the candy*'
   c. /wɔŋ/ 'person' + /ṭuwɔ/ 'old' →
      [wɔŋ-ṭuwɔ-ne], *[wɔŋ-ṭuwa-ne]   '*the parents*'

    d. /anḍa/ 'ladder' + /lanaŋ/ 'male' →
       [ɔnḍɔ-lanaŋ-e], *[anḍa-lanaŋ-e]   'the ladder (special kind)'
    e. /ṭukaŋ/ 'worker' + /ḍoɲa/ 'prayer' →
       [ṭukaŋ-ḍoɲɔ-ne], *[ṭukaŋ-ḍoɲa-ne]   'the prayer leader'
    f. /upa/ 'rice grain' + /ɟiwa/ 'soul' →
       [upɔ-ɟiwɔ-ne], *[upɔ-ɟiwa-ne]   'the search for life'
    g. /kanca/ 'friend' + /wiŋkiŋ/ 'back' >
       [kɔncɔ-wɪŋkɪŋ], *[kancawɪŋkɪŋ]   'wife' (old word)
    h. /kanca/ 'friend' + /lanaŋ/ 'male' >
       [kɔncɔ-lanaŋ], *[kanca-lanaŋ]   'boyfriend'
    i. /kaca/ 'glass' + /maṭa/ 'eye' >
       [kɔcɔ-mɔṭɔ-ne *[kaca-maṭa-ne]   'eyeglasses'

2. Other Possibile Compounds + -ne
    a. /ṭukaŋ/ 'worker' + /rasa/ 'taste' + /səga/ 'rice' + -ne →
       [ṭukaŋrɔsɔsəgɔne], [ṭukaŋrɔsɔsəgane]   'taster (by profession)'
    b. /raɟa/ 'king' + /kaya/ 'resemble' →
       [rɔɟɔkɔyɔne], [rɔɟɔkayane], *[raɟakayane]
                         'person who owns a lot of (stolen) livestock'

3. Reduplication + clitic
    a. /kanca/ 'friend' + -ku 'my' >
       [kɔncɔkancaku], [kancakancaku], [kɔncɔkɔncɔku]   'all my friends'
    b. /anḍa/ 'ladder' + -ne >
       [ɔnḍɔɔnḍɔne], [ɔnḍɔanḍane], [anḍaanḍane]   'the ladders'
    c. /apa/ 'what' + -ne >
       [ɔpɔɔpɔne], [ɔpɔapane], [apaapane]   'anything'

Intonation, information structure and the derivation of inverse VO languages*

Mara Frascarelli
Università degli Studi Roma Tre

The correspondence between grammatical and prosodic boundaries is widely acknowledged in the literature and a number of recent works have studied the syntax–prosody interface and its relation to information structure. In this line of analysis, this paper presents the results of a pioneering interface investigation (based on natural data) on two inverse VO languages, Tagalog and Malagasy. Crucial similarities and important asymmetries provide a contribution to the understanding of intonational properties and to the ongoing debate on word order derivation. In particular, prosodic evidence and information-structural considerations show that the V-initial order is derived through vP (remnant) movement in both languages. This movement, however, is not directly connected with focus, since it also occurs when the vP does not convey new information. A connection with an (extended) EPP requirement is therefore proposed as a property of 'predicate-fronting' languages.

1. Introduction

A large number of recent analyses have investigated the relation between syntax and phonology, having the aim to identify the principles of prosodic mapping on universal grounds.[1] In this area of research, the analysis of Focus constructions plays a major

---

* This work benefited from crucial support at the ZAS (Berlin); I wish to thank Hans-Martin Gärtner and Paul Law for their help and precious discussion and two anonymous reviewers for critics and suggestions. Many thanks to my informants Marites Navarro Alcaria, Carolyn Vargas, Annita Rasamoely and Emy Fernando for their patience in providing and checking the data used in this analysis.

1. According to the generative approach, there is a correspondence between grammatical and prosodic boundaries (Selkirk 1986, Nespor and Vogel 1986) and patterns of default phrase stress result from Spell-out conditions. In marked patterns, on the other hand, a base-generated extraposition has been invoked for [-focus] constituents, so that Foci always mark a major phrase boundary, while Topics form independent Intonational Phrases (Frascarelli 2000).

role, showing the existence of a significant connection between discourse grammar and PF-correlates (cf., among others, Kenesei & Vogel 1990, Frascarelli 2000, Samek-Lodovici 2005).

Prosodic properties are also important for a deeper understanding of word order variation. In this respect, intonation seems to support the association of information Focus with a pitch-lending accent both in VO and OV languages (Hayes & Lahiri 1990) and the existence of a common underlying order (in line with Kayne's 1994 assumptions). To the best of my knowledge, however, no systematic interface analysis has been carried out on *inverse* VO languages that – as is argued in Pearson (2000) – form a separate type within the VO class and show some striking asymmetries with respect to the direct VO group (cf. among others, Rackowski & Travis 2000, Carnie et al. 2005).

The aim of this paper is exactly to provide an interface analysis of broad and narrow Focus constructions[2] in two V-initial Austronesian languages, Tagalog and Malagasy, in order to shed some light on the interface interpretation of predicate fronting and consider its syntactic implications within a 'Phase-approach' (Chomsky 2001, 2005).[3] Mention to Italian data will also be present as a comparative element with a direct VO language.

2. The interface realization of focus

The association of Focus with a major tonal event in the sentence is widely acknowledged in the literature. In this respect, two main concerns can be identified, namely (a) the distinction between default and marked stress assignment, and (b) the connection between tonal events and syntactic structure.

Some authors have argued that there is no difference between the tonal event denoting the last accented syllable of a Broad Focus (BF) sentence and the pitch marking the tonic vowel of a Narrow Focus (NF; cf. Selkirk 1986). Along this line of analysis, Cinque's (1993) 'Nuclear Stress Rule' links main prominence assignment to the most embedded constituent in the sentence, independent of Focus structure. Recent analyses, however, have proven a substantial difference in the tonal properties of broad and narrow Focus constructions (cf., among others, Frota 2000, D'Imperio 2002), showing the necessity of a principled distinction, also in a syntax-phonology perspective (Frascarelli 2000, 2004).

In particular, research on intonation shows that in an SVO language like Italian, BF sentences exhibit a downgrading contour with a final fall on the last accented

---

2. Broad Focus sentences carry 'all new' information, whereas in Narrow Focus constructions, new information is restricted to a single constituent.

3. The relevant investigation is based on natural data (2 hours ca.), collected with the help of four native speakers (aged 30–35), who replied to questions inducing different Focus structures.

vowel (i.e., a complex tonal event of the H + L* type), while NF is always marked by a H* pitch (cf. D'Imperio 2002, Frascarelli 2004, Frascarelli & Trecci 2007).[4] This means that, contrary to Cinque's (1993) generalization, no pitch-accent can be found on the most embedded constituent of a BF sentence. This leads to the conclusion that, at least in Italian, broad Focus is not interpreted at the PF interface as the effect of an "extended Focus projection" (as is proposed in Selkirk 1986). Indeed, BF intonation appears as a 'default' tonal interpretation that arises in declarative sentences when the Focus field (Rizzi 1997) is not activated in the C-domain (cf. Frascarelli & Puglielli 2007). Consider, for instance, the following sentence (from Frascarelli 2004):[5]

(1) E   infatti quello mi   manca   molto.
     and in.fact that   to.me to be.missing.3SG much
     'In fact, I miss that a lot.'

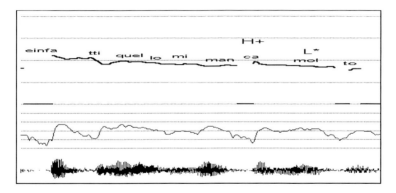

Figure 1. BF sentence in Italian (H + L*)

---

4. The description of intonational contours is based on Pierrehumbert's (1980) system – generally known as ToBI – in which tunes are described as sequences of *low* (L) and *high* (H) tones, which determine the shape of the F0 contour. According to this framework, pitch accents have a prominence-lending function on stressed syllables, while boundary tones delimit prosodic edges. In particular, there are six different types of pitch accent (two simple tones – High (H*) and Low (L*) – and four complex (bitonal) ones) and two boundary tones (the Intonational Phrase boundary (marked as H% or L%) and the Intermediate Phrase boundary (marked as H⁻ or L⁻)). In this paper I mainly focus on pitch-accents, though reference to boundary tones can be present, when relevant.

5. The list of abbreviations used in the glosses is the following: ACT = actor; DAT = dative; DET = determiner; DIR = direct object; FM = Focus marker; IMPF = imperfective; OBL = oblique; PERF = perfective; PL = plural; PRN = pronoun; PST = past tense; REC = recent; SG = singular; TH= theme; TR = trigger marker.

As we can see in example (1), the sentence, which conveys all new information, is realized by means of a gradual downgrading contour and no pitch can be found either on the last accented vowel (*mòlto*, which is marked by a Low tone), or on any other constituent.

Let us now consider the interface properties of BF sentences in inverse VO languages.

2.1 Broad focus sentences in Tagalog

The analysis of natural data shows that the unmarked word order in Tagalog is strongly based on argument structure. Specifically, BF sentences prefer the V-Actor-Theme order, independent of the 'trigger' (i.e., the constituent marked by *ang*, determining the Voice morphology of the verb), in line with Schachter's (1993: 1425) indications.[6]

Interestingly, with respect to intonational properties, BF sentences are characterized by a *rising tone on the verb*, which reaches its highest point on the post-tonic syllable (i.e., a complex tonal event of the L* + H type).[7] The rest of the sentence shows a downgrading (or flat) contour and no tonal event can be found on the trigger, independent of its argument role. After the rightmost constituent a minimum value of F0 is reached (the 'baseline'): For that position, we can posit the presence of a Low Intonational Phrase boundary tone (L%). Let us observe this pattern with verbs having different argument structures:

(2) *Dumating   ang kaibigan ko   kahapon.*
    TH.arrive.PERF TR friend   PRN.1SG yesterday
    'My friend arrived yesterday.'

---

6. I avoid reference to the syntactic notion of 'subject' in dealing with Tagalog. Indeed, there is considerable disagreement over which noun phrase has the strongest claim to being called the 'subject' in this language, if this notion is applicable at all. In short, the problem is that properties commonly associated with subjects are 'split' between two different NPs, namely the trigger and the Actor NP. The former launches floating quantifiers, is the target of raising, conjuction and relativization; the latter can be reflexified and bound from within the local clause (for discussion and references, cf. Klamer 2002, Gärtner et al. 2006). Given these 'distributed' properties, constituent order can be hardly stated in standard terms (i.e., using the S-V-O labels). Though important, this issue is immaterial for the purposes of the present analysis.

7. To produce the relevant sentences, informants were given a verbal form (e.g., *dumating* for sentence (2)) and asked to use it in answering questions like "What happened?", "What's the news?".

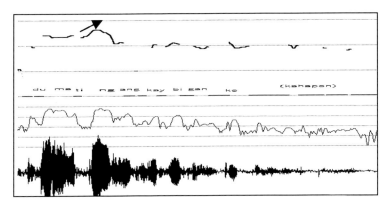

Figure 2. BF sentence in Tagalog – one-argument verb

(3) *Bumabasa   ang titser   ng diyaryo.*
    ACT.read.IMPF TR teacher DIR newspaper
    'The teacher is reading a newspaper.'

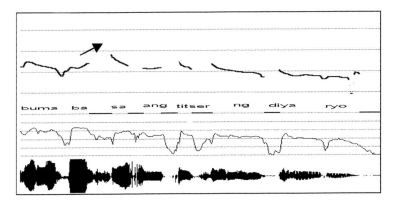

Figure 3. BF sentence in Tagalog – transitive verb, Actor trigger

(4) *Binabasa   ng titser   ang diyaryo.*
    TH.read.IMPF DIR teacher TR newspaper
    'A/the teacher is reading the newspaper.'[8]

---

8. As the translations indicate, the trigger argument is regularly interpreted as definite, a non-trigger Theme is indefinite and other non-trigger constituents are either definite or indefinite, in line with Schachter and Otanes (1972: 75, 96) and Schachter (1993: 1419).

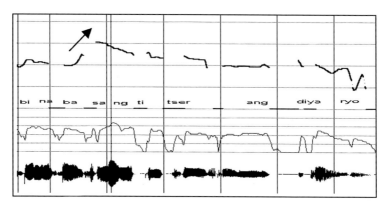

Figure 4. BF sentence in Tagalog – transitive verb, Theme trigger

As shown above, no major difference can be found in the general pattern described above.[9] We can therefore conclude that unlike in Italian BF sentences, in Tagalog BF sentences, a rising tone marks the verb, which forms a unique Intonational Phrase with the following arguments, independent of the θ-role of the trigger. The trigger, however, affects the formation of prosodic boundaries in ditransitive BF constructions, as shown below:

(5) *Nagbigay   ang titser   ng libro kay Juan.*
     ACT.give.PERF TR teacher DIR book DAT Juan
     'The teacher gave a book to Juan.'

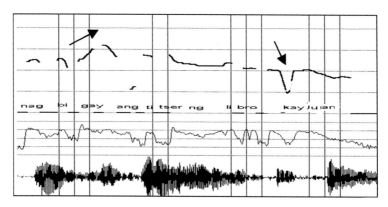

Figure 5. BF sentence in Tagalog – ditransitive verb, Actor trigger

---

9. Notice that the same pattern can be found with different types of mono-argumental verbs, in sentences like (i)-(ii) below. This shows that tonal properties do not depend either on the unaccusative/unergative distinction or on weather/impersonal verbs.

  (i) *natulog* (L* + H) *si Juan kahapon* ('John slept yesterday')
  (ii) *umulan* (L*+H) *nang madalas* ('it often rained')

(6) *Ibinigay   ng titser   ang libro kay Juan.*
    TH.give.PERF DIR teacher TR book DAT Juan
    'A/the teacher gave the book to Juan.'

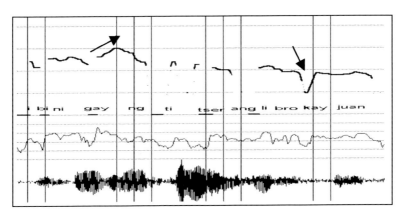

Figure 6. BF sentence in Tagalog – ditransitive verb, Theme trigger

As we can see, when the trigger is either the Actor or the Theme, ditransitive sentences show the tonal pattern illustrated above, that is to say, the rising verb is followed by a downgrading contour including both Actor and Theme (i.e., the direct arguments). Surprisingly, the indirect object is preceded by a clear break that can be interpreted as a prosodic boundary. Since it is not a major pause in durational terms and the intonational curve resumes its downgrading contour (after resetting), it is feasible to propose that the relevant prosodic boundary corresponds to an Intermediate Phrase (L⁻). From a syntax-prosody interface perspective, this means that a (prepositional) indirect object is not included in the prosodic phrase containing the verb and its arguments, as a sort of 'adjunct' (i.e., a PP merged outside the *v*P-phase; cf. also Rackowski 2002: 63).

Given this analysis, it is interesting to note that when the indirect object is the trigger, the relevant break disappears and the three arguments are all included in a unique prosodic unit:[10]

(7) *Binilhan   ng bulaklak ni Juan si Maria.*
    GOAL.give.PERF DIR flowers DIR Juan TR Maria
    'Juan gave some flowers to Maria.'

---

10. Notice that the trigger marker is realized as *si* with proper nouns.

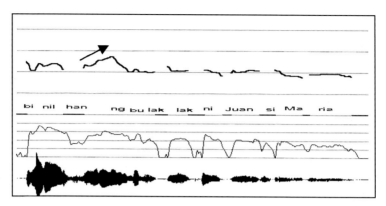

Figure 7. BF sentence in Tagalog – ditransitive verb, Goal trigger

These data lead us to the conclusion that indirect objects are merged in the *v*P-phase only when they are non-prepositional (i.e., when they are triggers). This suggests that the trigger function of a non-direct argument implies an increase in the argument structure of the verb. This proposal is supported by syntactic evidence concerning focalization: When indirect objects are realized as PPs, they are focused through simple fronting (cf. (8); Focus is capitalized, as in standard use), as are adjuncts (cf. (9a–b)). On the other hand, when an indirect object is the trigger, it is focused by means of a specific construction (cf. (10)) that is typical of direct arguments (cf. Section 3.2) and cannot be used for PPs (compare (8) and (11)):

(8) KAY PEDRO ibinigay ni Maria ang libro.
 DAT Pedro TH.give.PERF DIR Maria TR book
 'Maria gave the book TO PEDRO.'

(9) a. KAHAPON pumunta si Maria sa simbahan.
  yesterday ACT.go.PERF TR Maria OBL church
  'YESTERDAY Maria went to church.'

 b. SA BAHAY KO nagluto si Pedro ng isda.
  OBL house PRN.1SG ACT.cook.PERF TR Pedro DIR fish
  'AT MY PLACE Pedro cooked fish.'

(10) SI PEDRO ang binigyan ni Maria ng libro.
 TR Pedro TR GOAL.give.PERF DIR Maria DIR book
 'It's TO PEDRO that Maria gave a book.'

(11) *KAY PEDRO ang ibinigay ni Maria ang libro.
 DAT Pedro TR TH.give.PERF DIR Maria TR book

2.2 Broad focus sentences in Malagasy

The analysis of natural data show that BF sentences in Malagasy are strictly VOS (in line with standard assumptions, cf. Klamer 2002), where S is the trigger. As for intonational properties, they are also characterized by a *rising tone* (L* + H) but, differently from Tagalog, this is not invariably located on the verb: the maximum of F0 is reached on *the constituent preceding the trigger*. Finally, like in Tagalog, no tonal event marks the trigger, which is realized in the final part of a downgrading contour. After the trigger, the baseline is reached and a Low Intonational Phrase boundary (L%) can be identified. Let us consider the following examples:

(12) *Mivoavoa   ny   alika.*
     PST.ACT.bark DET(TR) dog
     'The dog barked.'

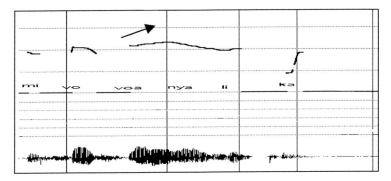

Figure 8. BF sentence in Malagasy – one-argument verb

(13) *Nahazo   mpangalatra ny   polisy.*
     PST.ACT.arrest thief   DET(TR) police
     'The police arrested the thief.'

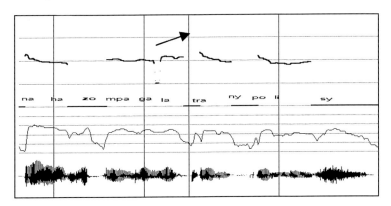

Figure 9. BF sentence in Malagasy – transitive verb

(14) *Nividy vonikazo hoan'i Maria i Joana.*
PST.ACT.buy flowers to Maria DET(TR) Joana
'Joana bought some flowers for Maria.'

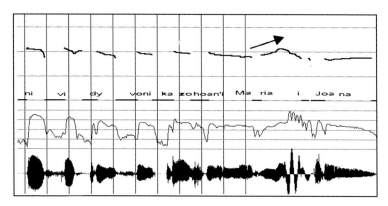

Figure 10. BF sentence in Malagasy – ditransitive verb

As shown in Figures 8–10, the relevant pattern is consistently found for one-argument (12), transitive (13) and ditransitive (14) verbs.

2.3 Preliminary conclusions

So far, we have seen that BF constructions are characterized by a rising tone and that the [verb-arguments] sequence forms an Intonational Phrase both in Tagalog and Malagasy. However, main prominence marks different elements in the two languages: the verb in one, the constituent preceding the trigger in the other. A number of questions thus arise: What interface interpretation can we provide for these data? How are these intonation patterns related to the pattern of a direct VO language like Italian? What do they show about the syntactic derivation at the moment of Spell-out? An answer to these questions can be found if the *predicate-fronting* quality of inverse VO languages (cf. Rackowski & Travis 2000, Pearson 2000) is considered in a Minimalist approach.

According to the Phase Impenetrability Condition (PIC; Chomsky 2004), only XPs located in an edge position are visible to operations at the next highest level. We can therefore assume that in inverse VO languages the *v*P moves to an edge position in the T-domain (a "Spell-out domain", cf. Chomsky 2005) and is visible to operations at the CP-level (where discourse-grammar and illocutionary Force are encoded). In particular, I propose that the *v*P enters an Agree relation with the Force head, which specified for a [+decl(arative)] feature and acting as a probe, yielding a rising tone on the rightmost constituent within the relevant goal.

Given the prosodic evidence analyzed above, this implies that *v*P movement is in fact an instance of *remnant* movement (as proposed in Pearson 2000 for Malagasy and in Massam 2000 for Niuean). Specifically, arguments evacuate the *v*P in Tagalog, scrambling to some licensing position (i.e., functional projections, FP) in the T-domain, so that only the verb is visible for main prominence assignment, while in Malagasy only the trigger scrambles out of the *v*P before *v*P movement.[11] This is illustrated in the Spell-out structure given below:

(15)

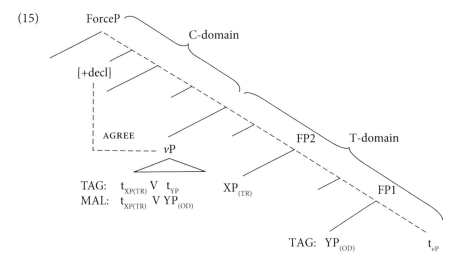

This analysis can provide an explanation for the difference between the intonational properties of inverse VO languages (like Tagalog and Malagasy) and an SVO language like Italian, in which no tonal event can be found in BF sentences (cf. Figure 1): Since Italian is not a predicate-fronting language, the *v*P stays low in the T-domain and, according to the PIC, it cannot be visible to operations at the next highest phase.

The prosodic evidence discussed above also provides important support in favor of an XP-movement analysis to derive the syntax of verb-initial languages, a major issue in recent works (cf. Carnie & Guilfoyle 2000). We can in fact conclude that what is visible for default stress assignment is the rightmost boundary of the *v*P located in an edge position. This requirement is particularly clear in Malagasy: Main prominence on the constituent preceding the trigger can be hardly accounted for in a V-movement approach. On the other hand, it can be argued that the rising tone on the verb in Tagalog may be the effect of X-movement to the head position of the relevant

---

11. A number of works have been dedicated to the syntactic position of the trigger (cf., among others, Guilfoyle et al. 1992, Pearson 2000, Rackowski 2002, Richards 2005). However, since this issue is far beyond the purposes of this paper, the relevant functional projection is simply indicated as FP2 in (15).

edge projection. This proposal, however, is immediately nullified by the interface analysis of BF sentences containing aspectual adverbs like *lamang*:

(16) *Kababasa   lamang ng titser   ng diyaryo.*
      read.REC.PERF just   DIR teacher DIR newspaper
      'The teacher has just read a newspaper.'

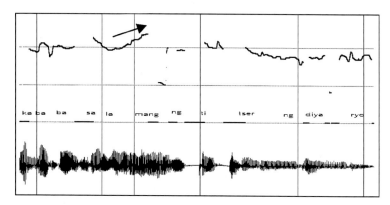

Figure 11. BF sentence in Tagalog (with *lamang*)

As shown in Figure 11, the verb is prosodically flat in the presence of *lamang* while the rising tone is aligned with the aspectual adverb. This is evidence that low adverbs like *lamang* move with the remnant *v*P (an *intraposition* movement of the 'onion-skin type' discussed in Rackowski & Travis 2000) and are therefore visible for main prominence assignment.[12]

Before turning to the analysis of NF constructions, a final comment about the trigger of *v*P movement is in order. Since the *v*P moves to an edge position and assumes scope over the T-domain even when it does not convey new information (see Section 3 below), predicate-fronting cannot be connected with Focus (*contra* Jelinek 2000). I therefore propose that this movement is motivated by the syntax-discourse requirement of establishing the predicate as the 'starting point' of the relevant

---

12. An anonymous reviewer points out that *lamang* is in fact a clitic forming a prosodic unit with the verb. Thus, s/he concludes that the rising pitch on the verb shown in Figures 2–7 corresponds to a rise on *lamang* in this case. Given this observation, X-movement could not be excluded. According to phonological tenets, however, prominence marks the *head* of a prosodic phrase (cf. Nespor and Vogel 1986, Selkirk 1986, Frascarelli 2000). Indeed, clitics are by definition unstressed and they never modify the location of prominence in the phonological word they attach to. Hence, if *kababasa lamang* forms a Clitic Group, the main prominence should fall on the verb. We might therefore conclude that *lamang* is not a phonological clitic (as is also suggested by its bisyllabic nature) and that its position (apparently following Wackernagel's law) depends on a syntactic requirement (to be explored). In this case its XP status can be maintained and the argumentation proposed is not challenged.

event (i.e., the constituent in *foreground*), which can be feasibly interpreted in the light of an 'extended' EPP feature. In other words, while the Subject Criterion (Rizzi 2006) pertains to *argument-fronting* languages (cf. Pearson 2000) and is connected with Nominative Case, the relevant edge position for our purposes is specific to *predicate-fronting* languages and is endowed with a predicative feature [+Pred] (cf. Massam 2000: 111) to be overtly checked by the *v*P. Since the Spec,IP (or Spec,TP) position is typically associated with argument-fronting, I therefore assume that the relevant edge position (undefined in (15)) corresponds to the *Predicative Phrase* (PredP) projection (cf. Pearson 2000).

The prosodic analysis of BF sentences and the syntactic interpretation provided allow for a number of predictions about the interface properties of NF constructions in Tagalog and Malagasy. As shown in the following sections, these predictions are borne out by data, providing substantial support to the present proposal.

3. Interface properties of narrow focus constructions

3.1 In situ focus

Since non-predicative XPs do not reach an edge position – they either scramble to licensing positions in the T-domain or are included in the *v*P –, the first prediction we can draw is that they are not visible to Agree operations with discourse categories (in the CP-phase). Hence, when they are focused *in situ*, they cannot be assigned a pitch. This is exactly the case in Tagalog. Consider the following question-answer pairs:

(17) Q: *Sino ang dumating?* ('Who arrived?')
    A: *Dumating* ANG KAIBIGAN KO.
       TH.arrive.PERF TR friend PRN.1SG
       'MY FRIEND arrived.'

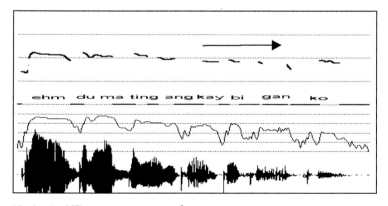

Figure 12. in situ NF – one-argument verb

(18) Q: *Ano ang binabasa ng titser?* ('What is the teacher reading?')
    A: *Binabasa   ng titser*   ANG DIYARYO.
       TH.read.IMPF DIR teacher   TR newspaper
       'A/the teacher is reading THE NEWSPAPER.'

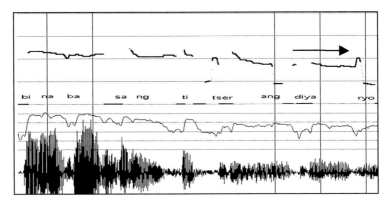

Figure 13. in situ NF on the Object

As we can see, no tonal event characterizes the relevant sentences: We can find neither a prominence on the verb, nor a pitch on the *in situ* Focus. This demonstrates, as expected, that the *v*P-initial position is not necessarily connected with a rising tone and that arguments embedded in the T-domain are not visible to PF operations. Both observations confirm the analysis proposed in the previous section: Main prominence assignment is the result of an Agree relation between a probe in the C-domain and a goal located in an edge position in the T-domain.

In this case, however, the discourse function that is activated in the C-domain is not declarative Force but the [+foc] feature located in the head of the *Focus Phrase* (FocP) projection (as assumed in a number of recent works; cf., among many others, Rizzi 1997, Frascarelli 2000). Consequently, since the raised *v*P is not the element that matches this feature in (17)-(18), no constituent receives the main prominence. This analysis is confirmed by data concerning *v*P-focusing:[13]

(19) Q: *Ano ang ginagawa ng titser?* ('What is the teacher doing?')
    A: BUMABASA   *ang titser*   NG DIYARYO.
       ACT.read.IMPF TR teacher   DIR newspaper
       'The teacher IS READING A NEWSPAPER.'

---

13. As noted by an anonymous reviewer, the NP *ang titser* would be more naturally substituted by a pronoun in (19A). I acknowledge this fact; however, informants were asked not to use pronouns for unfocused NPs in order to examine their intonational contour in full extent.

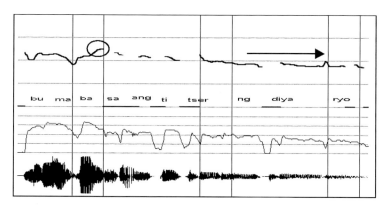

Figure 14. in situ NF on the *v*P

As we can see, while the verb is marked with a High tone, no pitch can be found on the embedded direct object, though it is also part of the new information. This is fully expected in the present analysis: The object scrambled in the T-domain cannot be visible to Agree operations, so that the (remnant) *v*P only can show the interface effects of the [+foc] feature:[14]

(20) [ForceP [Force'... [FocP [Foc' [+foc] [PredP [t_TR *BUMABASA* t_DO] [Pred'
[FP2 *ang titser* [F2' [FP1 *NG DYARYO* [F1' [t_*v*P]]]]]]]]]]]

Finally, notice that this type of tonal event is different from the one analyzed in Section 2.1. While the maximum of F0 is reached on the post-tonic syllable in BF sentences, the High tone only includes the tonic vowel in NF constructions (compare Figure 14 with Figures 3 and 4). The realization of broad and narrow Focus sentences is therefore distinguished at the PF interface: Whereas the former is a L* + H tone, the second can be described as a typical pitch accent of the H* type.

Let us now consider the interface properties of *v*P-focusing in Malagasy:

(21) Q: *Inona no nataon'ny polisy?* ('What did the police do?')
  A: *HAZON'   i   polisy   NY   MPANGALATRA.*
    PST.TH.arrest DET police DET(TR) thief
    'The police arrested the thief.'

---

14. As a result of this Agree requirement, in situ Focus for arguments is simply signaled by destressing of the predicate (cf. (17)-(18)). This does not mean that NF has no impact on the intonation of Tagalog, but simply that the derivation of the V-initial order has crucial consequences on the visibility of arguments at PF, which is expected in a phase framework.

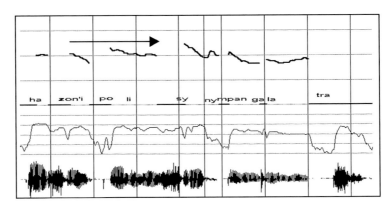

Figure 15. in situ NF on the *v*P

As is clear, no pitch is realized in the relevant sentence, neither on the agent, *i polisy*, even though it is the rightmost constituent within the raised *v*P, nor on the trigger, *ny mpangalatra*, even though it is part of the Focus.[15] This piece of evidence shows that in Malagasy, as in Tagalog, focused triggers are not visible for main prominence assignment (since they do not sit in an edge position). Moreover, a focused verb in Malagasy cannot receive a pitch as well, unlike in Tagalog, because it is *not the rightmost constituent* within the raised *v*P.

3.2 'Clefted' focus

The second prediction we can draw from the present analysis is that focused 'arguments' can only be assigned the main prominence when they are *fronted*, that is to say, when they are *predicates* in a *cleft-like construction*.

According to this analysis, (nominal) Focus is realized by means of reduced predication (i.e., a Small Clause), in which the Focus is merged in a predicate position, while the subject is a free relative clause, headed by a generic (null) NP of a restricted class (namely, 'PERSON', 'TIME', 'PLACE', etc.). From a semantic point of view, this amounts to saying that in an NF construction like 'MARY is intelligent', 'Mary' is not the subject of a categorical judgment and the *v*P has an NP-like denotation (a 'type-shifting' operation, cf. Partee 1987). In other words, this type of sentence implies the recognition of [someone who is intelligent] as the subject of the predication realized by [Mary] (for details and data in a cross-linguistic perspective, cf. Frascarelli 2010). In

---

15. Notice that, as a reply to question (21Q), the speaker has produced a sentence in which *polisy* (given information) is the *v*P-internal agent, while 'the thief' (which is part of new information) is promoted to the Subject-trigger role.

this construction, the predicate-NF moves to scope position and provides a value for the variable contained in the relative clause[16] (cf. also Frascarelli & Puglielli 2005):

(22)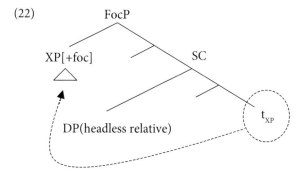

Significant syntactic evidence supports this analysis both in Malagasy (cf. Paul 2001, Potsdam 2006) and in Tagalog (cf. Frascarelli 2006, 2007). It is therefore unsurprising that 'clefted' Foci also behave like predicates with respect to intonation. They receive the main prominence of the sentence, bearing out the second prediction formulated above. Consider sentences (23) and (24) from Tagalog and Malagasy, respectively:

(23) ANG TITSER *ang nagbigay*   *ng libro kay Juan*.
      TR teacher TR ACT.give.PERF DIR book DAT Juan
      'THE TEACHER gave a book to Juan.'

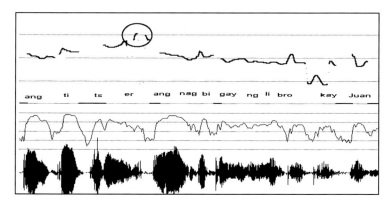

Figure 16. Fronted NF in Tagalog

---

16. The nominal nature of the presupposition is made clear by the presence of *ang* before the verb. Indeed, the trigger marker can only precede NPs and has often been considered as a specificity marker as well (cf. Himmelmann 2008), hence as an element located in the D° head.

(24) NY ALIKA no mivoavoa.
    DET(TR) dog FM PST.ACT.bark
    'THE DOG barked.'

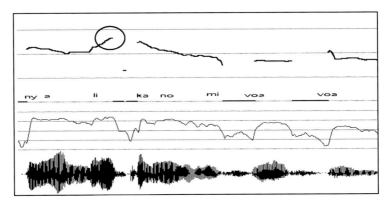

Figure 17. Fronted NF in Malagasy

We can conclude that in a cleft-like construction, the fronted Focus moves to position in the C-domain that is visible for [+foc] assignment, namely, to Spec,FocP, forming a Spec-head relation with the (overt/covert) Foc° head. Consistently, it is marked with a pitch accent (H*). The relevant structure is illustrated below for the Tagalog sentence in (23):

(23') [$_{FocP}$ ANG TITSER$_k$ [$_{Foc'}$ [+foc] [$_{SC}$ [$_{DP}$ ang [$_{CP}$ OP$_k$ [nagbigay VAR$_k$ ng libro kay Juan]]] t$_k$]]]

As a final support to the present analysis, it is important to note that the same (syntactic and intonational) pattern is found in wh-questions, for both languages. As illustrated in Figures 18 and 19 below, wh-constituents are assigned the main prominence of the sentence, which is also of the H* type. This is evidence that these elements are derived like clefted Foci and are likewise interpreted at the PF interface:[17]

(25) ANO ang ginagawa ng titser?
    what DET TH.do.IMPF DIR teacher
    'What is the teacher doing?'

(26) INONA no nataon' ny polisy?
    what FM PST.ACT.do DET police
    'What did the police do?'

---

[17] Also notice the presence of a final H% boundary tone in Malagasy, signaling the interrogative Force of the sentence.

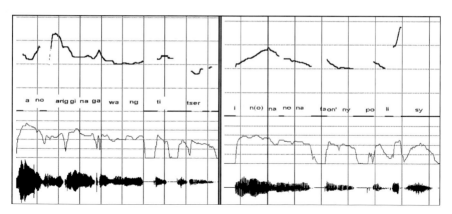

Figures 18–19. Wh-questions in Tagalog and Malagasy

4. Conclusions

The data discussed in this paper support an analysis of Tagalog and Malagasy as predicate-fronting languages, a syntactic requirement (an 'extended' EPP feature) that has crucial consequences for interface interpretation.

In BF sentences this property implies obligatory *v*P-movement to an edge position in the T-domain, where the *v*P enters an Agree relation with the [+decl] feature located in Force°. As a result, its rightmost boundary is marked with a L* + H tone, which is the main tonal event of the sentence. Triggers belong to the T-domain at Spell-out and, given the PIC, are not visible to interface operations. As for non-trigger XPs, they either scramble to some functional projection in the T-domain (Tagalog) or are 'frozen' in the fronted *v*P (Malagasy).

In NF sentences, on the other hand, predicate-fronting and the PIC derive a structure in which *in situ* arguments cannot be assigned a pitch. Only clefted Foci can move, because they are predicates in an SC construction. The target position is, in this case, the Specifier of the FocP, where the NF is marked with a pitch accent (H*).

Tonal events are therefore distinguished in Broad and Narrow Focus constructions, like in Italian (and a number of direct VO languages). This result supports recent analyses and is consistent with a cartographic approach in which different functional features in the C-domain correspond to specific interpretations at the PF-interface (cf. Frascarelli & Trecci 2007).

References

Carnie, A. & Guilfoyle, E. (eds). 2000. *The Syntax of Verb-initial Languages*. Oxford: OUP.
Carnie, A., Harley, H. & Dooley, S.A. (eds). 2005. *Verb First: On the Syntax of Verb-initial Languages* [Linguistik Aktuell/Linguistics Today 73]. Amsterdam: John Benjamins.

Chomsky, N. 2001. Derivation by Phase. In *Ken Hale. A Life in Language,* M. Kenstowicz (ed.), 1–52. Cambridge MA: The MIT Press.
Chomsky, N. 2004. Beyond explanatory adequacy. In *The Cartography of Syntactic Structures,* Vol. 3: *Structures and Beyond,* A. Belletti (ed.), 104–131. Oxford: OUP.
Chomsky, N. 2005. On phases. Ms, MIT.
Cinque, G. 1993. A null theory of phrase and compound stress. *Linguistic Inquiry* 24: 239–298.
D'Imperio, M. 2002. Italian intonation: An overview and some questions. *Probus* 14: 37–69.
Frascarelli, M. 2000. *The Syntax-Phonology Interface in Focus and Topic Constructions in Italian.* Dordrecht: Kluwer.
Frascarelli, M. 2004. L'interpretazione del Focus e la portata degli operatori sintattici. In *Il Parlato Italiano,* F. Albano Leoni, F. Cutugno, M. Pettorino & R. Savy (eds), B06. Napoli: M. D'Auria Editore – CIRASS.
Frascarelli, M. 2006. Intonation and Information Structure in V-initial Languages. An interface analysis of Tagalog and Malagasy. Paper presented at the *2nd Conference on the Typology of Tone and Intonation (TIE2),* ZAS, Berlin (September, 7–9 2006).
Frascarelli, M. 2010. Narrow focus, clefting and predicate inversion *Lingua* 120:2121–2147.
Frascarelli, M. & Puglielli, A. 2005. The focus system in Cushitic languages. In *Proceedings of the 10th Hamito-Semitic Linguistics Meeting* [Quaderni di Semitistica 25], P. Fronzaroli & P. Marrassini (eds), 333–358. Firenze: Università degli Studi di Firenze.
Frascarelli, M. & Puglielli, A. 2007. Focus in the force-fin system. In *Focus Strategies in African Languages. The Interaction of Focus and Grammar in Niger-Congo and Afro-Asiatic,* A. Enoch Oladé, K. Hartmann & M. Zimmermann (eds), 161–184. Berlin: Mouton de Gruyter.
Frascarelli M. & Trecci, A. 2007. Subjects in a pro-drop Language. Syntactic roles, discourse categories and the interpretation of pro. In *La Comunicazione Parlata. Atti del Convegno Internazionale (23-25 febbraio 2006),* M. Pettorino, A. Giannini, M. Vallone & R. Savy (eds), Tomo I, 587–625. Napoli: Liguori Editore.
Frota, S., 2000. *Prosody and Focus in European Portuguese: Implication for Intonation Theory.* New York NY: Garland.
Gärtner, H.-M., Law, P. & Sabel, J. (eds). 2006. *Clause Structure and Adjuncts in Austronesian Languages.* Berlin: Mouton de Gruyter.
Guilfoyle, E., Hung, H. & Travis, L. 1992. Spec of IP and Spec of vP: Two subjects in Austronesian languages. *Natural Language and Linguistic Theory* 10: 375–414.
Hayes, B. & Lahiri, A. 1991. Bengali Intonational Phonology. *Natural Language and Linguistic Theory* 9: 47–96.
Himmelmann, N.P. 2008. Lexical categories and voice in Tagalog. In *Voice and Grammatical in Austronesian Languages.* P. Austin & S. Musgrave (eds), Relations 247–293. Stanford CA: CSLI.
Jelinek, E. 2000. Predicate raising in Lummi, Straits Salish. In A. Carnie & E. Guilfoyle (eds), 213–234.
Kayne, R. 1994. *The Antisymmetry of Syntax.* Cambridge MA: The MIT Press.
Kenesei, I. & Vogel, I. 1990. Focus and phonological structure. Ms, University of Cambridge and University of Budapest.
Klamer, M. 2002. Ten years of synchronic Austronesian languages (1991–2002). *Lingua* 112(2): 933–965.
Massam, D. 2000. VSO and VOS: Aspects of Niuean word order. In A. Carnie & E. Guilfoyle (eds), 97–116.
Nespor, M. & Vogel, I. 1986. *Prosodic Phonology.* Dordrecht: Foris.

Partee, B.H. 1987. Noun phrase interpretation and type-shifting principles. In *Studies in Discourse Representation Theory and the Theory of Generalized Quantifiers*, J. Groenendijk, D. de Jongh & M. Stokhof (eds), 115–143. Dordrecht: Foris.
Paul, I. 2001. Concealed pseudo-clefts. *Lingua* 111: 707–727.
Pearson, M. 2000. Two types of VO Languages. In *The Derivation of VO and OV* [Linguistik Aktuell/Linguistics Today 31], P. Svenonius (ed.), 327–363. Amsterdam: John Benjamins.
Pierrehumbert, J. 1980. The Phonology and Phonetics of English Intonation. PhD dissertation, MIT.
Potsdam, E. 2006. The cleft structure of Malagasy wh-questions. In *Clause Structure and Adjuncts in Austronesian Languages*, H.-M. Gärtner, P. Law & J. Sabel (eds), 195–232. Berlin: Mouton de Gruyter.
Rackowski, A. 2002. The Structure of Tagalog: Specificity, Voice and the Distribution of Arguments. PhD dissertation, MIT.
Rackowski, A. & Travis, L. 2000. V-initial languages: X or XP movement and adverbial placement. In A. Carnie & E. Guilfoyle (eds), 117–141.
Richards, N. 2005. Person-Case Effects in Tagalog and the Nature of Long-distance Extraction. Ms, MIT.
Rizzi, L. 1997. The fine structure of the left periphery. In *Elements of Grammar. Handbook in Generative Syntax*, L. Haegeman (ed.), 281–337. Dortrecht: Kluwer.
Rizzi, L. 2006. On the form of chains: Criterial positions and ECP effects. In *Wh Movement: Moving on*, L. Cheng & N. Corver (eds), 97–133. Cambridge MA: The MIT Press.
Samek-Lodovici, V. 2005. Prosody-Syntax Interaction in the Expression of Focus. *Natural Language and Linguistic Theory* 23: 687–755.
Schachter, P. 1993. Tagalog. In *Syntax. An International Handbook of Contemporary Research*, J. Jacobs, A. von Stechow, W. Sternefeld & T. Vennemann (eds), 1418–1430. Berlin: Mouton de Gruyter.
Schachter, P. & Otanes, F.T. 1972. *Tagalog Reference Grammar*. Berkeley CA: University of California Press.
Selkirk, E. 1986. On derived domains in sentence phonology. *Phonology* 3: 371–405.

SYNTAX

The case of possessors and 'subjects'*

Cathryn Donohue and Mark Donohue
Australian National University

Possessors have often been treated as the 'subjects' of the DPs in which they appear, being analyzed as surfacing in [spec, DP] by analogy to the standard analysis for clausal subjects in a configurational framework of grammar. In this paper, we present a new descriptive generalization showing that there is in fact much variation in the coding of genitive phrases, and that the simple equation of subjects to possessors fails to capture the range of variation attested cross-linguistically. Examining a broad selection of Austronesian languages, we conclude that an understanding of the systemic oppositions in a particular language is essential to understanding the syncretisms found in that language and that while the subject/possessor syncretisms are widespread, the only clear generalization that can be drawn about possessors in Austronesian is that processors are marked using the 'default' case marker.

1. Case syncretisms: Subject = Possessor?

It is widely, and generally uncontroversially, believed that the 'subject' of a clause and the possessor of an NP share many properties (e.g., Abney 1987, Chomsky 1970, Giorgi & Longobardi 1990, Szabolcsi 1994, among others), including the commonly found case syncretisms. It is because of this that possessors are often treated as subjects. We present data from a range of Austronesian languages illustrating different case syncretisms involving the genitive, and conclude that the terms used to describe the syncretisms ('possessors as subjects') must be reinterpreted to correctly account for the data, since other, apparently contradictory, syncretisms are also found. While some subjects are syncretic with possessors, it is also true that some objects show syncretisms with possessors as well.

We discuss an analysis of these data that highlights the importance of considering case as part of the case system as a whole. While the cases used to mark 'subjects' and

---

* Many thanks to the audience at AFLA XIV, the anonymous reviewers and editors for their comments, and especially Raph Mercado for a particularly helpful discussion of the issues presented here. We remain solely responsible for the data and analysis presented here.

possessors are often the same, hence the proposed structural explanation, we argue that the correct generalization is purely morphological, that possessors are (often) syncretic with the *unmarked* (or default) argument in the system. We show how this cross-linguistic generalization can be naturally explained using Lexical Decomposition Grammar, a theory of case licensing within which it is straightforward to capture both the unmarkedness of the nominative in a nominative–accusative system, and the unmarkedness of the absolutive in an ergative–absolutive system.

2. Previous analyses

Syncretisms between the marking of the possessor in a noun phrase and the 'subject' of a clause, referring to either morphological or syntactic coding properties, have long been observed (e.g. Chomsky 1970, Abney 1987). It has been assumed that possessors are best conceptualized as structurally equivalent to subjects, perhaps in part due to the fact that the subject/possessor syncretism is widely attested. This analysis has been formally modeled by appealing to the parallel structures of subjects and possessors in the constituent structure (e.g. *Rome* in (2a) and (2b) respectively), as illustrated by the structures in (1) (we note that the morphological encoding of *Rome* is distinct in the two different phrases).[1]

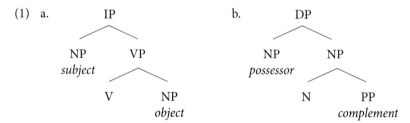

(2)   a.   *Rome destroyed Carthage.*   b.   *Rome's destruction of Carthage*

---

1. A more recent version of the structural relationships is shown in (i) and (ii). Although details of the architecture vary, the structural relationships remain essentially the same.

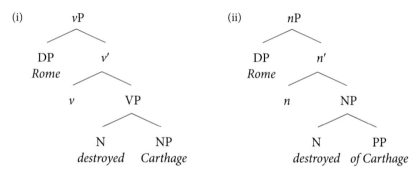

Even in languages for which these precise phrase-structural relationships are not obvious, it is claimed that underlying similarities between subjects and possessors can be attested in other parts of the grammar, such as case or agreement. This pattern, however, is not as universal a tendency as has been previously thought. This is demonstrated by an examination of data from a variety of Austronesian languages. We show that when a language shows syncretisms between a core argument and the genitive case marker, the case of the possessor is syncretic with the *default* case marker. In this paper, we first present data from a selection of representative Austronesian languages to establish the different patterns observed, before proposing an alternative account to capture this broader range of data.

3. Synthesis of the syncretism patterns

The key feature common to the syncretisms between the genitive case and a core argument illustrated here is that if there is syncretism in the case system, it is between the case of the possessor and the case that can be considered to be the default or 'unmarked' case. This is a purely morphological generalization, and one which is hard, if not impossible, to capture configurationally. This notion of a default case captures all of the examples, illustrated below in (i) – (iii).

i. Possessor and the 'subject': A/S grouping

Cross-linguistically the A/S, or 'nominative' category is often morphologically unmarked in a case system, and is certainly unmarked in terms of indicating two out of three core arguments. In Tinrin, of central New Caledonia (Osumi 1995), the overt case marker *nrâ* marks both the nominative and the possessive. Example (3) shows that the object of *nrorri*, *wake nrâ nrü* 'your work', does not take case marking, while the subject of *fwi* (as well as other subjects) must be case marked with *nrâ*. The same case marker is also used to indicate possession, as seen in the possessive phrase *nrâ nrü* and also in the phrases in (4), which show the use of *nrâ* to mark the arguments of a verb in a nominalization.

    Tinrin[2]
(3) *Tro nrorri* [*wake* [***nrâ nrü***]] *tra wei=fwi* [***nrâ** nrô*].
    AUG leave work POSS 2SG so.that 1SG.FUT=do NOM 1SG
    'Just leave your work, so that I myself may do it.'

---

2. The following abbreviations are used in this paper: A – most agentive argument of a bivalent verb; AUG – augment; AV – A-voice; CAUS – causative; COMP – completive; CORE – core case marker; D – recipient argument in a ditransitive verb; EX – exclusive; FUT – future; GEN – genitive; HR – highest role; IN – inclusive; LOC – locative; LR – lowest role; MUT – mutation; NOM – nominative; NONACT – non-active voice; OBJ – object; OBL – oblique; P – most patientive argument of a bivalent verb; PL – plural; POSS – possessive; PPr – P Prefix; PV – P-voice; R – realis; REL – relativizer; S – single argument of a monovalent verb; SG – singular; 1 – first person; 2 – second person; 3 – third person.

(4) Bee   ta [nrâ   pù]   [nrâ   ri]
    COMP   kill POSS flying.fox   POSS   1PL.IN
    'our killing of flying foxes'

ii. **Possessors and the absolutive case**: S/P grouping.

In a morphologically ergative language, the S/P grouping (absolutive) is considered the default, or unmarked case. In Nias, from western Indonesia, there is an overt absolutive case realized by 'mutation' (Brown 2001, Donohue & Brown 1999, Kähler 1936/7, Sundermann 1913). The mutation, realized on the vowel-initial words shown here as *n-*, is obligatory on a possessor.

Nias
(5) bavi n-ama-gu
    pig   MUT-father-1SG.GEN
    'my father's pigs'

The same mutation that is used for a possessor is also obligatory with absolutive arguments, S or P, as seen in the two examples below.[3]

(6) Manavuli sui n-ama-da   Tohönavanaetu ba   Maenamölö.
    return   again MUT-father-1PL.IN.GEN Tohönavanaetu LOC   Maenamölö
    'Ama Tohönavanaetu came back again to Maenamölö.'

(7) I-a   m-bavi   ama   Gumi.
    3SG.R-eat   MUT-pig father Gumi
    'Ama Gumi is eating/eats pork.'

iii. **Possessors and the 'object'**

In Tagalog (and most other northern Austronesian languages) the *ng*-marked argument is considered to be an 'object', regardless of the voice selected (see Donohue 2002, 2007 for a discussion of the terms). Thus in (8), the object of the clause is the theme 'book', while in (9) the object is the agent, 'child'. The same case marker that is used for objects is also used for genitives, shown in (10). It is crucial to note that 'object' can refer to the A in a non-Agent Voice (non-AV) verb and the P in a non-Patient Voice (non-PV) verb.[4]

Tagalog
(8) B⟨um⟩asa   ng   libro ang   bata.
    read⟨AV⟩   GEN   book   NOM   child
    'The child read a book.'

---

3. *Ama* 'father' is obligatorily used as part of male names in Nias. Similarly, the use of the 1PL.IN genitive suffix is customary, and does not necessarily indicate actual possession.

4. Alternating voice data is not presented for most of the languages described here, since most Austronesian languages do not employ morphologically-marked voice systems.

(9) B⟨in⟩asa **ng** bata ang libro.
    read⟨PV⟩ GEN child NOM book
    'The child read the book.'

(10) ang libro **ng** bata
     NOM book GEN child
     'the child's book'

Many, if not most, languages of the Philippines (and Formosa) display a distinct case marker for the non-subject non-agent in clauses such as (8). In this way, Tagalog is somewhat exceptional, and the more general characterization of this northern Austronesian syncretism is that the genitive case is syncretic with the Agent object, but not with the Patient object. The morphological shape of the genitive case is the default in all Philippine-type languages, regardless of any syncretisms involved in the case system. Furthermore, in contrast to the other case markers in the Tagalog system, *ng* is the case marker that cannot be easily defined, but must be treated as an 'elsewhere' category: The nominative *ang* is simply defined as the case marker used with the single most pragmatically important argument (the subject) in the clause, and the dative *sa* is used to indicate either (i) obliques or adjuncts; or (ii) highly salient non-subject arguments (salient either inherently because of the semantic type of argument, inherently because of the verb's lexical selection, or for pragmatic reasons). *Ng*, however, occurs in all other environments, and is the only core case marker that can occur multiple times in a single clause, marking terms, as in (11).

(11) P⟨in⟩a-basa **ng** guro ang bata **ng** libro.
     CAUS⟨PV⟩- read GEN teacher NOM child GEN book
     'The teacher made the child read the book.'

iv. **No possessive syncretism**

There are numerous examples of languages in which there is no syncretism between the genitive and another case. In the simplest form, this is apparent when there are no case markers, as in Indonesian, from the south-west of the Austronesian area. Here we see that none of the direct arguments of transitive or intransitive clauses take case marking, with SVO order alone differentiating the different syntactic roles. Similarly, in the possessive construction, the possessor NP follows the possessed noun with no morphology on either the possessor or the possessum.

Indonesian

(12) Udin makan roti.
     Udin eat bread
     'Udin ate bread.'

(13) Udin duduk di sana.
     Udin sit LOC there
     'Udin sat over there.'

(14) kucing Udin
      cat   Udin
      'Udin's cat'

In Tukang Besi the genitive *nu* is not syncretic with either the nominative *na*, the general core case *te*, or the oblique *i/di*, as shown in the following examples.

Tukang Besi

(15) Te   beka **nu** ama=su
      CORE cat GEN father=1SG.GEN
      'my father's cat'

(16) No-mbule **na**   La Udin **di**   kampo=no.
      3R-return NOM Mr Udin OBL:R village=3GEN
      'Udin returned to his village.'

(17) No-manga **te**   roti **na** La Udin.
      3R-eat   CORE bread NOM Mr Udin
      'Udin ate bread.'

(18) No-manga='e **na**   roti **te**   La Udin.
      3R-eat=3P   NOM bread CORE Mr Udin
      'Udin ate the bread.'

In connection with this, however, we note that a syncretism between the genitive and the Agent is often preserved in subordinate forms. Compare the complete lack of syncretism in case marking in (15) to (18) with the appearance of the genitive case syncretic with the marking of an Agent in the relative clause in (19) below (see Donohue 1999 for arguments against simply treating forms such as (19) as nominalizations).

(19) te   roti i-manga **nu** ama=su
      CORE bread PPT-eat GEN father=1SG.GEN
      'the bread that was eaten by my father'

Similar to the use of genitive agreement clitics in subordinate clauses in Tukang Besi, in Indonesian we can see that the genitive is used to indicate a third person Agent in a non-active construction, such as (21) (identical constructions are found in main clauses in Indonesian, which is not the case in Tukang Besi). The prefix *di-* is multifunctional, marking both the inverse and the passive (see van den Berg 1996 for the history of the prefix).

Indonesian

(20) roti yang di-makan   Udin
      bread REL NONACT-eat Udin
      'the bread that was eaten by Udin'

(21) roti yang di-makan-nya
      bread REL NONACT-eat-3SG.GEN
      'the bread that was eaten by her/him'

We also find this pattern appearing in subordinate clauses even in languages for which the genitive/Agent syncretism does not hold in main clauses. Palu'e does not use case or agreement morphology in main clauses (shown in (22) and (23)), and this lack of overt morphology is also possible in relative clauses, such as (24). At the same time, an alternative strategy for relative clauses sees the Agent marked on the verb with the genitive clitics that index possessors. (25) shows the use of the genitive clitics on nouns to index a possessor. (26) shows the optional use of genitive clitics to indicate the third person agent in a relative clause headed by an object. More specifically, (26a) shows the standard use of a third person genitive clitic with a third person Agent, while (26b) shows that this same 'third person' clitic can also be used with a first person subject.[5] This reflects a wider pattern in which the 'third person' genitive clitic has extended its range to include a more general sense of modification. In (27), we see that it is also possible for the agreeing first person genitive clitic to be used with a first person subject (but the 1SG -*gu* may not be used with a non-first person subject).

Palu'e

(22) a. *Lanu kha uvi.*
Lanu eat tuber
'Lanu ate tubers.'

b. *Uvi Lanu kha.*
tuber Lani eat
'Tubers were eaten by Lanu.'

(23) a. *Aku kha uvi.*
1SG eat tuber
'I ate tubers.'

b. *Uvi aku kha.*
tuber 1SG eat
'Tubers were eaten by me.'

(24) a. *uvi (vo) Lanu kha-n*
tuber REL Lanu eat-3GEN
'the tubers that Lanu ate'

b. *uvi (vo) aku kha-n*
tuber REL 1SG eat-3GEN
'the tubers that I ate'

(25) a. *Lanu uvi-n*
Lanu tuber-3GEN
'Lanu's tubers'

---

5. Alternating voice data is not presented for most of the languages described here, since most Austronesian languages do not employ morphologically-marked voice systems.

Table 1. Summary of syncretisms between genitive and other cases in Austronesian

	Language
GEN = NOM	Tinrin
GEN = ABS	Nias, (Tongan, Niuean)
GEN = Agent OBJ	(Northern Philippine languages)
GEN = OBJ	Tagalog
GEN ≠ syncretic	Indonesian, Tukang Besi, Palu'e

    b. *uvi-gu*
       tuber-1GEN
       'my tubers'

(26) a. *uvi (vo) Lanu kha-n*
       tuber REL Lanu eat-3GEN
       'the tubers that Lanu ate'

    b. *uvi (vo) aku kha-n*
       tuber REL 1SG eat-3GEN
       'the tubers that I ate'

(27) a. *uvi (vo) (aku) kha-gu*
       tuber REL 1SG eat-1GEN
       'the tubers that I ate'

    b. * *uvi (vo) Lanu kha-gu*

Table 1 summarizes the syncretisms that we have found in the Austronesian data. We do not exemplify the syncretisms found in agreement systems here, but simply summarize the results of the survey of case syncretism possibilities and note that the same syncretisms can be found in the domain of agreement systems (for further discussion, both diachronic and synchronic, see Donohue & Donohue [in preparation]). As suggested in the table, the languages that have been used for exemplification purposes here do not, by any means, exhaust the possible candidates displaying syncretisms in the Austronesian world, but a more complete survey of these patterns is beyond the scope of the current paper.

4. Explaining the full range of syncretisms

The notion of a default morphosyntactic case is intuitively easy to understand in any number of different systems of case oppositions. It is this concept which is crucial to understanding the full generalization about syncretisms that exist between the genitive case marker and core arguments as evidenced by the Austronesian data. This notion of 'default' case marker is readily modeled in frameworks that take into account the entire case system within which it occurs.

Lexical Decomposition Grammar (LDG; e.g. Wunderlich 1997, Kiparsky 2001) is a theory of case licensing that naturally accounts for the proposed generalization. Unlike most case theories which focus on the mapping between grammatical functions or structural configurations and thematic roles, LDG is a theory of case *licensing*, capturing the ternary relation between thematic roles (arguments), grammatical functions or 'abstract case' and morphosyntactic (and morphological) case. LDG has constrained principles for relating levels of abstract case and morphosyntactic case by defining them both with the same two relational features [±H(ighest) R(ole)] and [±L(owest) R(ole)]. The framework captures generalizations and predictions both about typologically diverse languages and highly complex phenomena within a specific language (e.g. see Donohue 2004). Additionally, positional licensing is also modeled in exactly the same way as morphological licensing in this framework (e.g. Kiparsky 1997) by defining certain configurations using the same features as one might for a case marker. In this way, LDG is a framework well suited to the investigation of the relation of subjects and possessors and possible case syncretisms.

We first outline LDG before returning to a discussion of how this theory enables us to capture the proposed generalization about possessor case syncretisms.

Semantic form

Following Bierwisch (1986 and elsewhere), LDG assumes a level of structure called semantic form (SF), which represents the grammatically relevant parts of a verb's conceptual structure. It consists of minimally decomposed expressions formulated in predicate logic and expressed using lambda-categorial expressions. SF representations are thus constrained to two basic types: Propositions (predicates), or *constants*, and individuals, or *variables*. Consider the verb 'show'.

(28)　*show*:　[x CAUSE [CAN [y SEE z]]]

In (28), the constants are the units of meaning (e.g. CAUSE, CAN, SEE) into which the predicate *show* is decomposed, and the variables are x, y, z, representing the participants. The variables are lambda-abstracted out of the SF, and the resulting lambdas are equivalent to thematic roles, where the (inside out) depth of embedding represents the thematic hierarchy for a given verb.

Abstract case

Abstract case is defined using the two aforementioned relational features. These are assigned to the 'thematic roles' according to their relative position in the semantic form. Once [+HR] and [+LR] have been assigned, the rest can be assigned implicationally.

(29) show: λz   λy   λx   [x CAUSE [CAN [y SEE z]]]
         $\begin{bmatrix}-HR\\+LR\end{bmatrix}$ $\begin{bmatrix}-HR\\-LR\end{bmatrix}$ $\begin{bmatrix}+HR\\-LR\end{bmatrix}$

With the highest and lowest roles identified, all other roles must be marked as non-highest role and non-lowest role to complete the feature specification. Once the abstract case is defined as in (30) below, the morphosyntactic case is assigned through simple unification. The relational case features cross-classify to define four abstract cases:

(30) i.   A: $\begin{bmatrix}+HR\\-LR\end{bmatrix}$

    ii. S: $\begin{bmatrix}+HR\\+LR\end{bmatrix}$

    iii. P: $\begin{bmatrix}-HR\\+LR\end{bmatrix}$

    iv. D: $\begin{bmatrix}-HR\\-LR\end{bmatrix}$

Morphosyntactic case

These features ([±HR], [±LR]) are also used to specify the morphosyntactic *structural* case (note that semantic case is *not* defined in this way). Typically the unmarked case nominative/absolutive is characterized by not having any specified features. The accusative is usually characterized as [–HR] and the ergative [–LR], while the dative is the most highly specified with negative values for both features. It is important to note that the presence or absence of features in the definition of the case marker does not imply the presence or absence of overt case morphology. Obviously these definitions must be tailored to suit the case system of the specific language. However, typical systems are shown below. In a typical morphologically ergative language with a structural dative, the structural case inventory would be as shown in (31).

(31) i.   Abs: [ ]
    ii. Erg: [–LR]
    iii. Dat: $\begin{bmatrix}-HR\\-LR\end{bmatrix}$

A typical morphologically accusative language would have the case inventory shown in (32).

(32) i.   Nom: [ ]
    ii. Acc: [–HR]

iii. Dat: $\begin{bmatrix} -\text{HR} \\ -\text{LR} \end{bmatrix}$

Two conditions govern the association of morphosyntactic case with abstract case. These are given in (33).

(33) i. Unification: Associated feature matrices must be non-distinct.
 ii. Specificity: Specific rules and morphemes block general rules and morphemes in the same context.

Thus, feature matrices will only unify if they are non-distinct. For example, typically the dative is defined as [–HR, –LR] and will unify with the middle role in a ditransitive verb:

(34) show: λz λy λx [x CAUSE [CAN [y SEE z]]]
$\begin{bmatrix} -\text{HR} \\ +\text{LR} \end{bmatrix}$ $\begin{bmatrix} -\text{HR} \\ -\text{LR} \end{bmatrix}$ $\begin{bmatrix} +\text{HR} \\ -\text{LR} \end{bmatrix}$

Dative morphosyntactic case [–HR, –LR] thus unifies with λy [–HR, –LR]. The less specific nominative case ([ ]) and ergative case ([–LR]), while able to, will not unify with this abstract case due to specificity: The more highly specified case available in the inventory [–HR, –LR] blocks the use of a more general morpheme in the same context. The theory also allows for case to be licensed positionally (see, e.g., Kiparsky 1997).

What is central about this approach to case is that a case marker is defined within the whole system of cases. Moreover, taking into account the morphological case inventory and set of oppositions (for core arguments) is necessary for determining how each case should be defined for a given language. We have described the typical case systems for morphologically ergative and accusative languages. That is, a language such as Tinrin has morphological case markers identified as in (32), repeated below as (35):

(35) i. Nom: [ ]
 ii. Acc: [–HR]
 iii. Dat: $\begin{bmatrix} -\text{HR} \\ -\text{LR} \end{bmatrix}$

This shows that the nominative case marker, the case of the A/S arguments, is (structuraly) the 'default' case marker. Note that the case marker need not be morphologically empty; we have seen that it is in fact morphologically overt in Tinrin. The lack of feature specifications simply captures its morphosyntactic status as the default case marker.

Nias has a case system like that illustrated in (31), repeated here as (36).

(36) i. Abs: [ ]
 ii. Erg: [–LR]
 iii. Dat: $\begin{bmatrix} -\text{HR} \\ -\text{LR} \end{bmatrix}$

As a typical ergative case system with a structural dative case, we see in (36) that there is a case marker to identify the very specific 'middle' role (e.g. recipient in a ditransitive verb), the case of the A (not overtly marked in Nias), and the 'elsewhere' or default case marker, which in this system is born by the S/P arguments.

Tagalog, and Philippine-type languages generally, are harder to characterize due to their complex voice systems. However, as noted above, what is not controversial is that the genitive case marker is the default case irrespective of voice, and as such would be assigned the empty morphosyntactic feature description:

(37) i. Gen: [ ]

In these languages, the genitive case marker is used to mark core arguments and *is* the morphosyntactic default case marker, not just syncretic with it.

It is important to note that this system of case licensing does not change the structural configuration in which possessors are generated (as [spec, *n*P]), nor is it at all incompatible with this. In fact, the theory allows for positional case licensing, so extra-clausal case markers such as special topic cases, would be assigned configurationally, along the usual assumptions. What this approach has in its favour for the data under consideration here, is that it is able to identify the natural class of case markers that show syncretism with the genitive case marker in Austronesian languages. What we do not address here is *why* we get the syncretisms, but we plan to develop this in future work (Donohue & Donohue, in preparation).

To recap, the 'default' or unmarked case is different for the various language types: It is typically the absolutive case (S, P) in an ergative language and the nominative case (A, S) in an accusative language and we have seen here that it is the genitive case in other Austronesian languages. It is important to emphasize that we are not referring to overt morphological marking – that is, the presence or absence of a case marker. Rather, we refer to the morphosyntactic status of the case marker in its system of oppositions. The generalization that emerged from examining the Austronesian data is that if the genitive case marker (potentially a separate case with its own morphosyntactic definition) is syncretic with the case marker of a core argument, that case marker is the *default* case marker. That is, the correct generalization is a morphological one, not a configurational one, and LDG is a theory that readily accommodates such a generalization.

The genitive case marker can have its own definition and be used in addition to core arguments, but it is useful to consider case in a framework like LDG when making sense of this range of syncretisms and unearthing the commonality of these otherwise seemingly disparate classes that are syncretic with the genitive. This generalization also underscores the importance of both taking morphology seriously and considering case markers as part of the system in which they occur (see also Donohue 2004, 2008).

5. Summary

There are Austronesian languages for which the subject = possessor syncretism, as it is usually described, is valid. However, we have shown that there are additional patterns of syncretism in the data as illustrated in (38):

(38) Possessor   = nominative
                      = absolutive
                      = agent
                      = object

These apparently conflicting patterns indicate that the simple syncretism shown structurally in (1) must be rethought in order to capture the syncretisms found in Austronesian languages. We have argued that the correct way of conceptualizing the syncretism is between the case of the possessors and the *default* case marker or the functionally unmarked case in the language. This natural class is readily identified in LDG, although why, exactly, we find the syncretism remains to be explained.

We are currently examining Austronesian agreement systems that exhibit genitive syncretisms to see how these bear on our analysis and plan to investigate three-way case systems. Once we have established the patterns exhibited in this wider range of languages, we hope to explain the diachronic development of these case and agreement syncretisms.

References

Abney, S. 1987. The English Noun Phrase in its Sentential Aspect. PhD dissertation, MIT.
Bierwisch, M. 1986. On the nature of semantic form in natural language. In *Human Memory and Cognitive Capabilities*, Vol. 2, K. Flix & H. Hagendorf (eds), 765-784. Holland: Elsevier.
van den Berg, R. 1996. The demise of focus and the spread of conjugated verbs in Sulawesi. In *Papers in Austronesian linguistics 3*, H. Steinhauer (ed), 89-114. Canberra: Pacific Linguistics A-84.
Brown, L. 2001. A Grammar of Nias Selatan. PhD dissertation, University of Sydney.
Chomsky, N. 1970. Remarks on nominalization. In *Readings in English Transformational Grammar*, R. Jacobs & P. Rosenbaum (eds), 184-221. Boston MA: Ginn.
Donohue, C. 2004. Morphology Matters: Case Licensing in Basque. PhD dissertation, Stanford University.
Donohue, C. 2008. Case selection in old and new Basque. In *Morphology and Language History*, C. Bowern, B. Evans & L. Miceli (eds), 269–280. Amsterdam: John Benjamins.
Donohue, M. 1999. *A Grammar of Tukang Besi* [Grammar Library series 20]. Berlin: Mouton de Gruyter.
Donohue, M. 2002. Developing accusativity: Tagalog revisited. Paper presented at the 9th International Conference on Austronesian Linguistics, Canberra, Australia.

Donohue, M. 2007. Word order in Austronesian: from north to south and west to east. *Linguistic Typology* 11(2): 351-393.
Donohue, C. & Donohue, M. In preparation. Default case, default agreement, and the genitive syncretisms in Austronesian.
Donohue, M. & Brown, L. 1999. Ergativity: some additions from Indonesia. *Australian Journal of Linguistics* 19(1): 57-76.
Giorgi, A. & Longobardi, P. 1990. *The Syntax of Noun Phrases*. Cambridge: CUP.
Kähler, H. 1936/7. Untersuchen über die Laut-, Wort-, und Satzlehre des Nias. *Zeitschrift für Eingeborenen-Sprachen* XXVII: 91-128; 212-288.
Kiparsky, P. 1997. The rise of positional licensing. In *Parameters of morphosyntactic change*, A. van Kemenade & N. Vincent (eds), 460–494. Cambridge: CUP.
Kiparsky, P. 2001. Structural case in Finnish. *Lingua* 111: 315-376.
Osumi, M. 1995. *Tinrin grammar*. Honolulu HI: Oceanic Linguistics special publications No. 25.
Sundermann, H. 1913. *Niassische Sprachlehre*. KITLV: Martinus Nijhoff's Gravenhage.
Szabolcsi, A. 1994. The noun phrase. In *Syntax and Semantics 27: The Syntactic structure of Hungarian*, S. Kiefer & É.K. Kiss (eds), 179-274. New York NY: Academic Press.
Wunderlich, D. 1997. Cause and the structure of verbs. *Linguistic Inquiry* 28: 27-68.

Genitive relative constructions and agent incorporation in Tongan*

Yuko Otsuka
University of Hawai'i at Mānoa

Polynesian languages commonly use the genitive relative construction (GRC) for non-subject relatives, in which the thematic subject of the relative clause is realized as a genitive that seemingly modifies the head noun. In Tongan, the GRC shows additional idiosyncratic properties: (a) The relative clause must contain a transitive verb; (b) the thematic subject of a relative clause must be pronominal; and (c) the genitive must be preposed. This study argues that these facts can be accounted for by assuming that (a) the relative clause of a GRC is an agentless transitive construction; (b) the genitive is base generated; and (c) the genitive is interpreted as the thematic subject of the relative clause through pragmatic rather than syntactic means.

1. Introduction

Polynesian languages, especially those of the Eastern Polynesian (EP) subgroup, commonly use a unique relativization strategy known as the genitive relative construction (GRC), in which the thematic subject of the relative clause is realized as a genitive that apparently modifies the head noun. Tongan, a Polynesian language of the Tongic subgroup, also makes use of the GRC, but with some language-specific restrictions that are not observed in EP or even in Niuean, the other member of the Tongic subgroup. First, the relative clause must contain a transitive verb. Second, the genitive can only be pronominal. Third, while Tongan permits both preposed and postposed genitives, only preposed genitives can be used in the GRC. This study argues that these idiosyncratic characteristics of the Tongan GRC can be accounted for by assuming (a) the relative clause of a GRC is an agentless transitive construction (to be defined in Section 4); (b) the genitive is base generated, i.e., not raised; and (c) coreference

---

* I would like to thank Raph Mercado, Eric Potsdam, and two anonymous reviewers for their helpful comments and suggestions on an earlier version of this paper. I am deeply grateful to Lose Kaufusi for her invaluable help with the Tongan data.

between the genitive and the thematic subject of the relative clause is pragmatic rather than syntactic in nature. The proposed analysis is discussed in full in Section 5.

2. The GRC in Polynesian

EP languages commonly use the GRC for non-subject relatives, in which (a) the head noun is seemingly modified by a genitive, (b) the relative clause lacks an overt subject, and (c) the genitive is interpreted as the thematic subject of the relative clause. This strategy is preferred to the regular gap strategy for non-subject relatives in Hawaiian (Hawkins 2000) and Māori (Bauer 1997).[1]

The thematic subject of the relative clause may be a pronoun, common noun, or proper name, as shown in the examples below.[2]

(1) Hawaiian
 a. ka hale āna   [e   kūkulu nei]
    the house POSS.3.S IMPERF build DEM.1
    'the house he is building'   (Hawkins 1982: 109)
 b. ka wā   a   Pākaʻa [i   haʻalele aku   ai
    the time POSS Pākaʻa PERF leave   DIR.2 AI
    iā   Waipiʻo]
    OBJ.PERS Waipiʻo
    'the moment when Pākaʻa left Waipiʻo'   (Hawkins 2000: 134)

(2) Māori
 a. Ka mōhio ahau ki te   tangata a   Hone [i   kōhuru ai]
    NS know 1.S to the   man   POSS John PERF murder AI
    'I knew the man that John murdered.'   (Bauer 1997: 570)
 b. Kei konei tooku   hoa   taau   [i   pātai mai   na]
    LOC here POSS.1.S friend POSS.2.S PERF ask   DIR.1 DEM.2
    'Here is my friend whom you asked.'   (Biggs 1998: 160)

---

1. Bauer (1997, 2007) notes that the use of the GRC is common in older texts and among older speakers, but has become rare among most younger speakers. According to Bauer, younger speakers tend to use the pronominal strategy (AI strategy) for object relatives, although this is impossible for older speakers.

2. The following abbreviations are used in this article: ABS = absolutive, C = common, DEF = definite, DEM = demonstrative, DIR = directional, DU = dual, ERG = ergative, EXCL = exclusive, FUT = future, GEN = genitive, IMPERF = imperfect, INCL = inclusive, INDF = indefinite, LOC = locative, NEG = negative, NFT = non-future, NS = non-specific tense, OBJ = object, P= pronoun, PERF = perfect, PERS = personal, PL = plural, POSS = possessive, PRED = predicate, PRS = present, PST = past, REF = referencial, S = singular, SBJV = subjunctive, 1 = first person, 2 = second person, 3 = third person.

In these examples, the genitive is postposed, i.e., follows the head noun. The relevant items are glossed as POSS, following the tradition in the descriptive grammars of Polynesian languages; the terms "genitive" and "possessive" are used interchangeably in the following discussion. EP languages also have preposed genitives, which can be pronouns, common nouns, or proper names.

(3) Māori (Biggs 1998: 46)
    a. te whakaaro o   te wahine   [postposed]
       the thought POSS the woman
       'the thought of the woman'

    b. to   te wahine whakaaro   [preposed]
       POSS the woman thought
       'the woman's thought'

(4) Hawaiian (Elbert 1970: 58)
    a. ke ka'a o   Pua   [postposed]
       the car POSS Pua
       'Pua's car'

    b. kō   Pua ka'a   [preposed]
       POSS Pua car
       'Pua's car'

Preposed and postposed possessive constructions show an interesting contrast when both the possessor and the possessee are common nouns. While both NPs are preceded by an article in postposed possessive constructions (3a), only the possessor has an article in preposed possessive constructions. In (3b), the possessee NP, *whakaaro* 'thought', without the article, *te*, immediately follows the possessor DP, *te wahine* 'the woman'. These languages seem to have developed what may be called a possessive article, which precedes the preposed possessor NP. Schematically, it is as if the postposed possessive phrase (i.e., [*o/a te* NP$_{POSSESSOR}$]) were inserted between the possessee NP and its article, [*te* [*o/a te* NP$_{POSSESSOR}$] NP$_{POSSESSEE}$], and subsequently, the sequence of the article and the possessive preposition were fused into a single item *to/ta*. In EP, preposed genitives can also be used in the GRC.

(5) Hawaiian (Hopkins 1992: 233)
    kā   Pua puke [i   kākau ai]
    POSS Pua book PERF write AI
    'the book that Pua wrote'

(6) Māori (Bauer 1997: 570)
    ka mōhio ahau ki tā   Hone tangata [i   kōhuru ai].
    NS know 1.S to POSS John man   PERF murder AI
    'I knew the man that John murdered.'

The GRC in Niuean (Tongic) shows basically the same properties as those in EP. First, this strategy can be used for a range of non-subject relatives, e.g., locatives (7a), oblique objects of semi-transitive verbs (7b), and absolutive (ABS) objects of transitive verbs (7c). Second, the genitive is not restricted to pronouns. Third, postposed genitive forms are preferred, although preposed forms may also be used, as in (7d).

(7) Niuean (Seiter 1980: 97–98)
    a. e   mena *hāu* [ne tunu ai e   moa]
       ABS.C thing your NFT cook AI ABS chicken
       'the thing you cooked the chicken in'
    b. e   tagata *he tau leoleo* [ne mumui tua ki ai]
       ABS person of PL police NFT follow.PL back to him
       'the person who the police are following'
    c. ... he tala *ha Mele* [ka talahau]
       LOC story of Mele FUT tell
       'with the story Mele's going to tell'
    d. Loga *ha Faliki a* kalahimu [ne moua] ...³
       many of Faliki POSS land.crab [NFT catch
       'Many were the land crabs which Faliki caught...'

3. The GRC in Tongan

The GRC also exists in Tongan, as shown in (8), but with some language-specific restrictions. First, it is only available for relative clauses involving transitive verbs. In oblique relatives with intransitive verbs, the thematic subject must occur inside the relative clause, as shown in (9b). As long as the relative clause is transitive, however, the GRC can be used for oblique relatives, as shown in (10). Thus, whether the GRC strategy can be used depends on the type of verb within the relative clause rather than the grammatical relation of the relativized position (contrary to Keenan & Comrie's (1977) observation regarding the choice between gap vs. pronoun strategies).

(8) Na'e lahi *'eku* fetu'u$_i$ [na'e lau t$_i$].
    PST much POSS.1.S star PST count
    'The stars I counted were many.'

(9) a. *Na'e hako *'eku* tahi$_i$ [na'e 'alu ki ai$_i$]
       PST rough POSS.1.S sea PST go to there
       'The sea I went to was rough.'

---

3. In Niuean, the preposed possessive is separated from the noun by a particle *a*, glossed here as POSS (Seiter 1980: 35).

b. Naʻe hako ʻa e tahi$_i$ [naʻa ku ʻalu ki ai$_i$]
PST rough ABS REF sea PST 1.S go to there
'The sea I went to was rough.'

(10) a. ʻeku loki$_i$ [naʻe fai ʻa e sivi ai$_i$]
POSS.1.S room PST do ABS REF exam there
'the room in which I took the exam'

b. ʻeku falemahaki$_i$ [naʻe ʻave ʻa e fefine ki ai$_i$]
POSS.1.S hospital PST take ABS REF woman to there
'the hospital to which I took a woman'

Second, unlike EP and Niuean, only the preposed genitives may be used to represent the thematic subject of the relative clause. Compare (8) above and the ungrammatical (11) with a postposed genitive.

(11) *Naʻe lahi ʻa e fetuʻu$_i$ ʻaʻaku [naʻe lau t$_i$].
PST much ABS REF star POSS.1.S PST count
'The stars I counted were many.'

Third, the thematic subject must be pronominal. Non-pronominal subjects must remain inside the relative clause, as in (12b).

(12) a. *Naʻe lahi ʻa e fetuʻu ʻa Sione [naʻe lau].
PST much ABS REF star POSS John PST count
Intended: 'The stars John counted were many.'

b. Naʻe lahi ʻa e fetuʻu [naʻe lau ʻe Sione].
PST much ABS REF star PST count ERG John
'The stars John counted were many.'

This constraint is due to the following two facts: (a) Only preposed genitives are allowed in the GRC (as observed above); and (b) unlike in EP and in Niuean, non-pronominal possessors cannot be preposed in Tongan. Although Tongan has a set of preposed possessive pronouns, it lacks possessive articles analogous to Māori *to* and Hawaiian *kō* discussed above. Hypothetical forms such as *ha* (= *he* 'REF' + *ʻa* 'POSS') do not exist in Tongan. Thus, common noun or proper name possessors can only be postposed, by means of possessive prepositions, as illustrated in (13).

(13) a. e tohi ʻa Mele
REF book POSS Mary
'Mary's book'

b. *ha Mele tohi
POSS Mary book
Intended: 'Mary's book'

Since postposed genitives are not allowed in the GRC and non-pronominal possessors can only be postposed, non-pronominal agents can never occur as a genitive in the GRC.

To summarize, any analysis of the Tongan GRC must account for the following: (a) The nature of the null agent of the relative clause; (b) the structural position of the genitive; (c) the mechanism of coreference; (d) why the relative clause must be transitive; and (e) why the genitive must be preposed (and hence, must be pronominal).

4. Agentless transitive constructions

Transitive verbs in Tongan may be used intransitively, i.e., occurring only with a single DP, which is marked as ABS. With the majority of transitive verbs, the ABS-marked DP in such constructions is interpreted as the theme/patient rather than the agent. Such constructions are called agentless transitive constructions (ATC) and are often translated in English as passive. Compare ergative (14a) and the corresponding ATC (14b).

(14) a. Te tau fai 'a e ngāue' 'apongipongi.
FUT 1.PL.INCL do ABS REF work.DEF tomorrow
'We will do the work tomorrow.'

b. 'e fai 'a e ngāue' 'apongipongi.
FUT do ABS REF work.DEF tomorrow
'The work will be done tomorrow.'
(Lit. '(someone) will do the work tomorrow')   (Churchward 1953: 68)

A possible analysis of the unexpressed agent in the ATC is that it is an instance of topic drop, with the null agent being a topic variable. Discourse topic variables are frequently used in Tongan. Unlike in Japanese and Chinese (Huang 1984, 1989), however, the use of topic variables is restricted to third person (Dukes 1996, Otsuka 2000). For first and second person discourse topics, clitic pronouns must be used (15a). On the other hand, topic variables are not subject to any Case constraints: They may occur as ERG as well as ABS arguments (15b, c).

(15) a. Na'a mau folau mama'o.
PST 1.PL.EXCL travel far
'oku *(mau) hela'ia.
PRS 1.PL.EXCL tired
'We traveled far. (We) are tired.'

b. Na'e folau mama'o 'a e siana'. 'oku (ne) hela'ia.
PST travel far ABS REF man.DEF PRS 3.S tired
'The man traveled far. (He) is tired.'

c. Na'e 'alu 'a e siana' ki tu'a.
   PST go ABS REF man.DEF to outside
   Na'e (ne) hua'i 'a e vai'
   PST 3.S pour.out ABS REF water.DEF
   'The man went outside. (He) poured out the water.'

The unexpressed agent in the ATC is different from a discourse topic variable in three respects. First, while the referent of a topic variable must be clearly known and identifiable from the context, the referent of the unexpressed agent in the ATC can be, and most of the time, is, unknown to both the speaker and the addressee. Second, when the context makes it possible to identify the referent of the unexpressed agent in the ATC, it is not restricted to third person, as shown in (16) from Dukes (1996: 152). The unexpressed agent is interpreted as coreferential with the possessor *'eku* 'my' in (16a) and the subject of the second clause *mau* 'we' in (16b).

(16) a. 'oku ou mahalo pē kuo 'ilo 'e he'eku
       PRS 1.S think just PERF know ERG POSS.1.S
       fa'ē [na'e 'ikai paasi 'eku sivi].
       mother PST NEG pass POSS.1.S exam
       'I think my mother knows that I didn't pass my exam.'

   b. [Na'e tāmate'i 'a e misini']
      PST kill ABS REF engine.DEF
      ka mau folau lā pē.
      and 1.PL.EXCL travel sail only
      '(we) turned off the engine and we traveled by sail alone.'

Third, unlike topic variables, which are not subject to any Case-related constraints, unexpressed agents must be ERG. In his corpus study, Dukes (1996) observes that null arguments in Tongan can be coreferential with first and second person arguments only when they are taken to be ERG arguments. He did not find any instance of the omission of first and/or second arguments that are ABS in his corpus.

A subset of transitive verbs, e.g., *'ilo* 'to find' in (17a), requires the ATC interpretation when used intransitively. With another subset of transitive verbs, such as *tāmate* 'to kill' in (17b), the ABS-marked DP is obligatorily interpreted as the agent (Tchekhoff 1973: 286).

(17) a. Na'e 'ilo 'a e fa'ee'.
       PST find ABS REF mother.DEF
       'The mother was found' (but not 'the mother found.')

   b. Na'e tāmate 'a Mele.
      PST kill ABS Mele
      'Mele killed' (but not 'Mele was killed.')

The distinction is reminiscent of Pawley's (1973) "obligatory transitive" and "optional transitive" in Oceanic. In Tongan, however, a majority of transitive verbs can occur in both the obligatory transitive pattern, in which the ABS-marked DP is interpreted as the patient, like in (17a), and the optional transitive pattern, in which the ABS-marked DP is understood as the agent, like in (17b). I propose that the intransitive use of optional transitive verbs arises due to object incorporation. The patient is therefore implicit and not overtly realized.

Note that the null object approach is not adequate for optional transitives in Tongan, as evidenced by the ABS marking on the overt DP. If there were a null object, the overt agent would be marked as ERG. Thus, it is not simply an instance of phonological suppression, but rather an instance of theta role absorption, which can be understood as incorporation of a null pronominal argument with unvalued phi-features.[4] Given that the remaining overt argument appears in ABS, I assume that incorporation takes place at the level of lexical syntax in the sense of Hale & Keyser (1993).

(18) Optional transitive and object incorporation

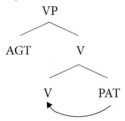

Along the same lines, I propose that the ATC is derived through incorporation of a phonetically null pronominal agent with unspecified phi-features. Although agent incorporation is generally taken to be impossible (Baker 1988), the proposed operation is compatible with Baker & Hale's (1990) observation that crosslinguistically, agent incorporation is permissible only in VSO languages and with pronominal agents.[5] Structurally, agent incorporation is possible in VSO languages if the V-initial order is derived due to V-to-T raising. As illustrated in (19), the agent argument is in a configuration from which incorporation to the raised V is possible.

---

4. This is in a sense similar to Rizzi's (1986) analysis of null objects in Italian in that the phonologically null object is taken to be a generic *pro*. The analysis discussed here is different from Rizzi's in that it also assumes incorporation of the postulated generic *pro*.

5. Van Valin (1992) notes that full noun subject incorporation is attested in Mayali (Australian, Evans 1990) and Boni (Eastern Cushitic, Sasse 1984).

(19) Obligatory transitive and agent incorporation

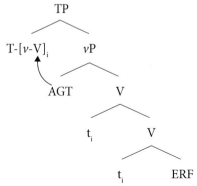

The incorporated agent can be interpreted as coreferential with a particular DP, if the context provides a potential antecedent (or "postcedent", as the cases below show). Otherwise, unvalued phi-features give rise to an indefinite interpretation (i.e., "someone"). Consider (16), repeated below (from Dukes 1996: 152), in which ATCs are indicated by square brackets.

(16) a. ʻoku ou mahalo pē kuo ʻilo ʻe heʻeku
      PRS 1.S think just PERF know ERG POSS.1.S
      faʻē [naʻe ʻikai paasi ___ *ʻeku* sivi].
      mother PST NEG pass POSS.1.S exam
      'I think my mother knows that I didn't pass my exam.'

b. [Naʻe tamateʻi ___ ʻa e misiniˊ]
      PST kill ABS REF engine.DEF
      ka *mau* folau lā pē.
      and 1.PL.EXCL travel sail only
      '(we) turned off the engine and we traveled by sail alone.'

Note that in both (16a) and (16b), the coreferent in italics occurs after the linear position in which the unexpressed agent is expected, indicated by the underscore. That is, it does not c-command the relevant position. This suggests that the coreference in question is not obtained syntactically, but pragmatically. And as expected of pragmatic coreference, if the possessive pronoun *ʻeku* is replaced with an article in (16a), the reference of the unexpressed agent becomes ambiguous: It could be 'I', 'my mother', or someone else.

(20) ʻoku ou mahalo pē kuo ʻilo ʻe heʻeku faʻē
      PRS 1.S think just PERF know ERG POSS.1.S mother
      naʻe ʻikai paasi (ʻa) e sivi].
      PST NEG pass ABS REF exam
      'I think my mother$_i$ knows that I/she$_i$/he didn't pass the exam.'

Note also that the presence of a possessive pronoun does not require such coreference. In (21) below, the verb *kaiha'asi* 'steal' makes the coreference between the unexpressed agent and the possessor *'eku* 'my' pragmatically infelicitous.

(21) 'oku ou 'ilo pē [na'e kaiha'asi 'eku me'alele].
 PRS 1.S know just PST steal POSS.1.S car
 'I know that someone/*I stole my car.'

5. Analysis of the Tongan GRC

With this analysis of the ATC in mind, I propose the following analysis of the GRC in Tongan. The relative clause in a GRC is an ATC, i.e., a clause containing an underlying transitive verb whose agent argument has been incorporated into the verb. The genitive pronoun in a GRC is base generated as D, external to the relative clause. In other words, the missing agent of the relative clause is not a trace that resulted from raising. The proposed analysis is schematically represented in (22) below. The internal structure of NP is ignored here for ease of exposition. It is also assumed that relativization involves movement of an empty operator (OP) rather than movement of the head noun, though it does not affect the analysis even if the latter were adopted (cf. Kayne 1994).

(22)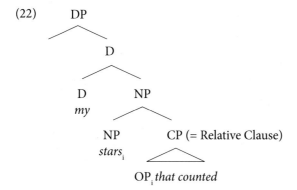

5.1 The GRC and the agentless transitive

If we take the relative clause of a GRC to be an ATC in Tongan, two facts about the Tongan GRC follow. First, oblique GRCs involving intransitive verbs such as (9a) are ruled out simply because it is impossible to derive an ATC from an intransitive construction. At the same time, the proposed analysis correctly predicts that the GRC can be used for oblique relatives as long as the verb is transitive. Second, the genitive is interpreted as the thematic subject of the relative clause in the GRC because the presence of the genitive creates a context in which it may serve as a potential antecedent for the incorporated agent of the ATC (relative clause) in a way similar to cases like (16) discussed above.

The hypothesis that intransitive verbs are incompatible with the ATC is empirically supported. Null subjects of intransitive verbs can never be interpreted as first or second person, as mentioned above (cf. Dukes 1996). Omission of intransitive subjects is possible only if their referent is known and is third person. This is unexpected if the ATC strategy is available for intransitive verbs. To illustrate, consider (23) below, which is parallel to (16a) above with the embedded clause containing a possessive pronoun that is coreferential with the matrix subject. Unlike (16a), however, the omitted agent in (23) cannot be coreferential with the matrix subject even though the context makes it a legitimate candidate. The difference between the two sentences is that the embedded verb is transitive in (16a), but intransitive in (23).

(23) 'Oku ou 'ilo   [na'e nofo 'i hoku   'api   'aneafi].
     PRS 1.s know PST stay in POSS.1.s home yesterday
     'I know he/*I stayed at my home.'

The incompatibility of the ATC and intransitive verbs can be explained if it is assumed, following Otsuka (2006), that in Tongan, intransitive subjects are generated VP-internally, unlike transitive subjects, which are generated in [Spec,*v*] (see also Wiltschko (2006) for a similar claim for Halkomelem Salish, another ergative language). If this analysis is correct, incorporation of intransitive subjects is then impossible in Tongan. Suppose intransitive subjects move to the edge of *v*P ([Spec *v*]) due to an EPP feature (as assumed by Otsuka (2005, 2006) for Tongan). Since such raising is an instance of phrasal movement, the moved element must be a maximal projection, and may not undergo incorporation, since incorporation is assumed to be an instance of head movement (Baker 1988). If intransitive subjects remain inside VP, incorporation is banned as well. Given the Phase Impenetrability Condition (PIC; Chomsky 2000, 2001), which states that only the head and the edge of a phase (*v*P or CP) are accessible to any operations at the next phase, VP-internal subjects are inaccessible to operations that take place at the CP-phase because they are not at the edge of *v*P. The agent incorporation proposed here takes place at the CP-phase, after V has moved to T. Therefore, intransitive subjects may not undergo this operation due to the PIC.

5.2 The nature of the null agent in the GRC

As for the nature of the null agent in the GRC, four alternative analyses exist, in which it is regarded as an instance of (a) an NP-trace, (b) a *wh*-trace, (c) a discourse topic variable, or (d) PRO. All of them are inadequate, however.

First, the NP-trace analysis fails to explain why the relevant movement (i.e., raising) is permissible only for pronominal transitive subjects. While generally restricted to subjects, raising is not known to distinguish pronominal from non-pronominal subjects or between subjects of intransitive verbs and of transitive verbs.

Second, the *wh*-movement analysis is untenable for two reasons. Such movement would violate the island condition (i.e., ban against the extraction of a DP out of a relative clause). Moreover, in Tongan, a *wh*-trace is licensed only in an ABS position (Otsuka 2006). Regular relativization in Tongan is restricted in the following manner: The gap strategy is used for ABS relatives, as illustrated in (24).

(24) a. Ko   e   fefine$_i$ [na'e kata   t$_i$]
     PRED REF woman   PST laugh
     '(It is) a woman who laughed.'

   b. Ko   e   fefine$_i$ [na'e fili   'e   Sione t$_i$]
     PRED REF woman   PST choose ERG John
     '(It is) a woman whom John chose.'

In contrast, relativization of ERG arguments requires a resumptive pronoun, a clitic attached to the tense aspect marker, as demonstrated in (25a). ERG relatives without a resumptive pronoun are ungrammatical, as exemplified in (25b).

(25) a. Ko   e   fefine$_i$ [na'a ne$_i$ kai 'a   e   ika]
     PRED REF woman   PST 3.S   eat ABS REF fish
     '(It is) a woman who (she) ate a fish.'

   b. *Ko   e   fefine$_i$ [na'e kai t$_i$ 'a   e   ika]
     PRED REF woman   PST eat   ABS REF fish
     Intended: '(It is) a woman who ate a fish.'

The pronoun strategy is also used for oblique relatives. The resumptive element is *ai* rather than any of the personal clitic pronouns.

(26) a. Ko   e   feitu'u$_i$ [na'e 'alu 'a   Sione ki *(ai$_i$)]
     PRED REF place   PST go   ABS John to there
     '(It is) a place to which John went'

   b. Ko   e   loki$_i$ [na'a ku mohe 'i *(ai$_i$)]
     PRED REF room   PST 1.S sleep in there
     '(It is) a room in which I slept'

Thus, a resumptive pronoun is expected in the relative clause if the genitive of the GRC indeed were to undergo *wh*-movement. Yet, in the GRC, a gap is permitted in the ERG position and moreover, it cannot occur in the ABS position (i.e., as intransitive subjects).

Third, topic variables in Tongan are restricted to third person as noted above, whereas the null subjects in the GRC can be of any person and number, e.g., first person singular as in (8). Note that this is a property of the implicit agent in ATCs, as discussed above.

Finally, PRO in Tongan is licensed only in the subject position of a transitive construction (Otsuka 2000). For the subject position of an intransitive construction, an overt pronoun must occur (27a). One may hypothesize that intransitive verbs are not permitted in the GRC because the null agent is a PRO. Unlike other instances of PRO, however, insertion of an overt pronoun does not improve grammaticality in the GRC, as exemplified by (27b).

(27) a. 'oku ou loto [ke u/*PRO 'alu]
       PRS 1.S want SBJV 1.S   go
       'I want to go.'

   b. *Na'e hako 'eku   tahi [na'a ku 'alu ki ai]
       PST rough POSS.1.S sea   PST   1.S go to there
       Intended: 'The sea I went to was rough.'

The fact that a resumptive pronoun is not possible in a GRC also supports the argument against the null subject being a *wh*-trace.

5.3 The position of the genitive in GRCs

In this subsection, I present some arguments to support the current analysis that the genitive in the GRC is base generated in D and demonstrate that this hypothesis also explains why the genitive in the Tongan GRC must be preposed and hence must be pronominal.

Let us first consider the position of the genitive within the projection of N. Tongan has two sets of possessive pronouns, preposed (28a) and postposed (28b). They may co-occur within a single noun phrase, as shown in (28c), when emphasis is intended as in 'my *own* book'. This suggests that there are two separate positions for preposed and postposed possessive pronouns.

(28) a. 'eku   tohi
       POSS. 1.S book
       'my book(s)'

   b. e   tohi 'a'aku
      REF book POSS.1.S
      'my book(s)'

   c. 'eku   tohi 'a'aku
      POSS.1.S book POSS.1.S
      'my own book'

Based on these facts, I propose that postposed possessive pronouns are in [Spec, Poss] whereas preposed possessive pronouns are base generated in D, as illustrated in (29).

(29)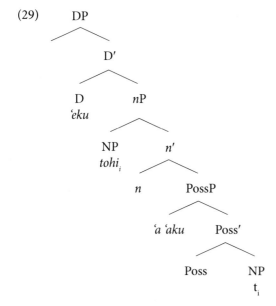

Recall that in Tongan, only pronominal possessors can be preposed. This fact can be nicely accounted for if it is assumed that preposed possessives are Ds. With pronouns as determiners (cf. Abney 1987), they may be base generated in D, but common nouns and proper names may not.

The hypothesis that preposed possessive pronouns are determiners is also supported by their morphology. Preposed possessive pronouns, except for second person, have two allomorphs, e.g., *'eku* and *he'eku* 'my', *'ene* and *he'ene* 'his/her'. The initial *he-* is homophonous with an allomorph of the referential article. The referential article has two allomorphs *he* and *e*. The former occurs after a preposition or Case marker ending in [e] or [i], and the latter occurs elsewhere. Possessive pronouns with initial *he-* show the same distribution as the article *he*, as illustrated in (30), suggesting that preposed possessive pronouns contain the referential article.

(30) a. ki he/*e fefine
       to REF woman
       'to a woman'

   b. ki he'eku/'eku tamai[6]
       to POSS.1.S father
       'to my father'

---

6. After a preposition ending in [i], possessive pronouns show free variation, i.e., the initial *he* can be optionally omitted. However, such free variation is not available in the environment where *he*-less forms are required. That is, optional addition of *he* is not permitted.

c. mo   e/*he fefine
    with REF   woman
    'with a woman'

d. mo   'eku/*he'eku tamai
    with POSS.1.S   father
    'with my father'

Note also that preposed possessive pronouns cannot co-occur with an article, as shown in (31), suggesting that they are indeed determiners.

(31) a. mo   (*e) 'eku   tamai
         with REF   POSS.1.S father

     b. *mo e he'eku tamai
         with REF POSS.1.S father

     c. ki (*he) he'eku   tamai
         to REF   POSS.1.S father

The forms of the second person possessive pronouns provide another piece of evidence to support this hypothesis. The relevant forms are *ho'o* 'your (S)', *ho'omo* 'your (DU)', and *ho'omou* 'your (PL)'. Note that the vowel following the initial *h* is [o] rather than [e]. This can be explained in terms of assimilation to the following vowel. However, such assimilation never occurs between the article *he* and the noun it modifies, e.g., *he/*ho 'ofa* 'the love', *he/*ho ongoongo* 'the news'. Furthermore, unlike other preposed possessive pronouns, second person possessive pronouns do not have an allomorph without the initial *ho*. Thus, in these forms, the referential article *he* has been fully integrated as part of the possessive pronouns.

Let us now return to the genitive in the GRC. The structure in (22) correctly predicts that no more than one preposed genitive may occur in the GRC, as in (32a), since there is only one D position in the whole noun phrase. It also correctly predicts that it is possible for a preposed possessive pronoun and a postposed genitive to co-occur, as in (32b). The postposed genitive is interpreted as the owner or the author of the book. The missing agent of the relative clause can be coreferential with the preposed genitive. (It can also be interpreted as indefinite "someone", in which case (32b) means 'your book of John (author) that someone read'.)

(32) a. *ho'o   'ene   tohi [na'e lau]
         POSS.2.S POSS.3.S book PST   read
         Intended: 'his book that you read'
         or 'your book that he read'

     b. ho'o   tohi 'a   Sione [na'e lau]
         POSS.2.S book POSS John   PST   read
         'John's book that you read'

One last point that needs to be explained is that postposed genitives may never be coreferential with the null agent of the relative clause. In (33), for example, the postposed possessive must be interpreted as the possessor. The missing agent of the relative clause cannot be coreferential with the postposed possessive, but can only be interpreted as indefinite "someone" (with the relative clause being an instance of the ATC) or as a third person whose reference is given (as a topic variable).

(33) Naʻe maumau ʻa e meʻalele ʻaʻau [naʻe fakaʻuli].
PST broken ABS REF car POSS.2.S PST drive
*'The car you drove was broken.'
'Your car that he/someone/*you drove was broken.'

There are two possible hypotheses for this fact, semantic and syntactic. The semantic hypothesis is that in Tongan, postposed genitives are restricted to possessors, whereas preposed genitives are "true" genitives in the sense that they can bear various semantic roles including possessor and agent. This is partially supported by the semantic difference between the two. Churchward (1953: 142) observes that postposed genitives are used to lay the emphasis on the possessive itself rather than on the noun which it modifies, e.g., '*my* shirt' as opposed to 'my *shirt*'. Similarly, my consultant gave me the following example to illustrate the difference between the two: The postposed possessives "emphasize the ownership".

(34) a. ʻene meʻalele
POSS.3.S car
'his car (which he uses, but may not own)'

b. e meʻalele ʻaʻana
REF car POSS.3.S
'his car (which he owns and uses)'

If this hypothesis is correct, then, it also explains why the thematic agent of the GRC cannot occur as a postposed genitive. Simply put: A postposed genitive cannot bear the semantic role of agent.

Another piece of evidence to support this hypothesis comes from the use of possessive pronouns in nominalization. Preposed possessives can be used in nominalization to refer to the agent, as shown in (35).

(35) a. ʻene kata
POSS.3.S laugh
'his/her laughing'

b. ʻene taki (ʻa e kakaiʻ)
POSS.3.S lead ABS REF people.DEF
'his/her leading (the people)'

On the other hand, it is ungrammatical to use a postposed possessive pronoun to express the agent of a nominalized verb. Consider the intransitive example in (36a) and the transitive example in (36b).

(36) a. *e   lele   'a'aku.
         REF run   POSS.1.S
         Intended: 'my running'

     b. *e   taki   'a'au   'a   e   fonua´
         REF lead   POSS.2.S   ABS   REF   country.DEF
         Intended: 'your leading the country'

The ungrammaticality of (36a) is alleviated if a preposed possessive pronoun is added (Churchward 1953: 142). However, the addition of a preposed genitive does not improve grammaticality if the verb is transitive.[7]

(37) a. 'eku   lele   'a'aku
         POSS.1.S run   POSS.1.S
         '*my* running'

     b. *ho'o   taki   'a'au   'a   e   fonua´
         POSS.2.S lead   POSS.2.S   ABS   REF country.DEF
         Intended: '*your* leading the country'

Likewise, postposed genitives cannot be used to represent non-pronominal agents if the verb is transitive, as shown in (38b).

(38) a. e   lele 'a   Sione.
         REF   run   POSS   John
         'John's running'

     b. *e   taki   'a   Sione 'a   e   fonua´
         REF lead   POSS John   ABS   REF   country.DEF
         Intended: 'John's leading the country'

---

7. In order to express the intended emphasis, the ergative marker 'e is used:

   (i) ho'o   taki   'e   koe   'a   e   fonua´
        POSS.2.S   lead   ERG   2.S   ABS   REF country.DEF
        'your leading the country'
        The same strategy is used to express non-pronominal agents of nominalized verbs. Compare (ii) with (38b).

   (ii) e   taki   'e   Sione 'a   e   fonua´
        REF   lead   ERG   John   ABS   REF country.DEF
        'John's leading the country'

The use of postposed genitives appears to be grammatical if the verb is intransitive, as in (38a). It should be noted, however, that the particle 'a in (38a) is ambiguous between the ABS Case marker and the possessive preposition, since they are homophonous.

Let us now turn to the syntactic account. One might hypothesize that the genitive must c-command the relative clause in order to obtain coreference. (This is assumed by Herd et al. (2004), as discussed below in Section 6). In the analysis presented here, postposed genitives are base generated in [Spec, Poss], which is inside the nP, to which the relative clause is adjoined. Therefore, postposed genitives do not c-command the relative clause and consequently, may not establish a syntactic relation necessary for coreference. Although it is a reasonable hypothesis, it contradicts the present proposal that the coreference between the genitive and the null agent in the relative clause in the GRC is pragmatic in nature. Moreover, c-command does not always license coreference between the genitive and the missing agent of a relative clause. These issues are taken up in the following section.

5.4 The mechanism of coreference

The hypothesis that coreference between the genitive and the null agent of the relative clause is pragmatic in nature predicts that long distance coreference is possible with the GRC. This prediction is borne out, as shown in (39). The genitive can be interpreted as the thematic subject of the verb *fili* 'choose' of the lower embedded clause CP2.

(39) 'eku   kaati$_i$ [$_{CP1}$ 'oku ke pehē [$_{CP2}$ na'e fili   t$_i$]]
      POSS.1.s card   PRS 2.s think   PST choose
      'the card you think I chose'

Surprisingly, however, in a similar construction, the genitive cannot refer to the subject of the verb *pehē* 'think' of the higher embedded clause.

(40) ho'o   kaati$_i$ [$_{CP1}$ 'oku pehē [$_{CP2}$ na'a ku fili   t$_i$]]
      POSS.2.s card   PRS think   PST 1.s choose
      Intended: *'the card you think I chose'

The sentence in (40) could mean "your card that (s/he) thinks I chose" with the genitive taken to be the possessor and the missing subject of *pehē* 'think', a topic variable. Crucially, however, the GRC interpretation is not available. That examples like (40) cannot have the GRC interpretation suggests that the null agent of a GRC requires more than just pragmatic coreference.

One possibility is that the genitive and the head noun of the relative clause must be associated with the same verb. If this hypothesis is correct, we expect it to be possible for the genitive to be coreferential with the missing agent of the higher embedded clause if that clause also contains the relativized position. Although it is difficult to find such examples (especially with two tensed clauses), elicited examples like (41) partially support this prediction. In (41), the null operator has been extracted from CP1 and the genitive is interpreted as the thematic subject of the verb *fili* 'choose' of that clause.

(41) 'enau siana$_i$ [$_{CP1}$ 'e fili t$_i$
POSS.3.PL man FUT choose
[$_{CP2}$ ke PRO$_i$ mali mo ho'o 'ofefine]]
SBJV marry with POSS.2.S daughter
'the man they will choose to marry your daughter'

We would also expect it to be impossible for the genitive to be interpreted as the agent of the lower embedded clause if the relativized position is in the higher embedded clause. Again, the prediction is borne out. The genitive cannot be coreferential with the missing agent of CP2 when the relativized position is in CP1. The genitive is obligatorily interpreted as the possessor.

(42) 'eku siana$_i$ [$_{CP1}$ na'a ke tala ange ki ai$_i$
POSS.1.S man PST 2.S tell DIR.3 to AI
[$_{CP2}$ 'e langa 'a e fale]]
FUT build ABS REF house
'my man$_i$ you told (to him$_j$) that he$_{i/j}$/*I will build a house'

It thus seems that coreference between the genitive and the null agent of the relative clause is more restricted than simple pragmatic coreference as exemplified by (16) above. Although both involve the ATC, sentences involving the GRC are different from those in (16) in one crucial manner: While the coreferent of the incorporated agent of the ATC is independently licensed (i.e., it has received a theta role) in sentences like (16), the genitive of a GRC is not independently licensed, not receiving a theta role in its base position. Thus, one may hypothesize that what motivates coreference in the GRC is not the need of the incorporated agent for a referent, but the need of the genitive for a theta role. I propose that the genitive acquires a theta role through pragmatic coreference with the incorporated agent of the relative clause. I elaborate on this mechanism below.

Recall that in the analysis of the ATC espoused here, the null agent of an ATC is understood as the result of the incorporation into the verb of a phonetically null pronoun with unspecified phi-features. This pronoun receives the agent theta role in its base position from the verb. Thus, as far as the Theta Criterion (Chomsky 1981) is concerned, this item is licensed. On the other hand, its referential interpretation depends on context: It can be coreferential with a pragmatic antecedent if the context provides one, but is otherwise interpreted as indefinite "someone". Since coreference in this case is pragmatic in nature, it can be established after syntax.

To account for how the genitive of a GRC acquires a theta role through coreference with the incorporated agent of the relative clause, I propose a system of coindexation between the verb, its theta roles, and the DPs to which these theta roles are assigned. For the sake of argument, I assume that theta roles are features and that each noun phrase has an uninterpretable theta-feature [$u\theta$]. For example, the verb phrase in the simple sentence *John pushed Mary* has three lexical items: *push$_i$* [$u\theta$:AGT$_i$, $u\theta$:PAT$_i$], *John* [$u\theta$], and *Mary* [$u\theta$]. When the verb assigns a theta role to a DP, the relevant theta-feature on the verb is checked and the theta-feature of the DP receives a value with the index: *push$_i$* [~~$u\theta$:AGT~~i, ~~$u\theta$:PAT~~i], *John* [AGT$_i$], and *Mary* [PAT$_i$]. In the ATC, the incorporated agent has the following features: [phi:__, AGT$_i$], where the underscore indicates that its value is unspecified. For independent ATCs, that is the end of the story. The agent theta role has been assigned and the phi-features receives either the default value [INDF, 3.S] or a specific value through pragmatic coreference.

Let us consider the GRC. In object relatives, for example, the head NP of the relative clause is coindexed with the null operator, whose theta-feature has received a value and an index, [PAT$_i$] from the verb. Within the relative clause, the theta-feature of the incorporated agent of the ATC has also received a value and an index, [AGT$_i$]. It also has unvalued phi-features [phi:__]. The genitive in D has an uninterpretable theta-feature [$u\theta$].[8]

Let us also assume that D and NP are coindexed by virtue of the head-complement relation. The theta-feature on D is thus indexed as [$u\theta_i$]. The theta-feature on D seeks an available theta-feature in the construction, that is, a theta-feature that has the same index *i* and is accessible. The incorporated agent in the relative clause is accessible, as it still needs to have its phi-features valued, and it has a theta-feature that is coindexed with that of the genitive. The genitive provides a specific value for the phi-features of the incorporated agent (i.e., pragmatic coreference). In return, the genitive's theta-feature receives a value from the theta-feature of the incorporated agent: [$u\theta_i$] → [AGT$_i$]. The relevant relations are schematized in (43) (irrelevant details are omitted). Note that the proposed feature-checking operations are assumed to be postsyntactic operations and therefore not subject to the PIC.

---

8. This feature may also be checked by the noun itself and receive the value [POSS]. I assume this to be syntactic theta-feature checking, an operation that takes place in narrow syntax. This raises an interesting question of whether the same theta-feature can be checked twice, once in narrow syntax and later post-syntactically. When this happens, the genitive is interpreted both as possessor and as implied agent of the relative clause. Since such an interpretation is available (e.g., *my book that I read*), I assume that a theta-feature on a genitive D can be checked either only in narrow syntax (possessor, but not agent), only postsyntactically (agent, but not possessor), or both (agent and possessor).

(43)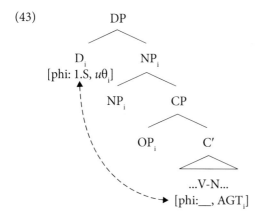

A stipulation that the unvalued theta-feature on D can only access those theta-features which have the same index ensures that the genitive and the head noun of a GRC are associated with the same clause. The idea of post-syntactic theta-feature checking has also been proposed by Bošković & Takahashi (1998) to account for long distance scrambling in Japanese. Their analysis is similar to the one proposed here in permitting the base generation of an argument in a non-theta position and postulating post-syntactic theta-feature checking (which, in their case, involves lowering of the theta-feature into an available theta position).

6. Comparison with Herd et al. (2004)

The analysis of the Tongan GRC proposed here is similar in many respects to Herd et al.'s (2004) approach to the GRC in Polynesian in general. Both argue (a) that the genitive is base generated (i.e., no raising) and (b) that the relation between the genitive and the thematic subject of the relative clause in a GRC is not syntactic.

Herd et al. (2004) argue that coreference is obtained through a special kind of semantic control, a relation holding between a DP and a theta-feature(cf. Manzini & Roussou 2000). Their version of semantic control does not involve a particular position or element, but assumes that the antecedent can control a position in a theta grid. This is mainly due to Māori data, which suggest that the relative clause in the GRC is intransitive (e.g., passive in the case of patient relatives) and therefore, does not have a structural position for the agent (Herd et al. 2004: 10–11). It is also assumed, though tentatively, that this special kind of semantic control can occur across the CP phase, enabling the genitive to control into the theta grid of the verb inside the relative clause.

Their idea of control into the theta grid is similar to the proposal here, in which the coreference between the genitive and the null agent is understood as a relationship between two theta-features rather than two DPs. The idea of pragmatic coreference explains why this operation may apply across the CP phase. A possible advantage of my approach is that it provides a mechanism to license a genitive that is base-generated in a non-theta position. The process of semantic control accounts for coreference, but does not explicitly explain how the genitive is licensed, specifically, by satisfying the Theta Criterion.

As for the structure of the GRC, the two analyses are alike in essence. They both assume (a) that the genitive agent is outside *n*P and (b) that the *n*P-internal PossP is reserved for possessors (though Herd et al. (2004) do not explicitly state this). There is a slight difference between the two approaches, however. As shown in (44) below, Herd et al. (2004: 4) postulate an extra PossP above *n*P and place the genitive in its Spec.

(44)

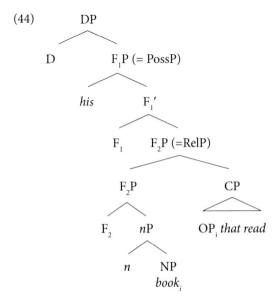

Their basis for this structure comes from Niuean data, in which the head noun of a GRC may be modified by another postposed genitive, e.g., *the son of Mary of John [that smacked]* meaning 'Mary's son that John smacked' (Herd et al. 2004: 6). Such data suggest that the genitive agent must be in a position other than the possessive position within the head noun phrase, the latter being reserved for the true possessor.

Differences between the analysis presented in this paper and that proposed by Herd et al. (2004) are due to the kind of data used in each study. Recall that the Tongan GRC is different from the GRC in other Polynesian languages in two respects: (a) The genitive in the Tongan GRC must be preposed; and (b) only pronominal genitives can be preposed. The latter fact suggests that preposed genitives are Ds in Tongan. Furthermore, because no more than one postposed genitive can occur in the Tongan GRC, there is no basis to postulate an external PossP in Tongan DPs. Considering these different syntactic constraints, it is plausible that the Tongan GRC and the GRC in other Polynesian languages have slightly different structures. Crucially, the structure in (44) fails to capture the relevant facts about the Tongan GRC.

7. Conclusion

The present study starts with two puzzling facts about Tongan GRCs: (a) The genitive must be preposed and pronominal; and (b) the relative clause must be transitive. These facts differentiate the Tongan GRC from the GRC in its cousin Polynesian languages. That the genitive must be preposed and pronominal has led to the conclusion that the genitive in the Tongan GRC is a D head. The fact that only transitive verbs may participate in the GRC in Tongan sheds light on how a genitive that is base-generated in a non-theta position is linked to the agent theta role of the verb of the relative clause. I have argued that agent incorporation makes the relevant theta-feature accessible to post-syntactic operations. Although the mechanism of post-syntactic theta-feature checking proposed here leaves room for further refinement, the idea is promising with implications for other instances of long distance coreference that do not seem to involve syntactic movement.

The analysis proposed above is in line with the one proposed by Herd et al. (2004) in assuming that (a) the genitive is base generated in its surface position; and that (b) the coreference between the genitive and the thematic subject of the relative clause is not syntactic in nature. At the same time, while Herd et al. (2004) account for the common properties of the GRC in Polynesian, their approach falls short in explaining the two idiosyncratic characteristics of the Tongan GRC. The Tongan data discussed in this study clearly call for an alternative analysis and suggest that crosslinguistically, there may be more than one type of GRC despite the apparent similarities.

References

Abney, S. 1987. The English Noun Phrase in its Sentential Aspects. PhD dissertation, MIT.
Baker, M. 1988. *Incorporation: A Theory of Grammatical Function Changing*. Chicago IL: University of Chicago Press.
Baker, M. & Hale, K. 1990. Relativized minimality and pronoun incorporation. *Linguistic Inquiry* 21: 289–97.
Bauer, W. 1997. *The Reed Reference Grammar of Māori*. Auckland: Reed.
Bauer, W. 2007. Typology to the rescue: Halting the infiltration of English into Maori syntax. A paper presented at the fourteenth meeting of the Austronesian Formal Linguistics Association. Montreal, McGill University.
Biggs, B. 1998 [1969]. *Let's Learn Maori*. Auckland: Auckland University Press.
Bošković, Ž., & D. Takahashi. 1998. Scrambling and Last Resort. *Linguistic Inquiry* 29: 347–366.
Chomsky, N. 1981. *Lectures on Government and Binding*. Dordrecht: Foris.
Chomsky, N. 2000. Minimalist inquiries: The framework. In *Step By Step*, R. Martin, D. Michaels & J. Uriagereka (eds), 91–155. Cambridge MA: The MIT Press.
Chomsky, N. 2001. Derivation by phase. In *Ken Hale: A Life in Language*, M. Kenstowicz (ed), 1–52. Cambridge MA: The MIT Press.
Churchward, C.M. 1953. *Tongan Grammar*. London: OUP.

Dukes, M. 1996. On the Nonexistence of Anaphors and Pronominals in Tongan. PhD dissertation, UCLA.

Elbert, S.H. 1970. *Spoken Hawaiian*. Honolulu HI: University of Hawai'i Press.

Evans, N. 1990. Noun incorporation, grammatical relations and valency change in Mayali. Ms, University of Melbourne.

Hale, K. & Keyser, S.J.. 1993. On argument structure and the lexical expression of syntactic relations. In *The View from Building 20: Essays in Honor of Sylvain Bromberger*, K. Hale & S.J. Keyser (eds), 53–109. Cambridge MA: The MIT Press.

Hawkins, E. 1982. *Pedagogical Grammar of Hawaiian: Recurrent Problems*. Mānoa: Hawaiian Studies Program, University of Hawai'i.

Hawkins, E. 2000. Relative clauses in Hawaiian. In *Leo Pasifika: Proceedings of the Fourth International Conference on Oceanic Linguistics*, S.R. Fischer & W.B. Sperlich (eds), 127–141. Auckland: Institute of Polynesian Languages and Literatures.

Herd, J., Macdonald, C. & Massam, D. 2004. Genitive-relative constructions in Polynesian. In *Proceedings of the 2004 Canadian Linguistics Association Annual Conference*, M.-O. Junker, M. McGinnis, & Y. Roberge (eds). <http://http-server.carleton.ca/~mojunker/ACL-CLA/pdf/Herd-MacDonald-Massam-CLA-2004.pdf>.

Hopkins, A. P. 1992. *Ka Lei Ha'aheo: Beginning Hawaiian*. Honolulu HI: University of Hawai'i Press.

Huang, C.-T. J. 1984. On the distribution and reference of empty pronouns. *Linguistic Inquiry* 15: 531–574.

Huang, C.-T. J. 1989. *Pro*-drop in Chinese: A generalized control theory. In *The Null Subject Parameter*, O. Jaeggli & K.J. Safir (eds), 185–214. Dordrecht: Kluwer.

Kayne, R. 1994. *The Antisymmetry of Syntax*. Cambridge MA: The MIT Press.

Keenan, E.L. & Comrie, B. 1977. Noun phrase accessibility and universal grammar. *Linguistic Inquiry* 8: 63–99.

Manzini, M.-R. & Roussou, A. 2000. A minimalist theory of A-movement and control. *Lingua* 110: 409–447.

Otsuka, Y. 2000. Ergativity in Tongan. PhD dissertation, University of Oxford.

Otsuka, Y. 2005. Two derivations of VSO: A comparative study of Niuean and Tongan. In *Verb First: On the Syntax of Verb Initial Languages* [Linguistik Aktuell/Linguistics Today 73], A. Carnie, S. Dooley-Collberg & H. Harley (eds), 65–90. Amsterdam: John Benjamins.

Otsuka, Y. 2006. Syntactic ergativity in Tongan: Resumptive pronouns revisited. In *Ergativity: Emerging Issues*, A. Johns, D. Massam & J. Ndayiragije (eds), 79–107. Dordrecht: Springer.

Pawley, A. 1973. Some problems in Proto-Oceanic grammar. *Oceanic Linguistics* 12: 103–188.

Rizzi, L. 1986. Null objects in Italian and the theory of *pro*. *Linguistic Inquiry* 17: 501–557.

Sasse, H.-J. 1984. The pragmatics of noun incorporation in Eastern Cushitic languages. In *Objects: Towards a Theory of Grammatical Relations*, F. Plank (ed.), 243–268. London: Academic Press.

Seiter, W. 1980. *Studies in Niuean Syntax*. New York NY: Garland.

Tchekhoff, C. 1973. Some verbal patterns in Tongan. *Journal of the Polynesian Society* 82: 281–292.

Van Valin, R.D. Jr. 1992. Incorporation in Universal Grammar: A case study in theoretical reductionism. *Journal of Linguistics* 28: 199–220.

Wiltschko, M. 2006. On 'ergativity' in Halkomelem Salish. In *Ergativity: Emerging Issues*, A. Johns, D. Massam & J. Ndayiragije (eds), 197–228. Dordrecht: Springer.

Possession syntax in Unua DPs*

Elizabeth Pearce
Victoria University of Wellington

The Unua dialect of Unua-Pangkumu, like other Oceanic languages of Vanuatu, has contrasting Direct and Indirect Possession constructions. Although these constructions are well-known from the literature, they have not yet been subsumed into a formal syntactic framework. In the terms of such a treatment, the present paper argues that in Unua the Direct Possessor argument is the syntactic complement of the head noun, whereas the Indirect Possessor argument is freely merged in an intermediate level of the DP structure. The "mirror-image" surface orderings of both types of possession constructions are then shown to be derivable by iterative phrasal movements on a right-branching base hierarchical structure conforming with the Linear Correspondence Axiom of Kayne (1994).

1. Introduction

The multiple possession systems of Oceanic languages have been described in accounts of individual Oceanic languages and in cross-linguistic analyses focusing on the nature of the constructions and their semantic characteristics and/or on their comparative reconstruction (Lynch 1982, 1996, 2001, Lichtenberk 1985, 2004, Palmer 2007). As yet, however, we do not have any accounts of how these systems might be treated in a generative framework. My aim in this paper is to develop such an account with respect to the syntax of possession in one Oceanic language, the Unua language of Vanuatu.

Unua is one of two dialects of Unua-Pangkumu spoken on the South-East coast of Malakula Island, Vanuatu. Following Lynch (2006, 2007) the languages of Malakula

---

* My research on Unua has been supported by the Marsden Fund of New Zealand grant UOW305/VUW311 in a research project initiated by the late Terry Crowley. I owe Terry my appreciation for his invaluable support and I wish to offer this paper in his memory. I also wish to thank the many Unua speakers, and especially Kalangis Bembe, who have provided me with data on their language, but who are not responsible for errors of interpretation or analysis in this paper. I thank Heidi Quinn and the participants at AFLA XIV for comments and discussion and two anonymous reviewers for further constructive comments.

belong to a Central Vanuatu sub-group of Southern Oceanic and, within Malakula, Unua belongs in a Central subgrouping of an Eastern Malakulan linkage. The figures from the 1999 Vanuatu census give 710 as the total population of the five Unua villages. The data that I present in this paper is based on field work that I have carried out between 2003 and 2007.

Unua is an SVO language which has the typical Oceanic encoding of singular/dual/plural along with inclusive/exclusive pronouns and quasi-obligatory subject-verb agreement in tense/aspect marking prefixes. The Unua DP has the "mirror-image" linear ordering: N – A – Num – Dem.

The central proposal of this paper is that Unua Direct and Indirect possessor DPs have syntactically distinct roles: Direct possessors are arguments subcategorized for by the head N and Indirect possessors are merged above the NP in the higher functional structure of the DP. Distinct morphology and linear ordering characteristics of Direct versus Indirect possessors are then accounted for in terms of iterative phrasal movement within the framework of the Linear Correspondence Axiom of Kayne (1994).

The paper has two main parts. Section 2 presents a description of the distinct characteristics of Direct and Indirect possession constructions. Section 3 develops the account of the syntax of the two kinds of possession constructions. Finally, the conclusions to this paper are set out in Section 4.

2. Forms of possession in Unua

2.1 Possession/association classes

In a DP with a 'Direct Possession Noun' (DPN) the possessor immediately follows the N either as a full DP (1a) or as suffix attached to the N (1b).[1]

(1) *DPN Construction:*
   a. vevne xina/mokiki/Sande
      sister 1SG/boy/Sande
      'my/the boy's/Sande's sister'
   b. vevno-g/vevna-m/vevne-n
      sister-1SG/sister-2SG/sister-3SG
      'my/your(sg.)/his or her sister'

---

1. The following abbreviations are used in glosses: (1/2/3)SG/DU/PL '(first/second/third person) singular/dual/plural', C 'complementizer', FOC 'focus', IO 'indirect object', IRR 'irrealis', NMZ 'nominalizer', REL 'relative clause marker'. In the present Unua spelling system ⟨ng⟩ is /ŋ/, ⟨b⟩, ⟨d⟩ and ⟨g⟩ are prenasalized stops, ⟨bb⟩ and ⟨rr⟩ are trills /ᵐB/ and /r/, <v> is /β/, <x> is /ɣ/ <r> is /ɾ/ and <j> is /tʃ/.

c. Vevne-*(n) i-xaxa   vex rites.
      sister-3SG 3SG-walk to LOC.sea
      'The/his/her sister walked to the sea.'

The possessor pronouns (e.g. *xina* in (1a)) are non-distinct from full form pronouns in other roles. The contrasting suffixed forms apply with singular possessors. With plural possessors, the full DP possessor is used, as with the singulars in (1a). In cases where the possessor is unspecified, *-n* serves as a default suffix, as in (1c).

With 'Indirect Possession Nouns' (IPNs) a linker *se* follows the N and the possessor follows the linker as a DP constituent (2a) or the possessor appears as a suffix on the linker (2b).[2]

(2) *IPN Construction:*
   a. naxat se xina/**se** mokiki/**se** Sande
      basket *se* 1SG/*se* boy/*se*   Sande
      'my/the boy's/Sande's basket'

   b. naxat so-**g**/so-**m**/se-**n**
      basket *se*-1SG/ *se*-2SG/ *se*-3SG
      'my/your(sg.)/his or her basket'

Except for their placement with respect to the linker, the forms of the possessors in the IPN construction are the same as those in the DPN construction.

The lexical semantics of the DPN/IPN distinction is discussed in more detail in Section 2.3. In general, however, DPN possessors are 'standard' inalienables: body parts and kin terms. Conversely, IPN possessors encode alienable ownership.[3,4]

The two kinds of possessive constructions are in contrast with other forms of noun-argument association: (i) a construction with a linker *nen*, (ii) a construction with a linker *nga*, and (iii) compound noun expressions. The possessive constructions are morphologically distinct from the other three types in that these latter do not occur with distinct suffixes.

The classificatory construction with the linker *nen* expresses purpose and other forms of N-DP/N-N association, as illustrated in the following.

---

2. The IPN linker *se* has an alternative form *xise*. *Xise* tends to be used in more formal registers and is hardly used in colloquial speech. In another use, *xise* serves as the pronominal possessor form corresponding to 'mine', 'yours', etc.

3. Lichtenberk (2004) shows how the kinds of meanings associated with 'possessive' constructions are many and varied cross-linguistically.

4. Unlike a number of other Oceanic languages, including some Malakula languages, Unua just has the one IPN construction which does not formally distinguish between different types of (alienable) possessor relation (see Palmer 2007 for an overall perspective on these types in Oceanic languages). In its lack of IPN differentiation, Unua patterns like four other languages of Malakula which are known to lack this distinction: Naman, Neve'ei, Avava (Crowley 2006a: 74) and Nese (Crowley 2006b: 54).

(3) a. xenen nen nani
　　　food *nen* coconut
　　　'coconut flesh'

　　b. nabbu nen nue
　　　bamboo *nen* water
　　　'bamboo for (carrying) water'

　　c. nemen nen netes
　　　bird *nen* sea
　　　'seagull'

In the second type of construction the relative clause linker *nga* is used with identifying place names:

(4) a. arres nga West Ambrym
　　　person *nga* West Ambrym
　　　'people of/from West Ambrym'

　　b. nutaim nga Kalele rin　　　　　　　　　　　　[Bembe 2005: Mark 1:39]
　　　village *nga* Galilee PL
　　　'villages of Galilee'

Finally, a variety of modifying relations are expressed in compound forms in which the head N precedes the identifying N:

(5) a. naxat vaiv
　　　basket pandanus
　　　'pandanus leaf basket'

　　b. bor　　[rrernge xasuv]
　　　mushroom ear　　rat
　　　'mushroom (kind)'

　　c. majo nut-bong
　　　star place-dark
　　　'Evening Star'

The semantics of the noun modification constructions shown in (3) – (5) do not include ownership relations and they are morpho-syntactically distinct from the two possession constructions in that they do not exhibit the suffixed/non-suffixed contrast. The focus of the present paper will be on the DPN/IPN possession constructions; therefore, I leave aside any further discussion of the construction types (3)–(5).

2.2　Direct versus Indirect possession

We have seen that both DPN and IPN constructions can have contrasting suffixed forms with singular possessors and that the IPN construction differs from the DPN construction in that it has a linker /se/. Two further differences between the two constructions are: (i) the DPN is inseparable from its possessor, whereas the IPN and its possessor can be separated by other material; and (ii) the IPN can occur without a possessor, whereas the DPN occurs only with a suffix (1b,c) or with a full DP possessor (1a).

The examples in (6) and (7) show the separability contrast: in the context of an adjective in (6) and under conjoining in (7).

(6) *Ordering with adjective*
    a. DPN: tasi   xai **kiki**
          younger brother 2SG little
          'your little younger brother'
          *tasi **kiki** xai

    b. IPN: (i) naxat   se xai **kiki**
                basket *se* 2SG little
                'your little basket'
                naxat **kiki** se xai

              (ii) naxat so-m **kiki**
                 basket *se*-2SG little
                 'your little basket'
                 naxat **kiki** som

(7) *Conjoining*
    a. DPN: [teme   rate] rroni [rrese   rate]
          father 3PL with   mother 3PL
          'their father and their mother'
          *[teme rroni rrese] rate

    b. IPN: (i) [bbue se xina] rroni [nato   se xina]
                pig   *se* 1SG with   chicken *se* 1SG
                'my pig and my chicken'
                [bbue rroni nato] se xina

              (ii) [bbue so-g]   rroni [nato   so-g]
                 pig   *se*-1SG with   chicken *se*-1SG
                 'my pig and my chicken'
                 [bbue rroni nato] sog

The tighter connection between the DPN and its possessor is observed in the behaviour of inalienable constructions cross-linguistically, as noted in Lyons (1999: 128), referring to 'Special inalienable possession constructions': "[...] in inalienable possession the structure is morphologically simpler or the possessive is in some way structurally closer to the head noun."

The contrasting properties of the DPN and IPN constructions are summarized in Table 1.

Table 1. DPN versus IPN characteristics

	DPNs	IPNs
linker se:	x	√
discontinuity option	x	√
requires possessor marking: (suffix or full DP)	√	x

2.3. The inalienable specification

The inalienables versus alienables distinction must be lexically specified although broadly semantically based as contrasting relational properties, because some apparently synonymous nouns have distinct DPN versus IPN characteristics.

Thus, with two words meaning 'bed', *mere* (DPN) and *mererr* (IPN), both forms may occur with an overt possessor (8), but the IPN form can be used when no possessor is implied (9).

(8) a. *DPN*
B-a-xa vex Lakatoro b-o-vr-i mero-g/mere **xina**.
IRR-1SG-go to Lakatoro IRR-1SG-buy-TR bed-1SG/bed 1SG
'I will go to Lakatoro to buy my bed.'

b. *IPN*
B-a-xa vex Lakatoro b-o-vr-i mererr **so-g/se xina**.
IRR-1SG-go to Lakatoro IRR-1SG-buy-TR bed se-1SG/se 1SG
'I will go to Lakatoro to buy my bed.'

(9) *IPN*
B-a-xa vex Lakatoro b-o-vr-i mererr b-i-soxa.
IRR-1SG-go to Lakatoro IRR-1SG-buy-TR bed IRR-3SG-one
'I will go to Lakatoro to buy a bed.'

Similarly contrasting forms are found also with nouns meaning 'blood' and 'food':

(10) *DPN*   *IPN*
a. *rrane*   *narra*
rrane xina   narra **se** xina   'my blood'
rrane xai   narra **se** xai   'your(SG) blood'
rrane xini   narra **se** xini   'his/her blood'
b. *nitaxe* *xenen*
nitaxe xina xenen **se** xina   'my food', etc.

The words for 'father' and 'mother' both occur in three forms, only one of which is a DPN:

(11)   DPN   IPN   IPN
   a.   *teme*   *mita*   *tata*
        teme xina   mita **se** xina   tata **se** xina   'my father'. etc.
   b.   *rrese*   *mira*   *mama*
        rrese xina mira **se** xina   mama **se** xina   'my mother', etc.

Other kin terms which are IPNs rather than DPNs are:

(12) *Some IPN kin terms:*
      ava se xina   'my older brother/sister'
      apu se xina   'my grandfather'
      metero se xina   'my nephew/niece'

In addition to the DPN forms for 'bed', 'blood' and 'food', further non-kin or non-body part nouns which are DPNs are as follows:

(13) *Non-kin/body part DPNs*
      dano xina   'my place'
      dovxi xina   'my grave'
      mavre xina   'my friend/other'
      nexse xina   'my name'
      rojo xina   'my goods'
      rrarrau xina   'my voice'
      sere xina   'my way'
      vuri xina   'my reward/wages'
      xuti xina   'my lice'

Therefore, on the basis of the evidence presented in this section, we conclude that the DPN/IPN assignment for individual nouns is not fully semantically transparent and must be viewed as lexically specified. In the next part of the discussion we will see how the distinct lexical specifications can be realized and how the morpho-syntactic outcomes can be derived.

3. DPN/IPN syntax

In this part of the paper I develop an account of DPN versus IPN syntax which will be based on the proposal that DPN possessors are merged as complements of the DPN, whereas IPN possessors are merged in a position external to the NP constituent within the extended DP:

(14) *DPN/IPN syntax*
      (i) DPN possessors are merged as complement arguments of the DPN.
      (ii) IPN possessors are merged in a higher location within the DP.

The analysis of how these contrasting syntactic positions are to be embedded in the syntax of the Unua DP is undertaken in the following sections of the paper.

3.1 Possessor role syntax

3.1.1 "Possessor" argument roles

Cross-linguistically, it is not uncommon to find special morpho-syntactic encoding applied to ownership possessor roles as well as to other kinds of relations between an argument and a noun.

In English, for example, a derived nominal can have an Agent or a Theme argument which is superficially non-distinct from a pre-N possessor (owner) argument:

(15) **John's** dog   OWNER

(16) a. **the enemy's** destruction of **the city**   AGENT... THEME
     b. **the city's** destruction   THEME

(17) The enemy destroyed the city.
     AGENT   THEME

Since the thematic roles of the arguments are parallel in (16) and (17), then we expect these arguments to be merged in parallel structural positions, as represented in (18a,b).

(18)

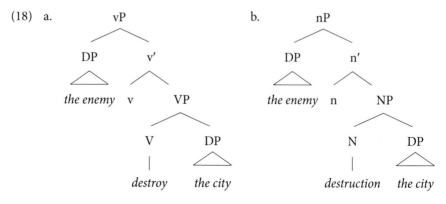

Alternatively, both structures in (18) could have an underspecified root head with the values for the relevant V versus N features written in through checking at some higher level in the structure. But it is evident that not all nouns in English allow for a full range of argument roles even in the case of 'picture' nouns, as is shown in the contrasting forms in (19) and (20).

(19) **John's** picture   OWNER/AGENT/THEME
     the picture of **John/the boy/me**   THEME

(20) **John's** book   OWNER/AGENT
     *the book of **John/the boy/me**

In English, "picture" nouns and derived nouns can have AGENT and THEME genitives and other kinds of nouns may have an AGENT but not a (human) THEME genitive.

Other examples of argument role distinctions with genitive morphology are seen in Eastern Polynesian languages which distinguish 'Controlling' versus 'Non-controlling' roles (see Bauer 1993, 1997, Harlow 2001). In the Māori examples in (22), the genitive marker with form *a* is assigned to a Controlling argument, whilst the genitive marker with the form *o* is applied to a Controlled argument.

(21) a. te rongoa **a** Mere
 the medecine *a* Mere
 'Mere's medecine' (Mere prescribed/made/owns the medecine)

 b. te rongoa **o** Pou
 the medecine *o* Pou
 'Pou's medecine' (Pou was given/inherited the medecine)

In DPs with nominalized verbs an overt Agent argument is marked with the Controlling genitive form *a*, whereas a Theme argument appears with the Non-controlling genitive marker *o*:

(22) *Māori*
 a. te patu-nga **a** Rewi i te poaka [Waititi 1974: 136]
 the kill-NMZ *a* Rewi ACC the pig
 'Rewi's killing the pig'

 b. te patu-nga **o** Paki e Rewi [Waititi 1974: 143]
 the kill-NMZ *o* Paki by Rewi
 'Paki's killing by Rewi'

Because of these morphological parallels, Waite (1994) and Pearce (1998, 2003) propose accounts of the contrasting genitive constructions in Màori whereby common nouns can accept arguments in Agent and Theme positions.

Obviously, different languages present different kinds of morpho-syntactic realizations of possessor/owner arguments within their DPs and they may also allow non-possessor arguments to appear in their genitive construction(s). As a consequence, we need to pay careful attention to the facts of the possessive constructions in the particular language being investigated, whilst we can still be alert to the possibilities for which we have evidence in other languages. The data that we have seen in this section supply some precedents for the assignment of Thematic argument roles within the NP structure. The next section develops a particular interpretation of the use of such a possibility in Unua.

3.1.2 *Possessor roles in Unua*

The preceding section showed alignments between possessor roles and other kinds of argument roles in genitive constructions in English and in Māori DPs. In that discussion, the relevant parallelisms derived from the fact that we could identify cases in which constructions with common nouns could be aligned with constructions headed by derived nominals. Can we find similar kinds of parallelisms in Unua?

Unua has verb-noun pairs which contrast as $[root]_V$ versus $[root\text{-}en]_N$. In one such case with the noun derived from the verb root *jirvar* '(tell) story', I have found examples in which the IPN linker *se* is used in one case with the DP argument referring to the teller of the story and in another case with the DP argument referring to what the story is about:[5]

(23) a. E, jirvar-en **se xina** soxa i-mre-n.
      e story-NMZ *se* 1SG one 3SG-like-this
      'E, a story of mine goes like this.'

  b. no-jajar ni b-e-jirvar ni jirvar-en **se demej xeru**.
     1SG-wish IO IRR-1SG-story IO story-NMZ *se* devil two
     'I would like to tell a story, a story about two devils.'

The data in (23) suggest that the IPN *se* linker does not have a function of distinguishing between Agent and Theme arguments with respect to the head N of a DP, although we are limited to a single derived noun form, and presently lack further evidence for the behaviour of potentially Agent/Theme arguments with derived nouns.

Further evidence that the possessors occurring in the IPN construction are not lexically specified for is seen in the fact that a DPN may occur both with its DPN "possessor" as well as with a further possessor in the IPN form:

(24) a. Bati-n i-merr.
      head-3SG 3SG-raw
      'The head is raw.'

  b. Bati naix i-merr.
     head fish 3SG-raw
     'The fish head is raw.'

  c. [Bati naix] so-g i-merr.
     head fish *se*-1SG 3SG-raw
     'My fish head is raw.'

---

5. Another example shows the linker *nen* with the argument referring to what the story is about:

  (i) Jirvar-en   **nen mokiki soxa** rroni vindra   demej soxa.
      tell.story-NMZ *nen* boy   one   with old.woman devil one
      'The story of a boy and an old devil woman.'

Unfortunately I do not have data testing whether or not both of the *se* possessor roles of (23a,b) may cooccur.

(25) a. Batu-g   i-se.
         head-1SG 3SG-bad
         'I have a head-ache.'

    b. Bati   xina i-se.
       head   1SG 3SG-bad
       'I have a head-ache.'

In (24b) and in (25a,b) the DPN *bati* has a single DPN possessor. In (24c) *naix* is the DPN possessor and *sog* is an IPN possessor. The availability of the two "possessive" arguments in (24c) lends further support to the interpretation that possessors in the IPN construction are freely merged within the DP structure above the NP.

There is another fact which is probative with respect to the possessor argument position in the DPN construction and it involves the forms of the possession constructions. This is the observation that suffixes occurring in the two possessive constructions are associated with complement arguments in other cases.

The suffixal forms occurring in the possession constructions are also found with certain prepositions and with verbs, and, just as in the possession constructions, the suffixes alternate with full form arguments.

The examples in (26) show such uses with two prepositions, *taxu* 'after' and *rotre* 'behind'.

(26) *Prepositions and suffixes*
      taxu: taxu-**g**   taxu xina   'after me'
                 taxu-**m**   taxu xai   'after you(SG)'
                 taxu-**n**   taxu xini   'after him-her'
      rotre: rotro-**g**   rotre xina   'behind me'
                 rotra-**m**   rotre xai   'behind you(SG)'
                 rotre-**n**   rotre xini   'behind him-her'

Most transitive verbs in Unua have a general object marker suffix with the form *-i*, as in (27).

(27) *Transitive verb*
      (xina)   no-ke-**i**   xai/xini   'I see you(SG)/him-her'
      (xai)   u-ke-**i**   xina/xini   'You(SG) see me/him-her'
      (xini)   i-ke-**i**   xina/xai/xini   'He/she sees me/you(SG)/him-her'

An older alternative form, however, uses the three-way distinct singular suffixes:[6]

---

6. Younger speakers also favour the use of the full form possessor in the DPN construction at the expense of the suffixed forms and, with the exception of one verb *-jbo-* 'alone', younger speakers no longer use agreeing suffixes with verbs. However, I do not have evidence on generational differences in the use of agreeing suffixes with the prepositions in (26).

(28) *Transitive verb (older speaker variants)*
i-xaj-i-g   (*xina)   'it bit me'
i-xaj-i-m   (*xai)   'it bit you(SG)'
i-xaj-i-n   (*xini)   'it bit him-her'

As indicated in the parentheses in (28), the agreeing suffix cannot cooccur with the full form argument, paralleling the possessive constructions.

With prepositions and with verbs, the agreeing suffixes encode (singular) person features of arguments which are complements of these heads. The generalizing of this head-complement relation to our interpretation of the syntactic relation between a lexical DPN head and the DPN possessor argument brings us to the conclusion that the DPN construction also involves a relation between a head and its complement. This is the proposal of (14i).

In the case of the IPN construction, although the suffixal forms with *se* are comparable to what we see with the other classes of constructions with agreeing suffixes, it remains to be considered exactly how such a 'complement' scenario is to be applied. In order to establish the merge location of IPN possessors, we will need to consider how these constructions are embedded within the processes applying in the derivation of the surface forms.

3.2 DP-internal syntax in Unua

3.2.1 *DP-internal mirror-image ordering*

In terms of Greenberg's Universal 20 (Greenberg 1966: 111), Unua DPs exhibit mirror-image ordering on the assumptions that the N is at the low end of the DP and that the hierarchical structures are right-branching, following Kayne (1994) and Cinque (1996, 2000, 2005).[7]

(29) N – A – Num – Dem:
    a. kuri   metmet   xeru   N – A – Num
        dog   black   two
        'two black dogs'
    b. namij   kiki   nge   N – A – Dem
        banana little this
        'this little banana'
    c. kuri   xeter   narag   N – Num – Dem
        dog   three   those
        'those three dogs'

---

7. Pearce (2007) undertakes analysis of further aspects of the Unua mirror-image ordering within the DP.

(30) N – A$_{Colour}$ – A$_{Size}$

   a. naxat   perrperr kiki   soxa   N – A$_1$ – A$_2$ – Num
      basket red   small one
      'a small red basket'

   b. *naxat kiki perrperr soxa   *N – A$_2$ – A$_1$ – Num

The English Dem – Num – A – N ordering is a direct reflection of the base merge ordering. With the reverse surface ordering that we see in (29) and (30), Unua is an exemplar of the "mirror-image" DP-internal ordering pattern, with respect to both Dem/Num/A/N ordering (30) and Size/Colour adjective ordering (31). I will follow Kayne (1994), Cinque (1996, 2000, 2005) and Shlonsky (2004) in assuming that iterative phrasal movements apply in the derivations of these mirror-image surface forms.[8]

3.2.2 Deriving the surface orderings: DPN constructions

Along with the assumption that the possessor argument is the complement of the N, the application of phrasal movement in the derivation of the DPN surface forms provides an immediate account of the lack of separability of the DPN and its possessor argument. Thus, in the derivation of (6a), repeated below as (31), the DPN raises together with its (possessor) complement, as shown in the two steps in (32).

(31) tasi   xai kiki
     younger brother 2SG little
     'your little younger brother'

(32) a. [[$_{AP}$ kiki] [$_{NP}$ tasi [$_{DP}$ xai]]]
    b. [[$_{NP}$ tasi [$_{DP}$ xai]]$_i$ [[$_{AP}$ kiki] t$_i$]]

From the structure obtained after the merge of the adjective shown in (32a), the NP constituent containing the possessor argument raises to a Spec position above the AP, producing (32b) corresponding to the surface ordering in (31). Further such raisings of whole phrases, successively around NumP and DemP will produce the surface mirror-image orderings shown in (29) – (30).

3.2.3 Deriving the surface orderings: IPN constructions

The task of identifying the precise location of the IPN possessor within the DP is somewhat more challenging, given the alternative positions with respect to the adjective, as in (6bi). Some further investigation of the variant surface order possibilities is required.

---

8. An alternative proposal put forward in Abels and Neeleman (2006) variously allows Spec positions to be right branches and requires fewer implementations of phrasal movement to derive the cross-linguistically attested DP-internal surface orderings. Lack of space prevents me from considering here how such an account might be pursued with respect to the derivation of the Unua surface forms. The account to follow will therefore be restricted to an analysis under the LCA approach to the underlying structures.

Whilst the mirror-image schema is attested for uninflected adjectives, adjectives carrying inflectional markings can be variously ordered, whether or not such adjectives occur inside relative clauses. My interpretation of these effects is that the ordering distinctions reflect differences between attributive and predicative adjectives: the attributive adjectives are uninflected and occur in a strict order after the noun and the predicative adjectives (which may or may not be inflected) are variably ordered in terms of their relative scope.[9] This distribution is summarized in (33).

(33) *Two classes of modifiers:*

	Inflection	Ordered
Attributive	–	+
Predicative	(+)	–

Compare the ordering of the uninflected Colour adjective with the inflected Colour adjective in (34a,b) and of the same adjective, *terrterr* 'strong', in uninflected form and inside a relative clause in (35a,b).

(34) a. kuri **metmet** totox soxa
    dog black big one
    'a big black dog'

  b. i-kare morin nga m-i-brov **i-porpor**
    3SG-wear shirt C REL-3SG-long 3SG-white
    'he wore a long white robe' [Bembe 2005, Mk 16:5]

(35) a. naxat **terrterr** nga m-i-ras
    basket strong C REL-3SG-big
    'a big strong basket'

  b. naxat totox **nga m-i-terrterr**
    basket big C REL-3SG-strong
    'a big strong basket'

In (35), in addition to the contrast in the form and placement of the adjective *terrterr* 'strong', we see that *totox* 'big', which has only an uninflected form, is "deselected" in the relative clause in (35a).

In unmarked patterns, the IPN possessor follows attributive adjectives and precedes predicative adjectives. The example in (36) shows the lack of variable ordering in the context of the adjective *-vo* 'good' which never occurs in an uninflected attributive use.

(36) a. kuri **so-g** i-vo
    dog *se*-1SG 3SG-good
    'my good dog'

---

9. For comparable conclusions with respect to adjectives in Javanese, see Ishizuka (2007). The attributive/predicative contrast of (33) may also correspond to the Direct versus Indirect modification discussed in Sproat and Shih (1991).

b. *kuri i-vo **so-g**

The variable ordering shown in (6bi) also requires some further analysis, because the adjective *kiki* appears variously in uninflected and inflected forms within DPs. Whilst it can be difficult to untangle particular discourse conditions at work, the examples in (37) show that, in the absence of contrast, in the unmarked ordering, the possessor follows the attributive adjective.

(37) a. No-jajar ni naxat kiki **so-m**.
    1SG-wish IO basket little *se*-2SG
    'I like your little basket.'

 b. No-jajar ni naxat so-m **kiki ngo**.
    1SG-wish IO basket *se*-2SG little the
    'I like **little** basket.'   = CONTRASTIVE

 c. No-jajar ni naxat kiki **so-m nu**.
    1SG-wish IO basket little *se*-2SG FOC
    'I like **your** little basket.'   = CONTRASTIVE

In combination with the evidence in (36), where the possessor precedes the predicative adjective, the placement of the possessor after the attributive adjective in (37) leads to the conclusion that the IPN possessor is merged within the DP above attributive adjectives and below predicative adjectives.

We also have some (mixed) evidence that the unmarked IPN possessor should be merged below NumP in the DP structure. Whereas a form with suffixed *se*- can only precede a cardinal number, the form with *se* + DP may be variably ordered.

(38) a. kuri **so-g** xeter
    dog *se*-1SG three
    'my three dogs'

 b. *kuri xeter **so-g**

(39) a. kuri **se xina** xeter
    dog *se* 1SG three
    'my three dogs'

 b. kuri xeter **se xina**

Instead of the ungrammatical suffixed *se*- form in (38b), the same ordering as in (39b) is grammatical with the suffixed form of *xise*-:

(40) kuri xeter xiso-g
    dog three *xise*-1SG
    'my three dogs'

Since *xise* is a marked form in the colloquial register, the use of this form in (40) suggests that the construction itself is marked in some way.[10] It would seem that special discourse conditions give rise to different ordering options for IPN possessors, but that in unmarked uses they are merged in the structure above attributive adjectives and below cardinal numbers and predicative modifiers.

Leaving aside the question of the positions for predictive modifiers and having reached the conclusion that the IPN possessor in the unmarked case is merged above attributive adjectives, we now come to the more difficult question of the treatment of the syntax of the IPN forms.

Under the type of schema that we are supposing, the AP is merged above the NP and the NP raises to a position above the AP (following Cinque 2005 I now identify that position as the Spec of an AgrP):

(41) a. [$_{SizeP}$ [$_{AP}$ kiki] [$_{NP}$ naxat]]   AP merged in Spec,SizeP
     b. [$_{AgrP}$ [$_{NP}$ naxat]$_i$ [$_{SizeP}$ [$_{AP}$ kiki] t$_i$]]   NP raises to Spec,AgrP

The unsuffixed forms of the IPN construction consist of two elements: *se* and a DP. The particle *se* has the appearance of a functional head which should be merged as a head in the extended DP structure. Let us label this projection 'Gen[itive]P'. Within this projection, the merge location for the accompanying DP should be Spec,GenP. By merging these items above the structure in (41b), we now have:

(42) [$_{GenP}$ [xai] se [$_{AgrP}$ [$_{NP}$ naxat]$_i$ [$_{SizeP}$ [$_{AP}$ kiki] t$_i$]]]   Mergers in GenP

If the derivation is now to proceed with another application of phrasal roll-up (the raising of AgrP), the output produced will have the wrong linear sequencing with *xai* preceding *se*. At this point, if the derivation is to converge, another process has to come into play.

In work on corresponding schema (Kayne 2000, Cinque 2000, Koopman & Szabolsci 2000), there is an option for the head of a projection to raise and merge above its XP. In the terms of Koopman & Szabolsci (2000), this option is forced through a restriction expressed as:

(43) *Generalized "Doubly Filled Comp Filter"*
     No projection has both an overt specifier and an overt head at the end of the derivation.   [Koopman & Szabolsci 2000: 4]

The raising of the *se* head from the structure shown in (42) voids the restriction expressed by (43):

(44) [$_{FP}$ se$_j$ [$_{GenP}$ xai   t$_j$ [$_{AgrP}$ [$_{NP}$ naxat]$_i$ [$_{SizeP}$ [$_{AP}$ kiki] t$_i$]]]]   Raising of *se*

The subsequent step in the derivation sees the AgrP complement phrase below the original position of the *se* head raising around the FP created in the step shown in (44):

---

10. See also note 2.

(45) [$_{AgrP}$ [$_{AgrP}$ [$_{NP}$ naxat]$_i$ [$_{SizeP}$ [$_{AP}$ kiki] t$_i$]]$_k$ [$_{FP}$ se$_j$ [$_{GenP}$ xai t$_j$ t$_k$]]]

AgrP raises to higherAgrP

With the implementation of the step shown in (45) we have obtained the correct surface ordering for all of the elements that have been entered into the computation. With the further introduction of a number and/or of a demonstrative, further iterative raisings will produce the unmarked mirror-image surface orderings including all of these constituents.

However, whilst the derivational processes that have just been sketched out are successful in producing the correct output, the approach that has been taken to the merge of the IPN items appears to be disadvantageous in that the merge locations of the different classes of suffixable heads now turn out not to be in parallel. That is, in the preceding discussion of DPN syntax, the argument of the DPN was merged as a complement to the right of the DPN head. This is different from the head and argument relation that obtains in (42) with the IPN *se* head.

However, we may maintain parallel structural relations between the different classes of arguments with suffixable heads with a reconsideration of the structure that is to be applied to the head-complement relation in general.[11] If in all cases the complement merges structurally as a specifier, we can obtain the desired across-the-board structural parallelism. A corollary of this approach is then that, as part of the derivational processes, other suffixable heads, including DPNs, will raise out the XP in which they are merged when their Specs have lexical content. Thus, in the case of the DPN at the lower end of (31):

(46) [$_{FP}$ tasi$_i$ [$_{NP}$ [$_{DP}$ xai] t$_i$]]

Although I am not attempting here to isolate the detailed workings of the feature checking processes that may be invoked as triggers in these derivations, it is possible that the raising process reflected in (46) is consistent with the presence of a dedicated *n* position in the extended NP structure. In any case, the derivation proposed in (46) preserves the integrity of the DPN unit as before.

3.2.4 *Constructions with conjoined DPNs/IPNs*

Recall from (7a,b) that another aspect of the inseparability characteristics of DPNs is that, in contrast with IPNs, two DPNs with the same possessor argument may not be independently conjoined. This fact is subsumed in our account since, in conformity with general restrictions imposed by X-bar theory, conjunctions are taken to be heads merging phrasal complements and specifiers (Kayne 1994, Progovac 1999, 2003). The lowest level at which two DPNs may be conjoined to the exclusion of a possessor argument is at the level of the N, as in (47). The illicit ordering in (7a) thus cannot be derived.

---

11. I wish to thank an anonymous reviewer for probative comments which have led me to reconsider the approach that I took to these structures in a preliminary version of this paper.

(47)

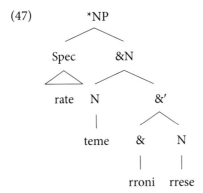

No such restriction applies in IPN constructions in which the possessor argument is outside the NP containing the IPN head.

3.2.5 *The suffixed forms*

There are different possibilities for the derivations of the suffixed forms, depending on whether one considers that the affix is merged as part of the content of the possessor DP or whether one takes the view that the affix is merged along with the head to which it attaches.[12] Whilst space constraints prevent me from investigating how such different approaches would work, I would like to bring into the discussion another possession construction in Unua which is relevant to the derivational processes.

A robustly attested possession construction in Unua presents an option in which the possessor argument occurs in DP-initial position. Here, overt post-N encoding of the possessor is obligatory, either as an affix or as the corresponding pronoun:

(48) DPN
    a. **xina tasi-g**
        1SG younger brother-1SG
        'my younger brother'

    b. **xina tasi xina**
        1SG younger brother 1SG
        'my younger brother'

(49) IPN
    a. **xina ava so-g**
        1SG older brother se-1SG
        'my older brother'

    b. **xina ava se xina**
        1SG older brother se 1SG
        'my older brother'

---

12. For a useful discussion of these two kinds of approaches see Julien (2002: 11–15).

The existence of forms like (48a) and (49a) might incline us to assume that the suffixes are merged with the head (the DPN in (48a) and *se* in (49a)) and that the preposed argument has raised from its merge position to a higher Spec position.[13]

The raising of the full DP then voids the illicit cooccurrence of the suffix and the overt possessor phrase following the relevant head. A mechanical treatment of this kind, however, will not of itself be adequate to account for the forms in (48b) and (49b) as it will require a different motivation for the preposing along with another kind of explanation for the in situ copy left behind. As it happens, alongside (48b) and (49b), a pronoun copy is used also when a non-singular preposed possessor DP has lexical content:[14]

(50) a. **namar xeru** vevne **raru**
       chief two   sister 3DU
       'the two chiefs' sister'   ['the sister of the two chiefs']

     b. **namar rin** vevne **rate**
        chief PL   sister 3PL
        'the chiefs' sister'   ['the sister of the chiefs']

In (50a,b), where the preposed possessors have lexical content, the copies appear in the form of the corresponding pronouns. In each of the three cases in (48)–(50), some copy of the preposed DP must be present at Spell Out, either in the form of the corresponding affix or of the corresponding pronoun. We could assume that this will entail particular realizations of uninterpretable features in the feeding to PF.

3.3 Summary

The principal claim developed in this section is that DPN possessors are subcategorized for and merged as complements of the head of the nominal projection, whereas IPN possessors are merged in the Spec of a GenP situated within the extended nominal projection (DP), above attributive adjectives. The unmarked mirror-image surface orderings are derived by iterative phrasal movements in a right branching base hierarchical structure. This account lends support to the view that it is possible for DPs to be merged within the argument structure of an N. It has also sketched out an analysis of

---

13. The question of the function labelling of this position would require further investigation. As other precedents, Giusti (2002) identifies Spec,DP (in her terms, Spec of the FP bearing referential features) as a target cross-linguistically for demonstratives and/or possessor arguments and Szabolsci (1983) has proposed CP/IP-like projections as the overlaying levels of the extended DP.
A reviewer suggests that a problem with the iterative movement approach to the derivations is that, prior to their extraction, the possessor DPs will have become quite deeply embedded in the structure. At this point, I must leave for future research the issue of the implications of the extraction processes involved, whether under the iterative movement approach or under other conceivable approaches.

14. Recall that in these cases a corresponding suffixed form is not available.

how the surface forms may be derived within the LCA approach to syntactic structure employing iterative phrasal movements as syntactic processes.

4. Conclusions

The general conclusions to this paper can be summarized as follows:

1. DPNs are lexically specified for a possessor.
2. A DPN possessor is merged as the complement of the N.
3. An IPN possessor is merged in the Spec of a projection which has a *se* head and which is located above lower APs in the extended DP structure.
4. Derivations involving phrasal movement can account for the obligatory contiguity of a DPN and its possessor in the surface ordering.
5. Unua possessor arguments can extract to a high Spec position in the DP extended structure.

The central proposal of this paper is that the DPN/IPN distinction in Unua is accounted for essentially as a contrast between whether or not the head noun selects/subcategorizes for an argument. Unua has lost the multiply differentiating IPN possession constructions which are still maintained in other related Oceanic languages. It will be of interest to determine how the differentiated IPN possession constructions are to be derived in other Oceanic languages and, in turn, to develop a characterization of the nature of the historical change implicated in the loss of the differentiation in Unua and in some of its neighbouring languages.

References

Abels, K. & Neeleman, A. 2006. Universal 20 without the LCA. *Glow Newsletter* 56: 16–17.
Bauer, W. (with W. Parker & Evans, Te K.) 1993. *Maori*. London: Routledge.
Bauer, W. (with W. Parker, Evans, Te K. & Teepa, Te A.) 1997. *The Reed Reference Grammar of Māori*. Auckland: Reed.
Bembe, K. 2005. Rejen nga mifo hise Iesu Kresto Mark iri (The Gospel of Mark]) Ms, Ruhumbo, Malakula.
Cinque, G. 1996. The antisymmetric program: Theoretical and typological implications. *Journal of Linguistics* 32: 447–464.
Cinque, G. 2000. On Greenberg's Universal 20 and the Semitic DP. *University of Venice Working Papers in Linguistics* 10(2): 45–61.
Cinque, G. 2005. Deriving Greenberg's Universal 20 and its exceptions. *Linguistic Inquiry* 36: 315–332.
Crowley, T. 2006a. *Naman: A Vanishing Language of Malakula (Vanuatu)*, J. Lynch (ed.). Canberra: Pacific Linguistics.

Crowley, T. 2006b. *Nese: A Diminishing Speech Variety of Northwest Malakula (Vanuatu)*, J. Lynch (ed.). Canberra: Pacific Linguistics.
Giusti, G. 2002. The functional structure of noun phrases: A bare phrase structure approach. In *Functional Structure in DP and IP,* Vol. 1, G. Cinque (ed.), 54–90. Oxford: OUP.
Greenberg, J.H. 1966. Some universals of grammar with particular reference to the order of meaningful elements. In *Universals of Language*, J.H. Greenberg (ed.), 73–113. Cambridge MA: The MIT Press.
Harlow, R. 2001. *A Māori Reference Grammar*. Auckland: Pearson Education.
Ishizuka, T. 2007. Internal structure of the DP in Javanese. Presented at *AFLA XIV (Austronesian Formal Linguistics Association)*, Montreal 4–6 May.
Julien, M. 2002. *Syntactic Heads and Word Formation*. Oxford: OUP.
Kayne, R.S. 1994. *The Antisymmetry of Syntax*. Cambridge MA: The MIT Press.
Kayne, R.S. 2000. *Parameters and Universals*. Oxford: OUP.
Koopman, H. & Szabolcsi, A. 2000. *Verbal Complexes*. Cambridge MA: The MIT Press.
Lichtenberk, F. 1985. Possessive constructions in Oceanic languages and in Proto-Oceanic. In *Austronesian Linguistics at the 15th Pacific Science Congress*, A. Pawley & L. Carrington (eds), 93–140. Canberra: Pacific Linguistics.
Lichtenberk, F. 2004. Inalienability and possessum individuation. In *Linguistic Diversity and Language Theories* [Studies in Language Companion Series 72], Z. Frajzngier, A. Hodges & D.S. Rood (eds), 339–362. Amsterdam: John Benjamins.
Lynch, J. 1982. Towards a theory of the origin of the Oceanic possessive constructions. In *Papers from the Third International Conference on Oceanic Linguistics* [Series C], P. Geraghty, L. Carrington & S.A. Wurm (eds), 259–287. Canberra: Pacific Linguistics.
Lynch, J. 1996. Proto-Oceanic possessive marking. In *Proceedings of the First International Conference on Oceanic Linguistics*, J. Lynch & F. Pat (eds), 93–110. Canberra: Pacific Linguistics.
Lynch, J. 2001. The development of morphologically complex possessive markers in the Southern Vanuatu languages. In *Issues in Austronesian Morphology: A Focusschrift for Byron W. Bender*, J. Bradshaw & K.L. Rehg (eds), 149–161. Canberra: Pacific Linguistics.
Lynch, J. 2006. Some notes on the linguistic history of Malakula. Paper presented at the *Terry Crowley Memorial Workshop on Vanuatu Languages*, Wellington 13–14 November. <http://www.vuw.ac.nz/lals/about/news-events.aspx>.
Lynch, J. 2007. The Malakula linkage of Central Vanuatu. Paper presented at *Seventh International Conference on Oceanic Linguistics*, Noumea 2–6 July.
Lyons, C. 1999. *Definiteness*. Cambridge: CUP.
Palmer. B. 2007. Semantically non-canonical possessive marking. Presented at *AFLA XIV (Austronesian Formal Linguistics Association)*, Montreal 4–6 May.
Pearce, E. 1998. The syntax of genitives in the Māori DP. *Canadian Journal of Linguistics/Revue canadienne de linguistique* 43: 411–434. (Special Issue on Syntax and Semantics of Austronesian Languages).
Pearce, E. 2003. Phrasal movement within the Māori DP. *Digests of Selected Papers Presented at AFLA X*, [Working Papers in Linguistics 34.2], 41–42. Honolulu HI: University of Hawai'i at Mānoa. <http://www.ling.hawaii.edu/afla/digests>.
Pearce, E. 2007. Constituent ordering within the Unua noun phrase. Paper presented at *Seventh International Conference on Oceanic Linguistics* (COOL 7), Noumea 2–6 July.
Progovac, L. 1999. Events and economy of coordination. *Syntax* 2: 141–159.
Progovac, L. 2003. Structure for coordination. In *The Second Glot International State-of-the-Article Book*, L. Cheng & R. Sybsema (eds), 241–287. Berlin: Mouton de Gruyter.

Shlonsky, U. 2004. The form of Semitic noun phrases. *Lingua* 114: 1465–1526.
Sproat, R. & C. Shih. 1991. The cross-linguistic distribution of adjective ordering restrictions. In *Interdisciplinary Approaches to Language: Essays in Honor of S.-Y. Kuroda*, C. Georgopoulos & R. Ishihara (eds), 565–593. Dordrecht: Kluwer.
Szabolcsi, A. 1983. The possessor that ran away from home. *The Linguistic Review* 3: 89–102.
Waite. J. 1994. Determiner phrases in Maori. *Te Reo* 37: 55–70.
Waititi, H.R. 1974. *Te Rangatahi: Advanced* 2. Wellington: Government Printer.

Seediq adverbial verbs
A review of the evidence*

Arthur Holmer
Lund University

This paper addresses adverbial verbs found in Formosan languages and evaluates two competing hypotheses which attempt to derive this phenomenon from other features of the language. The predication hypothesis links the phenomenon to verb-initial word order, while the adverbial heads hypothesis places them as heads of adverbial phrases within the backbone of the clause, along the lines of Cinque (1999). It is shown that the predictions of the latter hypothesis are empirically confirmed, although the former hypothesis is typologically more ambitious.

1. Introduction

During the past few years, attention has been increasingly focussed on the fact that the Austronesian languages of Taiwan (the Formosan languages) encode typically adverbial meanings by means of verbs, which serve as clitic hosts, and which bear distinctive verb morphology. This has been discussed in Chang (2006, 2007), Holmer (2002a, 2006), Liu (2003), Wu (2006) etc. An example of this phenomenon from the Atayalic language Seediq (spoken in central Taiwan) is given in (1a). A parallel example with a control verb is shown in (1b).[1]

---

* This paper is the partial result of fieldwork conducted in Taiwan within the research project *Adverbs as verbs in Formosan languages*, financed by the Bank of Sweden Tercentenary Foundation. I gratefully acknowledge this support. I also wish to thank Gilbert Ambrazaitis, Helen Avery, Mark Baker, Winifred Bauer, Henry Y.L. Chang, Mark Donohue, Niklas Jonsson, Paul Law and Eric Potsdam, as well as two reviewers and the AFLA XIV audience for helpful discussions and comments, which have radically improved my original paper. Any mistakes are mine and mine alone. Naturally, my deepest gratitude goes to the Seediq people whose kind cooperation made this work at all possible: Temi Nawi, Pawan Nawi, Dakis Pawan, Watan Pihu, Watan Diro, Iwan Iban, Pawan Torih and Awi Dakis. *Mhuwe namu!*

1. In the present paper, the following abbreviations are used: ABS = absolutive, ACC = accusative, AF = actor focus, BF = benefactive focus, CAUS = causative, CNG = connegative,

(1) a. Ini   =daha   kntte-i   m-ekan   beras baso,
       NEG   =3P.E   often-PF.CNG   AF-eat   grain sago
       pcnga-un   =daha m-ekan.
       sometimes-PF   =3P.E   AF-eat
       'They don't eat sago grain often, they eat it occasionally.'
   b. Ini   =mu   knkel-i   m-apa   rulu,
       NEG   =1S.E   able-PF.CNG   AF-carry   car
       anisa   knkel-un   =mu   m-apa   kulu   hlama.
       but   able-PF   =1S.E   AF-carry   box   steamed.rice
       'I can't carry a car, but I can carry a rice steamer.'

While the surface facts in themselves are clear, that adverbial meanings are grammatically encoded as verbs, it is not as clear in what sense they really are verbs. Is a verb a word which can bear verbal morphology or occur in a given syntactic distribution, or is a verb a word which has an argument structure of its own? Further, there is still no consensus as to what the above facts imply for language typology: whether we are dealing with a type of lexicalization pattern variation similar to that described by Talmy (1985) for the realization of motion expressions, or whether it is a syntactic phenomenon which can be derived from or correlated to other syntactic phenomena in the languages in question. On the theoretical level, the latter option would be preferable, insofar as it can dispense with one independent primitive, namely word class membership. The purpose of the present paper is to present a more detailed view of the patterns in Seediq, based on recent fieldwork, and to evaluate alternative models suggested in Holmer (2006). The structure of this paper is as follows. In Section 2, relevant data is presented showing that some of the properties of adverbial verbs are clearly the result of the structure in which they occur, and that they do not otherwise behave like prototypical lexical verbs. Section 3 addresses and evaluates two possible analyses of the facts. Finally, the conclusion in Section 4 summarizes the results and addresses and discusses further avenues of research.

2. Adverbs as verbs

In Seediq, while the adverbial is typically realized as the matrix verb of the clause, in that it attracts cliticization and bears voice and tense morphology, the semantic main verb of

---

CONT = continuous, COP = copula, DEM = demonstrative, DES = desiderative, DET = determiner, DU = dual, E = ergative, EXCL = exclusive, FEM = feminine, FUT = future, G = genitive, GEN = genitive, HORT = hortative, IF = instrument focus, INCL = inclusive, IND = indicative, LF = locative focus, MASC = masculine, N = nominative, NEG = negator, NOM = nominative, P = plural, PERF = perfect, PF = patient focus, PRES = present, PRF = perfective, PROGR = progressive, PROHIB = prohibitive, PST = past, QUOT = quotative, REL = relative, S = singular, UF = Undergoer focus. Figures refer to grammatical person.

the proposition is obligatorily realized in Actor Focus unmarked present tense, irrespective of the voice and tense/aspect of the clause as a whole (2a–d). This is what Chang (2007) refers to as the *AF-only restriction* and the *TAM-less Condition* respectively.

(2) a. M⟨n⟩hmet-an =mu m-imah sino kiya.
⟨PST⟩at.will-LF =1S.E AF-drink wine that
'I drank that wine with no thought about the consequences.'

b. N-mah-an =mu sino kiya.
PST-drink-LF =1S.E wine that
'I drank that wine.'

c. *M⟨n⟩hmet-an =mu mah-an/ n-mah-an/
⟨PST⟩at.will-LF =1S.E drink-LF PST-drink-LF
m-n-imah sino kiya.
AF-PST-drink wine that

This behaviour obtains for adverbials denoting manner, frequency and duration across Formosan languages, the major exception being Tsou, where voice morphology is shared across the clause by both adverbial and main verb.

The general lack of distinctive verbal morphology on subordinate verbs in Seediq (and other Formosan languages with the exception of Tsou) is readily accounted for under a structural approach where the adverbial is realized as a syntactic head (e.g. an auxiliary) that intervenes structurally between the main verb and inflectional morphology. This implies that it is the adverbial, not the main verb, which is the only possible candidate for distinctive verbal morphology. Similarly, when a negation is present, the verb may not realize any T/A marking. The assumed structure is shown in (3).[2]

(3)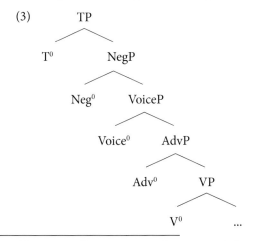

---

[2]. The category T represents tense/aspect morphology, whereas Voice represents the four-way focus distinction. Whether or not these are the best terms for the categories involved is not a relevant issue for our purposes. Similarly, we use the abbreviation Adv pretheoretically for adverbial verbs.

It follows from this account that Chang's AF-Only Restriction and the TAM-less Condition are not independent constraints, but rather an epiphenomenal consequence of the structure, no more remarkable than the use of infinitive marking on an English verb following a finite auxiliary.

Similarly, given that Neg° regularly causes the element in the Voice° head to be realized in connegative morphology (4a), this structure also explains why, when an adverbial is present, it is the adverbial that realizes connegative morphology (4b), not the main verb (4c).[3] Incidentally, it also explains why a negated verb bears no T/A morphology.

(4) a. Ini=mu mah-i sino kiya.
   NEG =1S.E. drink-PF.CNG wine that
   'I didn't drink that wine.'

   b. Ini =mu mhmet-i m-imah sino kiya.
   NEG =1S.E at.will-PF.CNG AF-drink wine that
   'I didn't drink that wine recklessly.'

   c. *Ini =mu mhmet-i/ mhemuc
   NEG =1S.E at.will-PF.CNG at.will.AF.CNG
   imah/ mah-i sino kiya.
   drink.AF.CNG drink-PF.CNG wine that

The only further assumption required is that AF be treated as the default (non-finite) value for a verb when no distinctive (i.e. non-default) voice morphology is available (in the same way as present tense and non-connegative forms are also default settings in their respective categories). There is nothing inherently problematic with this assumption, since AF is also the citation form of the verb. Further, while the other Focus categories (PF, LF and IF) are morphologically marked, in that they always display overt morphology, AF is in many cases morphologically unmarked. There are a number of very frequent verbs which do not realize the AF affix (except as a prefixed FUT marker), but the AF form of which is instead identical to the root. These include: *qduriq* 'flee' (5), *sluhe* 'learn' and *beebu* 'beat'. The same also holds for all causatives in Seediq.

(5) Wada qduriq ka dapa =su.
   PST flee.(AF) NOM buffalo 2S.G.
   'Your buffalo escaped.'

Thus, the morphological properties of constructions with adverbial verbs follow directly from the assumed structure, with no further stipulation required, other than the obvious issue that they are, in some relevant sense, verbs.

---

3. The behaviour of Atayalic connegatives is rather complex. These forms, which are identical in form with the imperative, are found with the negation *ini*, the prohibitive *iya* and the auxiliary *asi* 'just have to, spontaneously' (but not with the negation *uxe* 'will not, is not' which is used for nominal negation as well as for verbal negation in the future). For reasons of space, we will not touch on the mechanism deriving connegatives here.

It is not clear, however, what to be a verb really implies. In Seediq, adverbial verbs bear verbal morphology, but they are highly restricted in their distribution: usually, they must be accompanied by a main verb, unless the adverbial verb is serving as a proform for an entire VP (6a, b). Such constructions can not be rescued by a suitable context either, cf the dialogue in (6c).⁴

(6) a. M-urux =ku naq m-imah sino.
AF-alone =1S.N just AF-drink wine
'I drink wine alone.'

b. M-urux =ku naq (*sino).
AF-alone =1S.N just wine
'I'll just do it alone.' (≠ 'I do (something with) wine alone.')

c. – Bleq-i s⟨m⟩ino sama kiya!
well-PF.CNG ⟨AF⟩wash vegetables that
'Wash those vegetables well!'

– Un, bleq-un =mu *(s⟨m⟩ino).
yes well-PF =1S.E ⟨AF⟩wash
'Yes, I will!'

Further, while prototypical verbs in Seediq display a four-way voice distinction (AF, PF, LF, IF), adverbial verbs only distinguish AF and non-AF. Firstly, Instrument Focus appears to be lacking altogether (7a)⁵, and, when LF morphology occurs, the locative meaning never obtains, not even if semantically expected (7b); rather, the LF.PST signals simple non-AF past tense (cf. Holmer 2002b: 336–337 for a survey of the T/A use of focus in Seediq). Indeed, trying to force a locative reading by using LF.PRES leads to ungrammaticality, (7c).⁶

(7) a. *S-knteetu =daha m-ekan ido ka atak.
IF-often =3P.E AF-eat rice NOM chopsticks
'They often eat with chopsticks.'

---

4. Not all Formosan languages behave like this, however. One clear example of a language where adverbial verbs can take NP arguments in their own right is Paiwan (cf Wu 2003). We might speculate that adverbial verbs as in Seediq have two avenues of development: a) into fully-fledged verbs with their own argument structure (as in Paiwan); and b) into (non-verbal) adverbs, by losing their verbal inflection (as in Tagalog).

5. Some instances of the *s*-prefix are indeed found on adverbial verbs, but as optional affixes cooccurring with other focus markers. This is not relevant here.

6. Incidentally, we find the same functional distribution in Tsou (AF/non-AF on the adverbial verb). In Tsou this is even clearer, since focus morphology is not harnessed for other purposes, so the adverbial verb has only two possible forms, AF and non-AF (Szakos 1994).

b. !B⟨n⟩leq-an =daha t⟨m⟩inun ubung kiya.
⟨PST⟩-well-LF =3P.E ⟨AF⟩weave loom that
'!They have woven that loom well.'
(≠ 'They have woven well on that loom.')

c. *Bleq-an =daha t⟨m⟩inun ubung kiya.
well-LF =13P.E ⟨AF⟩weave loom that
('They weave well on that loom.')

Interestingly enough, this morphological restriction is not simply the consequence of realization as a coverb. While they are rather infrequent, spontaneous examples of IF on coverbs can be found (8a, b), while they can not even be elicited for adverbial verbs (data quoted from Tseng, to appear).

(8) a. Su-usa =daha m-angal qhuni mdengu.
IF-go =3P.E AF-take wood dry
'They went to fetch dry wood for it (to light a fire to heat it).'

b. Su-usa =daha c⟨m⟩uwaq qcurux yayung ma ruru.
IF-go =3P.E ⟨AF⟩-sprinkle fish river & stream
'They go to sprinkle with it over the fish in the rivers and streams.'

Thus, we see that the argument structure of adverbial verbs is not typical of verbs in general. The fact that they normally must cooccur with a main verb is reminiscent of auxiliaries, and the fact that the overt morphological voice marking (AF vs non-AF) of the adverbial verb corresponds to the relation between the NOM clause subject and the argument structure of the main verb (a situation analogous to long passivization) suggests that we are dealing with restructuring verbs similar to German *versuchen* 'try' (cf. Wurmbrand 2004).

The relevant issue for this paper is therefore to determine whether it is simply an isolated lexical fact that adverbial verbs in Seediq *are* restructuring verbs, or whether there is something in the syntax which can make them *behave like* restructuring verbs. In the former case, part-of-speech membership must be viewed as a primitive (partly) independent of semantics, while the second option allows us to account for the existence of adverbial verbs as a syntactic phenomenon. In the interests of keeping the number of assumed primitives at a minimum, as well as maximizing possibilities of cross-linguistic comparison, the second avenue, if viable, is to be preferred. This, however, raises the question of what kind of phenomenon could make an adverb behave like a restructuring verb. This will be the topic of the remainder of the paper.

3. Two analyses of the data

In Holmer (2002a, 2006), two alternative analyses of these facts are presented as possible syntactic mechanisms which could make adverbs behave syntactically like verbs. In this section, the predictions of these two analyses are tested empirically against one another.

3.1 Predication analysis

Jeng (1977), working on the syntax of Takbanuaz Bunun, was faced with two-verb constructions which display a mismatch between the argument structures of the respective verbs and the morphology they realize. Thus, in (9), it would seem obvious that it is the argument structure of the verb *baliv* 'to buy' rather than that of *tindangkul* 'to run' which should warrant the assignation of PF morphology. Nevertheless, the PF morphology is realized on the latter.

(9) tindangkul-un   ʔista ma-baliv   davus
     run-PF   3S.E AF-buy   wine
     'He runs to buy wine.'   (op. cit. 79)

Jeng's solution is to suggest that the whole of *mabaliv davus* 'to buy wine' is the sentential complement (and thus NOM subject) of the PF verb *tindangkulun*.

In Holmer (2002a, 2006), it is tentatively suggested that something akin to this analysis might be applied to the behaviour of adverbial verbs in Seediq, i.e., that the adverbial is a predicate, which either takes the main VP as one of its arguments (the agent being the other one) or the entire remainder of the proposition as its sole argument. In the latter case, if the adverbial verb is a raising verb, we get a situation that is superficially similar to restructuring. This would further capture the fact that these verbs cannot take NP arguments on their own, but require a lexical main verb as well (in Seediq, although clearly not universally, cf. Wu 2006).

This analysis could be interpreted as a purely lexical fact, i.e., that a certain set of meanings is simply realized lexically within a given word class (where English has adverbs, Seediq uses verbs). However, a quick look at the data suggests initially that this might not be an isolated occurrence. Another notable fact of Seediq and other Formosan languages is that weak quantifiers are often – and in some contexts obligatorily – realized as primary predicates (10).[7]

(10) a. Egu   [ka   preko   m-n-eyah   q⟨m⟩iyuc].
        many   NOM   mosquito   AF-PST-come   ⟨AF⟩-bite
        'Many are the mosquitoes that have come to bite.'

     b. *M-n-eyah   q⟨m⟩iyuc   egu   preko.
        AF-PST-come   ⟨AF⟩-bite   many   mosquito

Capturing these two facts under a single analysis becomes a question of isolating the common properties of the two constructions, namely, the tendency for clause-internal modifiers of different kinds (elements modifying NP or VP) to be construed as primary predicates and realized clause-initially. Trivially, of course, there is one further

---

7. A reviewer has commented that quantifiers can also be predicative in English. However, whereas this is a stylistic option in English, it is, in its context, obligatory in Seediq.

element which is prototypically a primary predicate and is normally realized clause-initially in Formosan languages, and that is the main verb itself.

The predication analysis seeks to link these three facts by proposing a macroparametric difference between languages like English, where primary predication holds between the most salient (phrasal) argument and the remainder of the proposition, and languages like Seediq, where predication singles out the most salient predicate instead. The "most salient predicate" would in most cases actually represent the adverbial. As already discussed in Holmer (2006), adverbials are particularly salient as predicates in that clausal negation most typically negates the adverbial (if one is present), or a modifier on an NP, rather than the main verb (although such a reading is also possible). The linear structure proposed is illustrated in (11).

(11) a. ARG_i - [V $\emptyset_i$ NP ADV]   (SUBJ)
     b. $PRED_i$ - [V NP NP $\emptyset_i$]   (ADVV)

Assuming that there is a left-right asymmetry between the single element selected for the establishment of the predication relation and the remainder of the proposition (i.e. the intuition underlying Kayne's (1994) concept of Antisymmetry), it would also follow that English type languages would tend to be subject-initial, and the Seediq type would (if no adverbial is present) tend to be verb-initial (or at any rate predicate-initial). This, in turn, establishes a correlation between the phenomenon of adverbial verbs and word order: the verbal realization of adverbial meaning in Seediq would be one possible consequence of its clause-initial realization as a predicate.

Note that realization as a clause-initial primary predicate does not automatically entail verbal status: such a predicate could just as easily be realized as a cleft. In fact, we can sketch a possible diachronic derivation from clause-initial predicate to verb. Assuming a verb-initial language which displays Wackernagel cliticization of certain elements to the first element in the clause (i.e. in practice usually the verb), it is a straightforward path of development for these elements (which would typically include clitic pronouns and aspectual markers) to be reanalysed as verbal morphology. The fronted element would then be reanalysed as a verb, in part due to its initial position, and in part due to the morphology it bears. For obvious reasons, this reanalysis as a verb would normally only be possible in a language which is verb-initial in itself (i.e. where clause-initial position is a typical verbal position), just as the clause-initial realization of such elements would also tend to co-occur with verb-initiality.[8]

Cross-linguistically, this model makes interesting predictions concerning the relation between verb-initiality on the one hand, and adverbial verbs – or other cases of predication involving elements other than prototypical verbs – on the other. These predictions gain some initial support from a quick overview of major verb-initial groups.

---

8. Note that while adverbial meanings are realized as verbs in Seediq, weak quantifiers are clefted with no corresponding reanalysis as verbs. In Tsou, on the other hand, the distributive quantifier *acɨhɨ/acɨha* 'all' is realized as a verb (Chang 2003).

Verb-initiality is particularly concentrated in certain language families or groups. Over and above Austronesian, we find verb-initiality in Semitic, Celtic and some other groups. In Semitic, exemplified here by Arabic, adverbial meanings are in fact regularly encoded as verbs with the semantic main verb serving either as the complement or the subject of the adverbial (12a–d).[9]

(12)   a.   Hasuna   dars-u-haa[10]
             well.PRF   study-N-3S.FEM
             'She studied well.'

       b.   sayaHsunu   dars-u-haa
             well.FUT   study-N-3S.FEM
             'She will study well.'

       c.   akthara   akl-a   as-samak-a
             often.CAUS.PRF.MASC   eat-ACC   DET-fish-ACC
             'He often eats fish.'

       d.   akthara-t   akl-a   as-samak-a
             often.CAUS.PRF-FEM   eat-ACC   DET-fish-ACC
             'She often eats fish.'

In Celtic, illustrated here by Scottish Gaelic, adverbial verbs do not occur. However, it is stylistically unmarked to cleft adverbials into predicates, (13a), although adverbials can also be realized within the clause. Further, weak quantifiers are regularly realized as predicates, (13b). In the case of Gaelic, we are dealing with a stylistic option which has apparently also made its way into English. Thus, Scottish Gaelic could be described as representing the other possible consequence of clause-initial realization as a predicate, i.e., clefting instead of reanalysis as a verb.

(13)   a.   Is   tric   [a   bheothaich srad   bheag   teine   mór].
             COP   often   REL   kindle   spark   small.FEM   fire   big
             'A small spark has often kindled a great fire.'

       b.   'S   iomadh   rud   [a   rinn   mi].
             COP   many   thing REL   do.PST   1s
             'Many's the thing I did.'

---

9. One reviewer questions the suitability of using Arabic as an example language, given that modern Arabic has SVO as an optional alternate order (and as the dominant order in many dialects). It should be recalled, however, that Classical Arabic was predominantly VSO, and the lexical facts described here hold equally for both modern and classical varieties. In fact, it appears that adverbial verbs were more frequent in Classical Arabic than in modern Arabic (Helen Avery, p.c.).

10. All examples from Helen Avery (p.c.).

There are some further examples of similar phenomena in the prototypical verb-initial areas of the world. Thus, in the verb-initial language Nootka (Wakashan: British Columbia), adverbs regularly bear tense and agreement morphology (14a, b), data from Wojdak (2005: 47).

(14) a. čamaqƛʔiš   titiqs Florence
čamaqƛ-ʔiiš   titiqs Florence
properly-3IND dry   Florence
'Florence is drying dishes properly.' [sic.]

b. wityáxits   waaɬšiƛ
wity'ax-mit-s   waɬ-[+L]-šiƛ
slow-PST-1S.ABS go.home-CONT-PERF
'I was going home slowly.'

The Nootka facts are actually the result of morphological linearization, in that finite morphology is always realized on the first element of the clause, which can be either a verb, an adverb, or a nominal predicate. This would represent the next step along the line of derivation towards the Formosan pattern, showing how verb-initiality can conspire with other phenomena to create what appears to be an adverbial verb, and can diachronically force a remapping of adverbial meanings into verbal form.

In the Austroasiatic VOS language Car Nicobarese, quantifiers are regularly realized as predicates (Gérard Diffloth, p.c.), and it appears that certain adverbial meanings (e.g. 'carefully') are expressed as verbs (cf. Braine 1961: 248). Finally, while I have found no evidence so far of adverbial verbs in Central American languages, it is clear that a plethora of adverbial meanings can be expressed as affixes on the verb in e.g. Choapan Zapotec (cf. Suárez 1983: 59). Under the common generative assumption that affixation is the result of verb incorporation into a superordinate head position (cf. Baker 1988), this is potentially a related phenomenon.

There is thus some anecdotal support for the predication model. However, in Austronesian itself (which is predominantly verb-initial), adverbial verbs are a typical feature of Formosan languages, although they are found in a couple of non-Formosan languages as well, such as Tukang Besi (Mark Donohue, p.c.). The extremely high level of Formosan within the sub-grouping of Austronesian, taken together with the sporadic extra-Formosan occurrences of adverbial verbs, suggests that the null hypothesis would be that adverbial verbs in Formosan are a retention from the earliest stages of Austronesian, while the phenomenon has been lost in most languages outside Taiwan.

Given that extra-Formosan languages are still predominantly verb-initial, it is potentially problematic for a typological approach that they do not display adverbial verbs to a greater extent than they do. The same principles holding in Formosan languages should be expected to hold outside Formosan. While we have been able to suggest a path for the development of adverbial verbs via reanalysis of fronted adverbs, we have yet to present a mechanism by which adverbial verbs may be lost without necessarily having to alter the basic structures of the languages involved.

One crucial mechanism is the morphology itself. Given that adverbial verbs are not prototypical verbs, as far as argument structure and distribution is concerned (cf. the discussion in Section 2), it is not surprising that they may lose morphological marking which is preserved on more prototypical verbs. This would be more or less what has happened to the negation verb in Finnish and Estonian. In Finnish, the negation is a verb which bears agreement morphology and prevents the main verb from bearing such morphology, (15a). Conversely, in Estonian, the verbal morphology of the negation has been lost, although it still prevents the main verb from realizing agreement morphology, (15b), while agreement morphology still exists for non-negated main verbs, as in (15c).

(15) a. Minä e-n   tule   Helsingi-stä.   *Finnish*
        1s   NEG-1s come Helsinki-from
        'I don't come from Helsinki.'

   b. Ma ei   tule   Tallinn-ast.   *Estonian*
        1s NEG   come Tallinn-from
        'I don't come from Tallinn.'

   c. Ma tule-n   Tallinn-ast.   *Estonian*
        1s come-1s Tallinn-from
        'I come from Tallinn.'

Once verbal morphology is selectively lost, the first step towards losing verbal status has been taken. For this to occur with adverbial verbs, as it has occurred with the Estonian negation, is, if not predictable, at any rate not particularly surprising. Therefore, the loss of adverbial verbs outside Formosan is not problematic for this analysis.[11]

However, the model, for all its elegant ambitions, faces more serious empirical problems at home when dealing with other facts in Seediq. Most crucially, it would imply that the predication mechanism could operate once per clause (just as externalization of a subject occurs once per clause in English). This, in turn, would entail that there can be no more than one instance of an adverbial verb in a given clause (nor indeed that an adverbial can cooccur with a verb-initial pattern). These predictions are contrary to fact (16).

---

11. More problematic might be the Bantu language Ibibio (Mark Baker, p.c.) and some other related languages, which are SVO but where something akin to adverbial verbs is attested. Cinque (1999: 70) analyses these as cases where the verbal morphology (seen as free morphemes or particles) can be cliticized linearly to constituents other than the verb, in essence the same as what is happening in Nootka. The exact distribution of this phenomenon in Bantu languages and possible reasons for it are deferred to future research.

(16) Kntte-un =daha mhemuc t⟨m⟩melux   m-ekan ucik qaun.
    often-PF =3P.E at.will.AF ⟨AF⟩on.its.own AF-eat chili
    'They often eat chili on its own for no reason.'

Further, if the proposition were the sole subject argument of the adverbial predicate, it would be predicted to be a syntactic island. However, relativization from a clause with an adverbial verb is perfectly grammatical (17), falsifying this prediction.

(17) Wada puq-un qtahi ka   hlama
    PST eat-PF ant NOM steamed.rice
    [ini=daha bleq-i   g⟨m⟩emuk].
    NEG=3P.E properly-PF.CNG ⟨AF⟩cover
    'The *hlama* which they didn't cover properly was eaten by ants.'

In addition, the correlation with predicative quantification is not entirely unproblematic. While predicative quantification is often obligatory in Seediq, a weak quantifier can appear within an NP in object position (18), and need not be realized predicatively in this context. In Henningsson & Holmer (2008), this is analysed as a restriction on weak quantifiers in prototypically definite positions (such as ERG agent and NOM subject). While other accounts are possible, the crucial point is that the realization of quantifiers as predicates in Seediq is not necessarily part of a generalized predication pattern (unless this is more complex than hitherto supposed).

(18) Mk-m-ari =ku egu blebun.
    DES-AF-buy =1S.N much banana
    'I want to buy many bananas.'

Finally, if the adverbial verb is the predicate of the clause, it would be expected to be intransitive and take the remainder of the clause as its sole argument. However, it regularly occurs in non-AF, exactly in cases where the NOM subject is a patient with respect to the argument structure of the main verb.[12] This behaviour is typical of restructuring verbs, not of monadic verbs with clausal arguments. For these reasons, the predication hypothesis as it stands proves to be empirically inadequate.

3.2 Adverbial heads

One alternative, presented and discussed at length in Holmer (2002a, 2006), would be to follow Cinque (1999) and propose that adverbs are located in a series of categories external to VP, within an extension of Split-INFL, in the backbone of the clause

---

[12]. One reviewer does, indeed, suggest that non-AF on the adverbial may reflect that the embedded clause (i.e. the remainder of the proposition) is a derived patient subject. However, it is difficult to envisage how to account for the AF/non-AF distinction on the adverbial verb under such an approach, and it would further seem a remarkable coincidence that this would always occur when a corresponding syntactic change has taken place *within* the embedded clause.

(although this does not necessarily imply following Cinque in assuming that these are uniformly ordered as the result of universal phrase structure).[13]

Under such an analysis, English realizes its adverbs in the phrasal Specifier positions corresponding to the relevant levels while Seediq (and other Formosan languages) realizes them as the heads. An analogy would be the behaviour of the negation verb in Finnish, which is partly verbal in that it displays subject agreement but no tense morphology, and which can be analysed as the realization of a head in Neg° (above T° but below Agr°) rather than a phrasal negation in SpecNegP, such as German *nicht*.

Cinque (2001) proposes that the corresponding head positions of these adverbial phrases are the locus of restructuring verbs. Given that adverbial verbs combine the syntactic behaviour of restructuring verbs with adverbial meaning, adverbial verbs would seem to be the most prototypical representatives of this category. In practice, adverbs, restructuring verbs and adverbial verbs are different manifestations of elements within the same syntactic domain. What is typical for Formosan languages is that they make use of the head positions rather than the Specifier positions of the relevant categories.

If adverbial verbs in Formosan are verbs by virtue of being elements realized in the heads of the adverbial levels in the sense of Cinque, it follows that (a) adverbial verbs are primarily heads, and secondarily verbs; and (b) adverbial verbs should be attested for a wide range of adverbial meanings. Further, if we do not strictly follow Cinque in assuming a universal ordering, only a universally available structural pattern, it would follow that we expect that variation in the internal ordering of adverbial verbs should be reminiscent of that of adverbs. Finally, we would also expect clauses with adverbial verbs to be monoclausal, i.e., the adverbial and the main verb should be located within the same minimal clause. We shall examine these predictions in turn below.

The first prediction involves the following rationale: assuming a plethora of syntactic positions above VP (simplified to two such positions in 19), which are responsible for a wide range of adverbial and modal meanings, and assuming that head movement is constrained by the Head Movement Constraint (cf. Travis 1984), it would follow that any head (illustrated here as Adv2°) which intervenes hierarchically between V° and the inflectional categories of the clause (shown here as Voice° and T°) is a potential host of verbal morphology (i.e. a verb). In contrast, a head located above these inflectional categories (shown here as Adv1°) is predicted not to surface as a verb.

---

13. Plausible alternatives, which place a lighter burden on Universal Grammar as an independent module, include a semantically based approach, as in Ernst (1997, 2002).

(19)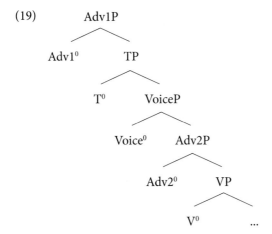

The relative height of adverbs can be independently determined semantically in terms of scope (cf. Ernst 1997). Therefore, the prediction implies that the higher an adverbial meaning, the less likely it is to be expressed as a verb.

This prediction is largely borne out. While lower types of adverbs such as manner and frequency are regularly coded as verbs, other adverb types do not bear verbal morphology, neither do they prevent the realization of distinctive morphology on the main verb (20a, b). Moreover, some adverbial meanings are expressed by subordinators or particles, which are not verbal as such, but which attract cliticization, a behaviour typical of syntactic heads in Seediq, (20c).[14] On a more theoretical level, perhaps, further adverbial meanings can be encoded by final particles, which are certainly not verbs, but arguably heads (20d, e), (cf. Holmer 2005 for a discussion).

(20) a. Hani =daha bale s⟨n⟩paq-an babuy nii.
just =3P.E very ⟨PST⟩-kill-LF pig this
'They have just killed this pig.'

b. Tena =ku m-n-eyah alang hini.
already =1S.N AF-PST-come village here
'I have already arrived in this village.'

c. Soo =ku hari uka pila.
like =1S.N a.bit not.have money
'Apparently I don't have money.'

d. Netun =su m-imah sino, bsukan =su dhenu.
if =2S.N AF-drink wine drunk =2S.N consequently
'If you drink wine, you will get drunk.'

---

14. For a discussion of this point and evidence that contemporary Seediq cliticization is not simply linear 2nd-position Wackernagel cliticization, but is sensitive to the category of the host, see Holmer (2005: 190) or Holmer (2006: 109ff).

e. M-iicu m-oda habung seediq peni.
AF-fear AF-pass grave person well.you.see
'You see, people are afraid of passing by a grave.'

As we have seen above, adverbials of a wide range of types are syntactically speaking heads in Seediq, but only a subset of these actually bear verbal morphology and appear to be real verbs. Incidentally, this same subset can be expected to intervene structurally between the V position and relevant inflectional categories. This bears out the first two predictions of the proposed model based on Cinque (1999).

The third prediction concerns ordering. If adverbial verbs are simply head realizations of the corresponding adverb positions in languages where adverbs are not verbal, it would follow that there should be clear parallels between the ordering variation patterns of the two types. This is what we seem to find: adverbial verbs can occur in fairly free order, with the ordering differences often reflecting scope (21a, b). However, some orders are impossible (21c, d), exactly in these cases where the corresponding ordering in English is aberrant.

(21) a. Mhmet-un =daha knteetu m-imah ka sino.
at.will-PF =3P.E often AF-drink NOM wine
'They never think of the consequences, just drink wine often.'

b. Kntte-un =daha mhemuc m-imah ka sino.
often-PF =3P.E at.will AF-drink NOM wine
'They often drink wine for no reason.'

c. *Tlmex-un =daha pcenga m-ekan ka ucik qaun.
on.its.own-PF =3P.E seldom AF-eat NOM chili
('??They do it on its own about eating chili seldom.')

d. Pcnga-un =daha t⟨m⟩-melux m-ekan ka ucik qaun.
seldom-PF =3P.E ⟨AF⟩on.its.own AF-eat NOM chili
'They seldom eat chili on its own.'

Note that a strict application of Cinque's universal ordering would still allow for a certain amount of order flexibility. The aim here is not to test the validity of a universal hierarchy, but rather to establish a parallelism with the ordering of (phrasal) adverbs.

Our final prediction concerns monoclausality. Unfortunately, not many tests for monoclausality are available in Seediq. Seediq lacks overt complementizers. In addition, Seediq has clitic climbing (22), so the realization of the clitic on the adverbial verb would be no evidence of monoclausality.

(22) Kla-un =su =mu m-n-eyah ciga.
know-PF =2S.N =1S.E AF-PST-come yesterday
'I know you came yesterday.' (Zhang 2000: 135)[15]

Similarly, the ordering variation with respect to negation (23a, b) does not count as evidence either way, cf. the fact that the same ordering variation occurs in the English translation, where a biclausal analysis would not usually be contemplated.

(23) a. Kntte-un =daha ini qita ka hido.
often-PF =3P.E NEG see.AF.CNG NOM sun
'They often don't see the sun (e.g. they don't notice it).'

b. Ini =daha kntte-i q⟨m⟩ita ka hido.
NEG =3P.E often-PF.CNG ⟨AF⟩-see NOM sun
'They don't often see the sun (e.g. it's often cloudy).'

Moreover, since we are dealing with restructuring verbs, we should be aware that any apparent evidence of monoclausality might be due to restructuring instead. Consider the following facts. If the main verb is in its own minimal clause, we would expect that relativization from the patient position of the main verb should be reflected by non-AF morphology within that minimal clause, i.e., on the main verb itself. This does not occur. Rather, the main verb is always realized in default AF (24a). This, however, is behaviour typical of restructuring, (cf. 24b), and thus not evidence of monoclausality per se.

(24) a. maha m-seang ka quyu [m⟨n⟩hmet-an =su beebu]
FUT AF-angry NOM snake ⟨PST⟩at.will-LF =1S.E hit.AF
'The snake which you beat for no reason will get angry.'

b. dass der Traktor zu reparieren versucht wurde
that DET tractor INF repair.INF try.PASS.PRT AUX
'that they tried to repair the tractor' (Wurmbrand 2004: 1008)

Therefore, given that evidence in favour of monoclausality is always the potential result of restructuring, it is more promising to look for evidence in favour of biclausality. One possible candidate is the following. Seediq has a generalized restriction on the realization of overt agents with the imperative, (25a). In most cases, this carries over to constructions with adverbial verbs as well, (25b). However, it is quite common for an overt agent pronoun to cooccur with an imperative adverbial verb, but only if it is attached to the main verb rather than to the adverbial verb (25c).

(25) a. Mah-i (*=su) ka sino!
drink-PF.IMP =2S.E NOM wine
'Drink the wine!'

---

15. For ease of comparison, the orthography has been adapted to conform with practice in the present paper.

b. Bleq-i   s⟨m⟩ino   ka   sama   kiya!
    well-PF.IMP ⟨AF⟩-wash   NOM vegetables that
    'Wash those vegetables properly!'

c. Thway-i   (*=su) hari   m-imah =su   sino!
    slow-PF.IMP =2S.E   a.bit AF-drink =2S.N wine
    'Drink wine a little more slowly!'

What these examples show us is that clitic climbing can sometimes be blocked. Here, the domain headed by the main verb must, at least in these cases, be a minimal clause which is capable of holding a clitic. Thus, it appears that the constructions involved presumably contain clausal boundaries, although this is concealed by clitic climbing and restructuring.[16]

If adverbial verb constructions are biclausal, we would expect the lower clause to be freely negatable. This is not the case, however. Certain adverbial verbs have a fixed position with respect to negation, (26a, b), surprisingly enough, even when the ungrammatical ordering would be semantically more expected. This might possibly indicate a preference for monoclausality, since what appears to be a straightforward biclausal solution is eschewed in favour of a total rephrasing (26c).

(26) a. Ini =su   mhemuc   m-usa m-eepah.
         NEG =2S.N at.will.AF.CNG   AF-go AF-work
         'You don't go to work just like that, unless you have reason to.'

     b. *M-mhemuc =su   ini   usa   m-eepah.
         AF-at.will =2S.N NEG   go.AF.CNG   AF-work
         ('For no good reason, you don't go/refrain from going to work.')

     c. M-bserux =su   m-usa m-eepah.
         AF-lazy   =2S.N AF-go AF-work
         'You are lazy/reluctant to go to work.'

It might be argued that this is not evidence of a preference for monoclausality, but rather that restructuring is creating an illusion of monoclausality. Prototypical restructuring verbs, however, do not behave like this: they do allow the lower clause to be negated (27a, b), although it is admittedly more common for the higher clause to be negated (27c).

---

16. This is of course assuming that (25c) has the same structure as (25b) or other adverbial verb constructions. While this is not self-evident, the same pattern can be found with a wide range of adverbial verbs like e.g. *pcenga/pcngai* 'seldom' and *bsiyaq/qbsyaqi* 'for a long time', suggesting that it is fairly general (except high adverbial heads which are incompatible with imperatives anyway, such as illocutionary adverbials).

(27) a. Quisiera   no ver-te.[17]   *Spanish*
       want.COND.1S NEG see.INF-2S
       'I would like not to see you.'

   b. Empez-ó   a   no hablar.   *Spanish*
      begin-PST.3S INF NEG talk.INF
      'He began not to talk.'

   c. No empez-ó   a   hablar.   *Spanish*
      NEG begin-PST.3S INF talk.INF
      'He didn't begin to talk.'

Thus, in cases where Seediq adverbial verbs diverge from the most prototypical type of restructuring verb, they err in the direction of apparent monoclausality. While the issue of clausal boundaries deserves further attention, the facts appear to fit rather neatly with both Cinque's (1999) proposal concerning adverb placement, as well as his (2001) analysis of restructuring verbs as elements base-generated in the head positions corresponding to the Specifiers hosting adverbs.

The other predictions were also more or less borne out. Of the two alternative accounts, therefore, the less ambitious predictions of the Cinque-based model fare better when dealing with Seediq data (although the status of clausal boundaries needs further investigation). At the same time, the model captures successfully the verbal nature of adverbial verbs by deriving it from the realization of syntactic heads within a relevant domain of the clause (viz. the domain intervening structurally between V and the head position responsible for inflectional morphology). What defines languages of the Formosan type is that adverbials are realized, not in the Specifier positions of the relevant categories in the backbone of the clause, but in the corresponding head positions instead.

4. Summary and conclusion

In the preceding sections, we have shown that adverbial verbs in Seediq conform rather neatly to what would be expected under the assumption that they are the lexical realization of heads in adverbial phrases of the type proposed by Cinque. So far, we have not examined any possible correlations of this with other facts in the languages concerned. Does anything else follow from the realization of heads rather than Specifiers of Cinque adverbial phrases?

It might be tentatively suggested that in English, the adverbial phrases can lexically realize both the Specifier positions (for adverbs) and the head positions (for restructuring verbs). In Seediq, in contrast, only the head positions are available (for restructuring verbs, including those which express adverbial meaning). It might

---

17. Quoted from Reider (1989: 284).

seem tempting to see this as evidence that the relevant Specifier positions are unavailable because they are required for other purposes, e.g., predicate raising of the type proposed in Pearson (1998) to derive VOS order, and in Rackowski & Travis (2000) to ensure the correct (reverse Cinque) ordering of adverbs. However, this connection is problematic for two reasons.

Firstly, the phenomenon is not restricted to VOS languages, but is found in both VOS and VSO languages. Here, it might be argued indeed that all languages which display adverbial verbs could be assumed to derive verb-initial order by some form of predicate raising in the sense of Pearson (1998), since most Formosan languages either allow for VOS as a word order option, or (like Bunun and Amis, cf. Zeitoun 2000: 65 and Wu 2000: 65, respectively) display subject-final word order in non-AF clauses. The first objection could therefore possibly be discounted.

More seriously, however, the Specifiers of the levels corresponding to the adverbial verbs are exactly the wrong Specifiers to be used for the rolling-up movement envisaged by Rackowski & Travis (2000). This type of movement (complement-to-Specifier) would raise the bulk of the clause past the relevant heads, leaving them in post-verbal or clause-final position, whereas adverbial verbs, crucially, occur in pre-verbal position. Therefore, the mechanisms of predicate raising can not be harnessed directly to derive adverbial verbs.

An alternative possibility is that the predication hypothesis, while not valid as a synchronic typological account, may still have something to offer as a possible diachronic explanation. If predicate fronting can place adverbials in clause-initial position where they can be reanalysed as verbs, these adverbials would retain their status as verbs, and would only be able to occupy the head positions of Cinque adverbial levels even when prevented from clause-initial realization by other factors. This issue must, however, be deferred to future research.

References

Baker, M. 1988. *Incorporation: A Theory of Grammatical Function Changing*. Chicago IL: University of Chicago Press.
Braine, J. 1961. Nicobarese Grammar (Car Dialect). PhD dissertation, University of California, Berkeley.
Chang, H.Y.-L. 2003. Distributivity, plurality, and reduplication in Tsou. *Tsing Hua Journal of Chinese Studies* 32 (2):1–30. (NSC 90–2411-H-194-028).
Chang, H.Y.-L. 2006. The guest playing host: Modifiers as matrix verbs in Kavalan. In *Clause Structure and Adjuncts in Austronesian Languages*, H.-M. Gärtner, P. Law & J. Sabel (eds), 43–82. Berlin: Mouton de Gruyter.
Chang, H. In press. On the syntax of Formosan adverbial verb constructions. In *Austronesialn and Theoretical Linguistics*. Mercado, R., E. Potsdam and L. Travis (eds.) 183–211. Amsterdam/Philadelphia. John Benjamins.
Cinque, G. 1999. *Adverbs and Functional Heads. A Cross-linguistic Perspective*. Oxford: OUP.

Cinque, G. 2001. 'Restructuring' and functional structure. *University of Venice Working Papers in Linguistics* 11: 45–127. (L. Brugé (ed.)).
Ernst, T. 1997. The scopal basis of adverb licensing. *Proceedings of NELS* 28: 127–142.
Ernst, T. 2002. *The Syntax of Adjuncts*. Cambridge: CUP.
Henningsson, L.-Å. & Holmer, A. 2008. The distribution of quantification in Seediq. *Working Papers* 53: 23–41. Lund: Dept. of Linguistics, Lund University.
Holmer, A. 2002a. The encoding of adverbs of manner in the Formosan language Seediq. Paper presented at International Symposium on Linguistics and Speech and Hearing Sciences, Kuala Lumpur, 2002.
Holmer, A. 2002b. The morphology and syntax of Seediq focus. In *The History and Typology of Western Autronesian Voice Systems*, F. Wouk & M. Ross (eds), 333–354. Canberra: Pacific Linguistics.
Holmer, A. 2005. Seediq: Antisymmetry and final particles in a Formosan VOS language. In *Verb First. On the Syntax of Verb-initial Language* [Linguistik Aktuell/Linguistics Today 73], A. Carnie, H. Harley & S.A. Dooley (eds), 175–201. Amsterdam: John Benjamins.
Holmer, A. 2006. Seediq – adverbial heads in a Formosan language. In *Clause Structure and Adjuncts in Austronesian Languages*, H.-M. Gärtner, P. Law & J. Sabel (eds), 83–123. Berlin: Mouton de Gruyter.
Jeng, H.-H. 1977. *Topic and Focus in Bunun* [Special Publication 72]. Taipei: Institute of History and Philology, Academia Sinica.
Kayne. R. 1994. *The Antisymmetry of Syntax* [Linguistic Inquiry Monograph 25]. Cambridge MA: The MIT Press.
Liu, E.E.-H. 2003. Conjunction and Modification in Amis. MA thesis, Tsing Hua University, Taiwan.
Pearson, M. 1998. Predicate raising and VOS order in Malagasy. *UCLA Occasional Papers in Linguistics* 20: 94–110.
Rackowski, A. & Travis, L. 2000. V-initial languages: X or XP movement and adverbial placement. In *The Syntax of Verb-initial Languages*, A. Carnie & E. Guilfoyle (eds.), 117–141. Oxford: OUP.
Reider, M. 1989. Clitic promotion, the evaluated proposition constraint, and mood in Spanish verbal complements. *Hispania* 72: 283–294
Suárez, J. 1983. *The Meso-American Indian Languages*. Cambridge: CUP.
Szakos, J. 1994. Die Sprache der Cou. Untersuchungen zur Synchronie einer austronesischen Sprache auf Taiwan. PhD dissertation, Friedrich-Wilhelms-Universität, Bonn.
Talmy, L. 1985. Lexicalization patterns: Semantic structure in lexical forms. In *Language Typology and Syntactic Description*, Vol. III, T. Shopen (ed.), 57–149. Cambridge: CUP.
Travis, L. 1984. Parameters and Effects of Word Order Variation. PhD dissertation, MIT.
Tseng, Temi Nawi C. to appear. *Saideke-ren de shenhua gushi* (Moral tales of the Seediq people).
Wojdak, R. 2005. The Linearization of Affixes. Evidence from Nuu-Chah-Nulth. PhD dissertation, University of British Columbia.
Wu, C.-M. 2006. Adverbials in Paiwan. Paper presented at 10 ICAL, Palawan, Philippines.
Wu, J.-L. 2000. *Amei-yu de cankao yufa* (Reference grammar of Amis). Taipei: Yuanliou.
Wurmbrand, S. 2004. Two types of restructuring – Lexical vs. functional. *Lingua* 114: 991–1014.
Zeitoun. E. 2000. *Bunong-yu cankao yufa* (Reference grammar of Bunun). Taipei: Yuanliou.
Zhang, Y.-L. 2000. *Saideke-yu de cankao yufa* (Reference grammar of Seediq). Taipei: Yuanliou.

On the syntax of Formosan adverbial verb constructions*

Henry Y. Chang
Academia Sinica

This paper deals with the adverbial verb construction (AVC) in Formosan languages. Three major issues concerning the AVC are addressed: (i) What syntactic relationship is involved in the AVC: Adjunction or complementation? (ii) What syntactic operation is taking place in the AVC: Control or raising? (iii) What is the syntactic status of adverbial verbs: Do they occur as functional heads, lexical heads, or something in between? Our findings suggest that (a) the AVC involves complementation rather than adjunction; (b) the AVC typically involves raising rather than control; (c) adverbial verbs are semi-lexical or quasi-functional rather than simply functional or lexical in nature.

1. Introduction

Recently, there is increasing evidence that adverbials involving notions such as manner and frequency typically surface as verbs in Formosan languages (L. Huang 1997, P. Li 2003, Liu 2003, H. Chang 2006a, Holmer 2006, among others). These adverbial expressions are referred to as adverbial verbs and the constructions they head are referred to as adverbial verb constructions (AVCs) in this paper.

The discovery of Formosan AVCs is typologically and theoretically significant. Typologically speaking, languages exhibiting AVCs differ systematically from languages

---

* This paper grew out of an invited talk given at AFLA-14, which was held at McGill University, Montreal, May 4–5. 2007. I am grateful to Lisa Travis for her invitation and her valuable comments on an earlier version of this paper. Thanks also go to two anonymous reviewers and the audiences at the conference, in particular, Mark Baker, Mark Donohue, Paul Kroeger, and Arthur Holmer. I would also like to express my gratitude to the following people for discussions of various issues with me: Chih-wei Chang, Chao-lin Li, Julia Su, Jane Tang, Chun-ming Wu, and Claire Wu. I am indebted to my major informants Haciang Pan (Kavalan), Pasuya Tiakiana (Tsou), and Mo'o Peonsi (Tsou) for sharing their linguistic knowledge with me. I also thank Chian-pang Wang and Cheng-chun Kuo for their typographical assistance. Any error remains mine.

that realize adverbials as adverbs in their morphosyntax. In this sense, AVCs can be regarded as a typological feature on a par with constructions like serial verb constructions (SVCs). Theoretically speaking, the discovery of AVCs can shed new light on the debate between the structure-based theory of adverbials as advocated by Cinque (1999) and the meaning-based theory of adverbials as initiated by Jackendoff (1972) and recently developed by Ernst (2002). We will return to this issue in Section 5.

Despite this important progress, the syntax of AVCs remains to be worked out. Research issues to be addressed might include:

a. What syntactic relationship is involved in AVCs: Adjunction or complementation?
b. What syntactic operation is taking place in AVCs: Verb serialization/Control, raising, or something else?
c. What is the syntactic status of adverbial verbs: Do they occur as functional heads, lexical verbs, or something in between?

This paper is organized with respect to these research questions. Section 2 will address question (A), Section 3 question (B), Section 4 question (C). In Section 5, we will discuss the typological and theoretical implications of this study, coupled with some suggestions for future research.

Before leaving this section, some clarification is in order. In Formosan languages, AVCs are by no means homogeneous; they vary from one language to another in how they are structurally represented. One aspect of this diversity is that different types of adverbial verbs involve different syntactic structures, as will be discussed in Section 3. Another aspect of the diversity concerns the syntactic relation of adverbial verbs to the lexical verbs. In this regard, Formosan languages with AVCs can be classified into four types. Type I includes Formosan languages such as Kavalan, Puyuma, Squliq Atayal, Seediq, etc., where adverbial verbs and the lexical verbs are simply juxtaposed without any intervening linking element. Take manner verbs for example:

(1) Kavalan (H. Chang 2006a: 46)
a. *paqanas*=iku t⟨em⟩ayta tu sulal.
   slow(AF)=1S.N see⟨AF⟩ OBL book
   'I read a book slowly.'
b. *paqanas-an*-ku t⟨em⟩ayta ya sulal.
   slow-PF-1S.GEN see⟨AF⟩ NOM book
   'I read the book slowly.'

As shown in (1), the manner adverbial verbs *paqanas* and *paqanasan* are present in sentence-initial positions, inflected for voice, and attract bound pronouns on a par with ordinary verbs, with the lexical verbs immediately following them.[1] Moreover, while the manner verbs can be inflected for either Actor Focus (AF) or Non-Actor

---

1. The terms voice and focus are interchangeable in this paper. Accordingly, AV is equivalent to AF, PV to PF, etc..

Focus (NAF), the lexical verbs can only bear the default marking (i.e., AF); in other words, the lexical verbs observe the AF-only Restriction.

In contrast, in Type II languages such as Paiwan, Amis, and Mayrinax Atayal, a linker intervenes between adverbial verbs and the lexical verbs. For instance:

(2) Paiwan (C. Wu 2004: 90)
    a. g-em-alu-aken   *a*   m-aljap tua kasiv.
       slowly-AF-1S.NOM LNK AF-take OBL stick
       'I slowly pick up the stick.'
    b. ku-galu-in   *a*   m-aljap a kasiv.
       1S.GEN-slowly-PF LNK AF-take NOM stick
       'I slowly picked up the stick.'

Note, however, that the AF-only Restriction on the lexical verbs is still in effect, regardless of the intervention of the linker.

Type III represents the Formosan language Tsou. Tsou manifests both the Kavalan-type and the Paiwan-type. On the one hand, Tsou adverbial verbs and the lexical verbs are connected by a subordinator, which appears to parallel the Paiwan-type.[2] For instance:

(3) Tsou
    a. mi-ta b-utas-o   ho mi-ta eobak-o ta oko
       AF-3S AF-violent-AF SUB AF-3S hit-AF OBL child
       'He hit the child violently.'

On the other hand, Tsou lexical verbs can be directly embedded to the adverbial verbs, as in the Kavalan-type. Note, however, that Tsou differs from the Kavalan-type in that it requires its lexical verbs to be voice-inflected in accordance with the adverbial verbs. Compare:

(3) Tsou (H. Chang 2005)
    b. mi-ta aha'-o   eobak-o ta oko.
       AF-3S suddenly-AF hit -AF OBL child
       'He suddenly hit a child.'

---

2. As will become clear in subsequent sections, examples like (3a) differ from constructions involving linkers in two important ways. First, the string following the subordinator *ho* does not observe either the AF-only Restriction or the Focus Harmony Restriction. Neither does it comply with the TAM-less Condition. Second, as pointed out in Tsai (2007:588), the *ho*-clause can be fronted, leaving the adverbial verb behind:

(i) ho mi-ta eobabak-o ta oko   mi-ta b-utas-o
   SUB AF-3S hit-AF OBL child   AF-3S AF-violent-AF
   'He hit the child violently.'

Thus, we do not identify Tsou as belonging to the Paiwan-type.

c. i-ta aha'v-a eobak-a 'e oko.
   NAF-3s suddenly-PF hit-PF NOM child
   'He suddenly hit the child.'

As illustrated in (3b), the manner verb *aha'o* is inflected for AF and so is the lexical verb *eobako*; in (3c), the manner verb *aha'va* appears in NAF, triggering the same voice marking of the lexical verb *eobaka*. In other words, lexical verbs must harmonize with the adverbial verbs in voice alternations, hence the term the Focus Harmony Restriction (FHR) (H. Chang 2005).

In the last type, adverbial verbs typically take a lexical prefix, which is copied from the lower verb. For instance:

(4) Bunun   (Nojima 1996: 17–18, Su 2008: 97)
   a. kis-asu-a=s   mabananaz=tia kis-laupa.
      stab-immediately=OBL man=that   stab-stab
      'Immediately after that, the man stabbed (the woman).'
   b. si-pusan-u=ku   silulu ca   lukic.
      pull-twice-PF=1s.GEN pull   NOM lumber
      'I pulled the lumber twice.'

As demonstrated in (4a), the aspectual verb *asu* is prefixed with the lexical morpheme *kis-*, which also appears on the following lexical verb *laupa*; in (4b), the cardinal frequency verb *pusan* takes the lexical prefix *si-*, which appears to be derived from the embedded lexical verb *silulu*. This phenomenon is dubbed as Prefix Harmony by Tsuchida (2000) and Anticipating Sequence by Adelar (2004). In this paper, we adopt Tsuchida's terminology and refer to the concord pattern as Prefix Harmony. Prefix Harmony is restricted to the Formosan languages spoken (or which used to be spoken) in central-southern Taiwan, such as Siraya (Tsuchida 1990, 2000, Adelaar 2004), Bunun (Nojima 1996, Su 2008), Saaroa (Radetzsky 2006, C. Li 2009), and Kanakanavu (C. Wu 2007).[3] Since it was first observed in Siraya by Tsuchida (1990), we label languages of this type as the Siraya-type. In this type, no intervening linker is attested but the AF-only Restriction is observed.

Here is a summary of the above classification:

---

[3]. Prefix Harmony has not been reported in the Tsou literature. Nevertheless, quite a few examples of Prefix Harmony are found in our recent field notes. For instance:

(i) yu-suhcu   yu-bankake   'o sbuku
    grow-gradually   grow-tall   NOM bamboo.shoot
    'The bamboo shoots grow taller gradually.'
(ii) mi-'o-cu   o-epxng-x   o-taseoni
     AF-1S.NOM-PFV   eat-finish-AF   eat-breakfast
     'I have finished eating breakfast.'

Since confirmation of this observation requires a more comprehensive investigation and it deserves another research paper, we will not identify Tsou as the Siraya-type at this moment.

Table 1. The classification of Formosan languages with AVCs

	Kavalan-type	Paiwan-type	Tsou-type	Siraya-type
Intervening linker	No	Yes	No	No
AF-only Restriction on the lexical verb	Yes	Yes	No	Yes
Prefix Harmony	No	No	Yes/No	Yes

Since Siraya-type languages uniquely exhibit the grammatical feature of Prefix Harmony, which goes beyond the scope of this paper, we will put them aside in this study; the remainder of this paper will be focused only on the first three types.

2. Syntactic relationships

In this section, we will address research question (A): What syntactic relationship is involved in AVCs: Adjunction or complementation? We will review the previous analyses first and then come up with our own analysis.

2.1 Previous analyses

2.1.1 *The adjunct/conjunct analysis (Liu 2003)*

In dealing with AVCs in Amis (Paiwan-type), Liu (2003) proposes a control adjunct analysis for manner verbs and a syntactic conjunct analysis for manner verbs affixed with *sa-/-sa*. Let us look at her control adjunct analysis first. Her control adjunct analysis mainly concerns examples such as (5):

(5) Amis (Liu 2003: 95)
  a. mi-palifud tu ci aki (a) mi-palu' ci kacaw-an.
    AV-violent PRF NOM aki A AV-hit ACC_1 kacaw-ACC_2
    'Aki violently hit Kacaw.'
  b. ma-palifud tu ni aki (a) mi-palu' ci kacaw.
    PV-violent PRF GEN aki A AV-hit NOM kacaw
    lit.: 'Kacaw was hit by Aki, and Aki was violent.'
    'Kacaw was violently hit by Aki.'

As shown in (5a–b), the manner verbs and the lexical verbs are connected by the linker *a*. The manner verbs entertain full-fledged inflection (including voice alternation and aspectual marking), while the lexical verbs are morphologically defective: they can only bear the default voice morphology (i.e., AF) and cannot take any aspectual marking. In view of the grammatical asymmetries, Liu treats the manner verbs as the main verbs of the clauses. In the meantime, Liu analyzes the phrases consisting of the lexical verbs as control adjuncts: they are analyzed as involving control because they observe the AF-only Restriction on a par with control complements; they are treated as adjuncts on the grounds that they are not semantically selected by the manner verbs.

As to the manner verbs affixed with *sa-/-sa*, Liu adopts Tsai & M. Chang's (2003) Neo-Davidsonian-syntax analysis and treats them as syntactic conjuncts. In her conjunct analysis, examples like (6) will have syntactic structures like (7a) or (7b) and a semantic structure like (8):

(6) Amis (Liu 2002:155)
naqun-sa (a) mi-pidpid ci aki tu lupas.
careful-SA A AV-pick NOM aki ACC peach
'Aki is picking peaches carefully.'

(7) Schematic syntactic structures of *sa-X-sa* AVCs in Amis (Liu 2003:158)
a. Syntax

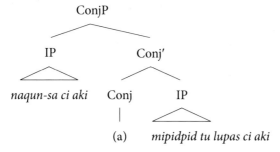

b. Syntax

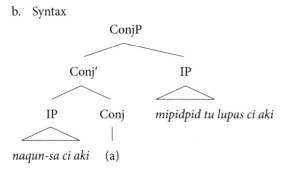

(8) Semantic representation of *sa-X-sa* AVCs in Amis (Liu 2003: 158)
∃e (picking (e) &Agent (e, Aki) &Theme (e, peaches) &careful (e))

While Liu's analysis of manner verbs as the main verbs is convincing, her treatment of lexical verbs as adjuncts is problematic. Among other things, the most challenging fact for her adjunct analysis is that NP arguments can be extracted out of the embedded clause, as illustrated in (5b) and will be discussed in detail in Section 3.

If the embedded clause were an adjunct, the extraction should not be possible, given that extraction out of an adjunct clause is generally banned by the island condition, i.e., the Condition on Extraction Domain (CED, J. Huang 1982). In this regard, Liu's adjunct analysis is inadequate. Moreover, her conjunct analysis is language-specific and cannot carry over to other Formosan languages, as noted in H. Chang (2006a).

2.1.2 *The complement analysis (H. Chang 2006a)*

In H. Chang (2006a), the phrase embedded to an adverbial verb in Kavalan is treated as a complement. This analysis is mainly based on the grammatical parallelisms between adverbial verbs and complement-taking verbs. In Kavalan, adverbial verbs such as manner verbs are reported to parallel complement-taking verbs such as *msiangatu* 'start' and *mrepun* 'finish' in the following respects:

(9) Kavalan (H. Chang 2006a)
    a. they must precede their complements;
    b. they can be inflected for AF and NAF, while their complement verbs observe the AF-only Restriction;
    c. they can take markings for tense/aspect/modality (TAM), while their complement verbs are unmarked for TAM;
    d. they can bear the imperative suffixes, while their complement verb cannot;
    e. they can attract pronominal clitics, while their complement verbs cannot.

Compare:

(10) Complement-taking verbs in Kavalan
    a. m-siangatu=pa=iku   t⟨m⟩ayta   tu   sulal.
        AF-start=FUT=1S.NOM   see⟨AF⟩   OBL   book
        'I will start to read books.'
    b. siangatu-an-ku=pa   t⟨m⟩ayta   ya   sulal
        start-PF-1S.GEN=FUT   see⟨AF⟩   NOM   book
        'I will start to red the book.'

(11) Adverbial verbs in Kavalan (H. Chang 2006a: 46) (=1)
    a. *paqanas*=iku   t⟨em⟩ayta   tu   sulal.
        slow(AF)=1S.N   see⟨AF⟩   OBL   book
        'I read a book slowly.'
    b. *paqanas-an*-ku   t⟨em⟩ayta   ya   sulal.
        slow-PF-1S.GEN   see⟨AF⟩   NOM   book
        'I read the book slowly.'

2.2 Our analysis

There are more grammatical parallelisms observed in other Formosan languages, which lead to a conclusion in support of the complement analysis. For instance, in Paiwan, adverbial verbs and the lexical verbs are connected in the same way that lexical verbs and their complements are linked – both by a linker. Compare:

(12) Paiwan (C. Wu 2005: 11–12)
   a. patagil-aken   a   k-em-an tua kinsa
      start(AF)-1S.NOM LNK   eat-AF OBL meal
      'I start to eat the meal.'
   b. ku-p-in-atagil   a   k-em-an a   kinsa
      1S.GEN-start-ASP.PF   LNK eat-AF NOM meal
      'I have started to eat the meal.'

(13) Paiwan (C. Wu 2005: 11)
   a. na-g⟨em⟩alu-aken   a   k⟨em⟩im   tua hung
      PERF-slowly⟨AF⟩-1S.NOM   LNK search⟨AF⟩   OBL book
      'I searched a book slowly.'
   b. ku-g⟨in⟩alu   a   k⟨em⟩im   a   hung
      1S.GEN-slowly⟨PERF.PF⟩   LNK search⟨AF⟩   NOM book
      'I searched the book slowly.'

In (12a), the aspectual verb *patagil* 'start' is connected to its complement by the linker *a*. Likewise, the manner verb *gemalu* 'slowly' and the lexical verb are linked by *a*, as shown in (13b). The same linking can also be found with their NAF counterparts, as in (12b) and (13b). Moreover, the grammatical asymmetries which are widely observed in Formosan AVCs (e.g. the AF-only restriction) are also attested here (Tang 1999 and C. Wu 2004, 2005).

Similar parallelisms are also attested in Tsou. In Tsou, aspectual verbs and their complement verbs must observe the Focus Harmony Restriction. For instance:

(14) Tsou
   a. mi-'o   ahoi   bon-x   ta   cnxmx.[4]
      AF-1S   start(AF)   eat-AF OBL banana
      'I start eating bananas.'
   b. os-'o   ahoz-a   an-a   'o   cnxmx.
      NAF-1S start-PF   eat-PF NOM banana
      'I start eating the bananas.'

---

4. For typographical convenience, we use the letter x to represent the high mid unrounded vowel ɨ in Tsou.

As shown in (14), the AF aspectual verb *ahoi* requires an AF complement verb *bony* and its NAF counterpart *ahoza* an NAF complement verb *ana*. The same restriction also holds of manner verbs and the lexical verbs, as already shown in (3). In the same fashion, the restriction also applies to frequency verbs and their complement verbs, as shown below:

(15) Tsou

    a. la-ta   asngxc-x eobak-o to   'o'oko.
        HAB-3s often-AF hit-AF OBL children
        'He hits his children often.'

    b. la-ta   asngxc-a eobak-a 'o 'o'oko.
        HAB-3s often-PF hit-PF NOM children
        'He hits the children often.'

In contrast, the Focus Harmony Restriction does not hold of adjuncts. Compare:

(16) Tsou

    a. mi-'o *kaeb-x* ho os-'o   *ait-i* suu.
        AF-1s happy-AF SUB NAF-1s see-LF 2s
        'I am happy when I see you.'

    b. os-'o takuv'-a ho o'a mi-ko *maine'e*.
        NAF-1 worry-PF SUB NEG AF-2 return(AF)
        'I was worried when you did not come home.'

These grammatical parallelisms follow naturally from the complement analysis but are unexpected in the adjunct/conjunct analysis. In addition, the aforementioned embedded NP extraction is also left unexplained in the adjunct/conjunct analysis but is nicely predicted by the complement analysis. Furthermore, the adjunct/conjunct analysis also fails to account for the word order restriction indicated in (9a), that is, the restriction by which adverbial verbs are required to precede the lexical verbs. In the adjunct/conjunct analysis, the reverse word order should be possible. However, the permutation is generally prohibited, as reported in C. Wu (2004), H. Chang (2006a), and C. Li (2009). The restriction, however, naturally falls out in the complement analysis, given that Formosan languages are mostly verb-initial languages. We thus conclude that the syntactic relationship involved in Formosan AVCs is complementation rather than adjunction/conjunction. It should be noted however that the complement analysis might face a problem which was noted in Liu (2003) – lexical verbs appear not to be semantically selected by the adverbial verbs in the normal sense. In Sections 3 and 4, we will tackle this problem and demonstrate that adverbial verbs do impose semantic selection upon the lexical verbs.

3. Syntactic operations

We now turn to the second research question: What syntactic operation is taking place in Formosan AVCs: Verb serialization/control, raising, or something else? In the Formosan literature, AVCs are usually identified as SVCs (L. Huang 1997, H. Chang 2006a, b). In this section, we will first show that the SVC analysis is untenable and that an alternative analysis is necessary.

3.1 Previous analyses: The SVC analysis

In L. Huang (1997), Formosan AVCs are all analyzed as SVCs, regardless of the presence/absence of an intervening linker. In H. Chang (2006a, b), Formosan AVCs without an intervening linker are identified as SVCs, whereas those with an intervening linker are not. The major evidence for the SVC analysis comes from the grammatical parallelisms between SVCs and AVCs, which are virtually equivalent to those indicated in (9):

(17) Grammatical parallelisms between SVCs and AVCs
 a. The first verb can be inflected for AF and NAF, while the second verb observes the AF-only Restriction;
 b. The first verb can bear markings for tense/aspect/modality (TAM), while the second verb is unmarked for TAM;
 c. The first verb can take imperative affixes, while the second verb cannot;
 d. The first verb attracts pronominal clitics, whereas the second verb normally does not.

Take Kavalan for example. Compare:

(18) SVCs in Kavalan (H. Chang 2006b)
 a. m-atiw=iku   m-ara   tu   sunis
    af-go=1s.NOM AF-take OBL child
    'I go and bring a child back.'
 b. qatiw-*an*-ku   m-ara   ya   sunis
    go-PF-1S.GEN   AF-take NOM child
    'I go and bring the child back.'

(19) AVCs in Kavalan (H. Chang 2006a: 7)
 a. *pataz-iku*   s⟨em⟩upas   tu   qRitun
    often(AF)-1S.NOM buff⟨AF⟩   OBL car
    'I buff cars often.'
 b. *pataz-an-ku*   s⟨em⟩upas   ya   qRitun
    often-PF-1S.GEN buff⟨AF⟩   NOM car
    'I buff my car often.'

At first glance, the AVCs in (19) are grammatically parallel to the SVCs in (18): the two verbs are placed one after another without any marker of syntactic dependency, with the first verb taking all the major morphological markings and the second bearing only the default AF morpheme. However, a closer inspection shows that AVCs are distinctive constructions from SVCs, as will be discussed shortly.

3.2 Problems with the SVC analysis

It is generally agreed that a construction can be identified as a SVC if and only if it satisfies all the following conditions (based on Foley & Olsen 1985, Sebba 1987, Baker 1989, Y. Li 1991, Seuren 1991, and Durie 1997):

(20) Diagnostics for SVCs
   a. Verbs or VPs are placed one after another without any marker of syntactic dependency (**the Linkerless Condition**);
   b. All component verbs should be interpreted within the same time frame/the sentential scope of negation, with grammatical markers of temporal reference/negation on one of the verbs or each of them (**the Same TAM/NEG Condition**);
   c. The structural relationship between component verbs or verb phrases is one of subordination rather than coordination (**The Subordination Condition**).
   d. Individual verbs should be lexical and can occur as a main verb in their own right (**the Lexical Verb Condition**);
   e. The first verb does not semantically select the phrase containing the second verb (**The Nonselection Condition**).
   f. Serial verbs must share at least one semantic argument (**The Argument-sharing Condition**).

The Kavalan-type, the Tsou-type, and the Siraya-type languages might satisfy condition (a), i.e. the Linkerless Condition, whereas the Paiwan-type languages will be excluded from serializing languages by this criterion in the first place. Formosan languages exhibiting AVCs can all meet the Same TAM Condition, given that TAM markings typically attach to adverbial verbs and extend their scope to the embedded clause, as illustrated in (13). AVCs will also be fine with the Subordination Condition, given that they involve complementation rather than conjunction, as discussed in the last section. As to the Lexical Verb Condition, the answer is not straightforward. It hinges upon how a lexical verb is defined. If a lexical verb is defined as a verb that can semantically select an argument, AVCs will meet this condition. We will elaborate on this point in the next section. However, conditions (e-f) might be problems.

As will become clear in the next section, an adverbial verb presumably has its own argument structure (though defective). Specifically, an adverbial verb can be analyzed as a one-place predicate:

(21) Argument structure of adverbial verbs
    a. manner verb (process)
    b. frequency verb (event)
    c. epistemic verb (proposition)

In this view, AVCs will fail to satisfy condition (e) and will be disqualified as SVCs. In the same vein, condition (f) will be violated as well. Note that the arguments which adverbial verbs select are different from those selected by lexical verbs: they are verbal arguments such as process/event/proposition rather than nominal arguments such as agent or patient. Accordingly, adverbial verbs will have no arguments to share with the lexical verbs.

As for syntactic operations, AVCs should be also distinguished from SVCs. Cross-linguistically, SVCs typically involve control (Law and Veenstra 1992, Collins 1997, among others). Accordingly, a theme-serial like (22a) will have a structure like (22b):

(22) Haitian   (Law & Veenstra 1992: 197, 202)
    a. Jan pran pen   coupe.
       Jan take bread cut
       'Jan cut the bread.'
    b. [$_{IP}$ Jan$_i$ [$_{VP}$ [$_{V'}$ [$_V$ pran pen$_j$] [$_{VP}$ O$_j$ [$_{VP}$ PRO$_i$ coupe t$_j$.]]]]

In particular, note that the subject and object of the first verb are not syntactically part of the second verb. Thus, in (22), both *Jan* and *pran* are base-generated in the matrix clause rather than derived from the embedded clause.

In contrast, AVCs normally undergo nominal argument movement from the embedded clause, yielding the syntax-semantics mismatches widely observed in the literature (L. Huang 1997, Liu 2003, H. Chang 2006a,b, Holmer 2006). Take frequency verbs for example:

(23) Frequency verbs in Kavalan   (H. Chang 2006a)
    a. *pataz-iku*   s⟨em⟩upas tu qRitun
       often(AF)-1S.NOM buff⟨AF⟩ OBL car
       'I buff cars often.'
    b. *pataz-an-ku*   s⟨em⟩upas ya qRitun
       often-PF-1S.GEN buff⟨AF⟩ NOM car
       'I buff the car often.'

Semantically speaking, the frequency verb *pataz* takes an event as its argument. It follows that the matrix nominal arguments in (23a–b) must be derived from the embedded clauses by nominal movement. To be more specific, the matrix subject in (23a) (represented by the clitic *iku*) is derived by long-distance cliticization, whereas the matrix subject *qRitun* in (23b) is derived by a syntactic process similar to long-distance passives (Wurmbrand 2001). It is obvious that the matrix arguments in AVCs are syntactically part of the adverbial verbs, though they are thematically related to the lexical verbs. The derivations can be roughly represented as follows:

(24) a.

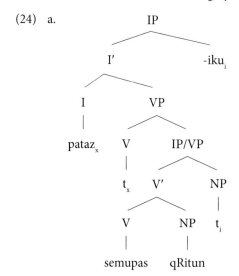

b.

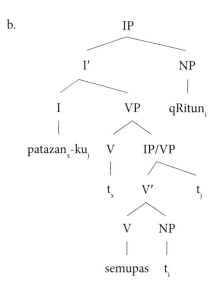

Similar operations can carry over to manner verbs:

(25) Kavalan (H. Chang 2006a: 46) (=1)
    a. *paqanas*=iku t⟨em⟩ayta tu sulal.
       slow(AF)=1S.N see⟨AF⟩ OBL book
       'I read a book slowly.'

b. *paqanas-an*-ku t⟨em⟩ayta ya sulal.
      slow-PF-1S.GEN see⟨AF⟩ NOM book
      'I read the book slowly.'

The movement of the object/patient is evidenced by the following case alternations:

(26) Kavalan
   a. *paqanas-an*-ku t⟨em⟩ayta ya sulal.
      slow-PF-1S.G see⟨AF⟩ NOM book
      'I read the book slowly.' (=1b)
   b. *paqanas-an*-ku t⟨em⟩ayta tu sulal.
      slow-PF-1S.GEN see⟨AF⟩ OBL book
      'I read books slowly.'

The two sentences in (26a–b) are thematically synonymous. The patient of the second verb remains *in situ* in the b-sentence but moves upward to the matrix subject position in the a-sentence. The alternation is in support of the long-distance nominal movement analysis.

Similar alternations are also attested in Amis, as shown below:

(27) Amis   (J. Wu 2006: 288)
   a. Kalamkam-en aku k-um-aˀen k-u hemay.
      fast-UV 1S.GEN eat⟨NEUT⟩ NOM-CN rice
      'I will eat the rice fast.'
   b. Kalamkam-en aku k-um-aˀen t-u hemay.
      fast-UV 1S.GEN eat⟨NEUT⟩ DAT-CN rice
      'I will eat the meal fast.'

It is noteworthy that there are some language-particular manifestations of the significant differences between AVCs and SVCs. Tsou is especially illustrative in this regard. In Tsou, the Focus Harmony Restriction is observed in AVCs, as discussed above. However, it is bypassed in SVCs. Compare:

(28) SVCs in Tsou
   a. os-ˀo tith-a *ma-hafo* to fˀue ˀo yungku
      NAF-1S use-PF AF-carry OBL sweet.potato NOM basket
      'I used the basket to carry sweet potatoes.'
   b. *os-ˀo tith-a *haf-a* to fˀue ˀo yungku
      NAF-1S use-PF carry-PF OBL sweet.potato NOM basket

As shown in the contrast in (28a–b), the second verb can only be inflected for AF in SVCs. In this regard, SVCs in Tsou do not differ from those in other Formosan languages. On the other hand, the parallelism suggests that AVCs should be distinguished from SVCs.

Last but not least, it is noteworthy that adverbial verbs in Tsou bear construction-specific morphology. Cardinal frequency adverbial verbs are typically prefixed with *i'-*, whereas other adverbial verbs are normally prefixed with *a-*. For instance:

(29) Cardinal frequency adverbial prefix in Tsou
    a. mi-ta i'-nxsk-x bait-o to tposx
       AF-3S ADV-once-AF see-AF OBL book
       'He read a book once.'
    b. i-ta i'-nxsk-a ait-i 'o tposx
       NAF-3S ADV-once-PF see-LF NOM book
       'He read the book once.'

(30) General adverbial prefix in Tsou
    a. la-ta a-sngxc-x bait-o to tposx
       HAB-3S ADV-often-AF see-AF OBL book
       'He reads books often.'
    b. la-ta a-sngxc-a ait-i 'o tposx
       HAB-3S ADV-often-PF see-LF NOM book
       'He reads the book often.'

The segmentation of the adverbial prefixes from adverbial verbs receives support from the alternations attested in AVCs. Adverbial prefixes can be replaced by lexical prefixes, giving rise to a morphologically complex verb. For example:

(31) Cardinal adverbial prefix in Tsou
    a. mi-ta *buh*-nxsk-x to tposx
       AF-3S see(AF)-once-AF OBL book
       'He read a book once.'
    b. i-ta *hu*-nxsk-i 'o tposx
       NAF-3S see(PF)-once-LF NOM book
       'He read the book once.'

As shown in (31a–b), adverbial prefixes are replaced by the lexical prefix *buh-* for AF adverbial verbs and *hu-* for NAF adverbial verbs. When the replacement takes place, the original lexical verbs will normally be left out.

Likewise, the prefix *a-* in (30a–b) is also replaceable, though the replacement might result in a slight change in meaning:

(32) Verb complex in Tsou
    te-ko e-sngxc-a 'o te-ko e'e-engh-a
    IRR-2S say-straight-PF NOM IRR-2S speak-use-PF
    'You should get it straight.'

Table 2. AVCs vs. SVCs

Constructions	AVCs	SVCs
Properties		
Whether 1st verb shares argument with 2nd verb	No	Yes
Whether 1st verb s-selects 2nd verb	Yes	No
What syntactic operation is involved	Nominal movement	Control
Whether the FHR is attested (in Tsou)	Yes	No
Whether there is special morphology	Yes (in Tsou)	No

The adverbial prefixes are exclusively used for AVCs; they are not attested elsewhere. This lends strong support to the independence of AVCs.

To sum up, AVCs should be distinguished from SVCs and treated as distinctive constructions.

4. Syntactic status of adverbial verbs

This sections addresses the last research question of this paper: What is the syntactic status of adverbial verbs: Do they occur as functional heads, lexical verbs, or something in between?

4.1 Previous analyses

4.1.1 *Adverbial verbs as functional heads*

Along the lines of Cinque (1999), Holmer (2006) analyzes Seediq adverbials as clause-level functional heads. His analysis is mainly based on the occurrence of voice morphology on adverbials in indicative and negative sentences. In indicative sentences, Seediq voice inflection is basically the same as that of other Formosan languages such as Kavalan, and Paiwan. For example:

(33) Indicative sentences in Seediq (Holmer 2006:90)
    a. skret-an=daha   m-ekuy quwaq salo.
       tight-LF=3PL.GEN AF-tie mouth pot
       'They tie the mouth of the pot tightly.'
    b. gguy-un=misu   s⟨m⟩neru
       secretly-PF=1SG>2SG ⟨AF⟩tell
       'I'll startle you.'

However, Seediq voice inflection is different in negative sentences: AF is not overtly marked, whereas PF is suffixed with -*i*. This has been dubbed as connegative morphology by Holmer. Compare:

(34) Negative sentences in Seediq (Holmer 2006:90)
    a. ini   burux   m-ekan   ka   seddiq cbeyo.
       NEG alone.CNEG AF-eat NOM person long.ago
       'The people of old didn't eat alone.'

    b. ini=daha   trmex-i   m-ekan.
       NEG=3PL.GEN on.its.own-PF.CNEG AF-eat
       'They don't eat chili on their own.'

As noted by Holmer and also discussed above, voice markers attach to adverbial verbs rather than the lexical verbs and occur once per clause. In light of these properties, Holmer treated adverbial verbs in Seediq on a par with the Finnish negative verb as clause-level functional heads.

4.1.2 *Adverbial verbs as predicates/lexical verbs*

As reviewed in Section 2.1.1, Tsai and M. Chang (2003) and Liu (2003) treat manner adverbials in Tsou and Amis as syntactic predicates as well as semantic predicates. Moreover, they hypothesize that the syntactic relationships between adverbial verbs and the lexical verbs develop diachronically from conjunction to adjunction.

In a slightly different vein, Tang (2001) analyzes adverbials in Paiwan as matrix predicates, taking the lexical verbs as their complements. Along a similar line of thought, I elaborate on the categorical status of adverbials in Kavalan and identify them as lexical verbs on the basis of their semantic properties and grammatical behavior (H. Chang 2006a). In particular, I point out that some manner verbs in Kavalan can take NPs as their complements without the help of a lexical verb. For instance:

(35) Kavalan (H. Chang 2006a : 46)
    a. paqasiR tu   *qRitun*
       fast(AF) OBL car
       'He drives fast.'

    b. paqasiR-i-ka ya   *qRitun*
       fast-NAF-IMP NOM car
       'Make the car (go) faster!'

    c. satawaR-ka   tu   *razing*
       careful-IMP(AF) OBL sea
       'Beware of the sea!'

    d. satawaR-i-ka   ya   *sunis-su*
       careful-NAF-IMP NOM child-2s.GEN
       'Take good care of your child!'

This lends strong support to the lexical analysis of adverbials.

4.2 Problems with the previous analyses

4.2.1 *Problems with the functional-head analysis*

Despite its cross-linguistic appeal, the functional-head analysis faces a number of important problems. First, it leaves unexplained the predicative properties of adverbial verbs. This is particularly obvious for manner verbs. In the Formosan languages we have investigated so far, manner verbs are consistently allowed to serve as the main predicate of a clause as well as adverbial modifiers without any modification in their forms. For instance:

(36) Kavalan
    a. m-qasiR   ti   utay
        AF-fast(AF) NOM Utay
        'Utay runs fast.'

    b. m-qasiR   m-RaRiw ti   utay
        AF-fast(AF) AF-run   NOM Utay
        'Utay runs fast.'

(37) Tsou
    a. mi-ta b-utas-o   ho mi-ta eobak-o ta   oko
        AF-3S AF-violent-AF SUB AF-3S hit-AF   OBL child
        'He hit the child violently.'

    b. mi-ta b-utas-o   eobak-o ta   oko
        AF-3S AF-violent-AF hit-AF   OBL child
        'He hit the child violently.'

(38) Amis   (Liu 2003:115)
    a. mi-naqun ci   aki.
        AV-careful NOM aki
        'Aki is careful.'

    b. mi-naqun ci   aki [(a) mi-pidpid tu   lupas].
        AV-careful NOM aki A   AV-pick   ACC peach
        'Aki picked peaches carefully.'

(39) Squliq Atayal   (Hsiao 2004:57)
    a. m-k'ial   qu' Tali.
        AV-violent NOM Tali
        'Tali is violent.'

    b. wal   m-k'ial   m-ihiy Tali qu' Yumin.
        PERF AV-violent AV-beat Tali NOM Yumin
        'Yumin beat Tali violently.'

As shown in (36–39), there appear to be no discernible meaning differences between the instances of manner verbs as main predicates and those as adverbial modifiers.

It is thus difficult to assign them two different entries, one as a lexical verb and another as a functional head. In other words, they seem to be indistinctive from lexical verbs with respect to their forms and meanings and should better be identified as the same category.

Another piece of evidence indicative of the predicative nature of manner adverbial verbs is their ability to take the morphological causative prefix *pa-*. For example:

(40) Kavalan (H. Chang 2006a)
pa-qasiR tu qRitun
CAUS-fast OBL car
'Make the car go faster!'

(41) Paiwan
pa-ka-tjaljav-u a dj⟨em⟩avac
CAUS-INCH-fast LNK walk⟨AF⟩
Lit. 'Make yourself walk faster!'
'Walk faster!'

(42) Mayrinax Atayal (C. Wu, p.c.)
pa-pa-k-hailag-ci' 'i' m-irai cu' kuru'
IRR-CAUS-INCH-fast-1S.NOM LNK AF-drive OBL car
lit.: 'I will make myself drive a car faster!'
'I will drive faster!'

(43) Kanakanavu (C. Wu, p.c.)
ni-pa-para'an=maku a-pa-supulu avia sinat isi,
PF-CAUS-fast=1S.GEN IRR-CAUS-read (AF) Avia book this
maka-sua=cu=ku puei tanasa
MAKA-SO=COS=1S.NOM come.back (AF) home
'I have made Avia quickly read the book, so I can come back home (soon).'

(44) Saisiyat (M. Yeh, p.c.)
pa-k-'alikaeh sowiti' manra:n
CAUS-INCH-fast a.little walk(AF)
'Walk a little faster!'

(45) Truku Seediq
p-slikaw nhari ka tdruy-su
CAUS-fast immediately NOM car-2S.GEN
lit.: 'Make your car go faster immediately!'
'Speed up your car right away!'

This suggests that manner adverbial verbs can represent events and that they can be associated with nominal arguments. In other words, they are lexical rather than functional.

Second, the functional-head analysis cannot correctly predict the presence/absence of the AF-only Restriction and the TAM-less Condition. In the functional-head analysis, adverbial verbs will be said to head their own functional projection: manner verbs will head AspP$_{celerative}$, frequency AspP$_{frequentative}$, and epistemic verbs ModP (Cinque 1999). Accordingly, lower functional projections headed by manner and frequency verbs will be expected to take non-finite complements. This prediction is borne out for manner verbs. As is well-known, the complements taken by manner verbs are subject to the AF-only Restriction and the TAM-less Condition. Nonetheless, as noted by H. Chang (2006a), C. Wu (2006), and C. Li (2007), frequency verbs can take complements which are inflected for NAF and TAM. Compare:

(46) Kavalan (H. Chang 2006a:50)
   a. pataz s⟨em⟩upas-ti-iku tu qRitun
      often(AF) buff⟨AF⟩-ASP-1S.NOM OBL car
      'I buffed a car often.'

   b. pataz *supas-an-ku-ti* ya qRitun
      often(AF) buff-PF-1S.GEN-ASP NOM car
      'I buffed my car often.'

(47) Kanakanavu (C. Wu 2006:13)
   pair-o *a-p-ukusa* avia
   often-imp fut-caus-go (AF) Avia
   'You must often encourage Avia to go!'

(48) Puyuma (C. Li 2007:15)
   m-(k)arayas *nu=pukpuk-aw=ku.*
   AV-often 2SG.GEN=hit-PV=1SG.NOM
   'You often hit me.'

The example in (47) is illuminatingly decisive: the complement verb is prefixed with the future tense marker *a-*, indicating that it is finite rather than nonfinite, contra the prediction made by the functional-head analysis.

Third, adverbial verbs differ from typical functional heads in their morphological markings. As repeatedly mentioned in the preceding sections, adverbial verbs can be inflected for voice and imperative. In contrast, except for Tsou, typical functional verbs are not eligible for voice and imperative inflection across Formosan languages. Compare:

(49) Kavalan H. Chang 1997:111)
   a. *mai*=iku t-em-ayta tu razat 'nay.
      NEG=1S.NOM see-AV ACC person that
      'I did not see that man.'

   b. *mai* tayta-an-ku ya razat 'nay.
      NEG see-PV-1S.GEN NOM person that
      'I did not see that man.'

(50) Seediq (H. Chang 1997:109)
 a. *wada-ku* beebu laqi.
   PST-1S.NOM beat (AF) child
   'I beat a child.'
 b. *wada*-ku-na bube-un na pawan ka yaku.
   PST-1S.NOM-3S.GEN beat-PV GEN Pawan NOM 1S
   'Pawan beat me.'

(51) Mayrinax Atayal (L. Huang 1995:167–168)
 a. kaa nubuwag cu' quwaw.
   NEG drink(AF) ACC.NRF wine
   'Don't drink wine!'
 b. kaa tuting-i 'i' ba'ay.
   NEG beat -PF NOM Ba'ay
   'Don't beat Ba'ay!'

The negator *mai* in Kavalan and the TAM marker *wada* in Seediq should be identified as clause-level functional heads, since they occupy the highest position of the clauses and are able to attract pronominal clitics/affixes. However, they are not inflected for voice; the voice distinctions are marked on the lexical verbs following them. Similar observations hold for the imperative negator *kaa* in Mayrinax Atayal, as illustrated in (51). The voice options are by no means arbitrary; they can be semantically or syntactically motivated. Our observation is that the more lexical a verb is, the more voice options it will entertain. We will return to this issue in the next section.

4.2.2 *Problems with the lexical-verb analysis*

If adverbial verbs are not functional heads, can they appear as lexical verbs? The answer to this question is not straightforward. For adverbial verbs that are able to serve as main predicates (e.g. manner verbs), the lexical verb analysis may be justified. But for adverbial verbs that lack of this property, there is no clear-cut grammatical evidence for the lexical-verb analysis. Frequency verbs are a case in point. Frequency verbs are presumably semantic predicates, taking events as their arguments. Take 'often' for example: it can be either a one-place predicate or a two-place predicate (de Swart 1993).

(52) a. often (event) Cardinal reading
  b. often (event$_1$, event$_2$) Quantificational reading

However, there seems to be no firm grammatical evidence which can be used to determine the syntactic status of frequency verbs. Unlike manner verbs, frequency verbs cannot occur as main predicates, although frequency verbs that are inflected for NAF parallel manner verbs in almost every aspect of their grammatical behavior: they can attract TAM markers and pronominal clitics/affixes; they require their complement verbs to be marked only for AF and unmarked for TAM (H. Chang 2006a, C. Wu 2006, C. Li 2007). Compare:

(53) Tsou
    a. la-ta   *asngxc-x* eobak-o to   oʹoko.
       HAB-3S often-AF hit-AF OBL children
       'He hits his children often.' (=15a)
    b. *la-ta *asngxc-x* ho la-ta   eobak-o to oʹoko.
       HAB-3S often-AF and HAB-3S hit-AF OBL children

Still, there is a grammatical property which might reveal the syntactic status of adverbial verbs. This concerns voice inflection. As mentioned in the previous section, the voice option of a verb correlates with its syntactic status. As is well-known, a lexical verb can entertain up to four voice options. This is best illustrated by verbs of cause-motion (see also H. Huang & S. Huang 2007). For instance:

(54) Tsou   (Zeitoun 2000:93–4; glosses mine.)
    a. mo *mo*-si ta pangka to emi ʹo amo
       AF AF-put OBL table OBL wine NOM father
       'Father puts wine on a table.'
    b. i-si   *si-a* ta pangka to amo ʹo emi
       NAF-3S put-PF OBL table OBL father NOM wine
       'The wine is put on a table by Father.'
    c. i-si   *si-i* ta amo ta emi ʹo pangka
       NAF-3S put-LF OBL father OBL wine NOM table
       lit.: 'The table is put wine by Father.'
       'Father puts wine on the table.'
    d. i-si   *si-eni* ta emi ta amo
       NAF-3S put-BF OBL wine OBL father
       lit.: 'He is put wine for by Father.'
       'Father puts wine for him.'

The verb meaning 'put' can be inflected for AF (*mosi*), as in (54a), for PF (*sia*), as in (54b), for LF (*sii*) as in (54c), and for B/IF (*sieni*), as in (54d).

In contrast, functional categories are normally unmarked for voice, with Tsou as the only exception, as noted above. Interestingly enough, adverbial verbs sit in between: they tolerate at most two voice options, i.e., AF and PF. For example:

(55) Tsou
    a. mi-ta *b-utas-o*   eobak-o ta oko
       AF-3S AF-violent-AF hit-AF OBL child
       'He hit the child violently.' (=38b)

b. i-ta   *utasv-a*   eobak-a 'e   oko
   NAF-3S violent-PF hit-PF   NOM   child
   'He hit the child violently.'

c. *i-ta   *utasv-i*   eobak-i ta   oko   'e   eona   bonx
   NAF-3S violent-LF hit-LF   OBL   child NOM   be.at   eat
   Intended for 'He hit the child violently at the restaurant.'

d. *i-ta   *utasv-eni* eobak-neni ta   oko   'e   kaapana
   NAF-3S violent-IF hit-IF   OBL   child NOM   stick
   Intended for 'He hit the child violently with the stick.'

As shown in (55a–b), the adverbial verbs can only exhibit a two-way voice distinction: AF (*butaso*) versus PF (*utasva*). The options of LF and B/IF are banned, as illustrated in (55c–d), though they are logically possible.

The morphological restriction is not absolute, though; it will be relaxed if the adverbial verbs function as main predicates. Compare:

(56) Tsou

a. mi-ta *b-utas-o*   ho   mi-ta poe'oh-x   ta   fatu
   AF-3S AF-violent-AF   and AF-3S remove-AF OBL   stone
   'He removed a stone with great effort.'

b. i-ta   *utasv-a*   'e   fatu ho   i-ta   poe'oh-a
   NAF-3S violent-PF NOM   stone and NAF-3S remove-PF
   'He removed the stone with great effort.'

c. i-ta   *utasv-eni* 'e   fatu ho   i-ta   poe'oh-a
   NAF-3S violent-IF NOM   stone and NAF-3S remove-PF
   'He removed the stone with great effort.'

The predicative status of adverbial verbs in (56) is evident. In (55a–b), where adverbial verbs occur as adverbial modifiers, there is only one instance of marking for TAM and a pronominal argument. In (56), however, there are two instances of TAM/pronominal marking: one for adverbial verbs and the other for the lexical verbs, with the conjunction *ho* intervening between them. This indicates that the sentences in (56) involve a bi-clausal structure and that adverbial verbs surface as main predicates in (56), as opposed to those in (55).

It is not immediately clear why the scalar voice inflection arises. However, given that it is regular and systematic, it suggests that adverbial verbs are distinct from functional heads on the one hand and from lexical verbs on the other. This is the line we would like to pursue shortly.

4.3   An alternative analysis: Adverbial verbs as an in-between category

Before proceeding any further, let us summarize the problems which the previous analyses face:

Table 3. Problems with the previous analyses

Analysis Property	Functional-head analysis	Lexical-verb analysis
Adverbial verb as main predicate	Problematic	OK (for manner verbs) Problematic (for frequency verbs)
Adverbial verbs bear rich semantic content	Problematic	OK
Evading AF-only Restriction and TAM-less Problematic Condition for complement verbs	OK	
Two-way voice inflection restriction (AF and PF only) for adverbial verbs	Problematic	Problematic

These problems can be resolved if we identify adverbial verbs as an intermediate category between functional category and lexical category. In this view, the distinctions between AVCs and SVCs summarized in Table 2 will also fall out naturally. It will be no surprise that adverbials occur as verbs in Tsou but bear special functional morphology in a similar manner as adverbs suffixed with -*ly* in English and adverbs suffixed with -*ment* in French.

As far as their hybrid nature is concerned, Formosan adverbial verbs are comparable to light verbs. As noted by Butt & Geuder (2001:355–356), adverbial modifiers and light verbs are both semantically dependent: Although they have their own argument structures, they must be interpreted in conjunction with the lexical verbs. This semi-lexical nature leads to the general patterns found across Formosan languages, that is, adverbial verbs are typically followed by lexical verbs, even when they occur as main predicates. Thus, the semantic structure of an adverbial verb will be represented in a Neo-Davidsonian style along the line of Parsons (1990), viz., it involves semantic conjunction (Tsai & M. Chang 2003 and Liu 2003). Take manner verbs for example:

(57) Semantic structure of a manner verb
Manner verb (process) & lexical verb (actor, (patient))

As shown in (57), a manner verb selects as its argument a process, which is expressed by the lexical verb. Despite the uniform semantics of AVCs, their syntactic realizations vary across Formosan languages. The syntactic structure is largely isomorphic to its semantic structure in the Paiwan-type, as adverbial verbs are connected to the lexical verbs by a linker. In the Kavalan-type, however, there arise noticeable syntax-semantics mismatches: adverbial modification is done through complementation rather than conjunction. In the Tsou-type, either structure is attested.

Owing to insufficient grammatical evidence, our discussion of this issue is limited and our analysis is far from mature. We would like to leave it for future research.

5. Concluding remarks

In the preceding sections, we have shown that: (i) AVCs mainly involve complementation rather than adjunction/conjunction; (ii) AVCs are distinctive constructions; their syntactic operations might be either raising or long-distance passive; and (iii) adverbial verbs are likely to be semi-lexical in nature. These findings have far-reaching implications. Let us consider first the typology of adverbials. While adverbials surface as adverbs/adjuncts in familiar languages like English, they typically occur as verbs in Formosan languages. This categorical division leads to a number of systematic grammatical differences widely observed between these two types of languages. The most noticeable differences are that Formosan adverbials bear verbal morphology and take the lexical verbs as their complements, whereas their English counterparts are unmarked for verbal morphology and do not take complements. In this sense, AVC can be regarded as a typological feature.

Let us now turn to the theory of adverbials. It appears that Cinque's analysis of adverbials as functional heads/specifiers does not work out nicely for Formosan languages (see also Tang 2008). In particular, it fails to account for the occurrence of Formosan adverbials as main predicates and the possibility for Formosan frequency adverbials to take finite clauses as their complements. From this perspective, Cinque's theory might require modification.

Many research questions arise in the wake of this study. The first concerns the nature of voice. Our finding that voice is able to induce long-distance nominal movement calls into question the standard analysis of voice as derivational (Starosta, Pawley, and Reid 1982). The scalar voice inflection also deserves more attention. In a recent paper, I attempt to account for the phenomenon in terms of what I dub the Split VoiceP Hypothesis (H. Chang 2008). In this analysis, voice is divided into two broad categories, namely, Agent voice (AV) versus Undergoer Voice (UV), with the voice morphology of each category heading a voice phrase (VoiceP). Furthermore, the UV category is argued to comprise two projections – an applicative phrase (ApplP) embedded to a higher VoiceP, with the applicative head responsible for the thematic operation of turning an oblique argument into a core argument (i.e. the applied object) through applicative feature checking and the voice head checking and attracting the applied object to its Spec position so that the applied object can move further upward to a case position. Since adverbial verbs do not involve thematic operations such as applicativization, it is reasonable to assume that they typically sit between the ApplP and the VoiceP. It follows that they can only be inflected for the two-way voice inflection.

Last but not least, recall the clitic-climbing and long-distance nominal movement as well as the "nonfinite" features of the complement clauses attested in AVCs. All of these properties hint at the existence of restructuring (Wurmbrand 2001, Cinque 2006). A closer look at this is also desirable.

Abbreviations

(The abbreviations listed below basically follow the Leipzig Glossing Rules.)

1.	first person pronoun
2.	second person
3.	third person pronoun
ACC	accusative
AF	Actor focus
ASP	aspect
BF	Benefactive focus
CAUS	causative
CN	common noun
DAT	dative
FUT	future tense
GEN	genitive
HAB	habitual
IF	instrumental focus
IMP	imperative
INCH	inchoative
IRR	irrealis
LF	locative focus
LOC	locative
LNK	linker
NAF	Non-Actor focus
NEG	negation
NEUT	neutral voice
NOM	nominative
OBL	oblique
PF	Patient focus
PFV/PERF/	perfective
PL	plural
PST	past tense
RED	reduplication
REL	relativizer
S	singular
SUB	subordinator
TAM	tense, aspect, and modal
TNS	tense
UV	Undergoer voice

References

Adelaar, K.A. 2004. The coming and going of 'lexical prefixes' in Siraya. *Language and Linguistics* 5(2): 333–362.
Baker, M. 1989. Object sharing and projections in serial verb constructions. *Linguistic Inquiry* 20: 513–553.
Butt, M. & Geuder, W. 2001. On the (semi)lexical status of light verbs. In *Semi-lexical Categories: The Function of Content Words and the Content of Functional Words*, N. Cover & H.C. van Riemsdjik (eds), 323–370. Berlin: Mouton de Gruyter.
Chang, H.Y. 1997. Voice, case, and agreement in Seediq and Kavalan. PhD dissertation, National Tsing Hua University, Hsinchu.
Chang, H.Y. 2005. Restructuring in Tsou. Paper presented at the 12th Annual Conference of Austronesian Formal Linguistics Association (AFLA-12), UCLA, April 30–May 2.
Chang, H.Y. 2006a. The guest playing host: Adverbial modifiers as matrix verbs in Kavalan. In *Clause Structure and Adjuncts in Austronesian Languages*, H.-M. Gaertner, P. Law & J. Sabel (eds), 43–82. Berlin: Mouton de Gruyter.
Chang, H.Y. 2006b. Syntax-semantics mismatches and complex predicate formation in Formosan languages. Invited speech delivered at AFLA-13, National Tsing Hua University, Hsinchu, Taiwan.
Chang, H.Y. 2008. Focus marking and phrase structure in Tsou. Paper presented at AFLA-15, University of Sydney, July 1–2.
Cinque, G.. 1999. *Adverbs and Functional Heads*. Oxford: OUP.
Cinque, G. 2006. *Restructuring and Functional Heads*. Oxford: OUP.
Collins, C. 1997. Argument sharing in serial verb constructions. *Linguistic Inquiry* 28: 84–119.
Durie, M. 1997. Grammatical structures in verb serialization. In *Complex Predicates*, A. Alsina, J. Bresnan & P. Sells (eds), 289–354. Stanford CA: CSLI.
Ernst, T. 2002. *The Syntax of Adjuncts*. Cambridge: CUP.
Foley, W.A. & Olson, M. 1985. Clausehood and verb serialization. In *Grammar inside and outside the Clause: Some Approaches to Theory from the Field*, J. Nichols & A. Woodbury (eds), 17–60. Cambridge: CUP.
Holmer, A. 2006. Seediq–adverbial heads in a Formosan language. In *Clause Structure and Adjuncts in Austronesian Languages*, H.-M. Gaertner, P. Law & J. Sabel (eds), 83–124. Berlin: Mouton de Gruyter.
Hsiao, S., I-Ling. 2004. Adverbials in Squliq Atayal. MA thesis, National Tsing Hua, Hsinchu.
Huang, C.-T. James. 1982. Logical Relations in Chinese and the Theory of Grammar. PhD dissertation, MIT.
Huang, L.M. 1995. *A Study of Mayrinax Syntax*. Taipei: The Crane Publishing.
Huang, L.M. 1997. Serial verb constructions in some Formosan languages: A typological view. Paper presented at the Eighth International Conference on Austronesian Linguistics, Academia Sinica, Taipei, December 28–30.
Huang, H. & Huang, S. 2007. Lexical perspectives on voice constriction in Tsou. *Oceanic Linguistics* 46(2): 424–455.
Jackendoff, R. 1972. *Semantic Interpretation in Generative Grammar*. Cambridge MA: The MIT Press.
Law, P. & Veenstra, T. 1992. On the structure of serial verb constructions. *Linguistic Analysis* 22: 185–217.

Li C. 2009. On lexical prefixes in Saaroa. Ms, National Tsing Hua University, Hsinchu, Taiwan.
Li, P., Jen-kuei. 2003. Verbs or adverbs in Thao? Paper presented at the second Workshop on Formosan Languages, Academia Sinica, November 1–2.
Li, Y. 1991. On deriving serial verb constructions. In *Serial Verbs: Grammatical, Comparative and Cognitive Approaches* [Studies in the Sciences of Language Series 8], C. Lefebvre (ed.), 103–135. Amsterdam: John Benjamins.
Liu, Emma En-hsing. 2003. Conjunction and modification in Amis. M.A. thesis: National Tsing Hua University, Hsinchu.
Nojima, M. 1996. Lexical prefixes of Bunun verbs. *Journal of the Linguistic Society of Japan* 110: 1–27.
Parsons, Terence. 1990. *Events in the Semantics of English: A Study in Subatomic Semantics*. Cambridge MA: The MIT Press.
Radetzky, P.K. 2006. The semantics of the verbal complex, with particular reference to Saaroa. Paper presented at 10-ICAL, Palawan, the Philippines.
Sebba, M. 1987. *The Syntax of Serial Verbs: An Investigation into Serialization in Sranan and Other Languages* [Creole Language Library 2]. Amsterdam: John Benjamins.
Seuren, P. 1991. The definition of serial verbs. In *Development and Structures of Creole Languages: Essays in Honor of Derek Bickerton* [Creole Language Library 9], F. Byrne & T. Huebner (eds), 193–205. Amsterdam: John Benjamins.
Su, Y. 2008. Adverbials in Takituduh Bunun. MA thesis, National Tsing Hua University, Hsinchu, Taiwan.
de Swart, Henriëtte. 1993. *Adverbs of Quantification: A Generalized Quantifier Approach*. New York NY: Garland.
Tang, C.J. 1999. On clausal complements in Paiwan. *Selected Papers from the Eighth International Conference on Austronesian Linguistics*, 529–578. Taipei: Academia Sinica.
Tang, C.J. 2001. Functional categories and adverbial expressions: A case study of Paiwan and Tsou. NSC project report.
Tang, C.J. 2008. Specifiers vs. non-specifiers: Evidence from adjuncts in Formosan languages, Chinese and English. Paper presented at A Dialogue Between Historical Linguistics and Theoretical Linguistics, July 14–16, Academia Sinica.
Tsai, W.D. & Chang, M.Y. 2003. Two types of Wh-adverbials: A typological study of how and why in Tsou. In *The Linguistic Variations Yearbook*, Vol.3, P. Pica & J. Rooryck (eds), 213–236. Amsterdam: John Benjamins.
Tsai, W.D. 2007. Conjunction reduction and its origin: A comparative study of A. Tsou & S. Atayal. *Oceanic Linguistics* 46(2): 585–602.
Tsuchida, S. 1990. Classificatory prefixes of Tsou verbs. *Tokyo University Working Papers* 89: 17–52.
Tsuchida, S. 2000. Lexical prefixes and prefix harmony in Siraya. In *Grammatical Analysis: Morphology, Syntax, and Semantics: Studies in Honor of Stanley Starosta*, V.P. de Guzman & B.W. Bender (eds), 109–128. Honolulu HI: University of Hawai'i Press.
Wu, C. 2004. A Study of Lexical Categories in Paiwan. MA thesis, National Chung Cheng University, Chiayi, Taiwan.
Wu, C. 2005. Adverbials in Paiwan. Ms, National Tsing Hua University, Hsinchu, Taiwan.
Wu, C. 2006. Verb serialization in Kanakanavu. Ms, National Tsing Hua University, Hsinchu, Taiwan.

Wu, C. 2007. Prefix copy in Kanakanavu. Ms, National Tsing Hua University, Hsinchu, Taiwan.
Wu, J.J. 2006. Verb Classification, Case Marking, and Grammatical Relations in Amis. PhD dissertation, the State University of New York at Buffalo, New York.
Wurmbrand, S. 2001. *Infinitives: Restructuring and Clause Structure*. Berlin: Mouton de Gruyter.
Zeitoun, E. 2000. *A Reference Grammar of Tsou*. Taipei: Yuan-Liou Publishing. (In Chinese).

Specification and inversion
Evidence from Malagasy*

Ileana Paul
University of Western Ontario

This paper analyzes specificational sentences in Malagasy and shows that such sentences involve obligatory inversion, marked by the topic particle *dia*. I argue that the topicalized element is a small clause predicate that inverts with its subject. Two competing analyses of this inversion are compared and contrasted. I conclude with a brief comparison of Malagasy and Tagalog.

1. Introduction

The goal of this paper is to investigate the syntax of specificational sentences in Malagasy. In particular, I am interested in examples such as those given in (1).[1]

(1) a. *Ny mahafinaritra dia izany vaovao izany.*
　　　 DET AT.happy　　　 TOP that news　 that
　　　 'What is pleasing is the news.'

　　 b. *Ny nahatongavany　　　dia omaly.*
　　　 DET PST.CT.arrive.3(GEN) TOP yesterday
　　　 'When he arrived was yesterday.'　　　　　　　　　　　[Rajaona 1972: 68]

---

* This paper would not have been possible without the help of the following people: Emma Mamifarananahary, Hasina Mihaingosoa, Dina Rakoto-Ramambason, Hanta Rakotoarivony, Georges Ralaisoa, Vololona Rasolofoson, Francine Razafimboaka, and Raphael Mercado. Unless otherwise indicated, all data are from my own fieldwork. I also acknowledge the very helpful comments and questions from two anonymous reviewers. Finally, I would also like to acknowledge the feedback from Diane Massam, Matt Pearson, Eric Potsdam and Lisa Travis, as well as from participants at the Stanford Austrofest 2005, AFLA XIV, and audiences at McGill, University of Toronto and University of Western Ontario. Any errors are my own. This research was supported by the Canada Research Chair program and a SSHRC Standard Research Grant (410-2005-1758).

1. Native speakers initially judge these examples to be slightly marked. I have found, however, several examples in written texts – a sample is provided in the appendix.

In these examples, the predicate (e.g. *ny mahafinaritra* 'what is pleasing' in (1a)) is a headless relative marked with the definite determiner *ny* and appears in the topic position. I show that in Malagasy, specificational sentences always involve inversion, as indicated by the topic particle *dia*. Moreover, I compare two analyses of this inversion. According to the first (Paul 2008), inversion results from the definiteness of the predicate. According to the second, based on den Dikken (2006), inversion is triggered by a null predicate within the headless relative.

2. Basic facts about Malagasy

Malagasy is a VOS language that lacks an overt copula – thus any lexical category can be the matrix predicate. Moreover, as is well known since Keenan (1976), subjects must be (formally) definite. Finally, Malagasy is famous for its complex grammatical voice system. The voice system is important for this paper, so I give a brief introduction here. Basically, there are three voices, as marked by morphology on the verb: Actor Topic, Theme Topic and Circumstantial Topic (examples from Keenan 1976: 256–257).

(2) a. Actor Topic: Agent is subject
    Manasa lamba Rasoa.
    AT.wash cloth Rasoa
    'Rasoa is washing clothes.'

b. Theme Topic: Theme is subject
    Sasan-dRasoa ny lamba.
    TT.wash-Rasoa DET cloth
    'The clothes are washed by Rasoa.'

c. Circumstantial Topic: Oblique is subject
    Anasan-dRasoa lamba ity savony ity.
    CT.wash-Rasoa cloth this soap this
    'This soap is being washed clothes with by Rasoa.'

For a more detailed discussion and analysis of this system, see Pearson (2005).
    The core examples in this paper are of nominal predication, so I turn to that topic in the next section.

2.1 Nominal predicates

Malagasy has what appears to be a Definiteness Restriction on the predicate position, such that nominal predicates are usually indefinite, even when semantically definite.

(3) a. [predicate *Mpanjaka*] [subject *Rakoto*].
           king   Rakoto
       'Rakoto is/was (the) king.'

    b. *Vadiko   izy*.
       spouse.1SG(GEN) 3(NOM)
       'S/he is my spouse.'

The example in (3b) is all the more striking because in a non-predicate position *vadiko* 'my spouse' must occur with a determiner (*ny vadiko* 'the my spouse').

As a result of the Definiteness Restriction, the sentences in (4) are ungrammatical: The predicate in (4a) is headed by a determiner and in (4b), the predicate is a proper name, *Rakoto*.

(4) a. **Ny   vadiko   Rakoto*
       DET spouse.1SG(GEN) Rakoto
       'Rakoto is my spouse.'

    b. *Rakoto Rabe
       'Rabe is Rakoto.'

This restriction raises the question: How are identity statements and specificational sentences expressed in Malagasy?

2.2 Definite nominal predicates

There appear to be two main strategies to obviate the Definiteness Restriction on predicates. First, if the subject is headed by the anaphoric determiner *ilay* or is a demonstrative pronoun, the predicate can be definite (compare (4a) and (5b)).

(5) a. *Izaho ity*.
       1SG   this
       'This/it is me.'   (e.g. pointing to a picture or when at the door)

    b. *Ny vadiko   ilay olona teto   omaly*.
       DET spouse.1SG(GEN) DEF person PST.here yesterday
       'The person who was here yesterday is my spouse.'   [Rajaona 1972: 68]

The reason for this exception is unclear and I set it aside here, but Rajaona notes that these are not true identity statements, but presentatives.

The second, and more productive, strategy is to use the topic marker *dia*.

(6) *Rakoto dia Rabe.*
    Rakoto TOP Rabe
    'Rabe is Rakoto.'

In the remainder of this paper, I focus on examples such as (6), and I propose that a nominal predicate (here *Rakoto*) has been topicalized.

3. The *dia* construction

Keenan (1976) notes that the particle *dia* normally marks topicalized elements.

(7) *Rakoto dia manasa lamba.*
    Rakoto TOP AT.wash cloth
    'Rakoto, he is washing clothes.'

As we have already seen, *dia* also occurs in many examples of nominal predication, where the predicate appears in the topic position. These examples can be divided into two groups. In the first, the predicate is a common noun (8a) or a proper name (8b).

(8) a. *Ny filoha dia Ravalomanana.*
       DET president TOP Ravalomanana
       'Ravalomanana is the president.'
    b. *Spiderman dia i Tobey Maguire ao amin'ilay sary mihetsika.*
       Spiderman TOP Tobey Maguire there P'DEF picture move
       'Spiderman is (played by) Tobey Maguire in this film.'

In the second group, the predicate is a headless relative (a predicate headed by the determiner *ny*). Note that in these examples, the post-*dia* element can be of any category.[2]

(9) a. *Ny tonga dia [ny ankizy]*$_{DP}$.
       DET arrive TOP DET child
       'The ones who arrived are children.'
    b. *Ny nahatongavany dia [tamin'ny Talata]*$_{PP}$.
       DET PST.CT.arrive.3(GEN) TOP PST.P'DET Tuesday
       'When he arrived was on Tuesday.'
    c. *Ny ataon-dRabe dia [manasa lamba]*$_{VP}$.
       DET TT.do.GEN-Rabe TOP AT.wash cloth
       'What Rabe is doing is washing clothes.'
    d. *Ny nariny dia [lafo]*$_{AP}$.
       DET PST.TT.lost.3(GEN) TOP expensive
       'What he lost was expensive.'
    e. *Ny tsy fantatro dia*
       DET NEG know.1SG(GEN) TOP
       [hoe iza no tonga]$_{CP}$.
       COMP who FOC arrive
       'What I don't know is who arrived.'

---

2. There is some inter-speaker variation in the possibility of an indefinite DP in examples such as (9a). Although some speakers (including one of the anonymous reviewers) prefer a definite DP, other speakers accept an indefinite.

Rajaona (1972: 67–84) discusses examples such as these and argues that the first element is the predicate and the second is the subject; he does not say anything about *dia*. In other words, his discussion seems to indicate that these examples have the standard predicate>subject word order of Malagasy. It can be shown, however, that in these examples, the normal new>old order has been reversed. The particle *dia* therefore plays an important role and also appears to still be a marker of topicalization.

(10) a. *Tonga ny ankizy.*
      arrive DET child
      'The children *arrived*.' (and not left)

   b. *Ny tonga dia ny ankizy.*
      DET arrive TOP DET child
      '*The children* arrived.' (and not the adults)

For example, *ny ankizy* 'the children' in (10b) is focused, while the predicate *tonga* 'arrive' is focused in (10a). (10b) can therefore be the answer to the question 'Who arrived?', but (10a) cannot. Drawing on similar observations, Dez (1980: Tome I, 304–306) criticizes Rajaona's analysis and claims that whatever is to the right of *dia* is the predicate. In what follows, I combine aspects of both Rajaona's and Dez' analyses.

4. Specification vs. predication

Before presenting my analysis, I discuss some parallels between the *dia* construction and pseudoclefts (Higgins 1979). As has long been noted, English pseudoclefts allow predicational and specificational readings.

(11) What Pervez is is interesting.   (ambiguous)
    i. The job that Pervez has is interesting.   (predicational)
    ii. Pervez is interesting.   (specificational)

The Malagasy *dia* construction also permits both readings (but I have not found any truly ambiguous examples parallel to English).

(12) a. *Ny nomeko azy dia ity peratra ity.*
      DET PST.give.1SG(GEN) 3(ACC) TOP this ring this
      'What I gave him was this ring.'   (specificational)

   b. *Ny nomeko azy dia lafo.*
      DET PST.give.1SG(GEN) 3(ACC) TOP expensive
      'What I gave him was expensive.'   (predicational)

These two readings are described below (see Paul 2008 for more detailed discussion).

4.1 Specification

In the specificational reading the pre-*dia* XP sets up a variable and the post-*dia* XP supplies the value for this variable.

(13) a. *Ny ilaiko dia fiara sy trano.*
DET need.1SG(GEN) TOP car and house
'What I need is a car and a house.'

b. {x: I need(x)} = {car, house}

Specifying the value for the variable is like enumerating items on a list: 'The list of things I need contains two items: A car and a house.' In English, the free relative sets up a variable, the value is supplied by post-copular XP. In other words, the variable is created by *wh*-movement.

(14) a. What Sandy is is important to herself.
b. Sandy is x, x = important to herself

In the Malagasy examples under consideration, there is no overt *wh*-word. Instead, the variable is set up by voice morphology, and the value is supplied by post-*dia* XP. For example, if the voice morphology is Actor Topic, as in (15a), the variable is an agent. Other examples of this "voice connectivity" are provided in (15b,c).

(15) a. ActorTopic (≈active): the agent
Ny manasa lamba dia Rabe.
DET AT.wash cloth TOP Rabe
'Who is washing clothes is Rabe.'

b. ThemeTopic (≈passive): the theme
Ny sasan-dRabe dia ny lambany.
DET TT.wash.GEN.Rabe TOP DET cloth.3(GEN)
'What Rabe is washing are his clothes.'

c. CircumstantialTopic (≈special passive): a circumstance
Ny anasan-dRabe lamba dia ny savony.
DET CT.wash.GEN.Rabe cloth TOP DET soap
'What Rabe is washing clothes with is the soap.'

Given that voice morphology plays the role of *wh*-movement, we have indirect evidence in favour of the A-bar analysis of voice ("wh-agreement"), as recently argued for by Pearson (2005).

The important role played by voice can also be seen in the following examples, discussed by Rajaona (1972: 75).

(16) a. *Ny tsy tiako dia ny tsy nahafahany fanadinana.*
DET NEG like.1SG(GEN) TOP DET NEG PST.CT.pass.3(GEN) exam
'What I don't like is his not passing the exam.'

b. *Ny   tsy   nahafahany   fanadinana dia
    DET NEG   PST.CT.pass.3(GEN)   exam   TOP
    ny   tsy   tiako.
    DET NEG   like.1SG(GEN)

To explain the contrast above, Rajaona claims that what he calls the predicate (the pre-*dia* XP) must have greater "extension". I believe that it is easier to understand the contrast as arising from the specificational character of this construction: The variable must be specified by an element of the correct value. In (16a), for example, the variable is the theme of *tiana* 'loved', as marked by Theme Topic morphology; the value is the event of him not passing the exam. Since it is possible to not like an event, the sentence is grammatical. In (16b), on the other hand, the variable is some circumstance related to the event of him not passing the exam (due to the Circumstantial Topic morphology); my not liking cannot fill this role and the sentence is ungrammatical (or perhaps uninterpretable). These examples illustrate an important difference between Malagasy and English: Specificational sentences in Malagasy are not reversible, unlike in English.[3] I return to this difference later.

4.2 Predication

I now turn to the predicational reading. Here, the pre-*dia* XP is simply an argument and the post-*dia* XP is predicated of this argument.

(17) a. *Ny nolazain-dRabe   dia marina.*
         DET PST.TT.say.GEN-Rabe TOP true
         'What Rabe said is true.'
     b. Rabe said(x) & true(x)

On the predicational reading, we do not learn what Rabe said, we simply learn that whatever it was, it is true. In these examples, the pre-*dia* XP is a DP argument (not a

---

3. Dez (1980: Tome I, 306) gives an example of a reversible specificational clause, but I have not been able to replicate his judgements with other speakers.

   (i) *ny tiako   dia ny mitsangatsangana.*
        DET like.1SG(GEN) TOP DET AT.walk
        'What I like is going for a walk.'
   (ii) %*ny mitsangatsangana dia ny tiako.*

True identity statements, however, are reversible:

   (iii) a. *Diego dia Antsiranana.*
             'Diego is Antsiranana.'
         b. *Antsiranana dia Diego.*
             'Antsiranana is Diego.'

predicate) and can appear in other argument positions; topicalization is therefore optional, as illustrated below.

(18) a. *Ny   nomeko   azy   dia lafo.*
         DET PST.TT.give.1SG(GEN) 3(ACC) TOP expensive
         'What I gave him was expensive.'

     b. *Lafo   ny   nomeko   azy.*
         expensive DET PST.TT.give.1SG(GEN) 3(ACC)
         'What I gave him was expensive.'

Because my focus in this paper is on specification, I set the predicational examples aside.

5. Structure

Before turning to the analyses, I mention some relevant facts about the structure of the *dia* construction.[4] As a starting point, it is easy to see that the pre-*dia* XP is topicalized – it appears immediately before the topic particle. The position of the post-*dia* XP is less obvious. In this section, I show that the post-*dia* XP is low in the structure, within the VP (i.e. it is not the matrix subject).[5]

5.1 Post-dia XP ≠ subject

In order to test for the position of the post-*dia* XP, I first turn to data illustrating modal and adverb placement. Malagasy has pre-VP elements (e.g *tokony* 'should') and post-VP elements (e.g. *foana* 'always'). Their respective positions can be seen in (19).

(19) a. *Tokony hilalao   baolina ny   ankizy.*
          should AT.play   ball   DET child
          'The children should be playing ball.'

     b. *Milalao baolina foana   ny   ankizy.*
         AT.play ball   always   DET child
         'The children are always playing ball.'

---

4. Most analyses of inversion provide data from extraction as evidence for a certain structure. For reasons internal to Malagasy syntax, I am unable to provide parallel data. First, extraction in Malagasy is highly restricted – only subjects and certain adjuncts can extract. Second, extraction involves focus, which always follows topics. As noted in footnote 10, it is impossible to get both topic and focus in the sentences under consideration in this paper.

5. As a point of clarification, here and in the following sections, I refer to VP. The actual label of the constituent is not important, however; what is crucial is that there is strong evidence in Malagasy for a syntactic constituent that includes the verb and the object and excludes the subject. Keenan (1995) refers to this constituent as "PredP". What is important, therefore, is that the post-*dia* material behaves as if it is within this constituent.

Crucially, these elements occur on either side of the post-*dia* XP (*ny ankizy* 'the children in (20)): *Tokony* 'should' precedes and *foana* 'always' follows.

(20) a. *Ny milalao baolina dia tokony ny ankizy.*
     DET AT.play ball   TOP should DET child
     'The ones who are playing ball should be the children.'

   b. *Ny milalao baolina dia ny ankizy foana.*
     DET AT.play ball   TOP DET child always
     'The ones who are playing ball are always the children.'

Moreover, *tokony* cannot follow *ny ankizy* and *foana* cannot precede *ny ankizy*.[6]

(21) a. **Ny milalao baolina dia ny ankizy tokony.*
     DET AT.play ball   TOP DET child should
     'The ones who are playing ball should be the children.'

   b. **Ny milalao baolina dia foana ny ankizy.*
     DET AT.play ball   TOP always DET child
     'The ones who are playing ball are always the children.'

Similarly, the post-*dia* XP can be negated, unlike argument DPs, including subjects:

(22) a. *Ny mihira dia tsy i Bakoly.*
     DET AT.sing TOP NEG Bakoly
     'The one who is singing is not Bakoly.'

   b. **Mihira tsy i Bakoly.*
     AT.sing NEG Bakoly
     (lit.) 'Not Bakoly is singing.'

If *i Bakoly* in (22a) is not an argument, then it cannot be a subject.

A third and final piece of evidence against treating the post-*dia* XP as a subject comes from pronouns. In Malagasy, the first person singular pronoun has two nominative forms: A 'default' form for subjects (*aho* in (23a)) and a 'strong' form for topic and focus (*izaho* in (23b)).[7]

(23) a. *Tsy mahalala izany aho.*
     NEG AT.know that 1SG(NOM)
     'I don't know that.'

---

6. Because the pre-*dia* material contains a VP (within the headless relative), it is always possible for *tokony* and *foana* to appear framing that VP. But these data are tangential to determining the nature of the post-*dia* material.

7. Malagasy does have other case forms (*ahy* is accusative and affixal *ko* is genitive). The data presented in this section show that whatever position is involved, it is neither accusative nor genitive.

b. *Izaho no tsy mahalala izany.*
   1SG FOC NEG AT.know that
   'It's I who doesn't know that.'

c. **Aho* no tsy mahalala izany.*
   1SG(NOM) FOC NEG AT.know that

The strong form of the pronoun is also used in the predicate position:

(24) *Izaho ilay notadiavina.*
   1SG DET PST.TT.look-for
   'The one being looked for was me.' [Dez 1980: Tome II, 207]

Turning now to the *dia* construction, we see that the strong form is required, and the default form is not possible. Given that subjects can always appear in the weak form (e.g. (23a)), the ungrammaticality of (25b) shows that the post-*dia* XP is not a subject.[8]

(25) a. *Ny mihira dia izaho.*
   DET AT.sing TOP 1SG
   'The one who is singing is me.'

b. **Ny mihira dia aho.*
   DET AT.sing TOP 1SG(NOM)

In sum, the data from modals, adverbs, negation and pronouns all show that the post-*dia* XP acts like a VP-internal element, not like a subject (see Dez 1980: Tome I, 304–306 for a similar conclusion).

5.2 *Dia* ≠ 'be'

Before concluding this section, I discuss the status of *dia* and show that it is not a copular verb. At first glance, it is tempting to treat *dia* as the equivalent of 'be' in English. The *dia* construction would have the following structure, where the pre-*dia* XP is a subject, *dia* is the predicate and the post-*dia* XP is the complement to *dia*.

(26) [$_{TP}$ [$_{DP}$ *Ny milalao baolina*] [$_{VP}$ *dia* [$_{DP}$ *ny ankizy*]]].
   DET AT.play ball BE DET child
   'The ones who are playing ball are children.'

As a first argument against this analysis, the proposed structure in (26) does not conform to the standard predicate-initial word order of Malagasy. One would have to stipulate that *dia* is a medial predicate.

---

8. Strictly speaking, these data show that the post-*dia* XP is not in the "normal" matrix subject position. It could be a subject that has moved, for example, to a clause-initial position below the topic. But we would then expect examples like (21a), where *tokony* 'should' precedes the XP, to be grammatical. Since this is not the case, I reject this possibility.

Second, the position of adverbs show that *dia* does not pattern with other predicates. Recall that there are pre-VP adverbs (e.g. *tokony* 'should') and post-VP adverbs (e.g. *foana* 'always'). We have already seen that these adverbs frame the post-*dia* XP, treating it like the predicate ((27a) and (27c)). Crucially, these adverbs do not frame *dia* ((27b) and (27d)).

(27) a. Ny milalao baolina dia tokony ny ankizy.
DET AT.play ball TOP should DET child
'The ones who are playing ball should be the children.'

b. *Ny milalao baolina tokony dia ny ankizy.
DET AT.play ball should TOP DET child
'The ones who are playing ball should be the children.'

c. Ny milalao baolina dia ny ankizy foana.
DET AT.play ball TOP DET child always
'The ones who are playing ball are always the children.'

d. *Ny milalao baolina dia foana ny ankizy.
DET AT.play ball TOP always DET child
'The ones who are playing ball are always the children.'

I therefore reject treating *dia* as a copular predicate and assume that it is always a topic particle.

6. Analysis 1

In this section, I consider one analysis of the *dia*-construction, proposed by Paul (2008). According to this analysis, the pre-*dia* XP is a headless relative that originates as the predicate of a small clause and undergoes topicalization. The post-*dia* XP is the small clause subject and remains in its base position. Topicalization, under this approach, is stipulated to be the result of the Definiteness Restriction on predicates, discussed in Section 2.1. Because definite predicates are ungrammatical, the headless relative must escape the predicate position and is topicalized.

6.1 Basic nominal predicates

The core of this analysis is that nominal predication involves PredP. The predicate head relates two DPs: One is referential, the other is predicational (see Moro 1997, Adger & Ramchand 2003, Mikkelsen 2004). When the predicate is an indefinite nominal, the referential DP raises to Spec, TP.

(28) a. Vadiko Rakoto.
spouse.1SG(GEN) Rakoto
'Rakoto is my spouse.'

b.

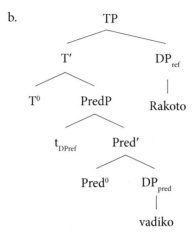

If the predicate nominal is definite, however, it is topicalized.[9]

(29) a. Ny vadiko dia Rakoto.
   DET spouse.1SG(GEN) TOP Rakoto
   'My spouse is Rakoto.'

b.

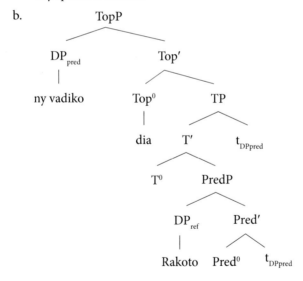

In the next section, I propose that the structure of *dia* examples is parallel to (29b).

---

9. For the purposes of this paper, I show topicalization as movement. It is possible, however, that the topic is base generated, coindexed with a null predicate. What is crucial for my analysis is that the subject position (Spec, TP) is not available – in these structures and in those in the next section, no other DP moves into the subject position. I also set aside here issues surrounding the motivation for movement.

6.2 Specificational sentences

We now can consider the *dia* construction in detail. As in the tree in (29b), the predicational DP is topicalized. The only difference is that in (30), the predicational DP is a headless relative.

(30) a. Ny mahafinaritra dia izany vaovao izany.
   DET AT.happy TOP that news that
   'What is pleasing is the news.'

   b.

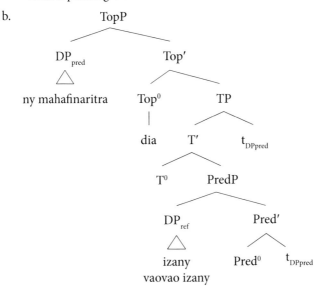

As mentioned earlier, I claim that topicalization occurs in (29) and (30) because the predicate is definite.[10]

---

10. An anonymous reviewer points out that Malagasy permits topicalization and focalization in the same clause (as seen in (i)) and asks whether similar stacking occurs in the specificational sentences discussed in this paper.

   (i) Ity radara ity dia ny Rosiana no nanao azy.
       this radar this TOP DET Russian FOC AT.make 3(ACC)
       'As for this radar, it was the Russians who built it.' [Keenan 1976: (69)]

In such cases, the focalized XP (e.g. *ny Rosiana* 'the Russians') must correspond to the grammatical subject. Given that in the structure proposed in this paper, it is the grammatical subject that has been topicalized, no other element is accessible for focalization. My analysis therefore (correctly) predicts the ungrammaticality of the following (though I suspect there are independent reasons why it is ungrammatical, in particular the stranding of the focus marker *no*):

   (ii) *Ny mahafinaritra dia izany vaovao izany no.
        DET AT. happy TOP that news that FOC

I also assume that topicalization is a two-step process: The predicative DP passes first through the subject position (see footnote 9). I discuss topicalization in more detail in Section 8.

7. Analysis 2

I would now like to consider a slightly different analysis of the Malagasy data, based on den Dikken (2006). Den Dikken argues that all identity statements involve inversion. That is, even in English sentences such as 'Cicero is Tully', the DP 'Cicero' has undergone inversion. According to den Dikken, the predicate DP in identity statements contains a headless relative and this headless relative inverts with the small clause subject. Inversion is driven by the need to properly license the null predicate (*pro*) adjoined to the headless relative.[11] Below, I provide the structure for Malagasy specificational sentences inspired by den Dikken's account, where R stands for Relator and is the head of the small clause. Note that the main difference between analysis 1 and analysis 2 is the labeling of particular nodes.

(31) a. *Ny mahafinaritra dia izany vaovao izany.*
DET AT.happy TOP that news that
'What is pleasing is the news.'

b.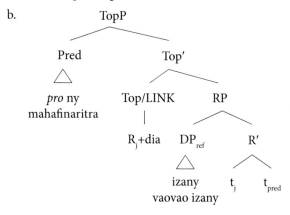

Following den Dikken, it is possible to treat *dia* as a "linker" – a functional head, typically spelled out as *be* in English, that provides a landing site for inversion.

---

11. Den Dikken posits the null predicate to account for the fact that a DP can fulfill a predicative function. The null predicate is overtly realized in certain languages, for example Scots and Irish Gaelic (Adger and Ramchand 2003).

8. Why topicalization?

I now turn to one unresolved issue in the analysis of the *dia*-construction. As has been clear, the predicate is always topicalized when definite. Which raises the question: Why can the predicate not remain in the subject position? In other words, why is (32b) ungrammatical?[12]

(32) a. *Ny mahafinaritra dia izany vaovao izany.*
     DET AT.happy   TOP that news that
     'What is pleasing is that news.'

   b. **Izany vaovao izany ny mahafinaritra.*
       that news that DET AT.happy
       'What is pleasing is that news.'

Note that analysis 1, as it stands, predicts (32b) to be grammatical – the headless relative *ny mahafinaritra* 'what is pleasing' moves out of the predicate position and into the subject position, avoiding the Definiteness Restriction. To account for the ungrammaticality of (32b) under analysis 1, an additional stipulation forcing topicalization is necessary. Paul (2008) suggests that the subject position is restricted to arguments and therefore a predicative element cannot appear there. As an example of this restriction, a measure phrase (a DP that does not get a theta-role and therefore is not an argument) cannot surface as the grammatical subject, as shown in (33).

(33) **Lanjain'ity   voankazo ity ny iray kilao.*
     TT.weigh.GEN'this fruit   this DET one kilo
     (lit.) 'One kilo is weighed by this fruit.'

If we assume that the headless relative in a specificational clause is a predicate and therefore does not receive a theta-role, then the ungrammaticality of (32b) falls out from an independent property of Malagasy grammar.

Analysis 2, on the other hand, can explain (32b) by invoking the notion of linker. Den Dikken (2006) argues that linkers are functional heads that provide a landing site for predicate inversion. He notes that linkers can be spelled out via different categories (e.g. a copula or an aspectual head). Given the lack of an overt copula in Malagasy, "inversion" of the predicate to the subject position (32b), is not marked by any linker and is therefore ungrammatical. Topicalization, however, provides the topic particle that can overtly mark inversion.

Looking cross-linguistically, however, it does not seem to be true that in languages that lack copulas, specificational sentences and identity statements must be overtly

---

12. This example is in fact structurally ambiguous: *Izany vaovao izany* could be the small clause subject or it could be the predicate. Under the latter parsing, (32b) would be ruled out by the Definiteness Restriction on the predicate position.

marked with a linker or other element. In Tagalog, for example, both specificational and identity sentences are possible with no overt topicalization or other linker.[13]

(34) a. *Ang karne ang nasunog.*
ANG meat ANG MA.burn
'What got burned is the meat.' [Schachter and Otanes 1972: 529]

b. *Si Tully si Cicero.*
'Cicero is Tully.' [R. Mercado, p.c.]

Moreover, these sentences maintain the unmarked comment>topic word order of Tagalog: Unlike in Malagasy, there is no visible inversion. In his discussion of nominal predication, Stassen (1997: 109) notes that identity statements are more likely to be marked with discourse-motivated elements such as topic and focus particles, and he suggests this marking arises due to the lack of grammatical relations (e.g. subject, predicate) in identity statements. But this is simply a cross-linguistic tendency, not a requirement. As we have just seen, Tagalog permits zero marking of identity statements.[14] The difference between Malagasy and Tagalog may be due to differences between the subject/topic position in these languages, but the Tagalog data suggest that an overt linker is not always necessary, a fact that calls into question the universality of den Dikken's claim that a linker must be spelled out.[15] In other words, it appears that whether or not a linker is pronounced is determined on a language-by-language basis and therefore the presence of *dia* in specificational sentences must simply be stipulated.

In sum, although den Dikken's analysis is initially appealing, it must resort to additional stipulations (the linker must be overt). Analysis 1, on the other hand, must stipulate that non-theta marked DPs cannot be subjects, but this is independently attested in the grammar. Therefore analysis 1 is more parsimonious of the two.

9. Conclusion

In this paper, I have claimed that specificational predication is inherently asymmetrical – one DP is the predicate and the other is the subject. In Malagasy, the predicate DP is topicalized, creating a structure that inverts the canonical comment>topic word

---

13. Topicalization is of course possible, but, crucially, it is not required.

14. Within Austronesian, some Polynesian languages such as Niuean (Massam, Lee and Rolle 2006), Maori (Bauer 1991) and Tuvaluan (Besnier 2000) pattern with Malagasy and require overt marking (*ko*) in identity statements. Fijian (Schütz 1985) is like Tagalog and permits simple juxtaposition (and no inversion).

15. Den Dikken (2006: 145–148) discusses contexts where an overt linker is not required, in particular in resultative constructions (e.g. *If Bill has an alibi for 6 p.m., that makes the murderer John*). His analysis crucially rests on the presence of an aspectual head that serves as the linker. Such an analysis does not easily extend to the Tagalog data.

order. Note that the resulting word order resembles inversion in English: The discourse familiar element appears first.

(35) Sitting in the garden was an old man. [Birner 1994: (4)]

The structure of English inversion is the subject of some debate; what is crucial for this paper is that word order and other tests indicate that in Malagasy the clause-initial constituent is a topic, not the subject. Whether or not specificational sentences in other languages involve inversion or require an overt linker remains open to further research. The Tagalog data tell us that, if inversion does obtain, it is not always overtly marked.

References

Adger, D. & Ramchand, G. 2003. Predication and equation. *Linguistic Inquiry* 34: 325–359.
Bauer, W. 1991. Maori *ko* again. *Te Reo* 34: 3–14.
Besnier, N. 2000. *Tuvaluan*. London: Routledge.
Birner, B. 1994. Information status and word order: An analysis of English inversion. *Language* 70: 233–259.
Dez, J. 1980. *La syntaxe du malgache*. Lille: Atelier reproduction des thèses, Université Lille III.
den Dikken, M. 2006. *Relators and linkers. The Syntax of Predication, Predicate Inversion and Copulas*. Cambridge MA: The MIT Press.
Higgins, R. 1979. *The Pseudo-cleft Construction in English*. New York NY: Garland.
Jedele, T.P. & Randrianarivelo, L.E. 1998. *Malagasy Newspaper Reader*. Kensington MD: Dunwoody Press.
Keenan, E. 1976. Remarkable subjects in Malagasy. In *Subject and Topic*, C. Li (ed.), 249–301. New York NY: Academic Press.
Keenan, E. 1995. Predicate-argument structure in Malagasy. In *Grammatical Relations: Theoretical Approaches to Empirical Questions*, C. Burgess, K. Dziwirek & D. Gerdts (eds), 171–216. Stanford CA: CSLI.
Massam, D., Lee, J. & Rolle, N. 2006. Still a preposition: The category of *ko*. *Te Reo* 49: 3–38.
Mikkelsen, L. 2004. Specifying Who: On the Structure, Meaning and Use of Specificational Copular Clauses. PhD dissertation, University of California at Santa Cruz.
Moro, A. 1997. *The Raising of Predicates: Predicative Noun Phrases and the Theory of Clause Structure*. Cambridge: CUP.
Paul, I. 2008. On the topics of pseudoclefts. *Syntax* 11: 91–124.
Pearson, M. 2005. The Malagasy subject/topic as an A-bar element. *Natural Language and Linguistic Theory* 23: 381–457.
Rajaona, S. 1972. *Structure du malgache: Étude des formes prédicatives*. Fianarantsoa: Librairie Ambozontany.
Schachter, P. & Otanes, F.T. 1972. *A Tagalog Reference Grammar*. Berkeley CA: University of California Press.
Schütz, A. 1985. *The Fijian Language*. Honolulu HI: University of Hawai'i Press.
Stassen, L. 1997. *Intransitive Predication*. Oxford: OUP.

Appendix: Examples from newspaper articles (Jedele and Randrianarivelo 1998)

(1) *Ny lazain'ny vahoaka dia izao*:
 DET TT.say.GEN'DET citizen TOP this:
 'What people are saying is this:'

(2) *Ny mampalahelo amin'izao fotoana izao mantsy dia mbola*
 DET CAUSE.sad p'this time this unfortunately TOP still
 mahazo vahana ny fijirihana ny asan'ny mpanakanto.
 get size DET theft DET work.GEN'DET musician
 'What is sad these days is that the theft of artists' work is continuing to increase.'

(3) *Ny voalohany dia ny hasin'ny firenena na ny voninahitry*
 DET first TOP DET dignity.GEN'DET nation or DET honor.GEN
 ny firenena.
 DET nation
 'The first is the dignity or honor of the nation.'

VSO word order in Malagasy imperatives*

Eric Potsdam
University of Florida

This paper accounts for an unusual VSO word order found in Malagasy imperative clauses to the exclusion of indicative clauses. It proposes that, what appears to be a subject in immediately post-verbal position is not a subject at all; rather, it is a vocative. Semantic and morphological characteristics of Malagasy vocatives support this claim. The paper argues against two alternative analyses: a scrambling analysis that derives VSO order from the canonical VOS via rightward scrambling, and a predicate-internal subject analysis that derives the VSO order by leaving the subject in its base position. I show that both alternatives are empirically and conceptually inferior to the vocative account proposed in the present work.

1. Introduction

Malagasy is an Austronesian language spoken by approximately 14 million people on the island of Madagascar. It is typically described as having basic VOS word order, (1a); while, VSO is generally not possible, (1b).[1,2]

---

* I would like to thank my Malagasy consultants Hantavololona Rakotoarivony, Raharisoa Ramanarivo, and Voara and Bodo Randrianasolo. I am also grateful to Lisa Travis, two anonymous reviewers, and audiences at AFLA XIV (McGill University, 2007) and the University of California, Santa Cruz for insightful comments and questions. This material is based on work supported by the U.S. National Science Foundation. Any opinions, findings, and conclusions or recommendations expressed in this material are those of the author and do not necessarily reflect the views of the U.S. National Science Foundation.

1. There is some debate over the exact status of the obligatory clause-final noun phrase, which Pearson (2005), following others, neutrally calls the TRIGGER. Under the traditional conception of Malagasy clausal organization, the trigger is the subject of the clause, yielding VOS word order. For ease of presentation, I will follow this line of description in what follows. Pearson (2005) develops an alternative conception of Malagasy word order in which the trigger is a clause-external topic linked to a clause-internal empty category. Under such an analysis, the basic word order is VSO, which can be seen when the trigger does not correspond to the subject (TT stands for the theme topic verb form):

(1) a. namaky   boky   ianao   VOS
        read.PAST   book   2SG
        'You read a book.'

    b. *namaky   ianao boky   *VSO
        read.PAST   2SG   book

In active imperatives, however, both VOS and VSO are freely allowed when there is an overt subject (Dez 1990, Koopman 2006). Compare (2c) with the ungrammatical (1b).

(2) a. mamakia   boky!
        read.IMP   book

    b. mamakia   boky   ianao!   VOS
        read.IMP   book   2SG

    c. mamakia   ianao boky!   VSO
        read.IMP   2SG   book
        'Read a book!'

The goal of this paper is to account for the additional word order option in (2c) by answering the following two, main questions. What is this immediately post-verbal subject position in imperatives? Can it tell us anything about Malagasy clause structure and the derivation of VOS/VSO more generally?

The paper is organized as follows: first, I consider two derivations for the VSO order in Section 2 and show that neither is empirically adequate. In Section 3, I argue in favor of a VOCATIVE ANALYSIS in which the immediately post-verbal subject is actually not a subject at all; rather, it is a vocative. In Section 4, I conclude that imperatives and indicatives actually do allow the same positional options for the subject and, thus, that imperatives do not differ from indicatives, at least not in this respect. Therefore, they do not tell us anything about Malagasy clause structure or the derivation of VSO/VOS. In the final section, I discuss several issues for further investigation.

2. Deriving VSO word order

The literature contains numerous proposals for deriving VSO word order within the Principles and Parameters framework (McCloskey 1991, 1996; Chung 1998, 2006; papers in Carnie & Guilfoyle 2000; papers in Carnie, Harley, and Dooley 2005; among

---

(i) novakin'   ny   mpianatra   ilay   boky
     read.TT.PAST   the   student   that   book
     'The student read that book.'

2. I use the following abbreviations in glossing: 1/2/3-person, DET-determiner, FOC-focus, FUT-future, IMP-imperative, LOC-locative, SG/PL-number, PASS-passive, PRES-present, Q-question, REFL-reflexive, REL-relative, VOC-vocative.

others). Two routes to VSO word order are SCRAMBLING of S and O with respect to the verb and use of the PREDICATE-INTERNAL SUBJECT POSITION. Sections 2.1 and 2.2, respectively, show that neither of these options can adequately account for the Malagasy VSO imperatives.

2.1 Rightward scrambling

If we assume that the basic word order in Malagasy is VOS, then VSO can be derived by "scrambling" the object rightward across the subject:

(3) [mamakia ~~boky~~]_VP ianao boky!
 read.IMP   2SG   book
 'Read a book!'

I use the term scrambling in a non-technical sense to describe the placement of a constituent at the right periphery of the clause, to the right of its normal position. Under a SCRAMBLING ANALYSIS of VSO for Malagasy, the VP-internal material scrambles over the subject, which is in its canonical position, as shown above. Such an analysis is a priori plausible as Malagasy independently allows rightward scrambling of various elements in indicative clauses relative to the subject (see Potsdam 2006 and Law 2007, where this phenomenon is called extraposition). (4) shows rightward displacement of a PP adjunct, an NP adverbial, and a CP complement, respectively.

(4) a. hanao izany (noho izaho) Rasoa (**noho izaho**)
 do.FUT that because 1SG Rasoa because 1SG
 'Rasoa will do that because of me.'

 b. namaky boky (omaly) ny mpianatra (**omaly**)
 read.PAST book yesterday the student yesterday
 'The student read a book yesterday.'

 c. mihevitra Rabe **fa nahita gidro**
 think.PRES Rabe that see.PAST lemur
 'Rabe thinks that he saw a lemur.'

Although I cannot conclusively eliminate the scrambling option to derive imperative VSO, such a solution would require a number of, at present, ad hoc restrictions. First, as we saw in (1b) above and as shown in (5) below, the VSO order is not permitted in indicatives. Such examples are robustly ungrammatical. In order to exclude (1b) and (5b) but permit (2c), the operation that scrambles NP objects would need to be restricted to imperatives. Although this could be implemented it would not be explanatory.

(5) a. namaky (ilay) boky Rabe
 read.PAST that book Rabe
 'Rabe read a/that book.'

b. *namaky Rabe (ilay) boky
   read.PAST Rabe that book

Second, a further restriction on imperative scrambling is necessary, namely, that it maintain base word orders. To illustrate, the base word order of ditransitives in both imperatives and indicatives is V NP PP (Pearson 2000):

(6) *imperative clause*
   a. V NP PP
      mametraha vilia eo ambonin' ny latabatra!
      put.IMP   plate LOC on   the table
      'Put a plate on the table!'
   b. *V PP NP
      *mametraha eo ambonin' ny latabatra vilia!
      put.IMP   LOC on   the table   plate

(7) *indicative clause*
   a. V NP PP
      nametraka vilia teo ambonin' ny latabatra Rabe
      put.PAST   plate LOC on   the table   Rabe
      'Rabe put a plate on the table.'
   b. *V PP NP
      *nametraka teo ambonin' ny latabatra vilia Rabe
      put.PAST   LOC on   the table   plate Rabe

The V NP PP order must also be maintained in imperatives with an overt subject, as exemplified in (8) below. (8a) is the baseline example with a clause-final subject. (8b) shows the post-verbal subject of interest. (8c) shows that, as in (6b), it is ungrammatical to have the alternative V PP NP order of the two complements.

(8) a. V NP PP *you*
      mametraha vilia eo ambonin' ny latabatra **ianao**!
      put.IMP   plate LOC on   the table   2SG
      'Put a plate on the table!'
   b. V *you* NP PP
      mametraha **ianao** vilia eo ambonin' ny latabatra!
      put.IMP   2SG   plate LOC on   the table
      'Put a plate on the table!'
   c. *V *you* PP NP
      *mametraha **ianao** eo ambonin' ny latabatra vilia!
      put.IMP   2SG   LOC on   the table   plate

If scrambling is responsible for (8b), it would have to maintain the pre-scrambled order of the NP and PP. This is a somewhat mysterious restriction that does not uniformly hold of scrambling in other languages.³

Finally, imperative scrambling would need to be semantically vacuous. As far as I have been able to ascertain, any type of object can appear before or after the imperative subject. As is expected, the scrambled object may be definite. The example in (9) illustrates a pronoun, name, and a demonstrative NP object.

   (9)   mamangia (ianao) ahy/an-dRabe/ilay havana (ianao)!
          visit.IMP 2SG me/Rabe/that relative 2SG
          'Visit me/Rabe/that relative!'

All other kinds of NPs, including indefinite and non-referential NPs, are allowed as well, however. (10) illustrates a bare noun, a free choice indefinite, a headless relative, a quantified NP, a reflexive, and an idiom chunk alternating on either side of the subject *ianao* 'you'.

   (10) a. misotroa (ianao) rano betsaka (ianao)!
              drink.IMP 2SG water much 2SG
              'Drink lots of water!'
       b. mandraisa (ianao) na vilia iza na vilia iza (ianao)!
              take.IMP 2SG or plate which or plate which 2SG
              'Take any plate!'
       c. mandraisa (ianao) izay tianao (ianao)!
              take.IMP 2SG REL want.2SG 2SG
              'Take whatever you want!'
       d. mamakia (ianao) ny boky rehetra (ianao)!
              read.IMP 2SG the book all 2SG
              'Read all the books!'
       e. manongoa (ianao) tena (ianao)!
              pinch.IMP 2SG REFL 2SG
              'Pinch yourself!'
       f. makà (ianao) rivotra (ianao)!
              take.IMP 2SG wind 2SG
              'Take a vacation!'

Such data are unexpected in that scrambling usually has some information structural effect and is often restricted to definite/specific NPs. For example, den Dikken (1992)

---

3. Such a pattern might be accounted for by "Shape Conservation" constraints that require movement-derived structures to maintain base word orders (Müller 2000, Williams 2003, Fox & Pesetsky 2006).

shows that objects in Dutch imperatives undergo exceptional rightward movement but they must be definite.[4]

To summarize, scrambling is able to account for the VSO word order in imperatives but the transformation would have to have unique properties that are not well motivated at this stage: (a) application restricted to imperatives, (b) maintenance of base word orders, and (c) semantic vacuity. I take these reasons to be sufficient to set aside the scrambling analysis in favor of the more principled solution in Section 3.[5]

2.2 Predicate-internal subject

A promising analysis of the imperative VSO order is proposed by Koopman (2006: 148). She capitalizes on the fact that the Predicate-Internal Subject Hypothesis (Kitagawa 1986, Kuroda 1988, Koopman & Sportiche 1991, and others) provides a second subject position that is farther leftward. According to the INTERNAL SUBJECT ANALYSIS of VSO, the imperative subject can remain in the predicate-internal position, which would be immediately post-verbal, as shown in (11).

(11) [mamakia ianao boky]$_{VP}$ ø!
 read.IMP 2SG book
 'Read a book!'

A concrete implementation of this clause structure originates in Guilfoyle, Hung, and Travis (1992) and Paul (2000). The predicate-internal subject position is Spec,vP and the verb raises to the left of the subject into I°, yielding the VSO order. Under this conception, the structure of imperatives differs from that of other clause types in that the subject need not externalize to the clause-final subject position, which the above researchers take to be a righthand specifier of IP.

---

4. See Saito (1989), Sauerland (1999), and references therein for the claim that Japanese scrambling is semantically vacuous.

5. There is an alternative instantiation of the scrambling analysis that, I believe, is subject to similar criticisms. The analysis derives the VOS word order from a base SVO word order via fronting of the VO predicate (Rackowski & Travis 2000, Aldridge 2004, Pearson 2005, Cole & Hermon 2008, and references therein). VSO is derived by scrambling the object leftwards out of the predicate, but to a position below the subject. and then fronting the predicate, which consists solely of the verb (Massam 2000, 2001, Chung 2005, and references therein). This leftward movement of the object does seem to be semantically vacuous in the VSO languages that use it, perhaps because it is obligatory. On the other hand, for the VOS language Malagasy, the leftward movement must still be restricted to imperatives and to maintaining base word orders when there are multiple internal arguments.

(12)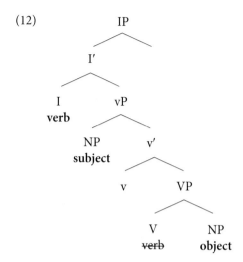

Such an analysis is not unprecedented. Henry (1995) argues for a predicate-internal subject in some Belfast English imperatives in which the subject appears immediately after the verb.

Two empirical arguments against the internal subject analysis follow. The first comes from word order possibilities for ditransitive imperatives. As we saw above, the subject in such examples can appear immediately after the verb or clause-finally, (13a,b). In addition, the imperative subject can appear between the internal arguments, (13c).

(13) a. mandidia **ianao** ilay mofo amin' ity antsy ity foana!
 cut.IMP 2SG that bread with this knife this always

 b. mandidia ilay mofo amin' ity antsy ity foana **ianao**!
 cut.IMP that bread with this knife this always 2SG

 c. mandidia ilay mofo **ianao** amin' ity antsy ity foana!
 cut.IMP that bread 2SG with this knife this always
 'Always cut that bread with this knife!'

This intermediate position in (13c) is not a position equatable to Spec,vP or Spec,IP, as seen in the structure in (14).

(14)

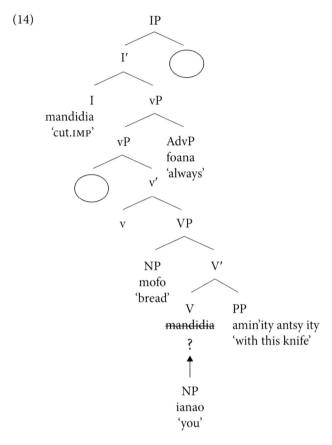

I use the VP-adverb *foana* 'always' in these examples to mark the right edge of the vP (Keenan 1995, Potsdam 2006). The position of this adverb ensures that the internal arguments have not scrambled over the subject to a position outside of the verb phrase. The structure in (14) shows that all complements should follow Spec,vP. Likewise, they should all precede Spec,IP. There is no structural position for the subject between the two complements. Not surprisingly, this position between internal arguments is not available to subjects in indicative clauses, (15a). Only the clause-final position is allowed, (15b).

(15) a. *nandidy ilay mofo **Rabe**
cut.PAST that bread Rabe
tamin' ity antsy ity foana
with this knife thisalways

b. nandidy ilay mofo tamin' ity antsy ity foana **Rabe**
cut.PAST that bread with this knife this always Rabe
'Rabe always cut that bread with this knife.'

The second argument against a vP-internal subject comes from non-active imperatives. If the internal subject analysis is correct, it can be paraphrased as saying that externalization of some element to Spec,IP is not required in imperatives and Spec,IP can remain empty (see the structure in (12)).[6] This general claim is incorrect, as we can see by looking at passive imperatives. Malagasy freely allows imperatives with the verb in the passive, or theme topic, form, (16). Such examples are quite usual and often preferred to active imperatives, as they are judged to be less direct.

(16) vakio   ilay boky!
     read.PASS.IMP that book
     lit. "That book be read!"
     'Read that book!'

In passive imperatives, the theme must be moved out of the vP to fill the subject position, Spec,IP. The passive imperatives in (17) and (18) illustrate this clearly because the theme must appear to the right of, and, thus, external to, vP-internal elements such as an oblique PP complement, (17), and the VP-adverb *foana* 'always', (18).

(17) a. didio   amin' ity antsy ity]$_{vP}$ ilay mofo!
        cut.PASS.IMP with this knife this   that bread
        lit. "That bread be cut with this knife!"
        'Cut that bread with this knife!'

     b. *didio   ilay mofo amin' ity antsy ity!
        cut.PASS.IMP that bread with this knife this

(18) a. ataovy   foana]$_{vP}$ ny enti-mody!
        do.PASS.IMP   always   the homework
        lit. "The homework always be done!"
        'Always do the homework!'

     b. *ataovy   ny enti-mody foana!
        do.PASS.IMP the homework always

Furthermore, Malagasy has a well-known formal requirement on its subjects, that they be morphosyntactically definite/specific (Keenan 1976, Law 2006, and others). Therefore, the subject must be a name, pronoun, or NP preceded by a determiner such as *ny* 'the' or *ilay* 'that', as in (19).

(19) mamaky   boky i Bao/izy/ny zaza/ilay zaza
     read.PRES book DET Bao/3SG/the child/that child
     'Bao/(s)he/the child/that child is reading a book.'

---

6. This characterization is neutral between treating the clause-final NP as a subject, as I do here, or as a topic, as in Pearson (2005) and note 1. The VSO word order indicates that this external position (subject or topic) is not occupied.

Bare noun phrases without an overt determiner are ungrammatical as subjects, (20). As seen in (19), objects are not so restricted and need not have an overt determiner.

(20) *mamaky boky olona/zaza
 read.PRES book person/child
 ('A person/child is reading a book.')

This restriction on subjects holds of the clause-final NP in passive imperatives, (21), confirming that it is indeed the externalized subject and that such externalization must therefore be obligatory.

(21) vakio *(ny) boky
 read.PASS.IMP the book
 'Read the book!'

I conclude that the internal subject analysis fails to account for the imperative word order facts and must be rejected. The imperative subject in VSO is not in its base position.

2.3 Intermediate summary

Thus far, I have rejected two derivational accounts for the VOS/VSO alternation in (22). Both scrambling and internal subject analyses of VSO proved to be empirically deficient.

(22) a. mamakia boky ianao! VOS
 read.IMP book 2SG
 b. mamakia ianao boky! VSO
 read.IMP 2SG book
 'Read a book!'

An important observation from the latter analysis however is worth highlighting: the word order variation is restricted to an unusual positioning of the agent in active imperatives. It does not affect the theme in passive imperatives. A passive imperative subject must appear in the canonical position. This suggests that the behavior is unique to agents or the imperative addressee. In the next section, I capitalize on this observation and offer an alternative analysis.

3. A vocative analysis

In this section, I propose that the post-verbal NP[7] in VSO imperatives is not a subject at all; rather, it is a vocative. By vocative, I mean a non-argument NP whose referent is

---

7. By "post-verbal", I mean all non-clause-final positions following the verb: the immediately post-verbal position but also the positions between internal arguments. Post-verbal excludes the clause-final position.

precisely the person or persons being addressed. Vocatives and subjects may be referentially identical but they are not the same. As we know from English and other languages, a sentence may easily have both: *Sandy, did you/Bill wash the dishes?*

For a number of reasons, it is often difficult to identify a vocative in an imperative and distinguish it from a subject. Nevertheless, there are useful criteria. The following are taken from Downing (1969) and Jensen (2003) and indicate that a variety of grammatical cues can be relied on to distinguish a vocative from a subject in a given case. One can use phonological, morphological, syntactic and/or semantic information.

(23) a. phonology: special pronunciation of NP
  b. prosody: special intonation contour, using/including a prosodic break
  c. morphology: special vocative case or other morphological marking
  d. syntax: cannot trigger 3rd person agreement, even when the vocative is 3rd person
  e. phrase structure: occupy a clause-external position
  f. semantics: reference exactly to the addressee

For Malagasy, (23c, f), the morphology and semantics of a vocative, will be particularly helpful. What we will see in the next two sections is that these two criteria unambiguously indicate that the post-verbal NP in the putative VSO imperatives is a vocative.

3.1 Morphology

Malagasy has specific morphology that identifies some vocative forms (Rahajarizafy 1960, Rajemisa-Raolison 1969, Dez 1990). Second person pronouns do not differentiate between vocative and non-vocative forms: *ianao* 'you.2SG' and *ianareo* '2PL' are both subjects and vocatives. With non-pronominals, however, the vocative determiner *ry* is used:

(24) a. ianao   'you (sg)'   vocative or non-vocative
  b. *ry ianao   –

(25) a. i Soa   'Soa'   non-vocative only
  b. ry Soa   'Soa!'   vocative only

(26) a. ny mpianatra   'the students'   non-vocative only
  b. ry mpianatra   'students!'   vocative only

The use of *ry* in a sentence is illustrated in (27).

(27) ry/*i   Soa, nividy   mofo ve ianao?
  VOC/DET Soa PAST.buy bread Q 2SG
  'Soa, did you buy bread?'

In addition, some nouns have suppletive vocative forms, (28). Instead of using the vocative determiner *ry*, the suppletive bare noun is used.

(28) a. ny zanaka/ankizy 'the child' non-vocative only
    b. *ry zanaka/ankizy –
    c. anaka/rankizy 'child!' vocative only

The vocative analysis correctly predicts that only the vocative forms of these noun phrases can appear in the VSO word order variant:

(29) a. mividiana **ry Soa** mofo!
       buy.IMP **VOC** Soa bread
       'Buy bread, Soa!'
    b. *mividiana (i) Soa mofo!
       buy.IMP DET Soa bread

(30) a. manaova **anaka/rankizy** enti-mody!
       do.IMP child.**VOC** homework
       'Do the homework, children!'
    b. *manaova (ny) zanaka/ankizy enti-mody!
       do.IMP the child homework

The data in (29) and (30) suggests that the post-verbal position is at least a vocative position. However, it could be the case that the post-verbal position is ambiguous between a vocative and a subject position and (29b) and (30b) are ungrammatical for an independent reason. Specifically, they might be ruled out because third person imperative subjects are ungrammatical in Malagasy. Some languages have restrictions on imperative subjects and limit them to second person pronouns. In fact, this scenario seems to be largely correct: such third person NPs are not allowed in the uncontroversial clause-final imperative subject position either, (31).[8] This leaves open the option that the post-verbal position might be a position for subjects *and* vocatives.

(31) a. *mividiana mofo i Soa!
       buy.IMP bread DET Soa
       ('Soa buy bread!')
    b. *manaova enti-mody ny zanaka/ankizy!
       do.IMP homework the child
       ('Children do the homework!')

---

8. Dez (1990: 21) gives a counterexample, which, as he indicates, can be used to avoid being too direct, (i). See also (37).

(i) avia i Koto!
    come.IMP DET Koto
    'Koto come!'
    "Que Koto vienne (c'est à dire: viens, Koto)"

We can make headway on this issue by avoiding third person NPs and making the subjects second person pronouns. Simple second person pronouns do not distinguish between subject and vocative forms but modified pronouns do. *Ianareo ankizy* 'you children' is the non-vocative form and *ianareo rankizy* 'you children.VOC' is unambiguously the vocative form. The modifier will allow us to determine whether the pronoun is functioning as a vocative or not. (32) shows that such modified pronouns are possible imperative subjects in the clause-final position.

(32) manaova enti-mody **ianareo zanaka/ankizy**!
do.IMP homework 2PL child
'Children (as opposed to others) do the homework!' picks out the group of children from the larger set of addressees

The non-vocative form of modified pronouns is not possible in the post-verbal position, (33), confirming that the post-verbal position is not a subject position.

(33) *manaova **ianareo zanaka/ankizy** enti-mody!
do.IMP 2PL child homework
('Children do the homework!')

Instead, the modifying noun in the post-verbal position must take a vocative form:

(34) a. manaova **ianareo anaka/rankizy** enti-mody!
do.IMP 2PL child.VOC homework

b. manaova enti-mody **ianareo anaka/rankizy**!
do.IMP homework 2PL child.VOC
'Do the homework, you children!'

Thus the first piece of evidence for the vocative analysis is that the post-verbal NP must take vocative morphology if it can. When the morphology allows us to differentiate subjects from vocatives, the post-verbal NP is unambiguously a vocative.

3.2 Semantics

The unique semantics of vocatives also allows us to identify the post-verbal NP as a vocative. By definition, vocatives are restricted to referring uniquely to the addressee. We will see that NPs that are unsuitable as vocatives because of their semantics are excluded from the post-verbal position even though they are acceptable as imperative subjects.

Some languages do not allow universally quantified vocatives such as *everybody* because they do not pick out a particular addressee. Greek is one language that does not, although English does, as witnessed by the acceptable translation in (35).

(35) *Kathenas, ela edho!   GREEK
everybody come.IMP.2SG here
('Everybody, come here!')

Malagasy is like Greek in not allowing universally quantified vocatives. *Ry rehetra* 'everybody.VOC' is not a possible vocative, regardless of its position:

(36) a. *** ry rehetra** misotroa rano betsaka!
VOC all drink.IMP water much

b. *misotroa rano betsaka **ry rehetra**!
drink.IMP water much VOC all
('Everybody, drink lots of water!')

As in English, however, *ny rehetra* 'everybody' is a possible imperative subject, (37). It can appear in the clause-final position with the non-vocative determiner *ny*.

(37) misotroa rano betsaka **ny rehetra**!
drink.IMP water much the all
'Everybody drink lots of water!'

When we turn to the post-verbal position, we see that neither *ry rehetra* 'everybody.VOC' nor *ny rehetra* 'everybody' is possible:

(38) a. *misotroa **ry rehetra** rano betsaka!
drink.IMP VOC all water much

b. *misotroa **ny rehetra** rano betsaka!
drink.IMP the all water much
('Everybody(,) drink lots of water!')

The ungrammaticality of (38a) is expected because *ry rehetra* 'everybody.VOC' is just not a possible vocative regardless of its position. The ungrammaticality of (38b) can be accounted for if we assume that the post-verbal position is simply not a subject position.

Observe that it is not the meaning of (38) that is the problem. A general audience vocative can be expressed using *ry vahoaka* 'people.VOC'. This can appear in post-verbal position but only as a vocative:

(39) a. misotroa **ry vahoaka** rano betsaka!
drink.IMP VOC people water much
'People, drink lots of water!'

b. *misotroa **ny vahoaka** rano betsaka!
drink.IMP the people water much
('You people drink lots of water!')

Thus, the second piece of evidence in favor of the vocative analysis comes from semantic restrictions on vocatives. Impossible vocatives are excluded from the post-verbal position but allowed in clause-final position. In summary, an NP in post-verbal position obligatorily has vocative morphology and obeys semantic restrictions specific to vocatives.

4. Conclusion

I conclude that the clause-internal agent NP that shows up in imperatives is really a vocative, not a subject.[9] Subjects in imperatives appear clause-finally, the canonical subject position in Malagasy, and clause-initially. The post-verbal position that would yield the VSO order is not available for subjects. Consequently, the position of subjects in imperatives is the same as the position of subjects in indicative clauses:

(40) *subject distribution in imperatives and indicatives*
 a. initial[10]
 b. *post-verbal
 c. final

(41) *imperative*
 (ny rehetra) mividiana (*ny rehetra) mofo (ny rehetra)!
 the all   buy.IMP   the all   bread the all
 'Everybody buy bread!'

(42) *indicative*
 (i Soa)   nividy   (*i Soa)   mofo (i Soa)
 (DET Soa buy.PAST   DET Soa   bread DET Soa
 'Soa bought bread.'

The conclusion reached in the present article is in line with work on imperative syntax in other languages, such as English and Dutch. Potsdam (1998) and Koopman (2007), respectively, argue that imperative clause structure should differ from that of other clauses only in principled ways. Contrary to some earlier work, imperatives should not be taken as peripheral constructions in the grammar allowing ad hoc rules.

In contrast to subjects, vocatives in imperatives can appear clause-initially, post-verbally, or clause-finally:

(43) *vocative distribution in imperatives*
 a. initial
 b. post-verbal
 c. final

(44) (ianao/ry Soa) mividiana (ianao/ry Soa) mofo (ianao/ry Soa)!
   2SG/VOC Soa   buy.IMP   2SG/VOC Soa   bread 2SG/VOC Soa
   'You/Soa, buy bread!'

---

9. Winifred Bauer (personal communication) indicates that the same is true of Maori imperatives.

10. SVO word order is allowed in indicative clauses under restricted circumstances when the subject is contrastive (Keenan 1976: 270–271, Paul 2001: 138, Pearson 2001: 214). I have not investigated clause-initial subjects thoroughly but I suspect that they are also possible in imperatives under similar circumstances.

The analysis of the original imperative paradigm from (2) is shown in (45). The clause-final position in imperatives is possible for vocatives or subjects. However, the post-verbal, clause-internal position is reserved for vocatives only.

(45) a. mamakia boky ianao! V O S/vocative
    read.IMP book 2SG.VOC/SUBJECT

  b. mamakia ianao boky! V vocative O
    read.IMP 2SG.VOC/*SUBJECT book
    'Read a book!'

I conclude with a challenge that sets up the agenda for future work. Given the above paradigms, a clear expectation is that the positioning of vocatives in indicative clauses will be the same as in imperative clauses: vocatives in indicatives should appear in clause-initial, post-verbal, and clause-final positions. My initial investigations suggest that this is not correct. Vocatives have a more restricted distribution in indicatives and, specifically, the post-verbal vocative position seen in imperatives is not available. This is the case for declaratives, yes/no questions, and wh-questions:

(46) a. (ry Soa) efa nividy (*ry Soa) mofo aho (ry Soa)
    VOC Soa already buy.PAST VOC Soa bread 1SG VOC Soa
    'Soa, I already bought bread.'

  b. (ry Soa) nividy (*ry Soa) mofo ve ianao/Rabe (ry Soa)?
    VOC Soa buy.PAST VOC Soa bread Q 2SG/Rabe VOC Soa
    'Soa, did you/Rabe buy bread?'

  c. (ry Soa) iza no (*ry Soa) nividy (*ry Soa) mofo (ry Soa)?
    VOC Soa who FOC VOC Soa buy.PAST VOC Soa bread VOC Soa
    'Soa, who bought bread?'

The indicative pattern is, in some sense, the expected pattern, as vocatives canonically appear in peripheral positions (Zwicky 1974, Lambrecht 1996, Leech 1999, Jensen 2003, Moro 2003). It is the post-verbal position of vocatives in imperatives that is somewhat unexpected and in need of an explanation. I leave the following questions for future work. What is the structure of imperatives, how should the post-verbal vocative position be analyzed, and why is this position only available in imperatives?

References

Aldridge, E. 2004. Ergativity and Word Order in Austronesian Languages. PhD dissertation, Cornell University.
Carnie, A. & Guilfoyle, E. (eds.). 2000. *The Syntax of Verb Initial Languages*. Oxford: OUP.
Carnie, A., Harley, H. & Dooley, S.A. (eds.) 2005. *Verb First: On the Syntax of Verb-Initial Languages* [Linguistik Aktuell/Linguistics Today 73]. Amsterdam: John Benjamins.

Chung, S. 1998. *The Design of Agreement*. Chicago IL: University of Chicago Press.
Chung, S. 2005. What fronts? On the VP raising account of verb-initial order. In *Verb First: Papers on the Syntax of Verb Initial Languages* [Linguistik Aktuell/Linguistics Today 73], A. Carnie, H. Harley & S.A. Dooley (eds), 9–29. Amsterdam: John Benjamins.
Chung, S. 2006. Properties of VOS Languages. In *The Blackwell Companion to Syntax*, M. Everaert & H.C. van Riemsdijk (eds), 685–720. Malden MA: Blackwell.
Cole, P. & Hermon, G. 2008. VP raising in a VOS language. *Syntax* 11: 144–197.
Dez, J. 1990. *Cheminements Linguistiques Malgaches*. Paris: Peeters.
den Dikken, M. 1992. Empty operator movement in Dutch imperatives. In *Language and Cognition 2*, D. Gilbers & S. Looyenga (eds). Groningen: Research Group for Linguistic Theory and Knowledge.
Downing, B.T. 1969. Vocatives and third person imperatives in English. *Papers in Linguistics* 1: 570–592.
Fox, D. & Pesetsky, D. 2005. Cyclic linearization of syntactic structure. *Theoretical Linguistics* 31: 1–45.
Guilfoyle, E., Hung, H. & Travis, L. 1992. Spec of IP and Spec of VP: Two subjects in Austronesian languages. *Natural Language and Linguistic Theory* 10: 375–414.
Henry, A. 1995. *Belfast English and Standard English: Dialect Variation and Parameter Setting*. Oxford: OUP.
Jensen, B. 2003. Syntax and semantics of imperative subjects. *Nordlyd* 31: 150–164.
Keenan, E.L. 1976. Remarkable subjects in Malagasy. In *Subject and Topic*, C.N. Li (ed), 247–301. New York NY: Academic Press.
Keenan, E.L. 1995. Predicate-argument structure in Malagasy. In *Grammatical Relations: Theoretical Approaches to Empirical Questions*, C.S. Burgess, K. Dziwirek & D. Gerdts (eds), 171–216. Stanford CA: CSLI.
Kitagawa, Y. 1986. Subjects in Japanese and English. PhD dissertation, University of Massachusetts at Amherst.
Koopman, H. 2006. Malagasy imperatives. In *UCLA Working Papers in Linguistics 12*, J. Heinz & D. Ntelitheos (eds), 141–160. Los Angeles LA: UCLA, Department of Linguistics.
Koopman, H. 2007. Topics in imperatives. In *Imperative Clauses in Generative Grammar: Studies in Honor of Frits Beukema* [Linguistik Aktuell/Linguistics Today 103], W. van der Wurff (ed), 153–180. Amsterdam: John Benjamins.
Koopman, H. & Sportiche, D. 1991. On the position of subjects. *Lingua* 85: 211–258.
Kuroda, S.-Y. 1988. Whether we agree or not: A comparative syntax of English and Japanese. *Lingvisticæ Investigationes* 12: 1–47.
Lambrecht, K. 1996. On the formal and functional relationship between topics and vocatives. Evidence from French. In *Conceptual Structure, Discourse, and Language*, A. Goldberg (ed), 267–288. Stanford CA: CSLI.
Law, P. 2006. Argument marking and the distribution of wh-phrases in Tagalog, Tsou, and Malagasy. *Oceanic Linguistics* 45: 153–190.
Law, P. 2007. The syntactic structure of the cleft construction in Malagasy. *Natural Language and Linguistic Theory* 25: 765–823.
Leech, G. 1999. The distribution and function of vocatives in American and British English conversation. In *Out of Corpora: Studies in Honour of Stig Johansson*, H. Hasselgård & S. Oksefjell (eds), 107–118. Amsterdam: Rodopi.
Massam, D. 2000. VSO And VOS: Aspects of Niuean word order. In *The Syntax of Verb Initial Languages*, A. Carnie & E. Guilfoyle (eds), 97–116. Oxford: OUP.

Massam, D. 2001. Pseudo noun incorporation in Niuean. *Natural Language and Linguistic Theory* 19: 153–197.
McCloskey, J. 1991. Clause structure, ellipsis, and Proper Government in Irish. *Lingua* 85: 259–302.
McCloskey, J. 1996. Subjects and subject positions. In *The Syntax of the Celtic Languages*, R. Borsley & I. Roberts (eds), 241–283. Cambridge: CUP.
Moro, A. 2003. Notes on vocative case: A case study in clause structure. In *Romance Languages and Linguistic Theory 2001* [Current Issues in Linguistic Theory 245], J. Quer, J. Schroten, M. Scorretti, P. Sleeman, & E. Verheugd (eds), 247–262. Amsterdam: John Benjamins.
Müller, G. 2000. Shape conservation and remnant movement. In *The Proceedings of NELS 30*, M. Hirotani, A. Coetzee, N. Hall & J.-Y. Kim (eds), 525–539. Amherst MA: GLSA.
Paul, I. 2000. Malagasy Clause Structure. PhD dissertation, McGill University.
Paul, I. 2001. *Ve* as a second-position clitic. *Oceanic Linguistics* 40: 135–142.
Pearson, M. 2000. Two types of VO languages. In *The Derivation of VO and OV* [Linguistik Aktuell/Linguistics Today 31], P. Svenonius (ed), 327–363. Amsterdam: John Benjamins.
Pearson, M. 2001. The Clause Structure of Malagasy: A Minimalist Approach. PhD dissertation, UCLA.
Pearson, M. 2005. The Malagasy subject/topic as an A'-element. *Natural Language and Linguistic Theory* 23: 381–457.
Potsdam, E. 1998. *Syntactic Issues in the English Imperative*. New York NY: Garland.
Potsdam, E. 2006. More concealed pseudoclefts in Malagasy and the Clausal Typing Hypothesis. *Lingua* 116: 2154–2182.
Rackowski, A. & Travis, L. 2000. V-Initial languages: X or XP movement and adverbial placement. In *The Syntax of Verb Initial Languages*, A. Carnie & E. Guilfoyle (eds), 117–141. Oxford: OUP.
Rahajarizafy, R.P.A. 1960. *Essai sur la Grammaire Malgache*. Antananarivo: Imprimerie Catholique.
Rajemisa-Raolison, R. 1969. *Grammaire Malgache*. Fianarantsoa: Librairie Ambozontany.
Saito, M. 1989. Scrambling as semantically vacuous A'-movement. In *Alternative Conceptions of Phrase Structure*, M. Baltin & A. Kroch (eds), 182–200. Chicago IL: University of Chicago Press.
Sauerland, U. 1999. Erasability and interpretation. *Syntax* 2: 161–188.
Williams, E. 2003. *Representation Theory*. Cambridge MA: The MIT Press.
Zwicky, A. 1974. Hey, Whatsyourname! In *CLS 10*, M.W. La Galy, R. Fox & A. Brock (eds), 787–801. Chicago IL: Chicago Linguistics Society.

A unified analysis of Niuean *Aki**

Douglas Ball
Truman State University

This paper re-examines the alternation in the Polynesian language Niuean involving the instrumental particle *aki* (Seiter 1980, Massam 1998), where *aki* can appear both as an apparent preposition and in the verbal complex, with its notional object having concomitantly different properties. A lexically-driven analysis is given for this alternation; namely, the morphosyntactic behavior of *aki* and its notional object in this alternation, as well as in long-distance dependency constructions, can be understood through the basic lexical entry of *aki* and its interaction with various other lexical operations, including argument structure extension, argument composition, and constraints on gap realization.

1. Introduction

In the Polynesian language Niuean,[1] instruments are marked by the word *aki*.[2] However, as first noted by (Seiter 1980: ch. 5), *aki* contrasts with the other 'case particles'

---

*   An earlier version of this work was presented at the 2007 LSA Annual Meeting. Thanks to the AFLA participants – especially Mark Baker and Mark Donohue – for their questions and comments, as well as to Peter Sells, Beth Levin, Aaron Broadwell, the Stanford Lexical Semantics Reading Group, the Stanford Syntax Workshop, and two anonymous reviewers. The usual disclaimers apply.
The following are abbreviations used in this paper: ABS = absolutive; ARG-ST = argument structure; COM = comitative; CN = common noun; DTRS = daughter nodes; ERG = ergative; ESS = essive; FUT = future; INST = instrumental; LDD = long-distance dependency; LN = local noun; LP = linear precedence; LOC = locative; MTR = mother node; NFUT = non-future; PL = plural; PN = proper noun/pronoun; PRON = pronoun; PRS = present; PRF = prefect; PST = past; SBJV = subjunctive; SG = singular; SYN = syntax; SEM = semantics; VAL = valence

1.   All Niuean examples are given in Niuean orthography, which is very much like the IPA except that {g} stands for the velar nasal and the sequence {ti} is pronounced [si].

2.   Cognates of *aki* are also found in Niuean's sister language, Tongan, and in a few select other languages far to the west, such as Tukang Besi (Evans 2003). *Aki* or a cognate form also occurs as an affix throughout the Oceanic branch, including Niuean, a use that is most likely historically

(prepositions) in Niuean: *Aki* can alternate between a realization where it looks more like a preposition and one where it is near the main verb.

In the first variant, which I refer to as the prepositional *aki* construction, *aki* appears to be a preposition. It surfaces before its notional object, which is marked by the absolutive case (to be discussed in depth in Section 2.1). *Aki* and its notional object form a contiguous unit, appearing at the end of the clause. It is exemplified in (1) where the *aki* phrase is in square brackets:

(1) Kua hele tuai e   Sione e   falaoa [aki e   titipi haana].
    PRF$_1$ cut PFT$_2$ ERG (name) ABS bread INST ABS knife his
    TAM V   NP[ERG]$_{agt}$ NP[ABS]$_{pat}$ PP[AKI]$_{inst}$
    'Sione has cut the bread with the knife.'   (Seiter 1980: 243)

In the second variant, which I henceforth call the applicative *aki* construction, *aki* appears near the main predicate, in what is called the verbal complex (following Seiter 1980). The notional object of *aki*, while still being marked with absolutive case, is not contiguous with *aki*, but appears later in the clause. This is illustrated in (2), where *aki* and its notional object are demarcated by square brackets:

(2) Kua hele [aki] tuai e   Sione [e   titipi haana] e   falaoa.
    PRF$_1$ cut INST PRF$_2$ ERG (name) ABS knife his   ABS bread
    TAM V aki   NP[ERG]$_{agt}$ NP[ABS]$_{inst}$ NP[ABS]$_{pat}$
    'Sione has cut the bread with his knife.'   (Seiter 1980: 243)

As (2) shows, there are two absolutive-marked DPs (*e titipi haana* and *e falaoa*) in a clause exhibiting the applicative *aki* construction, and, in fact, this is the only double absolutive (or what some might want to consider double object) construction in Niuean.

This alternation raises several questions about *aki* and the constructions it participates in. First, how is the absolutive case – exceptional for an object of a preposition, as I show later – licensed for prepositional *aki*'s complement? Second, and possibly related to the first question, how is the second absolutive licensed in the applicative *aki* construction, especially when this is the only instance of a double absolutive construction? Third, how is *aki* licensed to be in the verbal complex in the applicative *aki* construction? And finally, can an account of *aki*'s behavior in these two alternating constructions be extended to account for *aki*'s behavior in other constructions, like long-distance dependencies?

This paper presents answers to these questions. In particular, I propose that the crucial properties of these constructions follow from *aki*'s dependency potential, and its interaction with more general constraints on Niuean syntax, including case-licensing constraints, linear order constraints, available constructions, and constraints on long-distance dependency foot realization. I present my analysis within the framework

---

related to the word under discussion. However, I put affixal *aki* aside here; see Evans (2003) for a historical and comparative view of both affixal and 'free' *aki*.

of Head-driven Phrase Structure Grammar (HPSG) (Pollard & Sag 1994; Ginzburg & Sag 2000; Sag, Wasow & Bender 2003), although I draw on insights from previous analyses of *aki*. My analysis is relational (broadly construed) like that of Seiter (1980) (who worked in Relational Grammar), and draws on the lexical structure proposed for *aki* by Massam (1998) (working in early Minimalism).

First, though, I discuss the two *aki* expressions in more detail in Section 2. In Section 3, I present my account of *aki* and the constructions exemplified in (1) and (2). Section 4 discusses the long-distance dependency data and gives an analysis of it. Section 5 gives my conclusions.

2. More on the two *Aki* constructions

Having demonstrated many of the properties of the *aki* constructions in the introduction, I now return to them and discuss them in more detail, especially in light of the questions posed above. In the process, this section reviews the key findings of Seiter (1980: ch. 5). I begin with the prepositional *aki* construction before moving to the applicative *aki* construction.

2.1 Prepositional *Aki*

The prepositional *aki* construction exhibits some 'mixed' properties. In several ways, prepositional *aki* phrases are just like canonical prepositional phrases: The head immediately precedes its complement and the complete *aki*-phrase appears at the end of the clause. This is shown in (3), where the *aki*-phrase in (3a) has the same position in the clause as the benefactive *ma*-phrase in (3b), modulo the difference in verb transitivity between the two sentences.

(3) a. Kua hele tuai e Sione e falaoa [aki e titipi haana].
    PFT$_1$ cut PFT$_2$ ERG (name) ABS bread INST ABS knife his
    'Sione cut the bread with the knife' =(1)

   b. Gahua a au [ma e tagata kō].
    work ABS 1SG for ABS man that
    'I work for that man there.' (Seiter 1980: 36)

The syntax within the prepositional *aki* phrase itself, however, is much like the syntax within a phrase headed by a verb. This is evidenced by the object of *aki*, which shares both marking and behavioral properties with verbal objects.

First, the object of *aki* is marked just like an object of a verb, with absolutive case. In Niuean, as in other Polynesian languages, predicate-argument relationships are signaled by a word (or two) – a preposition and/or another prenominal word – at the left-edge of the nominal expression. The precise form (or forms) depends on both the kind of relationship (i.e. what case) and also on the type of noun (or noun phrase). The division in Niuean, as found elsewhere in the Austronesian family, is between common nouns (CNs) and proper nouns/pronouns (PNs). The relevance of noun type is evident below in (4), the paradigm of ergative and absolutive case forms:

(4)

	CNs	PNs
Ergative	he	e
Absolutive	e	a

The array of prenominal words for the objects of transitive verbs – these also hold for intransitive subjects – is exemplified in (5), where the objects are bracketed and prenominal words are italicized:

(5) a. Ne kai he pusi ia [e moa].
    PST eat ERG cat that ABS chicken
    'That cat ate the chicken.' (Seiter 1980: 29)

b. Ko e tele e Sione [a Sefa].
   PRS kick ERG (name) ABS (name)
   'Sione is kicking Sefa.' (Seiter 1980: 29)

The exact same array is found with complements of *aki*, as shown by the italicized words in (6) (the a and b examples correspond in (5) and (6)):

(6) a. ... aki e pene foou.
    INST ABS pen new
    '... with the new pen.' (Seiter 1980: 36)

b. ... aki a au.
   INST ABS 1SG
   '... with me.' (Seiter 1980: 84)

Aki contrasts with the other prepositions, which are split between two classes. One class, which includes *mo* 'COM', *ma* 'for', and *ko* 'ESS', shares its CN-marking with the absolutive (taking an *e*-marker), but has a different pattern with PNs (taking them 'bare'), as illustrated in (7):

(7) a. ... mo e vaka
       COM canoe
       '... with a canoe' (Seiter 1980: 37)

b. ... mo Maka
   COM (name)
   '... with Maka' (Seiter 1980: 37)

The other class, which includes the goal and locative prepositions, shares its CN-marking with the ergative (taking a *he*-marker). With these prepositions, PNs appear within an *a* phrase (looking like absolutive PNs), while a third class of nouns denoting locations – what Seiter (1980) calls local nouns (LNs) – are taken bare. The full paradigms for these two kinds of prepositions are given in (8); note that there are some formal idiosyncrasies in the CN-marking:

(8)

	CNs	PNs	LNs
goal	ke he	ki a	ki
locative	he	i a	i

Demonstrated using the goal preposition, the patterning for this class of prepositions is exemplified in (9):

(9) a. ... ke he fale-kava
         to   house-beer
         '... to the pub'   (Seiter 1980: 31)

   b. ... ki a   Sione
         to PERS (name)
         '... to Sione'   (Seiter 1980: 32)

   c. ... ki Niuē
         to (place)
         '... to Niue'   (Seiter 1980: 43)

A summary of the argument-marking possibilities with *aki*, verbs, and prepositions is given in (10):[3]

(10)

		Object	
Governor	CNs	PNs	LNs
Verb	*e* CN(P)	*a* PN	
aki	*e* CN(P)	*a* PN/LN(?)	
Prep Class I (*mo, ma, ko*)	*e* CN(P)	PN/LN	
Prep Class II (*ki/ke, i/∅*)	*he* CN(P)	*a* PN	LN

As (10) shows, there is a partial overlap among each of the patterns. However, *aki* matches exactly only the verb pattern. From this, it seems reasonable to conclude that

---

3. It is not clear from the data available to me what form *aki* requires of its local nouns, or even if *aki* can take local nouns.

the object of *aki* is marked using the verbal strategy. I label this strategy absolutive in the analysis to come, but the label could easily be different.

The class in which a preposition participates is conditioned by the (in some cases, historically present) final vowel of the preposition. Prepositions ending in a low or back vowel belong to Class I, whereas prepositions ending with a high vowel belong to Class II. This observation gives further evidence for the noteworthy nature of *aki*'s argument-marking pattern. *Aki* ends in a front vowel, yet it does not take the front vowel pattern with CNs (that is, it does not take CNs marked with *he*).[4] Thus, *aki*'s pattern must be analyzed as something different; a plausible way to do this is to assume that it takes absolutive case.

Moreover, the object of *aki* in the prepositional *aki* construction also shows one behavioral property of objects (I am not aware of it exhibiting other object behavioral properties in this construction): Objects of *aki* can 'launch' floated quantifiers. As Seiter (1980: 166–167) notes, both the ergative and absolutive arguments of a verb can float quantifiers, though phrases headed by oblique prepositions cannot. So, 'launching' quantifiers is a property of core arguments in Niuean. And it is also a property of the objects of prepositional *aki*, as shown in (11):

(11) a. Quantifier *in-situ*
To tā e ia e fale [aki e tau mena
FUT build ERG 3SG ABS house INST ABS PL thing
gahua *oti* nā]
work all that
'He will build the house with all those tools' (Seiter 1980: 251)

b. Floated Quantifier
To tā *oti* e ia e fale [aki e tau mena gahua nā].
FUT build all ERG 3SG ABS house INST ABS PL thing work that
'He will build the house with all those tools.' (Seiter 1980: 251)

Example (11a) shows the quantifier, *oti* 'all', *in-situ*, in its position near the end of the nominal expression. Example (11b) shows the floated quantifier variant, where the quantifier is next to the verb, *tā*, but the sentence on the whole has the same interpretation as (11a). From (11), we see that the object of *aki* has the object behavioral property of being able to 'launch' quantifiers.

Thus, even though prepositional *aki* phrases seem prepositional in their clause positioning, they seem quite verbal internally, as *aki*'s object is marked like a verbal argument, and that argument can also behave in one respect – quantifier float – like a verbal argument.

---

4. For discussion of the historical development of these alternations, see Clark (1976) and Seiter (1980: ch. 6).

2.2 Applicative *Aki*

Next, I move on to the properties of applicative *aki*. As this construction has two discontiguous parts – *aki* and its notional object (henceforth the applied object) –, I discuss the particulars of each part in turn. I begin with the positioning of *aki*.

2.2.1 *On the positioning and status of applicative* Aki

As (2) above illustrates, the usual place for *aki* in the applicative construction is immediately after the verb. This raises the question of whether applicative *aki* is an affix (or a tightly cohering clitic) to the verb. Once a greater range of data is consulted, though, I argue that *aki* in the applicative *aki* construction should be considered a separate word. A key piece of data is given in (12), which demonstrates that applicative *aki* can appear after some other verbal complex elements, such as the quantifier *oti*:

(12) To tā   oti *aki* e   ia e   tau mena gahua nā e   fale.
     FUT build all INST ERG 3SG ABS PL thing work that ABS house
     'He will build the house with all those tools.'   (Seiter 1980: 250)

Of course, separation by another element does not completely rule out the affixhood of *aki*; *oti* might also be an affix. However, investigation of *oti* reveals that *oti*, formally unchanged, can also appear as an NP modifier and as a main predicate (meaning 'finished') (Sperlich 1997: 251). This distribution seems to strongly indicate that *oti* is an independent word, because affixes generally do not have such a wide distribution, especially with an instantiation as the main predicate of the clause. Furthermore, the distribution of *oti* is unremarkable for a verb in a Polynesian language: Verbs in these languages regularly appear as main predicates (of course), postnominal modifiers, and postverbal modifiers.

So, if *oti* is an independent word, then *aki* likely is one as well, because, in canonical instances of affixation, no affix is ever separated from its base by an independent word. The data discussed here does not definitively rule out a 'phrasal affix' analysis (a possible analysis of English *'s*), but in the absence of morphophonological evidence for morphologization, it seems easiest to just consider *aki* an independent word. Of course, applicative *aki*'s general position near the verb does warrant some further analysis, and I return to this point in Section 3.

However, given the above conclusions about the status of *aki*, an analysis where *aki* is an Appl(icative) head (Pylkkänen 2002) and (as might be assumed) undergoes head movement into the verb is problematic, on the standard assumptions about head movement. Supposing that head movement involves the composition of a single X^0 element, it cannot be responsible for the positioning of *aki*, since *aki* and the verb are separate X^0 elements. Thus, the analysis of *aki* must involve something other than head movement.

2.2.2 Properties of the applied object

The other component of the applicative *aki* construction is the applied object. Much like its analogue in the prepositional *aki* construction, it has several object-like properties. In fact, the applied object appears to have all the properties of an ordinary core argument in Niuean, supporting the view that this object is truly an argument of the main predicate in the applicative *aki* construction. I illustrate this point using five types of evidence.

The first is marking, again. Like prepositional *aki*'s object, the applied object is marked with absolutive case. This is shown in (13) below, where the applied object (bracketed) begins with the absolutive marker *e* (also see (12), (15), and (19) for further examples):

(13) Kua hele aki tuai e   Sione [e   titipi haana] e   falaoa.
      PRF$_1$ cut INST PRF$_2$ ERG (name) ABS knife his   ABS bread
      'Sione has cut the bread with his knife.'   =(2)

As noted earlier, this creates the only double absolutive construction in Niuean. And observationally, it looks as if the verb is 'assigning' absolutive case to its complement (*e falaoa*), while *aki* is 'assigning' absolutive case to its complement (*e titipi haana*) (which it independently does, cf. Section 2.1); thus, there are the two absolutives.

The second object property of the applied object is ordering. In Niuean, the order after the verb is quite fixed (Seiter 1980: 56). The order is as follows: verb < ergative DP < absolutive DP < obliques. This is illustrated with a simple ditransitive in (14):

(14) Ne fakahū e   au e   tohi ke he kapitiga haaku.
      PST send   ERG 1SG ABS letter to   friend   my
      'I sent a letter to my friend.'   (Seiter 1980: 32)

In the applicative *aki* construction, the applied object usually appears as the second argument after the verb. The order, therefore, is verb < ergative DP < absolutive$_{applied}$ DP < absolutive$_{original}$ DP < obliques, as in (15), where the applied object has been bracketed:

(15) Ne hukui aki e   lautolu [e   tagata ia] a   au he gahuaaga.
      PST replace INST ERG 3PL   ABS man   that ABS 1SG LOC work
      'They replaced me with that man at work.'   (Seiter 1980: 257)

The ordering of the patient and the instrument in (15) is the reverse of their ordering with respect to each other in the prepositional *aki* construction (cf. (1)). The applied object's position, right after the ergative DP, makes it look like a normal object, such as *e tohi* 'the book', in (14). So, the applied object appears to have object-like ordering properties as well.

Thirdly, applied objects, like their prepositional counterparts, can also 'float' quantifiers. As noted in Section 2.1, the ability to 'float' quantifiers holds of core arguments (and the notional object of prepositional *aki*) in Niuean. Applied objects exhibit this property, too, as exemplified in (16):

(16) a. To tā aki e ia e tau mena gahua *oti* nā e fale.
FUT build INST ERG 3SG ABS PL thing work all that ABS house
'He will build the house with all those tools.' (Seiter 1980: 250)

b. To tā *oti* aki e ia e tau mena gahua nā e fale.
FUT build all INST ERG 3SG ABS PL thing work that ABS house
'He will build the house with all those tools.' =(12)

Like (11), (16) shows the two possible places for *oti*, with no change in thematic meaning (what relates to what). *Oti* can appear within the nominal phrase, as in (16a), or in the verb complex, as in (16b). So, applied objects share this behavioral property with canonical objects, too.

Fourthly, applied objects can undergo raising. In Niuean, as in most, if not all, other languages, certain predicates take nominal expressions that are understood as arguments of another predicate further embedded in the clause.[5] One such verb that allows raising in Niuean is *kamata* 'begin'. It can take a *ke*-clausal complement, with no raised argument, as in (17) (clausal complement bracketed here and elsewhere in this section):

(17) Kua kamata [ke hala he tama e akau].
PRF$_1$ begin SBJV cut ERG child ABS tree
'The child has begun to cut down the tree.' (Seiter 1980: 158)

Kamata can also take a nominal expression (the raised expression) and a *ke*-clause with a 'missing' argument. All core arguments (ergatives and absolutives) in Niuean have the potential to be the 'missing' argument, as exemplified in (18):

(18) a. Kua kamata e tama [ke hala e akau].
PRF$_1$ begin ABS child SBJV cut ABS tree
'The child has begun to cut down the tree.' (Seiter 1980: 158)

b. Kua kamata e akau [ke hala he tama].
PRF$_1$ begin ABS tree SBJV cut ERG child
'The tree has begun to be cut down by the child.' (Seiter 1980: 158)

Applied objects can also raise, as illustrated by the contrast between (19) and (20). In (19), *kamata* has no raised argument, just a clausal complement containing the applicative *aki* construction. The applied object is italicized.

(19) Kua kamata [ke hio aki e Sefa *e toki* e akau motua.]
PRF$_1$ begin SBJV chop INST ERG (name) ABS axe ABS tree old
'Sefa has begun to chop down the old tree with the axe.' (Seiter 1980: 250)

---

5. Whether the Niuean instantiation of raising should be analyzed on a par with raising as commonly discussed in the syntactic literature is a question I leave aside.

This contrasts with the raising example in (20). Here, the verb *kamata* is followed by the raised phrase *e toki* 'the axe', even though *e toki* is understood as the instrument of the lower predicate, *hio* 'chop'.

(20) Kua kamata e toki [ke hio aki e Sefa e akau motua.]
PRF₁ begin ABS axe SBJV chop INST ERG (name) ABS tree old
'Sefa has begun to chop down the old tree with the axe.' (Seiter 1980: 250)

So, the applied object, in addition to its marking, ordering, and quantifier floating properties, also joins canonical verbal objects in raising as well.

I turn briefly now to the fifth and last of the object properties: Applied objects have the same realization strategy in the termination of a long-distance dependency that objects do. This is an important part of Section 4, so I postpone discussion of this topic until then.

There appear to be no further available objecthood tests in Niuean, with the possible exception of noun incorporation. It is not clear how reliable noun incorporation is as a test for objects, because some 'middle objects' (S. Chung 1978) incorporate and their status is controversial (see S. Chung 1978, Seiter 1978, and Seiter 1980 for discussion of this issue). Applied objects do allow for incorporation (Massam 2001), so the controversy is immaterial for these instrumental expressions – either applied objects behave like canonical objects once again or the behavior of applied objects in incorporation does not matter. Overall, then, the data discussed above clearly show that the applied object has quite a few object properties – likely, in fact, all of them – a fact to be included in the analysis presented in Section 3.

3. An HPSG analysis: Part 1

In this section, I develop an analysis of the basic alternation in (1) and (2) in HPSG, a constraint-based lexicalist theory. HPSG is well-suited to the kind of analysis I propose here because the dependency potential (selectional properties) of a word and its phrase structure are separated, though related in a specific manner. This enables a straightforward account of both the formal requirements and the phrase-structural realizations of the different *aki* constructions. The analysis of the applicative *aki* construction given below can be viewed as a more formally developed version of the Seiter's Instrumental Advancement analysis (1980: ch. 5), that has been translated into the language and assumptions of HPSG. This analysis is also building on and making more explicit ideas noted in previous work by Massam (1998, 2006).

3.1 The basic lexical entry for *Aki*

Crucial to the account of all the constructions with *aki* is *aki*'s basic lexical entry, which is given in (21):

(21) $\begin{bmatrix} \text{word} \\ \text{FORM} \quad \langle \text{aki} \rangle \\ \text{SYN|CAT} \quad \text{prep} \\ \text{ARG-ST} \quad \langle \text{DP}[abs]_j \rangle \\ \text{SEM} \quad \text{use'}(i, j, (\text{verb'}(i,...))) \end{bmatrix}$

The entry in (21) says that *aki*'s syntactic category (the feature path SYN(tax)| CAT(egory)), is *preposition*. Because this feature is shared with higher projections of *aki* (in accordance with standard X-bar principles), this determines the external distribution of *aki* and the phrases it heads. This further allows for a simple account of the ordering generalization, whereby obliques appear at the end of the clause, as noted in Section 2.1.

(21) also indicates that *aki*'s combinatorial potential (the ARG(ument)-ST(ructure) list) lets it combine with an absolutive-marked DP, which is interpreted as the instrument: The absolutive-marked DP has the same index (*j*) as the object used in the semantic representation. The absolutive-marking is tied to *aki*'s semantics: *Aki* denotes the dyadic predicate *use'* and is required to modify another verbal relation (so the meaning is roughly like 'use while X-ing').[6] In general, in Niuean, affected second arguments of dyadic predicates are marked with the absolutive case. The manipulated second argument of the *use'* relation is among the affected second arguments of dyadic predicates. Therefore, the instrument is marked by the absolutive case. In a full HPSG analysis of Niuean, this case-marking generalization would not be specified on individual lexical items, as it appears to be in (21). Rather, it would be factored out as a higher-level constraint from which items like *aki* would inherit. Even so, (21) would remain a valid partial description of *aki*.

It must be noted that, modulo the representation conventions, the entry in (21) is very similar in content to the entry for *aki* given by Massam (1998: 18), shown in (22):

(22) *aki* {preposition/affix}, ([ABS case]) < *user, inst* >

Thus, it seems that something like (21) would form a foundation for almost any kind of analysis of *aki* and its alternation.

3.2 Allowing for the different frames

Having set out the foundational lexical entry in (21), I now discuss the means of licensing the two kinds of frames in which *aki* appears. Both are licensed by extensions to the verb's basic combinatorial potential. Within the specifics of the HPSG architecture,

---

6. In (21), the *use'* and the verb it modifies both have the same coindexed argument *i*. Any argument that comes to be identified as *i* thus will have to obey the thematic properties of both predicates. As long as *use'* is treated as an agent-patient kind of relation, this will capture the fact that *aki* only appears with 'agentive clauses' as noted in Massam (1998).

this involves manipulation of the ARG-ST list mentioned above. I begin with the analysis of the prepositional *aki* construction.

3.2.1 *Prepositional* Aki

The prepositional *aki* construction is licensed in a way that follows the common adjuncts-as-complements analysis in HPSG, as discussed in depth by Bouma, Malouf & Sag (2001). The intuition behind this analysis is that the difference between argument and adjunct is smaller than originally conceived, and many adjuncts can be more profitably viewed as optional arguments that appear if the verb's meaning and the overall context warrant them.[7]

Formally implementing this idea, I propose that the prepositional *aki* frame is licensed by the structure in (23), where a verb's base argument structure, [A], as seen in the D(augh)T(e)RS in (23), is extended by a full, saturated prepositional expression – a PP – headed by *aki*, as shown in the ARG-ST list of the M(o)T(he)R in (23). In (23), as well as in subsequent attribute-value matrices, such extensions are shown by the list addition operator, ⊕. Additionally, the identity of values are shown by boxed numbers (*1*); the identity of lists are shown by boxed letters (*A*).

$$(23) \begin{bmatrix} \text{MTR} \begin{bmatrix} \text{CAT} & 1\text{: verb} \\ \text{ARG-ST} & A \oplus \left\langle \begin{bmatrix} \text{CAT} & \begin{bmatrix} prep \\ \text{PFORM } aki \end{bmatrix} \\ \text{VAL} & \langle \rangle \end{bmatrix} \right\rangle \end{bmatrix} \\ \text{DTRS} \left\langle \begin{bmatrix} \text{CAT} & 1 \\ \text{ARG-ST} & A \end{bmatrix} \right\rangle \end{bmatrix}$$

How, though, does the ARG-ST list of the MTR in (23) actually figure in the generation of particular trees? Syntactic structure in HPSG is tied to the ARG-ST list of the head, though not directly, but through a related list of only surface-realizable elements, called the VAL(ence) list. The separation of ARG-ST from VAL allows for mismatches between the two, such as the one I show later in my discussion on long-distance dependencies. The general principles of HPSG ensure that every ARG-ST list member is either realized on the VAL list (and ultimately expressed in the surface syntax) or related to a filler by being classified as a *gap* (see Ginzburg and Sag 2000: ch. 5 for the technical details).

In the limiting case, the ARG-ST list and the VAL list of a head are identical, so a verb with the MTR's ARG-ST in (23) could have a VAL list with the same elements.

---

7. An analysis that also treats *aki*-PPs as adjuncts is also feasible. I choose the argument extension analysis mostly for uniformity with the analysis of the other variant; I presently do not know of any clear evidence from Niuean that would distinguish the two approaches to *aki*-PPs.

The verb can then combine with all its valents, using the *head-valents-phrase*. This phrasal schema licenses a local tree with a head and its VAL list elements, so it can license the combination of nouns with their complements, prepositions with their complements (including an *aki*-phrase), and a verb with its complements. A tree with two iterations of such a combination (one for *aki* and its complement, another for the verb and its valents) looks like the tree in (24), which is a representation of the critical part of the sentence in (1):

(24)

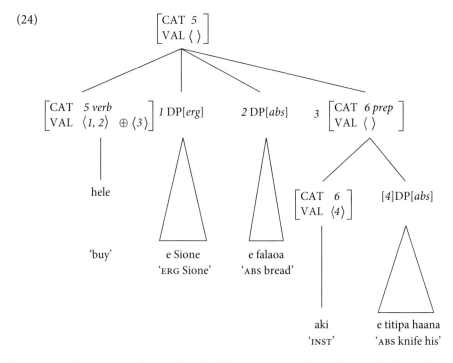

Observe that the main verb here, *hele* 'cut', has been extended with an *aki*-phrase, labeled 3 in (24), and that this *aki*-phrase appears as a sister of the verb and its other co-arguments (*e Sione* and *e falaoa*).

The structure depicted in (24) meets the two relevant constraints on linear ordering in Niuean. First, Niuean is head-initial. This is evident from all of the examples above, including (24) where the main verb *hele* precedes its sisters and the preposition *aki* precedes its sister. Such an ordering generalization is enforced in HPSG by a linear precedence (LP) constraint. The head-initial character of Niuean is captured by the constraint in (25), where X is a variable standing for any daughter that is not the head:

(25) [HEAD-DTR] < X
      "The head must be leftmost in a phrase"

Thus, (25) plays the same sort of role in an HPSG analysis as the head directionality parameter setting does in a Government and Binding framework analysis.

The second generalization, implicitly noted during the discussion on ordering in Section 2.2.2, is that the non-head daughters of a phrase are ordered according to decreasing obliqueness. Within this HPSG analysis, this ordering is enforced by a linear precedence constraint that requires that the order of the daughters in the phrase to be identical to the order of the corresponding elements on the VAL list. This LP constraint is given in (26). Independent motivation for ordering on the VAL list from least oblique to most oblique comes from co-argument binding (Pollard & Sag 1994).[8] Thus, (26) ensures that the non-head daughters of a phrase are likewise ordered according to decreasing obliqueness:

(26) $\begin{bmatrix} \text{HEAD-DTR|VAL} & \langle 1, 2, ..., n \rangle \\ \text{DTRS} & \langle 1, 2, ..., n \rangle \end{bmatrix}$

"The linear order of a phrase matches the order of the elements in the head's VAL list"

So, with (23), a standard HPSG mechanism for licensing structures from a head's combinatoric potential, and with the linear precedence constraints in (25) and in (26), prepositional *aki* constructions are licensed by the grammar.

3.2.2 *Applicative* Aki

The applicative *aki* construction poses a greater analytical challenge because any analysis needs a way to separate *aki* from its notional object in this construction. The intuition behind the analysis proposed here is that this separation comes about because the applicative *aki* construction involves a complex predicate. That is, the verbal predicate and *aki* combine to a form a single 'super predicate'. This single predicate's dependents are composed of both the verb's original dependents and the dependent of *aki*. So, the actual instrument is a dependent of a dependent in the prepositional *aki* construction, but a dependent of the main predicate in the applicative *aki* construction. This explains why applied objects display the host of object properties discussed in Section 2.2.2: they have literally become core arguments of the head verb.

I instantiate this intuition within HPSG with what is termed 'argument composition'. Such an analysis has first been proposed in HPSG for German verb stacking (Hinrichs & Nakazawa 1994), and has since been extended to a large number of other complex predicate phenomena: French auxiliaries and causatives (Abeillé, Godard & Sag 1998), Korean verb stacking (C. Chung 1998), and German particle verbs

---

8. In fact, in the version of HPSG I assume here, the ARG-ST list is crucially ordered for binding (following Manning and Sag 1998), and the order of the ARG-ST list is assumed to be the order of the VAL list unless otherwise stated, so the relationship is a bit indirect. Moreover, subjects are taken to be least oblique in HPSG, in contrast to the view in most neo-Davidsonian approaches to the syntax-semantics interface.

(Müller 2002). This analysis is nearly identical to the process of division in Categorial Grammar (Geach 1970), and is very similar to the concept of Clause Union in Relational Grammar (see Aissen & Perlmutter 1983).

Formally implemented within HPSG, argument composition is akin to (23). In this instance, though, a base ARG-ST list in the DTR ($\langle 1 \rangle \oplus A$) is extended by two items in the MTR. One item is the single word *aki*, the last element on the list of the MTR in (27). The other item is the list labeled B, a list of *aki*'s arguments, which, for independent reasons, contains just one argument. This list's placement in second position on the MTR's ARG-ST list allows for the ordering of the applied object, as discussed in Section 2.2.2. The full ARG-ST extension is given in the feature structure notation in (27):

$$(27) \begin{bmatrix} \text{MTR} \begin{bmatrix} \text{CAT} & 2 \\ \text{ARG-ST} & \langle 1 \rangle \oplus B \oplus A \oplus \left\langle \begin{bmatrix} P^0[aki] \\ \text{ARG-ST} & B\langle DP[abs] \rangle \end{bmatrix} \right\rangle \end{bmatrix} \\ \text{DTRS} \left\langle \begin{bmatrix} \text{CAT} & 2 \text{ verb} \\ \text{ARG-ST} & \langle 1 \rangle \oplus A \end{bmatrix} \right\rangle \end{bmatrix}$$

As the list [B] is the same for both *aki* and the main verb, the main verb inherits the absolutive case marking requirement from *aki*'s lexical entry. This licenses the exceptional second absolutive, and offers a reason why the double absolutives are remarkably allowed in this context: There are two absolutive case licensers present.

To integrate (27) into a larger structure, I again look at the limiting case, where the ARG-ST list of the MTR in (27) is identical to its VAL list. The main predicate and its valents then combine using two phrase structure rules. First, the verbal head combines with just *aki* using the *head-word-phrase*, which allows a head to combine with a copredicating single word argument (cf. *head-cluster-structure* in Müller 2002: 87). This 'early' combination of the verb and *aki* forces *aki* to be near the verb, thus capturing the property noted in Section 2.2.1, that *aki* is close, if not adjacent, to the verb in the applicative *aki* construction.[9]

Second, this larger verbal constituent combines with the other arguments using the *head-valents-phrase*, previously discussed in Section 3.2.1. The same linear ordering constraints – (25) and (26) – apply again, to both of these local subtrees. These constraints employed together yield the tree in (28), which is a representation of the critical part of (2):

---

9. An alternate approach would be to have the head combine with all its valents using the *head-valents-phrase* and capture the ordering through linear precedence constraints. A comparison of these two approaches involves more data and space than I have here, so I leave it as an open question which approach might ultimately give a more elegant account of Niuean grammar.

(28)

$\begin{bmatrix} \text{CAT} & 5 \\ \text{VAL} & \langle\,\rangle \end{bmatrix}$

$\begin{bmatrix} \text{CAT} & 5 \\ \text{VAL} & \langle 1, 2, 3 \rangle \end{bmatrix}$ *1* DP[erg]   *2* DP[abs]   *3* DP[abs]

$\begin{bmatrix} \text{CAT} & 5\ verb \\ \text{VAL} & \langle 1, 2, 3, 4 \rangle \end{bmatrix}$ *4* $\begin{bmatrix} word \\ \text{CAT} & prep \\ \text{VAL} & \langle 2 \rangle \end{bmatrix}$

                                 e Sione   e titipi haana   e falaoa
                                 'ERG Sione'   'ABS knife his'   'ABS bread'

hele   aki
'cut'   'INST'

Even though the applied object adds an additional daughter to the top node of the tree in (28), this analysis does not have to stipulate additional structure for this construction. Rather, the lexicon creates an ARG-ST list like that in (27), and the syntax interacts with it in the usual way. This contrasts with the analysis of *aki* sketched in Massam (2006), where additional functional heads or specifiers are suggested to account for the exceptional second absolutive. With a richer lexical structure, the need for such additional, and possibly undermotivated, structure is eliminated as are the issues over what causes various parts of the structure to move to give the attested ordering.

4. Long-distance dependencies (LDDs) with *Aki*

4.1 Data

As mentioned in Section 2.2.2, the notional object of *aki* also shows a fifth object-like property. This is apparent in long-distance dependencies (LDDs), like topicalization, content word questions, and relativization, where an argument is non-locally realized with respect to the predicate of which it is a semantic argument. In LDDs in Polynesian languages, as first noted by S. Chung (1978), the realization at the termination or foot of the LDD crucially depends on the relationship between the argument involved in the long-distance relationship and its local (downstairs) predicate. In Niuean, the foot of an LDD is sometimes indicated by a resumptive pronoun and sometimes by the absence of phonological material (a *gap*).

In LDDs with *aki*, the only possible foot realization is a gap. A realization with a putative resumptive pronoun is unacceptable. This is illustrated in (29):

(29) e   tagata ne   hukui aki e   lautolu {__ / *a   ia}
     ABS man   NFUT replace INST ERG 3PL   gap / ABS 3SG
     a   he gahuaaga
     ABS 1SG LOC work
     'the man who they replaced me with at work' (Seiter 1980: 250)

Also exemplified in (29) is the other important property of *aki*'s LDD behavior: *Aki* must appear in the verbal complex when its object is 'extracted'.

Aki's object patterns in LDD-foot behavior with core arguments (ergatives and absolutives), which likewise must be realized as gaps. One such example, with a single argument of an intransitive, is shown in (30) (see Seiter 1980: 94 for other core relations):

(30) e   tama ne   hau {__ / *a ia} i   Makefu
     ABS child NFUT come gap / ABS 3SG from (village)
     'the child who comes from Makefu'   (Seiter 1980: 246)

As in (29), (30) also shows that a realization with a putative resumptive pronoun is unacceptable for core arguments.

Aki's LDD-foot realization behavior contrasts with other obliques, all of which require a resumptive pronoun, and disallow a gap realization. This is demonstrated with the locative relation given in (31), which requires the resumptive pronoun *ai* 'there', as its foot realization (see Seiter 1980: 94–95 for other obliques):

(31) e   taga ne   tuku {ai / *__}   e   ia e   uga
     ABS bag NFUT put   there / gap   ERG 3SG ABS crab
     'the bag in which he put the coconut crab'   (Seiter 1980: 246)

So, in terms of LDD foot realization, *aki*'s notional object again patterns with core arguments. How might these facts be accounted for within the analysis being proposed here?

4.2 An HPSG analysis: Part 2

Aki in LDDs, such as (29), has previously been analyzed as a variable bound by an operator, the instrumental equivalent to the locative pronoun *ai* 'there' (Massam 1998). This analysis is motivated by a difference in the case of the single argument of intransitive verbs with *aki* in LDD and in non-LDD contexts, which suggests that *aki* is more 'inert' in the LDD context and perhaps does not have an argument at all. However, this operator bound-variable treatment does not treat all *aki*s uniformly. I propose that all *aki*s can be treated uniformly, including those in LDDs, through *aki*'s lexical entry, even while allowing for the case patterns that Massam (1998) describes.

First, though, let me set out a generalization present in the data given in (29)–(31): All phrases that are canonically marked with absolutive case are realized in LDDs as gaps (ergative DPs, too, can be realized as gaps, but they are not relevant to the topic at hand). This can be formalized by the constraint in (32).

(32) [ARG-ST ⟨...,DP[abs]$_k$, ...⟩] ⇒ [ARG-ST ⟨...,[gap]$_k$, ...⟩]

"If a lexical item has an absolutive-marked DP on its ARG-ST list, then the same lexical item can have a gap on its ARG-ST list, referring to the same semantic argument as the absolutive-marked DP did."

Aki, by its lexical entry in (21), is specified as [ARG-ST ⟨ DP[abs]$_j$ ⟩], so by (32), it can also have [ARG-ST ⟨ [gap]$_j$ ⟩]. It is this relationship that allows the complement of *aki* to behave like a core argument in LDDs.

As mentioned earlier, all ARG-ST elements are required to either be expressed in the surface syntax or be realized as a gap. When they are realized as gaps, they do not appear on the VAL list, due to what is known as the Argument Realization Principle (ARP), and so there is no corresponding overt element in the syntax. The actual long distance aspect of the dependency is handled by the SLASH feature in HPSG (see Ginzburg & Sag 2000: ch. 5 for an in-depth analysis). The presence of a gap on a given lexical item's ARG-ST list means that that item's SLASH attribute has as its value the semantic index of the gap.[10] This value then propagates up the tree, as shared information on the higher nodes' SLASH values, until the filler is reached. The path of propagation is similar to the path of moved elements proposed in movement-based accounts, but, here, the action lies entirely in the feature structures, and so there are no intermediate landing sites. In the subtree that includes the filler, the semantic index of the filler 'binds' the gap's index, ending the long-distance dependency.

This analysis not only predicts the unavailability of the resumptive pronoun strategy for *aki*'s argument, but also explains why *aki* must appear in the verbal complex in extraction contexts. Regardless of whether *aki*'s argument is composed onto the verb's ARG-ST by (27) or not, the verb has a single word *aki* expression on its ARG-ST and VAL lists, as in (33), when *aki* has a gap on its ARG-ST list, as permitted by (32):

(33) $\begin{bmatrix} \text{VAL} & A \oplus B \\ \text{ARG-ST} & A \oplus B \, \langle P^0[aki] \rangle \end{bmatrix}$

The convergence to these ARG-ST and VAL lists results from the interaction of the ARP and the extensions from Section 3.2, as I now show. Consider first the prepositional *aki* frame. In this instance, the gap on *aki*'s ARG-ST list is not composed to the verb's ARG-ST list; thus, only *aki*'s feature structure is of concern. By the ARP, the gap does not appear on the VAL list of *aki*. This yields a valent-saturated, yet single word *aki* in (34):

---

10. Due to the common use of resumptive pronouns in LDDs in Niuean, I assume that a SLASH attribute takes a set of indices as its value. Analyses of other languages in HPSG have assumed the value to be a larger data structure. The assumption that the value is an index is not crucial for the discussion here.

A unified analysis of Niuean *Aki* 267

(34) $\begin{bmatrix} word \\ \text{FORM} & \langle aki \rangle \\ \text{SYN} & \begin{bmatrix} \text{CAT} & prep \\ \text{VAL} & \langle \rangle \\ \text{SLASH} & \{j\} \end{bmatrix} \\ \text{ARG-ST} & [gap]_j \end{bmatrix}$

With respect to the applicative *aki* frame, here, the gap composes to the verb's ARG-ST list by (27). However, the ARP prevents the gap from being realized on the VAL list of both the verb and *aki*. So again, (34) is produced; this feature structure still meets the requirement for the *aki* expression on the verb's ARG-ST list in (27).

With the VAL list in (33), which has just the single word *aki*, the verb has to combine with *aki* using the *head-word-phrase*, resulting only in verbal complex *aki* in extraction contexts. The verbal complex then combines with the remaining verbal valents, the list [A], via the *head-valents-phrase*.

These two combinations license a structure very similar to (28) above, with two notable differences. First, the gap object is not realized, as it does not appear on any VAL list. Second, the index of the gap appears as the SLASH value of the verb, and also appears as the SLASH value of the two higher verbal phrases. An example of this structure is shown in (35), a tree of the crucial portion of (29) (illustrating an extraction from the prepositional *aki* frame):

(35)
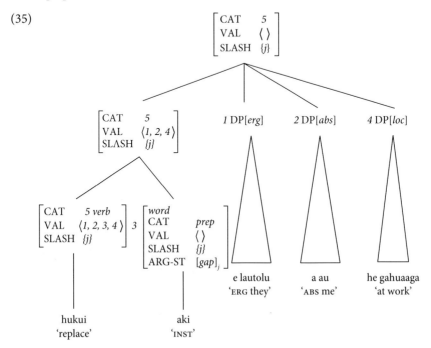

When the subtree in (35) is integrated with the rest of the LDD, the value of the highest node's SLASH, *j*, is identified, by general principles, with the SLASH value of the higher nodes. This percolation continues until the filler of LDD is reached, which crucially must also have the index *j*. The grammar ensures that the index is bound at the level of the filler, ending the long-distance dependency.

As sketched above and on the reasonable assumption that the applicative *aki* involves a case frame change when applied to an intransitive base verb (given the data discussed in Massam 1998: 16),[11] this analysis actually predicts that both absolutive and ergative external arguments are possible in extraction contexts. If the facts given in Massam (1998: 22–23) are precisely correct, and the ergative case is not allowed in clauses containing *aki* within extraction contexts, the analysis above needs some modification. To this end, I tentatively propose additional feature specification on one of the extensions to disallow that specific extension from relative clauses – the particular choice in extension and feature specification depends on the distribution of the two *aki* constructions and whatever might be motivating this distribution. However, given this phenomenon is not mentioned elsewhere in the Polynesianist literature and is only discussed briefly in Massam (1998), I refrain from taking a strong stand on how restricted to make the analysis and how to implement any restrictions until the precise details have been clarified further.

To conclude the LDD-foot realization discussion, on this account, *aki*'s core argument-like behavior in LDDs results from the relatively simple interaction of *aki*'s ARG-ST list, the general constraints on LDD-foot realization in Niuean, the extensions from Section 3.2, and the Argument Realization Principle that governs gap realization. These facets of the analysis allow LDD-foot behavior to be unified with the other aspects of *aki*'s grammar.

5. Conclusions

I have suggested that the dependency potential of the lexical item *aki* – that is, its ability to take the absolutive case, which stems from its lexical semantics – is key to understanding the behavior of *aki* and its argument. This ability allows for a crucial part of the prepositional *aki* frame by licensing *aki*'s exceptional absolutive case marking. This ability is also important for applicative *aki*: As information that is composed onto the verb's ARG-ST list, the *aki*'s original dependency potential licenses the second absolutive with applicative *aki*. Also through this composition, the notional argument of *aki* becomes a core argument of the main predicate, enabling the notional object to assume object properties such as an object-like position in canonical clauses, the ability to float quantifiers, and to raise. Finally, the dependency potential of *aki* also illuminates

---

11. Regrettably, a discussion of how to incorporate such a case frame change within the analysis here would require more space than is available.

LDD behavior. The absolutive case provides the necessary condition for gap realization in an LDD-foot. This realization then interacts with the modes of adding *aki* to the ARG-ST lists of the verbs and with the general constraints on LDD-foot realization to require that *aki* appear in the verbal complex in extraction contexts. Therefore, this specific property of *aki* together with more general syntactic constraints in Niuean come together to give a unified account of the varied behavior of prepositional *aki*, applicative *aki*, and *aki*'s LDD-foot realization.

References

Abeillé, A., Godard, D. & Sag, I.A. 1998. Two kinds of composition in French complex predicates. In *Complex Predicates in Nonderivational Syntax*, E.W. Hinrichs, A. Kathol & T. Nakazawa (eds), 1–41. New York NY: Academic Press.

Aissen, J.L. & Perlmutter, D.M. 1983. Clause reduction in Spanish. In *Studies in Relational Grammar* 1, D.M. Perlmutter (ed.), 360–403. Chicago IL: University of Chicago Press.

Bouma, G., Malouf, R. & Sag, I.A. 2001. Satisfying constraints on extraction and adjunction. *Natural Language and Linguistic Theory* 19: 1–65.

Chung, C. 1998. Argument composition and long-distance scrambling in Korean: An extension of the complex predicates analysis. In *Complex Predicates in Nonderivational Syntax*, E.W. Hinrichs, A. Kathol & T. Nakazawa (eds., 159–220. New York NY: Academic Press.

Chung, S. 1978. *Case Marking and Grammatical Relations in Polynesian*. Austin TX: University of Texas Press.

Clark, R. 1976. *Aspects of Proto-Polynesian Syntax*. Auckland: Linguistic Society of New Zealand.

Evans, B. 2003. *A Study of Valency-Changing Devices in Proto Oceanic*. Canberra: Pacific Linguistics.

Geach, P.T. 1970. A Program for Syntax. *Synthese* 22: 3–17.

Ginzburg, J. & Sag, I.A. 2000. *Interrogative Investigations: The Form, Meaning, and Use of English Interrogatives*. Stanford CA: CSLI.

Hinrichs, E.W. & Nakazawa, T. 1994. Linearizing AUXs in German verbal complexes. In *German in Head-Driven Phrase Structure Grammar* [CSLI Lecture Notes 46], J. Nerbonne, K. Netter & C. Pollard (eds), 11–37. Stanford CA: CSLI.

Manning, C.D. & Sag, I.A. 1998. Argument structure, valence, and binding. *Nordic Journal of Linguistics* 21: 107–144.

Massam, D. 1998. Instrumental *Aki* and the Nature of Niuean Transitivity. *Oceanic Linguistics* 37:12–28.

Massam, D. 2001. Pseudo noun incorporation in Niuean. *Natural Language and Linguistic Theory* 19: 153–197.

Massam, D. 2006. Neither absolutive nor ergative is nominative or accusative. In *Ergativity: Emerging Issues*, A. Johns, D. Massam & J. Ndayiragije (eds), 27–46. Dordrecht: Springer.

Müller, S. 2002. *Complex Predicates: Verbal Complexes, Resultative Constructions, and Particle Verbs in German* [Studies in Constraint-Based Lexicalism 13]. Stanford CA: CSLI.

Pollard, C.J. & Sag, I.A. 1994. *Head-driven Phrase Structure Grammar*. Chicago ILO: University of Chicago Press.

Pylkkänen, L. 2002. Introducing Arguments. PhD dissertation, MIT. (Published in 2008, Cambridge MA: The MIT Press).

Sag, I.A., Wasow, T. & Bender, E.M. 2003. *Syntactic Theory: A Formal Introduction*, 2nd edn. Stanford CA: CSLI.

Seiter, W. 1978. On the syntactic character of middle objects in Polynesian. In *Second International Conference on Austronesian Linguistics,* Fascicle 2, S.A. Wurm & L. Carrington (eds), 1289–1306. Canberra: Department of Linguistics, Australian National University.

Seiter, W. 1980. *Studies in Niuean Syntax*. New York NY: Garland.

Sperlich,W. 1997. *Tohi Vagahou Niue: Niue Language Dictionary*. Honolulu HI: University of Hawai'i Press.

Deriving inverse order
The issue of arguments

Diane Massam
University of Toronto

This paper explores word order in Niuean, a Polynesian language with VSO word order, within the context of theories that attempt to constrain the range and limits of possible word orders across languages (in particular Kayne 1994, Cinque 1999, 2005). First it is argued that V-initial order in Niuean is derived via verbal movement, through maximal predicate fronting. Following the predicate in Niuean are a sequence of inversely-ordered particles (Rackowski and Travis 2000). Various analyses are reviewed which attempt to account for the inverse ordering and to tie the V-initial word order to the inverse order of particles. Finally, the position of arguments is discussed. Their non-inverse ordering presents problems for inverse order derivations, assuming traditional theories of theta role assignment. It is proposed that we continue the trend towards separating arguments from their traditional theta role assigners and merge object arguments directly into specifiers of functional projections (as in, for example, Borer 2005). This allows for a comprehensive analysis of word order in Niuean.

1. Introduction

In this paper I consider word order in Niuean, a Polynesian language of the Tongic subgroup (Pawley 1966, 1967). The discussion is situated within attempts to constrain the range and limits of possible word orders across languages (e.g. Cinque 1999, 2005, Koopman & Szabolcsi 2000, Kayne 1994, and many others, rooted in Greenberg 1966, also Hawkins 1983). These frameworks adopt firm restrictions on phrase structure and movement; for example, they rule out adjunction on the right. Adopting the basic framework of Cinque (2005), and building on Rackowski & Travis (2000) and previous work on Niuean, I will first outline a derivation of Niuean predicate-initial word order, then I will discuss ordering of particles and adverbials, then turn to some problems posed by the positions of arguments, namely subjects, objects, and applied instruments, in inverse-order languages like Niuean.¹ (See also, for example, Thiersch 2006, Rackowski & Travis 2000, Rackowski 1998, Pearson 2000, 2001, Paul 2002, Shlonsky 2004). This paper is programmatic: I aim to bring to the fore a central problem in our understanding of the structure of Austronesian languages by articulating the issues and comparing various approaches. I will suggest a direction for future research, which involves the merging of all arguments in specifiers of functional heads.²

2. Basic sentential word order in Niuean

Niuean is a VSO language, with no inflection, and a rich particle/adverbial system. In previous work on this language I have argued for a base order of SVO (Massam 2000, 2001a, 2001b) with subsequent predicate fronting. Although termed 'VSO', Niuean is

---

1. This paper has a very particular, and somewhat narrow goal. It assumes the view that adverbs are in specifier positions of functional projections, rather than being adjoined (Cinque 1999, 2005, Alexiadou 1997, Laenzlinger 1996, 1998, Haumann 2007). These functional categories are merged in a universal order in accordance with their general scopal nature such that sententially scoping elements are higher than verbally scoping elements, for example. It further assumes that surface deviations from this order are due to movement and are limited by constraints on movement. In this paper I am not tackling the broader question of whether this essentially Kayne-based (1994) approach to adverb order is the right one for Niuean, as compared to others, such as Ernst (2002) and Alexiadou (2004). See Haumann (2007) for arguments in favour of the position adopted in this paper. This would make an interesting discussion, but it is beyond the scope of this paper. The focus on the Cinque/Kayne view is chosen because there is a body of work on inverse word order in this tradition, but most of it ignores or glosses over the placement of arguments. The purpose of this paper is to highlight the consequences of bringing arguments into this particular picture, not to argue for a particular analysis of adverbs. I would like to thank David Adger, Jila Ghomeshi, Peter Hallman, Jonathon Herd, Ofania Ikiua, Monica Irimia, Alana Johns, Arsalan Kahnemuyiour, Hilda Koopman, Raphael Mercado, Yves Roberge, Donna Starks, Lisa Travis, Jan-Wouter Zwart and two anonymous reviewers, all of whom have influenced my thinking in this work. Funding for this research was provided by a Social Sciences and Humanities Research Council of Canada Standard Research Grant "Featural Variation in the Left Periphery of a Verb-initial language".

2. Most data sources are listed in the references. (Ch: Chapin 1974, M: McEwen 1970, NAH: Niue A History, S: Seiter 1980, Sp: Sperlich 1997) Other data come from my own field notes (FN), or from the data generously provided by Donna Starks, University of Auckland from research on Languages of Manukau Region (LMR), as discussed in Bell et al. (2000). Abbreviations used in glossing and figures are as follows: ABS: Absolutive, ADV: adverb, APPL: Applicative, C: Common, DIR: Directional marker, EMPH: Emphatic, ERG: Ergative, FUT: Future, GEN: Genitive, INCL: inclusive, INSTR: Instrument, LOC: Locative, LNK: linker, MAN: manner, NFUT: Nonfuture, P: Proper, PERF: Perfect, PERS: Personal, PL: Plural, PST: Past, PRED: Predicative, Q: Question, RESPRON: Resumptive locative pronoun, SBJV: subjunctive, SG: Singular, TAM: Tense Aspect Mood, UQ, UnivQuant: Universal Quantifier, 3: third person, 2: second person, 1: first person.

more accurately a predicate-initial language, as the slot that is filled by the fronted verb can also be filled by various other predicate types, as is the case in other Polynesian languages (see recent discussions in Pearce 2002, 2003, Herd 2002, Lazard & Peltzer 1991). In (1a) we see an example where a V appears as the predicate. The predicate comes after the Tense Aspect Mood particle (TAM), which can be null in various contexts. The predicate also follows the negative marker if present, as in (1b), and certain modals, to be illustrated below, as well as various discourse elements. The predicate precedes a series of particles and adverbs (which also will be discussed in detail below), such as *foki* in (1a). The position between the TAM + (NEG) + (MOD) and the post-predicate particles and adverbs can be referred to as the predicate slot, as schematized in Figure 1 below.

(1) a. Ne **tutuli** foki he   tau tagata a   ia.
       PST chase also ERG.C PL person ABS.P 3.SG
       'The people also chased him.'   (NAH)

    b. Ne nākai **talia** he   papalagi nā ko   McFarland
       PST not accept   ERG.C European this PRED McFarland
       e   kupu he tau iki kafili.
       ABS.C word GEN PL chief judge
       'The European McFarland, refused to accept the word of the judges.'
                                                                         (NAH)

As discussed in Massam (2000, 2001a, 2001b), it is also possible to have maximal predicates that consist of a VP rather than V, provided the object within VP is a bare NP, rather than a KP or Case Phrase (i.e. does not contain left-peripheral material such as a case marker). This construction is termed pseudo-noun-incorporation (PNI). (2) shows a complex NP, which appears within the predicate slot with the verb.

(2) ...ke   [**kumi mena ke nonofo ai**] a   lautolu.
    ...SBJV seek thing SBJV settle there ABS.p 3.PL
    '...they sought a place to settle.'   (NAH)

The question that arises when examining (1a,b) vs. (2) is: How can the predicate be in a unique structural position, yet vary in status between being a head and a maximal projection (cf. Carnie 1995)? In earlier work I proposed that the answer to this question is that the predicate is in fact always a phrase, but in cases such as (1a,b), the case-marked object KP has necessarily escaped the VP prior to the (remnant)

Minimal Response/ Interjection	Typical Discourse Particle	Connective Complementizer	TAM	Neg	Modal	Pred	Post Verbal Particles	NPs

Figure 1. Niuean Surface Sentence Order (Massam, Starks and Ikiua 2006)

movement of this VP (cf. remnant movement analyses of Germanic languages, e.g. den Besten & Webelhuth 1987, 1990, Müller 2004, Zwart 2003, and other languages, for example Lee 2000). A bare NP, on the other hand, cannot move out of VP. This is derivationally schematised below for (1a) (without the particle *foki*). I assume, following many (e.g. den Dikken & Sybesma 1998, Harley & Noyer 1998, Marantz 1997) that all verbal phrases are headed by a light verb (with light core meanings such as BE, DO, MAKE, etc.), which contributes information about the basic nature of the verb. Since the light verb is null, it is not an empirical issue if it fronts with the VP or not, but I will assume here that it does (Massam, Lee & Rolle 2006). I follow standard current practice in merging the external argument in a position outside VP. See Figure 2 below.

In Figure 2, arguments surface in specifiers of projections containing case features, here labelled Erg and Abs between the vP and the PredP, the specifier of the latter being the destination of the moved vP predicate phrase.[3] As is standard, the external argument is merged external to VP, whereas the internal argument is merged within VP. I will return below to the issue of the position of arguments, and will note here only that the case system is an ergative one, in which case markers are inflected for a proper/common distinction (pronouns are classified as proper). The order of arguments is subject, object, indirect object, as illustrated in (3). Oblique PPs follow all arguments. I will not discuss PPs in this paper.

(3) *Ne tala aga e   ia   e   tala ke   he   tagata.*
    PST tell DIR ERG.P 3.SG ABS.C story GOAL.C LOC.C man
    'He told the story to the man.'   (FN:2001)

The predicate-fronting analysis presented briefly above explains the V and VP predicate examples. In both cases, it is vP that fronts, due to an [EPPv] feature in Pred^0,

$[_{VP}$ chase him$_i$ $]$
$[v\ [_{VP}$ chase him$_i$ $]]$
Abs$^0\ [v\ [_{VP}$ chase him$_i$ $]]$
$[$him$_i$ Abs$^0\ [v\ [_{VP}$ chase t$_i$ $]]]$
Erg$^0\ [$ him$_i$ Abs$^0\ [v\ [$ chase t$_i$ $]]]$
$[$the people Erg$^0\ [$him$_i$ Abs$^0\ [v\ [_{VP}$ chase t$_i$ $]]]]$
Pred$^0\ [$the people Erg$^0\ [$ him$_i$ Abs$^0\ [v\ [_{VP}$ chase t$_i$ $]]]]$
$[[_{VP}$ v chase t$_i$ $]$ Pred$^0\ [$the people Erg$^0\ [$ him$_i$ Abs$^0\ t_{VP}\ ]]]$

Figure 2. Niuean Transitive Clause (See (1a)) 'The people (also) chased him'

---

3. I use the labels ErgP and AbsP as neutral descriptive labels for the categories where the transitive subject is merged and to which the intransitive subject or object moves. These essentially correspond to other labels, such as VoiceP and vP, or AgrSP and AgrOP. Here, I assume external transitive arguments merge in ErgP, internal transitive objects merge in VP, and intransitive arguments merge in AbsP. I will focus on transitive clauses in this paper. See Massam (2006) for a discussion of Niuean ergativity.

[$_{PP}$ ko e kāmuta]
[$_{VP}$ BE [$_{PP}$ ko e kāmuta]]
Abs⁰ [$_{VP}$ BE [$_{PP}$ ko e kāmuta]]
[$_{AbsP}$ a au Abs⁰ [$_{VP}$ BE [$_{PP}$ ko e kāmuta]]]
Pred⁰ [$_{AbsP}$ a au Abs⁰ [$_{VP}$ BE [$_{PP}$ ko e kāmuta]]]
[[$_{VP}$ BE [$_{PP}$ ko e kāmuta]] Pred⁰ [$_{AbsP}$ a au Abs⁰ t$_{VP}$]]

Figure 3. Niuean Nominal Predicate Clause

with the difference being whether the object does or does not escape from VP prior to predicate fronting, which in turn depends on its categorical status (KP vs. NP).

As well as PNI maximal predicates, we also find maximal non-verbal predicates such as nominal predicates, which are marked with the prepositional case element *ko*, as in (4).

(4) *[Ko e fale ke lima aki] e fale i kō.*
    PRED C house SBJV five with ABS.C house LOC.P there
    'That house over there is the fifth house.'   (lit. "house to five with") (S:53)

Nominal predicate sentences as in (5) can be derived in similar fashion to other sentence-types, as outlined in Massam, Lee & Rolle (2006) and illustrated in Figure 3 above.

(5) *Ko e kāmuta a au.*
    PRED C carpenter ABS.P 1.SG
    'I am a carpenter.'   (S:53)

In (5), the nominal (PP) predicate is merged with a light BE verb and takes one argument (*a au* "I"). Intransitive subjects merge directly into AbsP (Massam 2006). The vP undergoes predicate fronting as in Figure 3 above to derive the predicate-first word order.

In summary, then, in this analysis, Niuean transitive clause structure involves merge in the order of [Pred⁰ Sbj-KP Erg⁰ Abs⁰ v⁰ V⁰ Obj-KP] with movement of object to specifier of AbsP and subsequent movement of vP to specifier of PredP (to check an EPP$_{pred}$ or v feature). This presents a fairly tidy analysis of Niuean word order, but there is an important ingredient that must yet be added in. As mentioned above, Niuean is a particle/adverbial rich language, and we must determine the place of particles and adverbials in the representation.

3. Verbal particles and adverbials in Niuean

3.1 The adverbials described

There are two main locations for particles in Niuean: pre-predicate and post-predicate. Figure 4 shows their order and placement.

Pre-predicate:

| TAM>Neg>Modal |

Post-Predicate:

| Dir>Man>InstrAppl>UnivQuant>ResPron>Advs>Emphs>Perf>Q |

Figure 4. Niuean Verbal Particle System

In the pre-predicate position we find the TAM particle followed by negation, as in (1b) above, and certain modal elements as listed in (6) and illustrated in (7). I will not be much concerned with the pre-predicate particles in this paper.

(6) Modals
fia "want", fā "habitual, typical", liga "likely", kamata, "begin", teitei "nearly", among others

(7) Ko   e tau aho oti ne   fā   hifo a   ia   ke
    PRED C PL day UQ NFUT habitual go   ABS.P 3.SG GOAL.C
    he   mataoneone i   Palitoa i   Avatele...
    LOC.C beach   LOC.P Palitoa LOC.P Avatele...
    'Every day, she would go down to the little beach at Palitoa in Avatele...'
    (NAH)

The elements following the predicate are more disparate, including mostly mono-morphemic items generally termed particles, and manner and aspectual adverbs. The distinction between particles and adverbials (if there is one) is not fully clear, and I use the terms loosely here. First, closest to the fronted verb, are direction particles, which generally indicate direction of movement with respect to discourse participants.

(8) Directional particles
mai "towards 1", atu "towards 2", age "towards 3", hake "upwards", hifo "downwards"

(9) Ne ō   mai a   lautolu ki   hinei.
    PST go.PL DIR ABS.P 3.PL   GOAL.P here
    'They came here.   (M:180)

These are followed by manner adverbials, a few of which are listed in (10), with an example in (11). The order between directional and manner modifiers can be reversed in certain cases (Seiter 1980:20).

(10) *Manner adverbials*
lahi "very, greatly", fakamitaki "well", fakaeneene "carefully", among others

(11) Kua hoge **lahi** e   motu.
     PERF starve very ABS.C island
     'The island is greatly starving.'   (Sp:172)

After the manner adverbials come three particles, each of which can also appear in other functions in Niuean grammar. First is found the instrumental applicative marker *aki* (12), second, the universal quantifier *oti*, (13), and third, the locative/temporal resumptive pronoun *ai* (14), in this order (Seiter 1980).

(12) *Kua hele **aki** tuai e Sione e titipi haana e falaoa.*
PERF cut with PERF ERG.P Sione ABS.C knife 3.SG.GEN ABS.C bread
'Sione has cut the bread with his knife.' (S:244)

(13) *Ne kai **oti** e Sione e tau apala.*
PST eat UQ ERG.P Sione ABS.C PL apple
'Sione ate all the apples.' (FN:1997)

(14) *Ka e leva lahi e tau magaaho ke taute **ai**.*
but take very ABS.C PL time SBJV cook there
'But it took a very long time for it to be cooked.' (lit. "to cook in") (Ch:23)

As well as being an applicative marker, *aki* can act as an instrumental preposition (Massam 1998, Ball this volume). As well as being a floated quantifier, *oti* can act as a nominal modifier, or as a verb of completion (Massam 2002). As well as being a temporal/locative resumptive pronoun, *ai* can act as an indicator of discourse temporal continuity, and can appear after a locative preposition (contra Abels 2001) (Massam & Roberge 1997, Chapin 1974).

Following *aki*, *oti*, and *ai*, we find aspectual/temporal adverbs as shown in (15).

(15) Aspectual Adverbs
tūmau "always", hololoa "frequently", agaia "still", agataha "immediately", among others

(16) *Mitaki, feleveia **tūmau** nakai a koe mo e*
good, meet always Q ABS.P 2.SG with
haau a tau mamatua motua?
2.SG.GEN LNK PL parent elder
'Right, do you meet all the time with your older relatives?' (LMR)

The emphatic particles come after the aspectual adverbs. They are shown in (17) and an example is given in (18), including two emphatic particles *nī* and *noa*.

(17) Emphatic Particles
noa "only", nī "indeed", foki "also", lā "just" (ia), koa "indeed"

(18) *Ka ko e tau tupua toko-lima ne mahani **nī***
But PRED C PL tupua PERS-five NFUT habit indeed
*a lautolu ke nonofo **noa** nākai kau ke he*
ABS.P 3.PL SBJV stay just not give GOAL.C LOC.C

> tau tauteaga   galue.
> PL preparation feast
> 'But the five tupua (legendary individuals) made it a habit to make no contribution to the feast preparations.' (NAH)

The perfect marker is *tuai*, and it usually partners with the pre-verbal TAM *kua* to indicate that an event occurred in the past but has continuing relevance (Seiter 1980, Sperlich 1997). This marker is exemplified in (19).

> (19) *Kua keli **tuai** e   ia   e   feke   ti   mate.*
>   PERF beat PERF ERG.P 3.SG ABS.C octopus then die
>   'She beat the octopus and it died.' (NAH)

The final post-verbal element is the question marker, *nakai*, or *kia*.

> (20) *a,   fai   magaaho **nakai** a   koe ne   nofo ai*
>   mmm have time   Q   ABS.P 2.SG NFUT stay there
>   *a   koe   i,   i   Niue ...?*
>   ABS.P 2.SG LOC.P, LOC.P Niue
>   'mmm, was there a time that you stayed in, in Niue...?' (LMR)

These particles and adverbs appear in the order given, as discussed in Seiter (1980: 16–27).[4] It is rare to find more than 2 or 3 particles after a predicate.

3.2 Analyzing the adverbials

3.2.1 *Inverse order*

In their paper on Malagasy and Niuean, Rackowski & Travis (2000) (henceforth R&T 2000) note that the Niuean post-verbal particles are in inverse order to the hierarchy proposed in Cinque (1999), in that those categories that Cinque proposes to be semantically high are low (on the right) in Niuean word order, and those that Cinque proposes to be semantically low are high (on the left) in Niuean word order (see also Jackendoff 1972, Ernst 2002, Rice 2000, and references in Alexiadou 2004). Indeed, VP modifiers (directional and manner adverbs) appear to the left of modifiers that

---

4. This order is supported by fieldwork and by data searches through texts. However, in his field notes from 1981, graciously provided to me by Chris Lane, it is indicated that *aki* and *oti* can appear in either order (*aki>oti* and *oti>aki*) in some sentences. If this is true for some speakers, and given the possibility of order variation with the directional and manner adverbs mentioned above, it would seem that what gets ordered are in fact the five domains, which are, starting with the lowest: (i) VP scoping: direction and manner, (ii) Argument scoping: *aki* and *oti* (iii) Indirect/Oblique scoping: *ai*, (iv) Aspect or IP scoping: adverbs, emphatics, *tuai*, and (v) Sentence or CP scoping: Q. Within each domain, some reordering options are possible. Given the essentially domain-based nature of adverbs (see Alexiadou 2004 and references therein), this seems plausible.

1	2	3	4	5	6	7	8	9	10
(Speech Act)>	Generally>	Neg>	Already>	Still>	(at all)>	Anymore>	Always>	Completely>	Well

Figure 5. Cinque's (1999) Universal Hierarchy of Adverbs (as given in Rackowski and Travis, 2000)

3	2		NoNum	10	NoNum	9	NoNum	8,5	7,6	4	1
Neg	Modal	//VERB//DIR	MAN	Appl	UQ	Respron	Adv	Emph	Perf	Q	

Figure 6. Niuean adverb order with corresponding Cinque numbers (NoNum = not discussed in Cinque, hence No Number)

make reference to arguments (*aki*, *oti*), which appear to the left of the modifier referring to locatives (*ai*), which in turn appears to the left of aspectual modifiers (adverbs and emphatic markers, and *tuai*). Last in the sequence comes the question particle, which has very high semantic scope, usually placed in CP.

The ordering proposed by Cinque, as given in R&T, is as in Figure 5 above.

While Rackowski and Travis are right in their observation that Niuean modifiers are in general inversely ordered as compared with Cinque, they do not examine the correspondences in detail, and they do not include all the Niuean particles and adverbials in their discussion. In fact, making detailed correspondences poses some problems. Figure 6 above shows the correspondences in more detail, using the system laid out in R&T.

Cinque (1999:106) also gives a more comprehensive hierarchy, consisting of 30 elements. This is given (with less commentary) in Figure 7 below. The bold elements correspond to elements in the Niuean adverbial system.[5]

There are two types of problems in setting up these equivalencies. First, there are mismatches in inventory. As indicated in Figure 6 with the label "No Num" (for No Number), some Niuean elements have no equivalent in Cinque's system. These are directional markers, the applicative (*aki*), and the locative/temporal resumptive pronoun (*ai*). In addition, within the various Niuean classes there are individual members which are not discussed by Cinque (e.g. the modal "want", various emphatics, some of the manner adverbs). In addition, there are elements in Cinque's system that

1. Frankly 2. Fortunately 3. Allegedly 4. **Probably** 5. Once 6. Then 7. Perhaps
8. Necessarily 9. Possibly 10. **Usually** 11. **Again** 12. **Often** 13. Intentionally
14. **Quickly** 15. Already 16. No longer 17. **Still** 18. **Always** 19. Just (Pst)
20. Soon 21. Briefly 22. Characteristically 23. **Almost** 24. **Completely (pl)**
25. **Tutto** 26. **Well** 27. Fast/early 28. **Again** 29. Often 30. Completely (sg)

Figure 7. Adverbial Hierarchy

---

5. The notions not in bold are expressed in a variety of ways in Niuean; for example in prepositional phrases, or as independent predicates.

do not appear in Niuean, as indicated in Figure 7. The meanings of these items are expressed by verbs or prepositional phrases in Niuean. I set these issues aside, since clearly languages can differ in their morpho-syntactic inventories; for example, not every language has an adverb meaning "fortunately". There is also the problem of determining whether the lexical semantics of an adverb in one language actually matches with a potential equivalent in another language. Since languages can bundle features differently, we must expect cross-classification of concepts and parts of speech.

The second type of problem involves outright ordering discrepancies. Some of these might also arise from bundling variations from one language to another, mentioned in the previous paragraph. To take an extreme example, if one language categorizes a concept as a predicate (e.g. "fortunately" in Niuean), and another language categorizes the concept as an adverb (e.g. "fortunately" in English), clearly they will be merged differently and they will not follow the hierarchy in Figure 7. One issue possibly of this type involves the Niuean modals, which pose problems for Cinque's more detailed system in Figure 7. Within the Niuean modals, we find a fair amount of chaos. Figure 8 below shows the numbers of the Niuean elements with correspondences in the hierarchy in Figure 7. There is no significance to the ordering within each class. It can be seen that there is a general descent in numbers from left to right (top to bottom in Figure 8, that is, Manner to Perfect), as we would hope, but the modals do not fit the pattern, since they express meanings from a variety of places in Cinque's hierarchy. Since Niuean modals are poorly understood in general (being considered variously to be compounded with the verb, or separate verbs (Sperlich 1997)), and since they are pre-verbal and arguably a different category, they do not fall within the restricted domain of this paper, hence I put this problem aside for future exploration. Negation, also pre-verbal, I similarly put aside here.

There are also some slight ordering discrepancies in the R&T system (Figure 6), in that the Niuean adverbial class 8 includes elements from Cinque's class 8, namely *tūmau* "always", exemplified in (19), but also from class 5 (*agaia* "still"), exemplified in (21).

(21) *nofo* **agaia** *nā* *au* *i* *Niue...*
     stay   still   EMPH   1.SG   LOC.P   Niue
     'I was still living in Niue...' (LMR)

This discrepancy seems corrected in the more detailed system of Figures 7 and 8.

        Modals: 4, 10, 11, 23, 28
        Manner: 26
        Oti: 25, 24
        Adverbs: 18, 17, 14, 12, 11
        Emphatics: (not mentioned in Cinque)
        Perf: (not mentioned in Cinque)

Figure 8. Correspondences between Niuean words and Cinque Hierarchy Items

> Q > Perf > Emphs > Advs > ResPron > UQ > InstrAppl > Man > Dir

Figure 9. Proposed merge order for Niuean post-predicate adverbials (cf. Figure 4)

We can see that no matter what system we use, there are problems in making exact correspondences between the Cinque system and Niuean word order. Nonetheless, given the vast historical distance between Polynesian languages and the languages discussed in detail by Cinque, R&T's observation that the order is opposite to Cinque's proposal is impressive, and it is maintained in the second system as outlined in Figures 7 and 8. And if we consider the important cross-linguistic ordering to be determined by scope, with the possibility of variations within a scopal domain (see Note 4), it is very clear that Niuean postverbal elements are in inverse order. Although we must allow for some of the details to be obscured by cross-linguistic variation in categorization and feature bundling, it must be emphasized that these variations deserve further exploration. For now, I will take the broad view that the Cinquean order is the universal merge order, in which case the merge order for Niuean is inverse to the surface order, as in Figure 9 above.[6]

Our next question then is: How might we derive the correct word order, within the stated assumptions of this paper, namely that adverbs are not adjoined, but are in specifiers of functional heads? There are several possibilities, which will be outlined in the following subsections.

3.2.2 *Head Movement*

In a head movement analysis, the V head would undergo head movement to left-adjoin to the first modifier (Dir), then the resulting complex head would undergo further head movement to adjoin to the next modifier (Man) and so on, as in Figure 10 below.

This type of analysis is not possible however, for sentences such as (20) above, and (22) and (23) below, where the fronting predicate in Niuean is not V but a maximal PP or VP and thus cannot be assumed to undergo head movement to achieve initial position.

(22) ko   e vagahau Niue tūmau kia a   koe.
     PRED C language Niue always Q ABS.P 2.SG
     '(When you are angry) is it always Niuean that you speak?'   (LMR)

               Prt1 Prt2 Prt3 V
               Prt1 Prt2 V + Prt3
               Prt1 V + Prt3 + Prt2
               V + Prt3 + Prt2 + Prt1

Figure 10. Successive Head Movement of PRED all the way up to the top

---

6. As discussed above in note 4, this can also be expressed more broadly in terms of domains, namely, sentential, aspectual, locative, argument, and VP domains.

(23) *Takafaga ika tūmau nī   a   ia.*
     hunt fish always EMPH ABS.P 3.SG
     'He is always fishing.'   (S:69)

Furthermore, it might also be the case that even predicates overtly consisting of just V are also maximal vPs, assuming the remnant vP analysis outlined above.

Another possible head-movement analysis would involve head movement only among the modifiers, not including the V, where first vP is merged, then the modifiers one by one. As each new modifier is merged, the immediately lower modifier undergoes head movement, successively, to form a complex bundle of adjoined modifier heads at the top of the tree. Then, when $Pred^0$ is merged at the top, the vP undergoes long movement to the specifier of PredP, as in Figure 11 below. (By "long movement" I mean direct movement of A to B, as opposed to successive head-to-head or roll-up movement.)

This analysis was assumed in Massam (2000). The problem with this analysis is that it fails to tie together inverse order with vP-fronting, that is, inverse particle order with VSO. If inverse order is associated with head-initial order as it seems to be, as discussed in Pearson (2000) (and see also Greenberg 1966, Koopman & Szabolcsii 2000, Johns 2007, Cinque 2005), this analysis is flawed in that respect. In the next subsection we see two proposals that make the connection.

3.2.3 Two alternatives to standard head-movement

Herd (2003) analyzes the order of post-predicate adverbial elements in Maori, and proposes that they should be considered second position clitics, and that their surface inverse order is related to their prosodic deficiency. Working within Distributed Morphology, and adopting a version of Prosodic Inversion (Halpern 1995), Herd proposes that phonological exponents are inserted derivationally into terminals working upwards from the most deeply embedded category. The clitics, specified as deficient, cannot be lexically inserted, thus they are skipped and the system moves upwards until the verb, which has undergone syntactic predicate fronting, is lexically inserted. After this, the system returns to the lowest clitic, whose requirement to be enclitic to a phonological phrase can now be met. The lowest clitic is thus inserted adjacent to the predicate. When the next (higher) clitic is treated, it will also cliticize to the [predicate + clitic] complex, thus reversing the merge order of the two clitics, as in Figure 12. This analysis has an advantage of adhering to the proposed constraint on head movement of Chomsky (2001) that it be limited to the domain of PF.

                         Prt1 Prt2 Prt3 PRED
                         Prt1 Prt3 + Prt2   PRED
                         Prt3 + Prt2 + Prt1 PRED
                         PRED Prt3 Prt2 Prt1 $trace_{PRED}$

Figure 11. Successive Head Movement of Particles, followed by long XP movement of PRED (Massam 2000 (for Niuean))

1. Initial structure at PF:
   PRED Prt1 Prt2 Prt3
2. Lexical Insertion of Particles is skipped, lexical insertion of verb takes place:
   "PRED" Prt1 Prt2 Prt3
3. Return to Particles, start with lowest, insert it and meet prosodic clitic requirement:
   "PRED Prt3" Prt1 Prt2
4. Next lowest particle is inserted:
   "PRED Prt3 Prt2" Prt1
5. Highest particle is inserted:
   "PRED Prt3 Prt2 Prt1"

Figure 12. Herd (2003) Prosodic Inversion analysis of inverse order (Maori)

Prt1 Prt2 Prt3 PRED
PRED Prt1 Prt2 Prt3
PRED + Prt3 Prt 1 Prt 2
PRED + Prt3 + Prt2 Prt1
PRED + Prt3 + Prt2 + Prt3

Figure 13. Long Head Movement of XP PRED, followed by movements and tuckings-in of Particles, starting with lowest – "Attract Selector" (Johns 2005 (Inuktitut))

Johns (2005) proposes an analysis for Inuktitut morpheme order in noun-incorporation structures, in which the root V (or N, in noun-incorporation) undergoes long movement first, in order to satisfy a Root First requirement, then the other elements, one by one, in bottom-up fashion, undergo long movement to a position to the right of the root, with each successive element undergoing tucking in to derive inverse order of the post-root elements. These later movements are triggered by a feature [S], which requires each element to be adjacent to its selector, as in Figure 13 above. See also Johns (2007).

These analyses avoid the problems of head movement discussed above, since they would allow for the maximal predicate to undergo long movement independently of the adverbials, and yet they do tie these independent movements together, either by the prosodic deficiency of the modifiers (Herd) or by a requirement that each element be adjacent to its selector (Johns). However, in Niuean, it is not clear that the post-predicate elements are clitics, since many are multi-syllabic, and some are derived; for example, those formed with the adverb-deriving prefix *faka-* and with reduplication (e.g. *faka-eni-eni* "carefully" (Sperlich 1997)). It is difficult to consider such items clitics, though further study may reveal that they are phonologically deficient in some way. Johns is also working within morphology, since Inuktitut is a highly synthetic language. For her, the initial movement is of a root, which is not the case in Niuean where maximal predicates are moved. However, in her system, the second sequence of movements is triggered by Attract Selector, which is syntactic for Johns, hence could be adopted for Niuean; but in essence, the system seems tied to a morphological requirement in a way that does not seem fully justified in Niuean, an isolating language. In summary, these approaches do not transfer directly to Niuean, but are worthy of further consideration.

3.2.4 *Roll-up movement analyses*

Let us now return to the analysis proposed by Rackowski & Travis (2000). They suggest an analysis in which the modifiers in Niuean are merged in head positions, then the inverse order is achieved by successive complement to specifier movement, as schematized in Figure 14 below. I refer to this kind of movement, where all material ends up in a left branch, as roll-up or snowball movement.

This analysis (see also Kahnemuyipour & Massam 2006) runs into problems, however, in cases where either the moving element moves over a maximal element, arguably not in head position, or where the moving element moves across a head which has an overt specifier of its own (putting aside the possibility of multiple specifers). We find the former case in Niuean nominal phrases, where nouns can move across complex adjectival phrases, and we find the latter in sentences with the particle *aki*, an instrumental applicative, which arguably has an applied argument in specifier position (see also Koopman & Szabolcsi 2000).

The applicative examples will be discussed further below. An example of a complex adjective, over which a nominal moves, is given below. Here, a subjunctive relative acts as modifying adjective phrase (not as a relative clause, which cannot occur within an incorporated nominal) and appears within the roll-up domain, to the right of the pseudo-incorporated noun. An example of such a nominal (in a noun incorporation context) appears in (2) above, schematized below, where the subjunctive relative clause "to settle there" is to the right of the noun it modifies, necessitating that the noun has moved across it.[7]

(24) Moving entity can move over maximal projections
...ke   [kumi [mena$_{NP}$ ke   nonofo ai t$_{NP}$]] a   lautolu.
...SBJV seek   thing   SBJV settle there   ABS.P 3.PL
'...they sought a place to settle.'   (NAH)

[_ etc [ManP _ Man [DirP _ Dir [Pred]]]]

Figure 14. Roll-up Movement (Rackowski and Travis 2000)

---

7. An anonymous reviewer asks why the subjunctive relative cannot be merged on the right of the noun. Part of the reason it is not so merged is because subjunctive relatives are different from tensed relative clauses, for example, in their ability to appear within the predicate. In this respect, they are like regular modifiers, and not like relative clauses, hence they are merged in pre-nominal modifier position in Massam and Kahnemuyipour (2006).

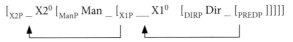

Figure 15. Roll-up Movement (Cinque 2005)

For some theorists, there are also difficulties with such an analysis as outlined in Figure 14. For example, Abels (2003) and Grohmann (2003) argue that complement to specifier movement within a single XP is ruled out in principle by anti-locality. (Grohmann also rules out movement within the same domain, larger than XP.) Thus, on both empirical and theoretical grounds, this analysis is dispreferred.

Another option, which allows for movement over complex elements and does not violate at least Abels' (2003) theory of antilocality, is that of Cinque (2005), who argues that the overt modifiers are in fact in Specifier positions. Between each phrase with overt content, there is a phrase with no merged content. Movement proceeds as in Figure 15 above, shown for the first two steps only (see also Koopman & Szabolcsi 2000, Pearson 2000 for similar analyses). I am simplifying aspects of this type of analysis here; see the originals for full details.

The derivation in Figure 15 has an advantage in that it allows for a unified analysis of inverse order in nominal and verbal clauses in Niuean, and in that it allows for a connection to be made between the predicate-initial order of Niuean and the inverse order of the modifiers. In addition, it avoids the problems raised by theories of anti-locality. The question remains as to whether this approach is preferable to one with long vP movement and inversion of the adverbials alone. And, a further more difficult question is: To what extent is this an empirical issue?

There is a problem, however, which is faced by both the analysis in Figure 14 and the analysis in Figure 15. This problem, discussed extensively in Thiersch (2006) has to do with the place of arguments in the clause. We now turn to a discussion of arguments in the Niuean clause.

4. Placing arguments

Niuean direct arguments are of three types: subjects, objects, and applied instrument objects. All other nominals are expressed as prepositional phrases. External arguments do not necessarily pose a particular problem for a roll-up analysis. In current standard views, external arguments are merged as specifiers of functional heads, external to the verbal domain. Thus, it is possible to simply consider external arguments to be merged in a position higher than all of the roll-up domains except for the final movement, as schematized in Figure 16 below.

$$[DP_{EA} \ X^0 \ [_{\text{rollup domain edge} \ldots}]]$$

Figure 16. External Arguments Outside the Roll-up Domain

Direct and applied objects, however, differ from external arguments in that they are considered to be thematically associated with overt elements that appear within the roll-up domain. The direct object is associated with the transitive V, and the applied instrument argument is associated with *aki*, the applicative morpheme (which is also used as an instrumental preposition). I will discuss these two argument types in turn. Let us first consider the applied argument.

The Niuean instrumental applicative argument is a high applicative (Pylkkänen 2002), hence the instrumental ApplP is properly merged above VP. If we adopt the now standard analysis, the instrument would merge into specifier of this phrase, which has *aki* as its head. Assuming the merge order proposed in Figure 9, the complement of ApplP would be ManP, as in Figure 17 below.

If this is correct, the existence of an argument in the specifier of one of the modifiers in the roll-up domain renders the complement-to-specifier analysis of R&T virtually impossible for Niuean, since the specifier that the complement (DirP) would move into is filled by a KP, the instrument argument.

In the Cinque system, the roll-up could proceed across the argument, since it would involve the movement of ManP to the specifier of a higher XP, rather than into the specifier of the ApplP itself. However, another problem arises with this analysis: the instrumental argument becomes trapped in the specifier of the instrument Appl phrase, becoming successively more deeply embedded within the roll-up domain as the movements continue. The result, if no further steps are taken, is the wrong word order, as in Figure 18 below.

This would incorrectly mean that the sentence in (12) would have the order [* cut [his knife with] Perfect Sione bread].

There are three possible solutions to this problem. First, we might simply allow the argument to undergo roll-up and then, when roll-up is complete, posit a rule of Argument Evacuation, which will pull the snowballed arguments up to specifiers of functional heads to the left of the roll-up domain, before a final movement of the roll-up complex to the left of the arguments. A variant of this is found in Mercado (2005) for Tagalog, where he posits the verb to undergo head movement within vP, prior to general argument evacuation, which itself occurs before the fronting of the XP remnant predicate. This last analysis faces the problems of head movement for Niuean, discussed above.

$$[_{ApplP} \quad KP_{Instr} \quad aki \quad [_{ManP} \ldots$$

Figure 17. Merge of ApplP and ManP

$$[Dir>Man>[KP + InstrAppl]> UQ\ldots]$$

Figure 18. Result of Roll-up Movement – Wrong Word Order

A similar issue arises with the direct object (see Rackowski 1998, and possibly Rackowski & Travis 2000).[8] Assuming the traditional view, it would be merged in the complement position of V. Given that it surfaces on the right of the subject and of the applicative object if there is one (as in (12)), we have the same options as outlined above for the applicative argument, so that we might allow it also to undergo roll-up within the VP, with final Argument Evacuation.

As for the external argument, we now have two choices. It could, like the other arguments, be merged below the modifiers, undergoing the same evacuations as the instrument and the direct object, or, since it is external, it might be merged high, as discussed above.

The problem with final Argument Evacuation, illustrated in Figure 19 overleaf, is that it violates long-standing assumptions about possible movements, in that it allows movement from a complex specifier, that is, from inside a specifier to a higher specifier position (as also discussed in detail in Thiersch 2006). Indeed, it allows movement from within a specifier of a specifier of a specifier etc. in the case of applicatives, while in the case of the object, it allows movement from the complement of an element in a specifier of a specifier, etc. An additional problem lies in making sure that final Argument Evacuation pulls each argument up to the correct specifier, so that [S Instr O] order results. Under usual assumptions about Merge, the lowest (rightmost) argument position would merge first, namely the object. In this case, given usual locality constraints, we would expect a feature on the head of this argument projection to pull up the closest argument, which would be either the subject (if it is in the roll-up domain) or the instrument. The object would in fact be the most deeply embedded; hence we predict object-initial order, contrary to fact. While it might be possible to articulate a theory of movement unique to roll-up contexts, it seems undesirable to open up such possibilities in languages where otherwise such movement does not seem to be licit (Thiersch 2006). Final Argument Evacuation is schematized in Figure 19.

A second option would involve successive Spec-to-Spec movement of the arguments to heads interspersed between the modifier phrases and the XPs, with subsequent repeated remnant movement across the arguments, as in Figure 20 overleaf. This option avoids the complex specifier violations discussed above, but it is unclear what would motivate the arguments to successively escape the roll-up domain (See Koopman & Szabolcsi 2000, Thiersch 2006).

A third option arises, once we have introduced the idea that the external argument might be merged high, outside the roll-up domain, which is to break with traditional assumptions about argument structure, and to posit that in fact all arguments are merged high, to the left of the roll-up domain, with one final movement of the roll-up constituent across the arguments to achieve the predicate-initial order. R&T

---

8. It is not clear whether this problem arises in Rackowski and Travis (2000) as this paper does not clearly specify whether the object is merged in traditional position inside the VP, or merged high, outside VP.

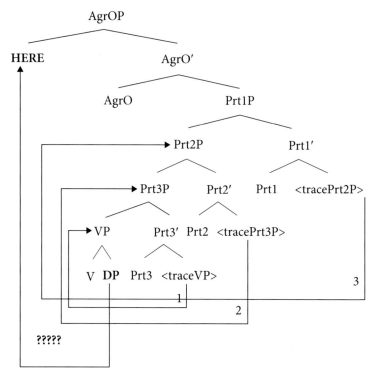

Figure 19. Final Argument Evacuation (variant in Mercado 2005, R&T 2000, Rackowski 1998, see Thiersch 2006 for discussion)

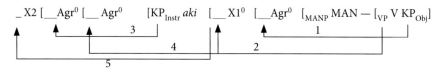

Figure 20. Successive Argument Evacuation (Koopman and Szzzabolsci 2000)

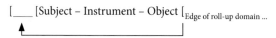

Figure 21. High Argument Merge

(2000) appear to posit this, but without discussion. This in fact fits in with some traditional grammatical views of Oceanic languages, which refer to the verbal complex as the verb phrase, and consider that the verb phrase does not contain the object (Harrison 1978, Oda 1977, as cited in Hale 1999, and see also Biggs 1971). This view essentially suggests that the verbal particles and modifiers are derivational in the sense that the 'verb' is not fully constructed until after they are added to it. It also presents an interesting new approach to the concept of 'flat' VSO languages (recently, see for example, Bresnan & Zaenen 1990, Carnie 2006, Dukes 2000, Kroeger 1993, Woolford 1991). In this view, like the flat view, basic argument word order is generated as such, but unlike most flat structures, constituency and c-command relations are nonetheless respected. Figure 21 on the previous page schematizes high merge.

Within this view, the next question to explore is whether there are in fact argument positions inside the roll-up domain, and if so, what they are filled with.

If there are argument positions inside the roll-up domain, one option is to posit empty pro DP arguments within the predicate domain (cf. Jelinek 1984, 1990, Jelinek & Demers 1994, Compton 2006, Baker 1996). Within this scenario, interestingly, Niuean emerges as similar to a polysynthetic language notwithstanding the fact that it is isolating. However, a key difference is that the high arguments are not adjunct-like in Niuean, since they can undergo raising and are null under relativization (unlike adjuncts, Seiter 1980), and their order is firmly fixed, rather than being distributed according to discourse criteria such as focus and topic, etc. as in polysynthetic languages.

Another option is to posit variables (Hallman 2005, Keenan 1987, Keenan & Westerstahl 1997) inside the predicate domain, co-indexed with the arguments that are merged high, as illustrated in Figure 22 below from Hallman 2005 in his discussion of quantifiers. The order of arguments would be taken care of by something like Hallman's constraint in Figure 23 below.

Also possible is to posit theta features on verbs, rather than argument positions in the predicate domain. These features would be part of the lexical entries of the elements theta-associated with the arguments, namely *v*, V and *aki*. These features require some form of checking, and have the property of being able to be satisfied late by high-merged arguments (Manzini & Roussou 2000, Hornstein 2001, Herd in prep.). This checking would not face the locality problems of movement, since feature percolation is a possibility in this case.

This view is possibly supported by the existence of long distance arguments in Niuean, such as in the Genitive Relative Construction (Herd, Macdonald & Massam 2004, Herd in prep), where external arguments appear to be merged well outside their traditional theta domains. In (25a) and (25b), the external argument appears as a genitive outside the clause (demarcated by the TAM) within which its theta role originates.

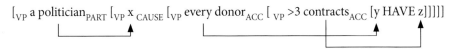

"A politican gave every donor more than three contracts."

Figure 22. Argument Variable Binding (Hallman 2006)

Thematic relations established in phase n must persevere in every phase containing n.

Figure 23. The Cyclic Linking Constraint (Hallman 2006)

(25) a. ko   hai   haau   ne   lagomatai.
       PRED who 2.SG.GEN NFUT help
       'Who did you help?' (FN:2001)

   b. a   mena haau   ne   tunu ai   e   moa.
       ABS.C thing 2.SG.GEN NFUT cook there ABS.C chicken
       'The thing you cooked the chicken in.' (S:97)

This view might also receive support from the fact that in Niuean it is possible for non-themes (in particular, instruments) to appear in direct object position and to undergo fronting with the predicate (via instrumental PNI – see Herd 2006 on similar Maori data). In such constructions, the object appears in its usual absolutive argument position. These structures are problematic under traditional argument structure assumptions, but if object KPs merge directly into specifier of AbsP, such structures can be explained by leaving the sister of V position free to host a direct (in the case of regular PNI) or an indirect object (in the case of instrumental PNI) in a modificational role.

(26) To   kai titipi mo e huki e   tautolu   e   vala povi.
     FUT eat knife and C fork ERG.P 1.PL.INCL ABS.C piece beef
     'We will eat the beef with knife and fork.' (S:73)

Another intriguing option is to posit diminished null nominal phrases, possibly NPs rather than DPs as in Jelinek, inside the predicate domain (Sportiche 1998, Cummins & Roberge 2004, 2005).

We have discussed a range of options that suppose that the source of the thematic role of the object and the applied instrument is lexical, appearing either on the verb or the applicative marker. There is another option, though, which is to consider that the internal role, like the external role, is assigned, not by a lexical item but by a functional head, in partnership with its complement. Just as the external theta role is assumed to be assigned by voice (in conjunction with its complement), so might an internal role be assigned by a light verb projection, possibly with an aspectual role. This possibility, developed in recent work (Borer 2005, Bowers 2004), is a natural extension of the neo-Davidsonian trend of separating thematic roles from lexical items, which began with the positing of Inflection as the mediator between verb and subject. It avoids the problem of setting up movement or checking relations from high positions into constituents embedded in specifiers, but whether it can account for all aspects of the verb-object relation remains to be determined.

Each of the possibilities mentioned here avoids the problem of having to somehow extract by movement the arguments out of the roll-up domain, but each also presents challenges to be overcome in future research.

5. Conclusion

In the end, then, we are left then with two basic options for deriving Niuean word order within the Kayne/Cinque context of assuming a universal base order for adverbials and particles. The first is to maintain traditional views of argument structure, and to consider that the long predicate fronting movement is separate from the roll-up head movement of the adverbials. The challenge here is to determine the nature of what appears to be the inter-connectedness between these separate movements (i.e. of the verb, and of inverse adverbs (Pearson 2000)). A theoretical disadvantage might be that this analysis involves at least two types of movement of complements: long movement for the predicate movement, and some version of head movement or roll-up movement for the adverbials (as well as the Spec to Spec movement of the object shift). This type of analysis avoids the problems of argument placement, since it is only the particles and adverbials which are undergoing movement, leaving the arguments at rest in their merged or simply-derived specifier positions.

The second option is to adopt some version of roll-up movement. This has the potential advantage of the 'extraordinary simplicity' (Stabler 1999, re: Koopman & Szabolcsi 2000) of the computations of a reduced theory of movement. But given the fact that the Niuean arguments would traditionally be assumed to have a thematic place within the roll-up domain, yet they appear phonologically outside of this domain, the theory must be augmented. This could be done with some version of Argument Evacuation, which would either necessitate the development of a theory of movement to explain why movements from within possibly deeply embedded specifiers are allowed just in case of roll-up evacuation, or necessitate an understanding of why arguments must successively evacuate the roll-up domain (Thiersch 2006).

Alternatively, the remnant movement approach could adopt High Argument Merge, a view of argument structure in which all arguments are merged in specifiers of functional projections which are separated from their traditional theta sources. In this approach, the decision must be made whether there are independent argument positions or theta features within the predicate domain. If so, the arguments would be featurally linked by Agree or linked by coindexing to their traditional theta-assigners. The structural conditions on this linking might problematically be the same as those required for Argument Evacuation, but since Agree does not involve movement, percolation is possible, hence locality issues might not be an issue. Another option within the High Argument Merge view is to consider that internal arguments, like other arguments, receive their theta roles directly from functional heads, and any relation with the complement of that functional head is provided compositionally. Given the independent movement towards this view (e.g. Borer 2005), which builds on the idea that thematic roles are largely aspectual, this is worth further exploration.

This last option seems to be the most promising in that it extends the ongoing separation of arguments from their traditional theta sources. For example, external arguments are routinely now merged in specifier of a functional head, following ideas of Davidson (1967), Kratzer (1996), Hale & Keyser (1993), and Chomsky (1995), among others. Internal arguments (objects) have for many years now been assumed to move to a specifier of a functional head, following ideas of Chomsky (1995), Runner (1998), Ritter & Rosen (2001), Travis (2000) among others, while in more recent work many argue that internal arguments are merged directly into a specifier of a functional head (e.g. Borer 2005, Bowers 2004, Basilico 1998, Hallman 2005). As for applicatives, recent work merges them in the specifier of a functional head (e.g. Pylkkänen 2002, Cuervo 2003, McGinnis 2001). It remains only to claim that the head containing the Appl morpheme (*aki* in Niuean) is removed from this argument assigning head (*aki*) position.

To sum up, this paper has examined three aspects of word order in Niuean, which have relevance for our understanding of Austronesian grammar. First, we reviewed the analysis that Niuean predicate fronting involves (remnant) movement of a maximal projection. Second, we elaborated on Rackowski & Travis's (2000) observation that particles and adverbials are inversely ordered in Niuean. It seems clear that the first two facts are connected to each other (Pearson 2001, Cinque 2005). We considered various ways that these two aspects of Niuean word order might be analyzed in a unified fashion. A prominent possibility is to adopt a roll-up analysis, but the position of arguments raises problems for such analyses (Thiersch 2006). The strengths and problems of various possible alternative analyses were discussed, but which analysis is to be preferred remains to be settled by future research on theories of movement from specifier position, or on theories of theta theory and argument structure.

References

Abels, K. 2001. *[P clitic]! – Why? Investigations into Formal Slavic Linguistics: Contributions of the Fourth European Conference of Formal Description of Slavic Languages (FDSL)*. Frankfurt: Peter Lang.

Abels. K. 2003. Successive Cyclicity, Anti-locality, and Adposition Stranding. PhD dissertation. University of Connecticut.

Alexiadou, A. 1997. *Adverb Placement: A Case Study in Antisymmetric Syntax* [Linguistik Aktuell/Linguistics Today 18]. Amsterdam: John Benjamins.

Alexiadou, A. 2004. (ed.) *Taking up the Gauntlet: Adverbs across Frameworks*. Lingua 114(6). (Special Issue).

Baker, M. 1996. The *Polysynthesis Parameter*. Oxford: OUP.

Basilico, D. 1998. Object position and predication forms. *Natural Language and Linguistic Theory* 16: 541–595.

Bell, A., Davis, K. & Starks, D. 2000. *The Languages of the Manukau Region: Woolf Fisher Research Report*. Auckland: Woolf Fisher Research Centre, University of Auckland.

Den Besten, H. & Webelhuth, G. 1987. Remnant topicalization and the constituent structure of VP in the Germanic languages. Paper presented at the GLOW colloquium, Venice.

Den Besten, H. & Webelhuth, G. 1990. Stranding. In *Scrambling and Barriers* [Linguistik Aktuell/Linguistics Today 5], G. Grewendorf & W. Sternefeld (eds.), 77–92. Amsterdam: John Benjamins.

Biggs, B. 1971. The languages of Polynesia. In *Linguistics in Oceania* [Current Trends in Linguistics 8], T. Sebeok (ed.), 426–465. The Hague: Mouton.

Borer, H. 2005. *Structuring Sense: The Normal Course of Events*. Oxford: OUP.

Bowers, J. 2004. Toward a unified theory of argument structure and grammatical function changing morphology. Paper presented at the Workshop on Argument Structure, University of Tromsø.

Bresnan, J. & Zaenen, A. 1990. Deep unaccusativity in LFG. In *Grammatical Relations*, K. Dziwirek, P. Farrell, & E. Meijas-Bikandi (eds.), 45–57. Stanford CA: CSLI.

Carnie, A. 1995. Non Verbal Predication and Head Movement. PhD dissertation, MIT.

Carnie, A. 2006. Flat structure, phrasal variability and non-verbal predication in Irish. *Journal of Celtic Linguistics* 9: 13–31.

Chapin, P.G. 1974. Proto-Polynesian *ai. *Journal of the Polynesian Society* 83: 259–307.

Chomsky, N. 1995. *The Minimalist Program*. Cambridge MA: The MIT Press.

Chomsky, N. 2001. Derivation by phase. In *Ken Hale: A Life in Language*, M. Kenstowicz (ed.) 1–52. Cambridge MA: The MIT Press.

Cinque, G. 1999. *Adverbs and Functional Heads: A Cross-linguistic Perspective*. Oxford: OUP.

Cinque, G. 2005. Deriving Greenberg's Universal 20 and its exceptions. *Linguistic Inquiry* 36: 315–332.

Compton, R. 2006. Word phases and linearization in Inuktitut. PhD Generals Paper, University of Toronto.

Cuervo, M.-C. Datives at Large. PhD dissertation, MIT.

Cummins, S. & Roberge, Y. 2004. Null objects in French and English. In *Contemporary Approaches to Romance Linguistics* [Current Issues in Linguistic Theory 258], J. Auger, J. C. Clements, & B. Vance (eds), 121–138. Amsterdam: John Benjamins.

Cummins, S. & Roberge, Y. 2005. A modular account of null objects in French. *Syntax* 8: 44–64.

Davidson, D. 1967. The logical form of action sentences. In *The Logic of Decision and Action*, N. Reschler (ed.), 81–95. Pittsburgh PA: University of Pittsburgh Press.

den Dikken, M. & Sybesma, R. 1998. Take serials light up the middle. Paper presented at the 20th GLOW meeting, Tilburg.

Dukes, M. 2000. The morphosyntax of 2P pronouns in Tongan. In *Proceedings of the LFG98 Conference: Workshop on Voice and Grammatical Functions in Austronesian*, M. Butt & T. Holloway King (eds.), 63–80. Stanford CA: CSLI.

Ernst, T. 2002. *The Syntax of Adjuncts*. Cambridge: CUP.

Greenberg, J. 1966. *Language Universals: With Special Reference to Feature Hierarchies*. The Hague: Mouton.

Grohmann, K. 2003. *Prolific Domains: On the Anti-locality of Movement Dependencies*. Amsterdam: John Benjamins.

Hale, K. & Keyser, S. J. 1993. On argument structure and the lexical expression of syntactic relations. In *The View from Building 20: Essays in Linguistics in Honor of Sylvain Bromberger*, K. Hale & S.J. Keyser (eds.), 111–176. Cambridge MA: The MIT Press.

Hale, M. 1999. Diachronic aspects of Micronesian clause structure. *Canadian Journal of Linguistics* 43: 341–358.

Hallman, P. 2005. Case, scope and linking. Ms, UCLA.

Halpern, A. 1995. *On the Placement and Morphology of Clitics*. Stanford CA: CSLI.

Harley H. & Noyer, R. 1998. Licensing in the non-lexicalist lexicon: Nominalizations, vocabulary items and the Encyclopedia. *MIT Working Papers in Linguistics* 32: 119–137.

Harrison, S. 1978. Transitive marking in Micronesian languages. In *The Second International Conference on Austronesian Linguistics*, S.A. Wurm & L. Carrington (eds), 1072–1127. Canberra: Pacific Linguistics C-61.

Haumann, D. 2007. *Adverb Licensing and Clause Structure in English* [Linguistik Aktuell/Linguistics Today 105]. Amsterdam: John Benjamins.

Hawkins, J.A. 1983. *Word Order Universals*. New York NY: Academic Press.

Herd, J. 2002. Deriving the Maori Clause: A Predicate-fronting Analysis. MA thesis, University of Toronto.

Herd, J. 2003. Deriving prosodic inversion: Clitics, cyclicity and the organization of post-syntactic interfaces. In *Proceedings of the Fourth Annual Meeting of the Niagara Linguistic Society: Toronto Working Papers in Linguistics*, Vol. 21, M. Barrie, M. Haji-Abdolhosseini & J. Herd (eds.). Toronto: University of Toronto.

Herd, J. 2006. Revisiting Polynesian pseudo noun-incorporation: Root modification and other problems. Paper presented at AFLA, Taiwan.

Herd. J. In preparation. Genitive Argument Constructions in Polynesian. PhD dissertation. University of Toronto.

Herd, J., MacDonald, C. & Massam, D. 2004. Genitive relatives in Polynesian. In *Proceedings of the 2004 Canadian Linguistics Association Annual Conference*, M.-O. Junker, M. McGinnis & Y. Roberge (eds.). Winnipeg: Canadian Linguistics Association.

Hornstein, N. 2001. *Move! A Minimalist Theory of Construal*. Oxford: Blackwell.

Jackendoff, R. 1972. *Semantic Interpretation in Generative Grammar*. Cambridge MA: The MIT Press.

Jelinek, E. 1984. Empty categories, case, and configurationality. *Natural Language and Linguistic Theory* 2: 39–76.

Jelinek. E. 1990. Grammatical relations and coindexing in inverse systems. In *Grammatical Relations*, K. Dziwirek, P. Farrell & E. Meijas-Bikandi (eds), 45–57. Stanford CA: CSLI.

Jelinek, E. & Demers, R. 1994. Predicates and pronominal arguments in Straits Salish. *Language* 70: 697–736.

Johns, A. 2007. Restricting noun incorporation: Root movement. Ms, University of Toronto.

Johns, A. 2008. Restricting noun incorporation: Root movement. *Natural Language and Linguistic Theory* 25: 535–576.

Kahnemuyipour, A. & Massam, D. 2006. Patterns of phrasal movement: The Niuean DP. In *Clause Structure and Adjuncts in Austronesian Languages*, H.-M. Gaertner, P. Law & J. Sabel (eds), 125–150. Berlin: Mouton de Gruyter.

Kayne, R. 1994. *The Antisymmetry of Syntax*. Cambridge MA: The MIT Press.

Keenan, E. 1987. Semantic case theory. In *Proceedings of the Sixth Amsterdam Colloquium*, J. Groenendijk, M. Stokhof & F. Veltman (eds.), 33–56. Amsterdam: University of Amsterdam.

Keenan, E. & Westerståhl, D. 1997. Generalized quantifiers in linguistics and logic. In *Handbook of Logic and Language*, J. van Benthem & A. ter Meulen (eds), 837–893. Amsterdam: Elsevier.

Koopman, H. & Szabolcsi, A. 2000. *Verbal Complexes*. Cambridge MA: The MIT Press.

Kratzer, A. 1996. Severing the external argument from its verb. In *Phrase Structure and the Lexicon*, J. Rooryck & L. Zaring (eds.), 109–138. Dordrecht: Kluwer.

Kroeger, P. 1993. Phrase Structure and Grammatical Relations in Tagalog. PhD dissertation, Stanford University.

Laenzlinger, C. 1996. A feature-based theory of adverb syntax. In *Adverbials: The Interplay between Meaning, Context and Syntactic Structure* [Linguistik Aktuell/Linguistics Today 70], J. Austin, S. Engelberg & G. Rauh (eds), 205–252. Amsterdam: John Benjamins.

Laenzlinger, C. 1998. *Comparative Studies in Word Order Variation: Adverbs, pronouns and clause structure in Romance and Germanic* [Linguistik Aktuell/Linguistics Today 20]. Amsterdam: John Benjamins.

Lazard, G. & Peltzer, L. 1991. Predicates in Tahitian. *Oceanic Linguistics* 30: 1–31.

Lee, F. 2000. Remnant VP-movement and VSO in Quiaviní Zapotec. In *The Syntax of Verb Initial Languages*, A. Carnie & E. Guilfoyle (eds), 143–162. Oxford: OUP.

Marantz, A. 1997. No escape from syntax: Don't try a morphological analysis in the privacy of your own lexicon. In *University of Pennsylvania Working Papers in Linguistics* 4(2), A. Dimitriadis, L. Siegal, C. Surak-Clark & A. Williams (eds), 201–225. Philadelphia PA: University of Pennsylvania.

Manzini, M.-R. & Roussou, A. 2000. A minimalist theory of A-movement and control. *Lingua* 110: 409–447.

Massam, D. 1998. *Aki* and the nature of Niuean transitivity. *Oceanic Linguistics* 37: 12–28.

Massam, D. 2000. VSO is VOS: Aspects of Niuean word order. In *The Syntax of Verb Initial Languages*, A. Carnie & E. Guilfoyle (eds), 97–117. Oxford: OUP.

Massam, D. 2001a. Pseudo noun incorporation in Niuean. *Natural Language and Linguistics Theory* 19: 153–197.

Massam, D. 2001b. On the status of subject in Niuean. In *Objects and Other Subjects*, W. Davies & S. Dubinsky (eds), 225–246. Dordrecht: Kluwer.

Massam, D. 2002. Some notes on the quantifier *oti* in Niuean *Rongorongo Studies: A Forum for Studies in Polynesian Philology* 12: 56–65.

Massam, D. 2006. Neither absolute nor ergative is nominative or accusative. In *Ergativity: Emerging Issues*, A. Johns, D. Massam, & J. Ndayiragije (eds), 27–46. Dordrecht: Springer.

Massam, D. & Roberge, Y. 1997. Operator bound clitics and Niuean ai. In *Clitics, Pronouns and Movement* [Current Issues in Linguistics Theory 140], J. Black & V. Motapanyane (eds), 273–300. Amsterdam: John Benjamins.

Massam, D., Lee, J. & Rolle, N. 2006. Still a preposition: The category of *ko*. *Te Reo: Journal of the New Zealand Linguistics Association* 49: 3–38.

Massam, D., Starks, D. & Ikiua, O. 2006. On the edge of syntax: Discourse particles in Niuean. *Oceanic Linguistics* 45: 198–212.

McGinnis, M. 2001. Phases and the syntax of applicatives. In *Proceedings of NELS 31*, M.-J. Kim & U. Strauss (eds), 333–349. Amherst MA: GLSA.

McEwen, J.M. 1970. *Niue Dictionary*. Wellington: New Zealand Department of Maori and Island Affairs.

Mercado, R. 2005. Remnant movement and V1 in Tagalog. Ms, McGill University.

Müller, G. 2004. Verb second as vP first. *Journal of Comparative Germanic Linguistics* 7: 179–234.

Niue: A History of the Island. 1982. Alofi, Niue: Institute of Pacific Studies of the University of the South Pacific and The Government of Niue.

Oda, S. 1977. The Syntax of Pulo Annian: A Nuclear Micronesian Language. PhD dissertation. University of Hawai'i.

Paul, I. 2002. An explanation of extraction asymmetries in Malagasy. *Linguistic Variation Yearbook* 2: 33–122.

Pawley, A. 1966. Polynesian Languages: A subgrouping based on shared innovations in morphology. *Journal of the Polynesian Society* 75: 39–64.

Pawley, A. 1967. The relationships of the Polynesian Outlier languages. *Journal of the Polynesian Society* 76: 259–96.

Pearce, E. 2002. VP versus V raising in Maori. In *MIT Working Papers in Linguistics 44: Proceedings of AFLA VIII: The Eighth Meeting of the Austronesian Formal Linguistics Association*, A. Rackowski & N. Richards (eds), 225–240. Cambridge MA: MIT.

Pearce, E. 2003. Phrasal movement within the Maori DP. *University of Hawai'i Working Papers in Linguistics* 34(2): *Digests of Selected Papers Presented at AFLA X*, 41–42. University of Hawai'i at Mānoa.

Pearson, M. 2000. Two types of VO languages. In *The Derivation of VO and OV* [Linguistik Aktuell/Linguistics Today 31], P. Svenonius (ed.), 327–365. Amsterdam: John Benjamins.

Pearson, M. 2001. The Clause Structure of Malagasy: A Minimalist Approach. PhD dissertation, University of California, Los Angeles.

Pylkkänen, L. 2002. Introducing Arguments. PhD dissertation, MIT.

Rackowski, A. 1998. Malagasy adverbs. In *The Structure of Malagasy*, Vol. II, I. Paul (ed.), 11–33. Los Angeles CA: UCLA Occasional Papers in Linguistics, University of California.

Rackowski, A. & Travis, L. 2000. V-initial languages: X or XP movement and adverb placement. In *The Syntax of Verb Initial Languages*, A. Carnie & E. Guilfoyle (eds), 117–142. Oxford: OUP.

Rice, K. 2000. *Morpheme Order and Semantic Scope: Word Formation in the Athapaskan Verb*. Cambridge: CUP.

Ritter, E. & T. Rosen, S. 2001. The interpretive value of object splits. *Language Sciences* 23: 425–451.

Runner, J. 1998. *Noun Phrase Licensing and Interpretation*. New York NY: Garland.

Seiter, W. 1980. *Studies in Niuean Syntax*. New York NY: Garland.

Shlonsky, U. 2004. The form of Semitic noun phrases. *Lingua* 114: 1465–1526.

Sperlich, W. 1997. *Tohi Vagahau Niue: Niue Language Dictionary*. Honolulu HI: University of Hawai'i Press and the Government of Niue.

Sportiche, D. 1998. *Partitions and Atoms of Clause Structure: Subjects, Agreement, Case, and Clitics*. London: Routledge.

Stabler, E. 1999. Remnant movement and structural complexity. In *Constraints and Resources in Natural Language: Studies in Logic, Language and Information*, G. Bouma, H. Hinrichs, G.J. Kruijff, & R. Oehrle (eds.), 299–326. Stanford CA: CSLI.

Thiersch, C, 2006. Three systems of remnant movement. In *Clause Structure and Adjuncts in Austronesian Languages*, H.-M. Gärtner, P. Law, & J. Sabel (eds.), 233–280. Berlin: Mouton de Gruyter.

Travis, L. 2000. Event structure in syntax. In *Events as Grammatical Objects: The Converging Perspectives of Lexical Semantics and Syntax*, C. Tenny & J. Pustejovsky (eds), 145–185. Stanford CA: CSLI.

Woolford, E. 1991. VP internal subjects in VSO and non-configurational languages. *Linguistic Inquiry* 22: 503–540.

Zwart, J.-W. 2003. Agreement and remnant movement in the domain of West-Germanic verb movement. In *Germania et alia: A Linguistic Webschrift for Hans den Besten*, J. Koster & H. van Riemsdijk (eds.). Groningen: Department of Linguistics, University of Groningen.

The impersonal construction in Tagalog*

Paul Law
City University of Hong Kong

This paper argues that the impersonal construction in Tagalog, in which a formally invariant predicate *may/mayroon* 'exist/have' is followed by a thematic predicate, is structurally related to the existential construction and the possessive construction both employing the same predicate *may/mayroon*. A variety of different facts including interpretation, NP distribution, patterns of argument-marking, word-order, pluralization, multiple occurrence of adverbials, long-distance construal of adverbs, locality and extraction are shown to follow from the analysis.

1. Introduction

In Tagalog, verb morphology in most cases requires a particular argument of the verb to be preceded by the morpheme *ang*. Thus, the form *nagluto* of the transitive verb root *luto* 'cook' requires that the Actor argument be preceded by *ang*, and the Patient argument with *ng* (pronounced as [na ŋ]):

(1) a. nagluto   ang/*ng guro   ng/*ang isda.
        cooked.AF   NOM/GEN teacher GEN/NOM fish
        'A/the teacher cooked fish.'

---

*   I would like to thank the participants for the 14th Annual Conference of the Austronesian Formal Linguistics Association for very helpful comments and suggestions and, Raph Mercado for editorial help and for having clarified a number of points with me. I am indebted to Joy Caban, Nestor de la Cruz, Karen Francisco, Carolyn Vargas for sharing their native judgments with me. All errors of fact and interpretation are my responsibility.
  Abbreviations. AF = actor focus, DAT = dative, GEN = genitive, GF = goal focus, LNK = linker, LOC = locative, NOM = nominative, PF = patient focus, PL = plural, RP = recent past, S = singular, 1 = first person. These labels are for glossing purposes, and the translations are mostly idiomatic. These have no theoretical implications for the formal analysis of the original Tagalog examples. Thus, the labels active and passive are not meant to imply that they are same as English active and passive.

b. niluto ng/*ang guro ang/*ng isda.
   cooked.PF GEN/NOM teacher NOM/GEN fish
   'The fish was cooked by a teacher.'

The form *niluto* of the same verb root requires that the Patient argument be preceded by *ang*, and the Actor argument with *ng*. Exchanging *ang* for *ng* or vice versa would lead to ungrammaticality, as the contrasts in (1) show. I follow Schachter (1987) in calling the argument preceded by *ang* **the trigger**.

Post-verbal word-order is rather free. The examples in (1) may have variants in which the arguments appear in the opposite word-order. For a three-place verbal root like *bigay* 'give', there are six logically possible post-verbal word-orders for any particular verb form (Schachter and Otanes 1972: 83), and the marking of the arguments is the same (the Goal argument is preceded by *sa* if it is not the trigger argument):

(2) a. nagbigay ng libro sa babae ang lalaki.
       gave.AF GEN book DAT woman NOM man
       'The man gave the woman a book.'
    b. nagbigay ng libro ang lalaki sa babae.
    c. nagbigay sa babae ng libro ang lalaki.
    d. nagbigay sa babae ang lalaki ng libro.
    e. nagbigay ang lalaki ng libro sa babae.
    f. nagbigay ang lalaki sa babae ng libro.

There is a type of construction that does not adhere to this kind of argument-marking. That construction begins with a formally invariant predicate *may* or *mayroon* 'exist/have', followed by a thematic predicate and its arguments, as in (3) and (4):[1]

(3) a. may/mayroong nagluto-ng guro ng isda.
       exist   cooked.AF-LNK teacher GEN fish
       'There was a teacher who cooked fish.'
    b. *may/mayroong nagluto ang guro ng isda.
        exist   cooked.AF NOM teacher GEN fish
        'There was a teacher who cooked fish.'

(4) a. may/mayroong niluto-ng isda ng guro.
       exist   cooked.PF-LNK fish GEN teacher
       'There was fish that a teacher cooked.'

---

1. The expression *mayroong* is a combination of the predicate *may* 'exist/have', the locative *doon* 'there', whose first consonant is realized as [r] when it immediately follows a vocalic segment, and the linker *-ng* encliticizing to the locative. The linker *-ng* cannot appear right-adjacent to *may* (see endnote 10 for examples with the linker *na*), however, for reasons that are unclear. For simplicity's sake, *mayroong* is treated here on a par with *may*, i.e., not morphologically analyzed. The discussion in the text is not affected by this treatment, as far as I can tell.

b. *may/mayroong niluto   ng guro   ang isda.
    have   cooked.PF GEN teacher NOM fish
    'There was fish that a teacher cooked.'

c. may/mayroong niluto-ng   isda ang guro.
    have   cooked.PF-LNK fish NOM teacher
    'The teacher cooked fish.'

From the perspective of (1), the argument-marking in (3) and (4) is quite surprising. The Actor *guro* 'teacher' of the form *nagluto* is preceded by *ang* in (1a), but not in (3b). Similarly, the Patient *isda* 'fish' of the form *niluto* in (1b) may be preceded by *ang*, but not in (4b). Even more surprising is (4c) where the Actor is preceded by *ang*, which is impossible in (1b).

The examples in (3a) and (4a) have the variants in (5), where the trigger appearing at the end is preceded by *na*, which is impossible in (1a):

(5) a. may/mayroong nagluto   ng isda na guro.
       exist   cooked.AF GEN fish LNK teacher
       'There was a teacher who cooked fish.'

    b. may/mayroong niluto   ng guro   na isda.
       exist   cooked.PF GEN teacher LNK fish
       'There was some fish that a teacher cooked.'

In fact, the arguments need not be present at all, ordinarily impossible with other sentences:

(6) may/mayroong nagluto.
    exist   cooked.AF
    'There was someone who cooked.'

For descriptive convenience, I henceforth refer to the examples in (3) to (6) as **the impersonal construction** (IC).[2]

The IC has been mentioned by Ramos (1971) and Schachter & Otanes (1972) (see also Kroeger 1993: 49). But it has not been systematically investigated since then:

(7) a. may nagnakaw ng pera ko.   (Ramos 1971: 161)
       exist stole.AF GEN money my
       'Somebody stole my money.'

---

2. The nomenclature IC is most suitable for examples like (6) where the trigger argument is not overt, but is less so for those in (3a) and (4a) where it is overt. Since I argue that the IC in fact has the same structure as that of an EC or PC, the IC as such is therefore not an independent construction. The various labels are for descriptive convenience and have no bearing on the formal analysis.

      b. mayroong tumatakbo sa kuwarto.
         exist   runs.AF   LOC room
         'There is someone running in the room.'

(8) a. may dumating na istudyante kahapon.
       exist arrived.AF LNK student   yesterday
       'A student arrived yesterday.'   (Schachter and Otanes 1972: 277–278)
    b. may susulatan   ako.
       have will.write.GF 1S.NOM
       'I have someone that I will write to.'
    c. may/mayroong niluto.
       exist   cooked.PF
       'There was something that was cooked.'

The question that arises is whether the IC is a special construction having its own properties, or is related to other constructions with similar properties.

In this paper, I argue that the IC is syntactically related to the existential construction (EC) and the possessive construction (PC), both of which employ the same predicate *may/mayroon* as the IC:

(9) a. may/mayroong guro.   (EC)
       exist   teacher
       'There is a teacher.'
    b. may/mayroong bahay ang guro.   (PC)
       have   house NOM teacher
       'The teacher has a house.'

I show that what follows the predicate *may/mayroon* in the IC is either (A) one syntactic constituent that independently has NP distribution, the same as the sole argument of the EC in (9a), or (B) two syntactic constituents that are similar to the arguments in the PC in (9b), one being an NP argument and the other the possessor argument that is the trigger. The key to the syntactic analysis of the IC is an understanding of various forms of Tagalog relative clauses (RCs), even though it is not immediately obvious how RCs are related to the IC.

While I have no specific proposal to make for the syntactic structures of the EC (see Sabbagh 2005) and the PC, especially for the issue of whether or how the two are related, I argue that many syntactic facts concerning the IC including argument-marking, word-order, the interpretation and multiple occurrence of adverbials, and extraction can be accounted for only if it has the same syntactic structure as the EC or the PC.

My analysis for the Tagalog IC consists of three parts. I first discuss the various forms and properties of RCs (Section 2), and then consider some morphosyntactic properties of the EC and the PC (Section 3). I show that the syntactic structure of the IC is the same as that of the EC or that of the PC (Section 4). This is but a natural consequence of the possible forms of RCs and the independent properties of the EC and the PC (Section 5).

2. Relative clauses and the distribution of NPs

In this section, I consider the different forms of the RC, the patterns of argument-marking and word-order in the RC, the locality condition and its NP distribution.

2.1 The forms of the RC

The RC in Tagalog may have one of four forms. The two more familiar forms are those in which the RC precedes or follows the overt head noun (Schachter & Otanes 1972: 123):[3]

(10) a. [NP [CP [IP nagbabasa ng diyaryo] -ng] babae]
 reads.AF GEN paper LNK woman
 'Woman reading a paper.'

b. [NP babae [CP [-ng [IP nagbabasa ng diyaryo]]]]
 woman LNK reads.AF GEN paper
 'Woman reading a paper.'

Cases like (10) are commonly known as externally headed RCs.

The other two, less familiar variants of the RC are those in which the head noun occurs in the RC (see Aldridge 2003), known as internally headed RCs, as in (11a), or those in which the head noun is not overtly realized, known as free/headless RCs, as in (11b):

(11) a. kilala ko ang [NP [CP [IP nagbabasa-ng **babae** ng diyaryo]]]
 know 1S.GEN NOM reads.AF-LNK woman GEN paper
 'I know the woman who is reading a paper.'

---

3. The linker -*ng* in (10) is a velar nasal. It encliticizes to the preceding segment if the segment is a vowel or [n]; otherwise, it surfaces as *na*. For clarity, it is sometimes represented as being separated from the preceding expression. Some speakers prefer the linker *na* instead of -*ng* even when the preceding segment is [n] or a vowel, especially when it is not adjacent to the verb.
  It is worth noting that the linker -*ng/na*, which precedes the head of the internally headed RC, differs from the case marker *ng* (pronounced [naŋ]), which precedes a non-trigger argument in the declarative sentence. The case marker never shows up as *na*, even when the preceding segment is not a vowel or [n]:

(i) a. nagbigay si Fred ng/*na bulaklak sa babae.
 give.AF NOM Fred GEN/LNK flower DAT woman
 'Fred gave a flower to the woman.'

b. ibinigay ng/*na lalaki ang bulaklak sa babae.
 give.PF GEN/LNK man NOM flower DAT woman
 'The flower was given to the woman by the man.'

b. kilala ko   ang [$_{NP}$ Ø$_N$ [$_{CP}$ [$_{IP}$ nagbabasa ng   diyaryo]]]
   know 1s.GEN NOM   reads.AF   GEN paper
   'I know the one who is reading a paper.'

For lack of space, I do not go into the details of the analysis of RCs.[4]

However, I would like to briefly consider the constraints on RCs as these have a crucial bearing on the structure of the PC, EC and IC that are our central concern here.

As is well-known, the head of the RC is related to the trigger argument of the predicate (see Keenan & Comrie 1977, Schachter 1987, and the extensive theoretical literature on the restriction on extraction, e.g., Aldridge 2004, Nakamura 1998, Rackowski & Richards 2005). Thus, in (11) the head of the RC is related to the Actor argument of the active verb *nagbabasa* 'is reading', which is the trigger argument of the active verb, and in (12) the head of the RC is related to the Patient argument of the passive verb *binabasa* 'is being read', which is the trigger of the passive verb:

(12) a. interesante ang [$_{NP}$ [$_{CP}$ [$_{IP}$ binabasa-ng **diyaryo** ng   babae]]]
        interesting NOM   reads.PF-LNK paper   GEN woman
        'The paper the woman is reading is interesting.'

    b. interesante ang [$_{NP}$ [$_{CP}$ [$_{IP}$ binabasa ng   **babae**]]]
       interesting NOM   reads.PF GEN woman
       'The one the woman is reading is interesting.'

In cases where the head of an RC is related to an argument of an embedded clause, the matrix clause (in the RC) cannot have a DP/NP trigger (see Schachter 1996, Kroeger 1993, Rackowski & Richards 2005).[5] The constraint holds of both externally (13) and internally (14) headed RCs:

---

4. For clarity, the head of the RC, including the phonetically empty head, is set in boldface. As post-verbal word-order is relatively free in Tagalog, the internal head of the RC may end up being at the end of the NP. I assume that it is still inside the RC CP, and such RCs are internally headed, i.e., these are not externally headed RCs with a pre-nominal CP.

Since the constraints discussed below hold of overt movement as well, it is clear that movement of some sort takes place in RCs. However, for the sake of simplicity, I do not indicate the details of such movement. I leave aside here the various issues concerning RCs, e.g., the analysis of the linker *-ng/na*, especially when it is not adjacent to the verb (I thank a reviewer for raising this issue), the issue of whether the overt external head of the RC is base-generated in its surface position as in the traditional analysis or raised from within the RC (Vergnaud 1974, Kayne 1994 and Aldridge 2003), and the issue of how the internally headed RCs are related to the externally headed ones. What is most relevant for my purposes here is that the (outermost) brackets in (10) and (11) constitute a nominal phrase, which I assume is an NP. As far as I can determine, these various details have no specific bearing on the analysis of the IC, which is the main concern of the paper.

5. It is an independent issue whether the CP in (13a) and (14a) is the trigger of the matrix clause. The examples in (i) suggest that the CP plays the same syntactic and semantic role as that

(13) a. [_NP **babae** [_CP [-ng [_IP sinabi ni Fred [_CP na [_IP nagbabasa
woman   LNK   said.PF GEN Fred   LNK   reads.AF
ng   diyaryo]]]]]
GEN   paper
'Woman who Fred said is reading a paper.'

b. *[_NP **babae** [_CP [-ng [_IP nagsabi si Fred [_CP na
woman   LNK   said.AF NOM Fred   LNK
[_IP nagbabasa ng diyaryo]]]]]
reads.AF   GEN paper
'Woman who Fred said is reading a paper.'

(14) a. [_NP [_CP [[_IP sinabi ni Fred
said.PF GEN Fred
[_CP na [_IP nagbabasa-ng **babae** ng diyaryo]]]]]]
LNK   reads.AF-LNK woman GEN paper
'Woman who Fred said is reading a paper.'

b. *[_NP [_CP [[_IP nagsabi si Fred
said.AF NOM Fred
[_CP na [_IP nagbabasa-ng **babae** ng diyaryo]]]]]]
LNK   reads.AF-LNK woman GEN paper
'Woman who Fred said is reading a paper.'

As we see below, these same constraints hold of the EC, PC and IC as well.

2.2 Argument-marking and word-order in the RC

It is of some significance that the pattern of argument-marking in the internally headed RCs is quite different from that in the declarative.

The trigger argument may be preceded by *ang* in the declarative in (15), but not in the RC in (16):

---

of a DP/NP trigger and hence is arguably the trigger of the matrix predicate, as Raph Mercado (personal communication) points out:

(i) a. sinabi   ni   Fred ang pangalan ko.
said.PF GEN Fred NOM name   1SG.GEN
'Fred said my name.'

b. sinabi ng ale   ang katotohanan.
said.PF GEN woman   NOM truth
'The woman said the truth.'

The relevant point here, however, is that some variants of the EC, PC and IC exhibit the same constraint on the relationship between the head of the RC and the argument it is related to. For a view of how the status of the embedded CP being a trigger bears on this relationship, see Rackowski and Richards (2005).

(15) a. nagluto   ang/*ng   guro   ng/*ang isda.   (=(1))
        cooked.AF   NOM/GEN   teacher   GEN/NOM fish
        'A/the teacher cooked fish.'

    b. niluto   ng/*ang   guro   ang/*ng isda.
        cooked.PF   GEN/NOM   teacher   NOM/GEN fish
        'The fish is cooked by a teacher.'

(16) a. kararating ng [$_{NP}$ [$_{CP}$ [$_{IP}$ nagluto   -ng/*ang **guro**   ng isda]]]
        arrive.AF.RP GEN   cooked.AF -LNK/NOM teacher   GEN fish
        'The teacher who cooked fish has just arrived.'

    b. masarap ang [$_{NP}$ [$_{CP}$ [$_{IP}$ niluto   -ng/*ang **isda** ng   guro]]]
        delicious NOM   cooked.PF   LNK/NOM   fish   GEN teacher
        'The fish cooked by a teacher is delicious.'

The fact that the trigger argument cannot be preceded by *ang* in (16) thus indicates that it does not have the same syntactic properties as the trigger argument of a declarative clause.

As the post-verbal word-order is rather free in Tagalog (see (2)), the arguments in the RC may appear in different positions. The RC in (11a) may have the variant in (17a), but the linker is *na* instead of *-ng* when the head of the RC is not adjacent to the verb (see endnote 3) (see (17a) vs (10a)):

(17) a. kilala ko   ang [$_{NP}$ [$_{CP}$ [$_{IP}$ nagbabasa ng   diyaryo na   **babae**]]]
        know   1S.GEN   NOM   reads.AF   GEN paper   LNK woman
        'I know the woman who is reading a paper.'

    b. kilala ko   ang [$_{NP}$ [$_{CP}$ [$_{IP}$ nagbigay na   **lalaki** ng
        know   1S.GEN   NOM   gave.AF   LNK man   GEN
        libro sa   babae]]]
        book   DAT   woman
        'I know the man who gave the woman a book.'

    c. kilala ko   ang [$_{NP}$ [$_{CP}$ [$_{IP}$ nagbigay ng   libro na
        know   1S.GEN   NOM   gave.AF   GEN book   LNK
        lalaki sa   babae]]]
        man   DAT   woman
        'I know the man who gave the woman a book.'

For three-place predicates, there are more word-order variations in the RC. The sentences in (17b) and (17c) are just two of the six possible word-orders (see (2)).

2.3 Non-contiguous RCs and stacked RCs

Two less known facts about RCs in Tagalog are (A) that the RC and the head noun it modifies need not be adjacent; and (B) that RCs may be stacked.

Thus, while the RC may appear adjacent to the noun it modifies, as is familiar (see (18a)), it may also be separated from it (see(18b)):

(18) a. kumain ng [_{NP} **isda** [_{CP} -ng [_{IP} niluto]]] ang guro.
      ate.AF GEN fish LNK cooked.PF NOM teacher
      'The teacher ate fish that was cooked.'

   b. kumain ng [_{NP} **isda**] ang guro [_{CP} na [_{IP} niluto]]
      ate.AF GEN fish NOM teacher LNK cooked.PF
      'The teacher ate fish that was cooked.'

The relationship between (18a,b) is reminiscent of RC extraposition in English:

(19) a. The teacher met [a student [who he knows]] yesterday.
   b. The teacher met [a student] yesterday [who he knows]

It has been well-known since Ross (1967) that rightward extraposition of the sort in (19) is subject to the Right-roof Constraint, i.e., clause-bound, whence comes the contrast in (20):⁶

(20) a. ?The teacher said [that [_{IP} [_{DP} a [_{NP} student [_{CP} who he knows]]]] will come]] twice.
   b. ?The teacher said [that [_{IP} [_{DP} a [_{NP} student]] will come [_{CP} who he knows]]]] twice.
   c. *The teacher said [that [_{IP} [_{DP} a [_{NP} student]] will come]] twice [_{CP} who he knows]

In (20b), the RC CP is extraposed from a position adjacent to the head noun *student* it modifies but is still within the embedded clause. In (20c), the CP appearing after the matrix adverb *twice* is outside the embedded clause, violating the Right-roof Constraint.

The same constraint holds in Tagalog as well. An RC cannot be related to a head noun across a clause boundary:

(21) a. ?sinabi ni Pedro [_{CP} na [_{IP} kumain ng [_{NP} **isda**
       said.PF GEN Pedro LNK ate.AF GEN fish
       [_{CP} -ng [_{IP} niluto]]] ang guro]] kay Fred.
       LNK cooked.PF NOM teacher DAT Fred
       'Pedro told Fred that the teacher ate fish that was cooked.'

---

6. The examples in (20a) and (20b) are (slightly) degraded, most probably due to the matrix adverb *twice* being linearly close to the embedded predicate *come* and hence possibly being taken to modify it rather than the linearly farther away matrix predicate *say*. In any event, there is a clear difference between these and (20c). The same point holds of the Tagalog examples in (21a) and (21b). Their slightly degraded grammaticality is due to the Goal argument *kay Fred* of the matrix predicate *sinabi* 'say' being separated from *sinabi* by the embedded clause.

b. ?sinabi ni Pedro [_CP_ na [_IP_ kumain ng [_NP_ **isda**]
   said.PF GEN Pedro   LNK   ate.AF   GEN   fish
   ang guro [_CP_ na [_IP_ niluto]]]] kay Fred.
   NOM teacher LNK   cooked.PF   DAT Fred
   'Pedro told Fred that the teacher ate fish that was cooked.'

c. *sinabi ni Pedro [_CP_ na [_IP_ kumain ng [_NP_ **isda**]
   said.PF GEN Pedro   LNK   ate.AF   GEN   fish
   ang guro]] kay Fred [_CP_ na [_IP_ niluto]]
   NOM teacher DAT Fred   LNK   cooked.PF
   'Pedro told Fred that the teacher ate fish that was cooked.'

In (21a,b) the RC is in the same clause as the head noun *isda* 'fish' it modifies. In (21c), however, the RC modifying the head noun *isda* 'fish' in the embedded clause is in the matrix clause after the matrix Goal argument *kay Fred*, in violation of the Right-roof Constraint.

Moreover, the head noun can be modified by two or more possibly non-adjacent RCs:

(22) a. kumain ng [_NP_ [_NP_**isda** [_CP_ -ng [_IP_ binili   ni   Pedro]]]
        ate.AF GEN   fish   LNK   bought.PF GEN Pedro
        [_CP_ na [_IP_ niluto   ni   Anna]]] ang guro.
              LNK   cooked.PF GEN Anna   NOM teacher
        'The teacher ate fish that was bought by Pedro, that was cooked by Anna.'

    b. kumain ng [_NP_ **isda** [_CP_ -ng [_IP_ binili   ni   Pedro]]]
       ate.AF GEN   fish   LNK   bought.PF GEN Pedro
       ang guro [_CP_ na [_IP_ niluto   ni   Anna]]
       NOM teacher   LNK   cooked.PF GEN Anna
       'The teacher ate fish that was bought by Pedro, that was cooked by Anna.'

In both cases, the two RCs are in the same clause as the head noun *isda* 'fish', which they modify in observance of the Right-roof Constraint.

2.4 RCs and the distribution of NPs

That the (outermost) bracketed phrases in (17) are NPs is further supported by their occurrence in positions where NPs occur.

Thus, apart from (possibly) being part of a trigger NP as in (16)-(17), these can also be part of a non-trigger NP, e.g., part of a possessor argument, an object of a preposition or a (non-trigger) Patient argument of a verb. I illustrate this point here with the less familiar internally headed RC and headless RC:

(23) a. bahay ng   guro.
        house GEN teacher
        'The teacher's house.'

    b. bahay ng [_{NP} [_{CP} [_{IP}nagluto-ng   **guro**   ng   isda]]]
       house GEN   cooked.AF-LNK teacher GEN fish
       'The house of the teacher who cooked fish.'

(24) a. nagkuwento si   Bob sa   akin tungkol sa   pagkain.
       told.AF   NOM Bob DAT me   about   DAT food
       'Bob told me about food.'

    b. nagkuwento si   Bob sa   akin tungkol sa [_{NP} Ø_N [_{CP} [_{IP} niluto]]]
       told.AF   NOM Bob DAT me   about   DAT   cooked.PF
       'Bob told me about what was cooked.'

(25) a. kilala   ng   babae   ang   guro.
       know.PF GEN woman NOM teacher
       'The woman knows the teacher.'

    b. kilala   ng [_{NP} [_{CP} [_{IP}nagbabasa ng   diyaryo na
       know.PF GEN   reads.AF   GEN paper   LNK
       babae kahapon]]] ang   guro.
       woman yesterday   NOM teacher
       'The woman who was reading a paper yesterday knows the teacher.'

The interpretation of the NP and its selectional restrictions demonstrate that the empty head noun external to the RC is indeed related to the trigger argument in the RC. The verb *tumakbo* 'run' may predicate of a being that may run on the ground, but not of one that may not, as the contrast in (26) shows:

(26) a. tumakbo ang   guro/#isda.
       ran.AF   NOM teacher/fish
       'The teacher/fish ran.'

    b. tumakbo ang [_{NP} Ø_N [_{CP} [_{IP} nagluto/#niluto]]]
       ran.AF   NOM   cooked.AF/cooked.PF
       'The one that cooked/was cooked ran.'

    c. tumakbo ang [_{NP} [_{CP} [_{IP} nagluto   -ng   **guro**   kahapon]]]
       ran.AF   NOM   cooked.AF LNK teacher yesterday
       'The teacher who cooked yesterday ran.'

    d. #tumakbo ang [_{NP} [_{CP} [_{IP} niluto   -ng   **isda** kahapon]]]
       ran.AF   NOM   cooked.PF LNK fish   yesterday
       'The fish that was cooked yesterday ran.'

The contrast in the headless/free RC in (26b) as well as that between the internally headed RCs in (26c,d) are understandable, given that the head of the RC is related to the trigger argument of the verb. The trigger argument of the verbal root *luto* 'cook' in the active form is the Actor, here a being that may run on the ground, and hence is compatible with the predicate *tumakbo* 'run'. But the trigger argument of the verb in the passive form is the Patient argument, here a being that may not run on the ground, and hence is incompatible with the predicate *tumakbo* 'run'.

Examples with the verbal root *hati* 'divide' illustrate the same point. It is fine to divide something like fish into two plates, but it is odd to do so to a man:

(27) a. pinaghati sa dalawa-ng pinggan ang [$_{NP}$ [$_{CP}$ [$_{IP}$ niluto-ng   isda]]]
divided.PF DAT two-LNK plate   NOM   cooked.PF-LNK fish
'The fish that was cooked was divided into two plates.'

b. #pinaghati sa dalawa-ng pinggan ang
divided.PF DAT two-LNK plate   NOM
[$_{NP}$ [$_{CP}$ [$_{IP}$ nagluto-ng   **lalaki**]]]
           cooked.AF-LNK   man
'The man who cooked was divided into two plates.'

c. pinaghati sa dalawa-ng pinggan ang isda/#lalaki.
divided.PF DAT two-LNK plate   NOM fish/man
'The fish/man was divided into two plates.'

d. pinaghati sa dalawa-ng pinggan ang [$_{NP}$ Ø$_N$ [$_{CP}$ [$_{IP}$
divided.PF DAT two-LNK plate   NOM
niluto/#nagluto]]]
cooked.PF/cooked.AF
'The one that cooked/was cooked was divided into two plates.'

The contrast between (27a) and (27b) as well as those in (27c) and (27d) all have the same explanation as those in (26) in terms of selectional restrictions.

Lastly, if the bracketed phrases in these examples are NPs, then we would expect that they can be pluralized. The expectation is indeed borne out:

(28) a. umalis ang mga/dalawa-ng [$_{NP}$ [$_{CP}$ [$_{IP}$ nagluto-ng
left.AF NOM PL/two-LNK   cooked.AF-LNK
guro kahapon]]]
teacher yesterday
'The teachers/two teachers who cooked yesterday left.'

b. guro   ang mga/tatlo-ng [$_{NP}$ Ø$_N$ [$_{CP}$ [$_{IP}$ hinuli]]]
teacher NOM PL/three-LNK   arrested.PF
'The ones/three who were arrested were teachers.'

c. umalis ang mga/dalawa-ng [$_{NP}$ **guro** [$_{CP}$ -ng [$_{IP}$ nagluto   kahapon]]]
left.AF NOM PL/two-LNK   teacher` LNK   cooked.AF yesterday
'The teachers/two teachers who cooked yesterday left.'

The NPs in (28a,b) can be pluralized, just like the NP with an overt head noun in (28c).[7]

---

7. For concreteness, I assume that the plural morpheme *mga* and the numeral is outside of the NP. Nothing crucially hinges on this assumption. I thank a reviewer for raising this issue.

In the next two sections, I bring RCs to bear on the EC, the PC and the IC.

3. Some morphosyntactic properties of the existential and the possessive constructions

There can be no doubt that *guro* 'teacher' and *bahay* 'house' are of the category noun. Thus, in the EC and PC, these can be modified by a relative clause, just as they can be in other constructions:

(29) a. may/mayroong [$_{NP}$ **guro** [$_{CP}$ -ng [$_{IP}$ nagluto   ng   isda]]]   (cf. (9))
    exist   teacher   LNK   cooked.AF GEN fish
    'There is a teacher who cooked fish.'

    b. may/mayroong [$_{NP}$ **bahay** [$_{CP}$ na [$_{IP}$ ginawa   ng
        have   house   LNK   made.PF GEN
        pamahalaan]]] ang   guro.
        government   NOM teacher
        'The teacher has a house that was built by the government.'

The examples in (29) of course have the variants in which the RC is to the left of the head noun that they modify, as in (30) (cf. (10)):

(30) a. may/mayroong [$_{NP}$ [$_{CP}$ [$_{IP}$nagluto   ng   isda] na] **guro**]
    exist   cooked.AF GEN fish   LNK teacher
    'There is a teacher who cooked fish.'

    b. may/mayroong [$_{NP}$ [$_{CP}$ [$_{IP}$ ginawa ng   pamahalaan] na
        have   made.PF GEN government] LNK
        bahay] ang   guro.
        house   NOM teacher
        'The teacher has a house that was built by the government.'

Two relevant facts regarding multiple occurrence and extraction of adverbials bear on the structures in (29) and (30).

3.1 Multiple occurrence and extraction of adverbials

Two adverbials of the same type may not co-occur in the same (minimal) clause. Thus, two time-conflicting temporal adverbials, two location-conflicting locative PPs, or two benefactive PPs cannot appear in the same clause:[8]

---

8. Raph Mercado (personal communication) points out that sentence (31c) is grammatical on the reading where one of the two PPs is understood to be 'on behalf of', and that in that case, the

(31) a. (*sa bahay) pinabayaan ng guro sa lansangan ang aso.
LOC house abandoned.PF GEN teacher LOC street NOM dog
'The dog was abandoned in the street (in the house) by the teacher.'

b. (*ngayon lang) niluto ng guro kahapon ang isda.
now only cooked.PF GEN teacher yesterday NOM fish
'The teacher cooked the fish yesterday (just now).'

c. binili ni Fred ang libro para kay Anna (*para kay Maria).
buy.PF GEN Fred NOM book for DAT Anna for DAT Maria
'Fred bought a book for Anna (for Maria).'

But two adverbials of a particular type may occur in the examples in (32):

(32) a. sa bahay may/mayroong [$_{NP}$ **aso** [$_{CP}$ -ng [$_{IP}$
LOC house have dog LNK
pinabayaan sa lansangan]]] ang guro.
abandoned.PF LOC street NOM teacher
'The teacher has in the house a dog that was abandoned in the street.'

b. ngayon lang may/mayroong [$_{NP}$ **guro** [$_{CP}$ -ng [$_{IP}$
now only exist teacher LNK
nagluto ng isda kahapon]]]
cooked.AF GEN fish yesterday
'There was just now a teacher who cooked fish yesterday.'

The contrast between (31) and (32) follows from the fact that two adverbials of the same type are in the same clause in (31) and in different clauses in (32).

Extraction out of syntactic islands like RCs is generally impossible (Ross 1967). The lack of the interpretation in (33) in which the *wh*-phrase adverbial *kailan* 'when' is related to the predicate *nagluto* 'cook' in the RC can be taken to be evidence that the adverbial cannot move out of the RC. Such movement would be in violation of Huang's (1982) Condition on Extraction Domain (CED):

(33) kailan darating ang [$_{NP}$ **guro** [$_{CP}$ -ng [$_{IP}$ nagluto ng isda]]]?
when will.arrive.AF NOM teacher LNK cooked.AF GEN fish
'When will the time *x* be such that the teacher who cooked fish will arrive at *x*?'
NOT 'When was the time *x* such that the teacher who cooked fish at *x* will arrive?'

The EC in (34a) and the PC in (34b) are no exceptions; they show the same restriction. The *wh*-phrase *kailan* 'when' cannot be taken to be related to the predicate in the RC:

---

two PPs may be in different structural positions. The point is well-taken but I have to leave the discussion of the structural positions of the two PPs for future research.

(34) a. kailan may/mayroong [_NP_ **guro** [_CP_ -ng [_IP_ nagluto   ng   isda]]]?
        when   exist   teacher   LNK   cooked.AF   GEN fish
        'When is the time *x* such that there exists at *x* a teacher who cooked fish?'
        NOT 'When was the time *x* such that there exists a teacher who, at *x*, cooked fish?'

   b. kailan may/mayroong [_NP_ **bahay** [_CP_ na [_IP_ ginawa
        when   have   house   LNK   made.PF
        ng   pamahalaan]]] ang guro?
        GEN   government   NOM teacher
        'When is the time *x* such that the teacher has, at *x*, a house that was built by the government?'
        NOT 'When was the time *x* such that the teacher has a house that was built at *x* by the government?'

The facts regarding multiple occurrence and extraction of adverbials in (32) and (34) are not specific to the EC and the PC. They hold of other structures with an RC as well (see (33)).

3.2 Three properties specific to the EC and the PC

Both the EC and the PC have three properties that most other constructions do not share. First, they begin with a formally invariant predicate *may* or *mayroon*, unusual given that verbal predicates in Tagalog morphologically inflect for aspect (Schachter & Otanes 1972: 65):

(35) a. may/mayroong guro   sa   parti bukas.
        exist   teacher LOC party   tomorrow
        'There will be a teacher at the party tomorrow.'

   b. may/mayroong bahay ang guro   noong   nakaraang taon.
        have   house NOM teacher then   past.LNK   year
        'The teacher had a house last year.'

The same form of the predicate *may/mayroon* 'exist/have' is used whether the sentence as a whole is interpreted as future, as in (35a), or as past, as in (35b). This is most evident with a temporal adverb.

Second, the sole argument *guro* 'teacher' of the EC is not preceded by *ang*, in sharp contrast with other one-place predicates (see also endnote 1):[9]

---

[9] The common understanding of the argument preceded by *ang* is that it is generally interpreted as definite (Schachter and Otanes 1972: 65) (see Adams and Manaster-Ramer (1988: 83–97) and Law (2006: 163–164), for examples of *ang*-marked triggers that are not definite, however). The exclusion of *ang* in (36a) thus follows from definite NPs being barred in the EC.

(36) a. may/mayroong (*ang) guro.
       have   NOM teacher
       'There is a teacher.'

   b. dumating *(ang)/*ng guro.
      arrived.AT NOM/GEN teacher
      'The teacher arrived.'

The sole argument of other one-place predicates is obligatorily preceded by *ang*, just the opposite of that in the EC, as illustrated by the pair of sentences in (36).

In the PC, e.g., (35b), while it is perhaps unsurprising that the possessor argument is preceded by *ang*, like the Actor argument of other two- or three-place predicates (see (1)–(2)), it is somewhat unexpected that the other argument of *may* cannot be preceded by *ng*, in contrast with the non-trigger argument of other two- or three-place predicates:

(37) a. may (*ng) bahay ang guro.
       have GEN house NOM teacher
       'The teacher has a house.'

   b. nagluto   *(ng) isda ang guro.
      cooked.AF   GEN fish NOM teacher
      'The teacher cooked fish.'

Moreover, the form *mayroong* in (38a) arguably consists of the predicate *mayroon*, to which the linker *-ng* cliticizes:[10]

(38) a. mayroong bahay ang guro.
       have   house NOM teacher
       'The teacher has a house.'

---

10. A reviewer gives the example in (ia), arguing that the linker *-ng* in the EC is not the same as the case marker, *ng*, which precedes a non-trigger argument of other predicates. The same fact holds of the PC in (ib):

(i) a. mayroon sa bahay na manok.
       exist   LOC house LNK chicken
       'There are chickens in the house.'

   b. mayroon ang guro   na manok.
      exist   NOM teacher LNK chicken
      'The teacher has chickens.'

The examples in (i) thus imply that the string *na manok* contains an RC (see Section 2.1, especially the examples in (5), see also those in (11a), (12a) and (14)). However, it is not clear whether *manok* 'chicken' is the head noun or the predicate in the RC. Unfortunately, I do not have any insight to offer to resolve this issue here. I expressly thank Raph Mercado for clarifying this point to me.

b. *nagluto-ng isda ang guro.
   cooked.AF-GEN fish NOM teacher
   'The teacher cooked fish.'

c. *niluto-ng guro ang isda.
   cooked.AF-GEN teacher NOM fish
   'The teacher cooked fish.'

But the *ng* that precedes a non-trigger argument of a two-place predicate, like that in (38b,c), cannot phonologically cliticize to the predicate (see endnote 3).

Third, the EC and the PC exhibit a peculiar pattern of extraction. In the EC, extraction of the sole argument is possible only with *mayroon*, not with *may*, while both *may* and *mayroon* are possible if an adverbial is extracted:[11]

(39) a. ilang bahay mayroon/*may dito?
        how.many.LNK house exist here
        'How many houses are there here?'

   b. saan mayroong/may bahay?
        where exist house
        'Where are there houses?'

---

11. Raph Mercado (personal communication) informs me that the examples in (39), in his dialect of Tagalog, are marginal, and that they sound better with *ang* intervening between the *wh*-phrase and the predicate *mayroon/may*:

(i) a. ilang bahay ang mayroon/*may dito?
        how.many.LNK house NOM exist here
        'How many houses are there here?'

   b. saan ang mayroong/may bahay?
        where NOM exist house
        'Where are there houses?'

I believe that the structure for the sentences with *ang* in (i) is different from that for the sentences in (39) without *ang*. In the former, what follows *ang* is an NP; more precisely, it is a headless RC. Thus, the *wh*-phrases in (i) do not originate from a position after *may/mayroon* as they do in (39), as extraction out of RCs is generally impossible. In other words, the structure of the sentences in (i) is the same as that for the sentence in (iia):

(ii) a. sira ang mayroon dito.
        broken NOM exist here
        'The things that exist here are broken.'

    b. *sira mayroon dito.
        broken exist here
        'There exists broken here.'

The grammatical contrast between (iia) and (iib) clearly shows that the two do not have the same structure. It remains unclear to me why some speakers do not readily allow direct extraction of the Theme/Patient or locative *wh*-phrase in (39).

In the PC, extraction of either argument is possible. Again, extraction of the non-trigger argument is possible only if the predicate is *mayroon* 'have', while extraction of either the possessor trigger argument or an adverbial is possible for both *may* and *mayroon*:[12]

(40) a. ilang   bahay mayroon/*may si   Pedro?
       how.many.LNK house have   NOM Pedro
       'How many houses does Pedro have?'

    b. si   Pedro$_i$ ay mayroong/may bahay t_i
       NOM Pedro AY have   house
       'Pedro has a house.'

    c. saan$_i$ mayroong/may bahay si   Pedro t_i?
       where have   house NOM Pedro
       'Where does Pedro have a house?'

As my concern here is the syntax of the IC, I do not pursue here the question of why the EC and the PC have the three properties discussed above, especially the issue of why *mayroon* contacts with *may* in (39a) and (40a) with respect to extraction of the non-trigger argument. (see Sabbagh 2005 for a formal account). I now proceed to show that given the independently possible forms of the RC, the structures and properties of the EC and the PC, the IC is structurally an EC or a PC.

4. The syntactic structure of the impersonal construction

It is easy to see that the IC has a syntactic structure similar to that of an EC or a PC, given the forms of the RC as well as the structures and properties of the EC and the PC.

    Superficially, the bracketed phrase in (41b), repeated from (23b), looks exactly like that in (41a), repeated from (3a); there is thus no reason why they should not be assigned the same structure:

(41) a. may/mayroong [$_{NP}$ [$_{CP}$ [$_{IP}$ nagluto-ng   **guro**   ng   isda]]]   (=(3a))
       exist   cooked.AF-LNK teacher GEN fish
       'There is a teacher who cooked fish.'

---

12. The examples in (40b) with the morpheme *ay*, which is untranslated here, are known as the *ay*-inversion construction. According to Schachter and Otanes (1972: 485), it is characteristic of formal style and is more common in writing than in ordinary conversation. The construction is a most reliable diagnostic for movement, since it can never be related to a pronoun in argument position. That is, (40b) is ungrammatical if the third person singular pronoun *siya* appears in a postverbal position.
    The extraction of the sort in (40a) is problematic for current accounts of the restriction on extraction in Tagalog. In most cases, only the NP trigger argument of a specific form of the verb may be moved to a preverbal position. The exceptional patterns of extraction in (40) may be due to the predicate *may/mayroon* being formally invariant, in contrast with most other verbs.

b. bahay ng [$_{NP}$ [$_{CP}$ [$_{IP}$ nagluto-ng **guro** ng isda]]] (=(23b))
   house GEN   cooked.AF-LNK teacher GEN fish
   'The house of the teacher who cooked fish.'

c. may/mayroong [$_{NP}$ [$_{CP}$ [$_{IP}$ niluto-ng **isda** ng guro]]] (=(4a))
   exist   cooked.PF-LNK fish GEN teacher
   'There is fish cooked by a teacher.'

In other words, the phrase that follows the predicate *may/mayroon* in (41a) is an NP; it is an internally headed RC, just like the bracketed phrase in (41b). The example in (4a) similarly has the structure in (41c). The structures in (41a,c) are exactly the EC in which the predicate *may/mayroon* is followed by an NP (see Section 3).

Since the head of the NP modified by an RC need not be overt (see (11b)), the example in (6) may be assigned the structures in (42) on a par with that in (11b):

(42) a. may/mayroong [$_{NP}$ Ø$_N$ [$_{CP}$ [$_{IP}$ nagluto]]] (=(6))
        exist   cooked.AF
        'There was someone who cooked.'

     b. may/mayroong [$_{NP}$ Ø$_N$ [$_{CP}$ [$_{IP}$ niluto]]]
        exist   cooked.PF
        'There was something that was cooked.'

The empty head noun in (42) is related to the trigger argument in the RC, just like that in (11b).

The example in (4c), repeated in (43a), cannot be an instance of the EC since it has two arguments. It resembles the PC, however, in that it too has an *ang*-marked argument in addition to the formally invariant predicate *may/mayroon* 'have' in the beginning:

(43) a. may/mayroong [$_{NP}$ [$_{CP}$ [$_{IP}$ niluto-ng **isda**]]] ang guro. (=(4c))
        have   cooked.PF-LNK fish   NOM teacher
        'The teacher cooked fish.'

     b. may/mayroong [$_{NP}$ [$_{CP}$ [$_{IP}$ niluto-ng **isda** ni
        have   cooked.PF-LNK fish GEN
        Pedro]]] ang guro.
        Pedro   NOM teacher
        'The teacher has fish that was cooked by Pedro.'

Moreover, given that the non-possessor argument of the PC is an NP (see (9b)), which may independently have a structure of an internally headed RC, the non-possessor argument of the IC, an NP, may have the structure indicated in (43a). Literally, then, the sentence in (43a) means that the teacher has fish that was cooked.[13] This conclusion

---

13. The translations in (43a) and (44a) (=(4c)) as declarative sentences with *ang guro* 'the teacher' being the Actor of the verbal root *luto* 'cook' are given by my consultants. Given that the

is supported by the fact that the Actor argument of the predicate *niluto* 'cooked' in the RC can be overt, as in (43b).

A number of facts about the IC now follow from its syntactic structure being either an EC or a PC. These include the interpretation of the NP argument of the predicate *may/mayroon*, argument marking, word order, pluralization, multiple occurrence of adverbs, long-distance construal of adverbs as well as locality. In fact, the IC also has the three properties of the EC and the PC that most other constructions do not exhibit (see Section 3.2).

4.1 Interpretation and pluralization

The interpretive difference between (41a) and (41c) is due to the internal head of the RC being related to the trigger argument in the RC. In (41a), the head is related to the Actor argument of the verb in the active form, while in (41c), the head is related to the Patient argument of the verb in the passive form (see the discussion of (12a)). The interpretive difference between (42a) and (42b) has the same explanation, even though they formally differ from (41a) and (41c) in that they have empty heads.

The examples in (44) and (45) are instances of the PC, where the bracketed phrases are interpreted in the same way as those in (41) and (42):[14]

(44) a. may/mayroong [$_{NP}$ [$_{CP}$ [$_{IP}$ niluto-ng   isda]]] ang
          have   cooked.PF-LNK fish   NOM
          guro.   (=(4c)/(43a))
          teacher
          'The teacher cooked fish.'

    b. may/mayroong [$_{NP}$ Ø$_N$ [$_{CP}$ [$_{IP}$ nagluto   ng isda]]] ang guro.
          have   cooked.AF GEN fish   NOM teacher
          'The teacher has someone that cooked fish.'

---

thematic predicate in the RC can have its own Actor argument, as can be seen in (43b), it should be possible for the Actor of the thematic predicate in the RC in (43a) and (44a) to be someone other than the matrix subject (see (43b)). Two of my consultants insist that this is impossible. I thus have no explanation for why *ang guro* 'the teacher' is necessarily understood to be the Actor of the passive verb *niluto* 'cook', even though it is not the syntactic argument of the verb. These remarks apply to the sentences in (46a) and (56a) below as well.

Given the interpretation of (44a), it is hardly surprising that a context is required to interpret the Actor of the verbal root *luto* 'cook' in (44b) and (45b) to be someone other than the matrix subject *ang guro* 'the teacher'. For instance, these interpretations are possible in a context where the teacher has several servants, one of them cooked and the others did something else, or one of them cooked fish, and the others cooked something else. I thank Raph Mercado for clarifying this point.

14. It should be noted here that the sense of 'have' in (44b) is more like 'have a certain relationship with' (e.g., that between employer and employee). I thank Raph Mercado for clarifying this point.

(45) a. may/mayroong [$_{NP}$ Ø$_N$ [$_{CP}$ [$_{IP}$ niluto]]] ang guro.
       have   cooked.PF NOM teacher
       'The teacher has something that was cooked.'

   b. may/mayroong [$_{NP}$ Ø$_N$ [$_{CP}$ [$_{IP}$ nagluto]]] ang guro.
      have   cooked.AF NOM teacher
      'The teacher has someone that cooked.'

The interpretations of the bracketed phrases in (44a) and (45a) are parallel to that of (41c) in that the head of the RC is related the Patient argument of the verbal root *luto* 'cook'. In contrast, the interpretations of the bracketed phrases in (44b) and (45b) are respectively parallel to those of (41a) and (42a) in that the head of the RC is related the Actor argument.

Additional evidence showing that the bracketed phrases in (44) and (45) are NPs comes from the fact that they can be pluralized, as in (46a,b), just as they can be pluralized in the EC in (46a',b'):

(46) a. may/mayroong dalawa-ng [$_{NP}$ Ø$_N$ [$_{CP}$ [$_{IP}$ niluto]]] ang guro.
       have   two-LNK   cooked.PF NOM teacher
       'The teacher cooked two things.'

   a'. may/mayroong dalawa-ng [$_{NP}$ Ø$_N$ [$_{CP}$ [$_{IP}$ niluto]]].
       have   two-LNK   cooked.PF
       'There are two things that were cooked.'

   b. may/mayroong mga [$_{NP}$ Ø$_N$ [$_{CP}$ [$_{IP}$ nagluto]]] ang guro.
      exist   PL   cooked.AF NOM teacher
      'The teacher has some people who cooked.'

   b'. may/mayroong mga [$_{NP}$ Ø$_N$ [$_{CP}$ [$_{IP}$ nagluto]]]
       exist   PL   cooked.AF
       'There were some who cooked.'

The pluralization in (46a,b) is evidence that the bracketed constituent in the IC is an NP with an RC, just as the bracketed constituent in the EC in (46a',b') and those in (28).

4.2 Argument-marking and word-order

In the IC that has the structure of an EC, the string after the predicate *may/mayroon* exhibits the same pattern of argument-marking and word-order as that of an RC.

The trigger argument in (3a) and (4a), repeated in (47), cannot be preceded by *ang*, since it is the internal head of an RC and not in a declarative sentence:

(47) a. may/mayroong [$_{NP}$ [$_{CP}$ [$_{IP}$ nagluto -ng/*ang **guro**
       exist   cooked.AF -LNK/NOM teacher

          ng   isda]]]   (=(3a))
          GEN   fish
          'There is a teacher who cooked fish.'
      b. may/mayroong [$_{NP}$ [$_{CP}$ [$_{IP}$ niluto   -ng/*ang **isda** ng
          exist   cooked.PF -LNK/NOM   fish   GEN
          guro]]]   (=(4a))
          teacher
          'There is fish that was cooked by a teacher.'

The contrasts in (47) are just the same as those in (16).

The postverbal word-order in the IC that has the structure of the EC is rather free; specifically, the trigger argument may appear at the end, just as in other cases, e.g., (17a):

(48) a. may/mayroong [$_{NP}$ [$_{CP}$ [$_{IP}$ nagluto   ng   isda na   **guro**]]] (cf. (41a))
          exist   cooked.AF GEN   fish LNK   teacher
          'There is a teacher who cooked fish.'
      b. may/mayroong [$_{NP}$ [$_{CP}$ [$_{IP}$ niluto   ng   guro   na   **isda**]]] (cf. (41c))
          exist   cooked.PF GEN   teacher LNK   fish
          'There is fish that was cooked by a teacher.'

The trigger argument in the IC – *guro* 'teacher' in (48a) and *isda* 'fish' in (48b) – is in fact the head of the RC. Not being adjacent to the verb in the RC, it is preceded by *na*, just as in (17a).

4.3 Multiple occurrence of adverbials and long-distance construal of adverbials

As the IC contains an RC, no problem arises from the multiple occurrence of adverbials of the same type. Thus, two time-conflicting adverbials or two location-conflicting locative PPs may occur in the IC as long as one PP is in the matrix clause, and the other is in the RC:

(49) a. bukas   may [$_{NP}$ [$_{CP}$ [$_{IP}$ niluto   kahapon   na
          tomorrow   exist   cooked.PF   yesterday LNK
          isda]]] (sa party)
          fish   LOC party
          'Tomorrow (at the party) there will be fish that was cooked yesterday.'
      b. bukas   may [$_{NP}$ [$_{CP}$ [$_{IP}$ niluto   kahapon   ni
          tomorrow   have   cooked.PF   yesterday GEN
          Pedro na   **isda**]]] ang guro.
          Pedro LNK   ish   NOM teacher
          'Tomorrow, the teacher will have the fish that Pedro cooked yesterday.'

c. sa bahay may [$_{NP}$ Ø$_N$ [$_{CP}$ [$_{IP}$ iniwanan   sa
   LOC house have   left.behind.PF LOC
   lansangan]]] ang guro.
   street   NOM teacher
   'The teacher has in the house something that was abandoned in the street.'

The examples in (49) are grammatical, just as those in (32) are.[15]

The lack of the interpretation in which the clause-initial adverbial is understood to be related to the predicate in the RC in (50) is similar to the facts found in (34):

(50) a. dalawa-ng beses sa   bahay mayroong [$_{NP}$ Ø$_N$ [$_{CP}$ [$_{IP}$
        two-LNK   time LOC house exist
        nagluto   (ng isda)]]]
        cooked.AF   GEN fish
        'There was twice in the house someone who cooked (fish).'
        NOT 'There was someone in the house who twice cooked (fish).'

    b. dalawa-ng beses mayroong [$_{NP}$ [$_{CP}$ [$_{IP}$ niluto-ng
        two-LNK   time have   cooked.PF-LNK
        isda]]] ang guro.
        fish   NOM teacher
        'The teacher twice had fish that was cooked.'
        NOT 'The teacher had fish that was twice cooked.'

Indeed, several other facts concerning extraction follow from the syntactic structure of the IC being the same as that of the EC or the PC.

4.4 Extraction

The IC exhibits two patterns of extraction. On the one hand, extraction of the NP argument is possible with the predicate *mayroon* but not with *may*. On the other hand, extraction of an adverbial or the possessor argument is possible with either *mayroon* or *may*, just like in the EC in (39) or the PC in (40):

(51) a. [$_{NP}$ ilang [$_{CP}$ [$_{IP}$ niluto-ng   isda]]]$_i$ mayroon/*may t_i?
        how.many.LNK cooked.PF-LNK fish   exist
        'How many fish that was cooked are there?'

    b. [$_{NP}$ ilang [$_{CP}$ [$_{IP}$ niluto-ng   isda]]]$_i$ mayroon/*may
        how.many.LNK cooked.PF-LNK fish   have

---

15. A reviewer does not find sentences (49a) and (49b) grammatical. For my language consultants, they initially hesitate but finally accept them. According to them, the sentences are confusing but acceptable. I am inclined to think that this is mostly due to processing and the general preference for N-initial RCs. In (49a) and (49b) there is no clear indication that one of the two time-conflicting adverbials is in an embedded clause.

t_i ang guro?
NOM teacher
'How many fish that was cooked does the teacher have?'

(52) a. saan$_i$ mayroong/may [$_{NP}$ Ø$_N$ [$_{CP}$ [$_{IP}$ nagluto kahapon]]] t_i?
where exist cooked.AF yesterday
'Where are there those who cooked yesterday?'

b. ang guro$_i$ ay mayroong/may [$_{NP}$ [$_{CP}$ [$_{IP}$
NOM teacher AY have
niluto-ng isda]]] t_i.
cooked.PF-LNK fish
'The teacher has fish that was cooked.'

c. saan$_i$ mayroong/may [$_{NP}$ [$_{CP}$ [$_{IP}$ niluto-ng isda]]] t_i ang guro?
where have cooked.PF-LNK fish NOM teacher
'Where does the teacher have fish that was cooked?'

Furthermore, as we may expect, phrases related to the thematic predicate in the IC cannot be moved to the left of the predicate *may/mayroon*, while the possessor argument can:

(53) a. *ang/ng isda$_i$ ay mayroong [$_{NP}$ [$_{CP}$ [$_{IP}$ niluto t_i ng
NOM/GEN fish AY exist cooked.PF GEN
babae]]] (see (40b))
woman
'There was fish that was cooked by a woman.'

b. *ng/ang babae$_i$ ay mayroong [$_{NP}$ [$_{CP}$ [$_{IP}$
GEN/NOM woman AY have
niluto-ng isda t_i]]] ang guro.
cooked.PF-LNK fish NOM teacher
'The teacher has fish that was cooked by a woman.'

c. ang guro$_i$ ay mayroong [$_{NP}$ [$_{CP}$ [$_{IP}$ niluto-ng
NOM teacher AY have cooked.PF-LNK
isda ng babae]]] t_i
fish GEN woman
'The teacher has some fish that was cooked by a woman.'

The sentences in (53a) and (53b) are excluded because extraction out of RCs is generally barred. Moreover, the movement of the non-trigger argument in (53b) also violates the well-known restriction in Tagalog and many other Austronesian languages that no NP argument other than the trigger argument may be extracted (see endnote 11, however). The contrast in (54) shows that quite generally the extracted NP must be the trigger argument:

(54) a. ang isda$_i$ ay niluto ng babae t$_i$
NOM fish AY cooked.PF GEN woman
'The fish was cooked by the woman.'

b. *ang/ng babae$_i$ ay niluto t$_i$ ang isda.
NOM/GEN woman AY cooked.PF NOM fish
'The fish was cooked by the woman.'

Long-distance construal of adverbials shows the same effect. The adverbial *wh*-phrase in (55) can only be understood to be related to the matrix predicate *may*, and not to the embedded predicate *niluto* 'cook':[16]

(55) a. kailan$_i$ may [$_{NP}$ [$_{CP}$ niluto ni Pedro kahapon na
when have cooked.PF GEN Pedro yesterday LNK
isda]] ang guro t$_i$?
fish NOM teacher
'When will the teacher have fish that was cooked yesterday by Pedro?'

b. *kailan$_i$ may [$_{NP}$ [$_{CP}$ niluto ni Pedro na **isda**
when have cooked.PF GEN Pedro LNK fish
t$_i$]] ang guro bukas?
NOM teacher tomorrow
'When will the teacher have tomorrow fish that was cooked by Pedro?'

The contrast in (55) is the same contrast as that in (34).

4.5   Non-contiguous and stacked RCs

Facts regarding non-contiguous and stacked RCs corroborate the syntactic structure of the IC being that of either an EC or a PC.

The RC can be adjacent to the head noun it modifies, or separated from it by the possessor argument. The non-contiguity of the RC to the head noun it modifies in (56b) is the same as in (18b):

(56) a. may [$_{NP}$ isda [$_{CP}$ -ng niluto]] ang guro.
have fish LNK cooked.PF NOM teacher
'The teacher cooked fish.'

b. may [$_{NP}$ isda] ang guro [$_{CP}$ na niluto]
have fish NOM teacher LNK cooked.PF
'The teacher has fish that was cooked.'

---

16. A reviewer does not find sentence (55a) grammatical. My language consultants find it on a par with those in (49a) and (49b). The remarks concerning the processing difficulty mentioned in endnote 15 apply here as well.

Non-contiguous RCs in the IC too are subject to the Right-roof Constraint. The grammaticality of the examples in (57) and in (58) is exactly the same as that in (21):

(57) a. ?sinabi ni Pedro [_CP na [_IP may [_NP isda [_CP -ng
said.PF GEN Pedro that exist fish LNK
niluto sa party]]] kay Fred.
cooked.PF LOC party DAT Fred
'Pedro told Fred that there was fish that was cooked at the party.'

b. ?sinabi ni Pedro [_CP na [_IP may [_NP isda] sa party
said.PF GEN Pedro that exist fish LOC party
[_CP na niluto]]] kay Fred.
LNK cooked.PF DAT Fred
'Pedro told Fred that there was fish at the party that was cooked.'

c. *sinabi ni Pedro [_CP na [_IP may [_NP isda]] sa
said.PF GEN Pedro that exist fish LOC
party] kay Fred [_CP na [_IP niluto]]
party DAT Fred LNK cooked.PF
'Pedro told Fred that there was the fish at the party.'

(58) a. ?sinabi ni Pedro [_CP na [_IP may [_NP isda [_CP -ng
said.PF GEN Pedro that have fish LNK
niluto]] sa bahay ang guro]] kay Fred.
cooked.PF LOC house NOM teacher DAT Fred
'Pedro told Fred that the teacher has at home fish that was cooked.'

b. ?sinabi ni Pedro [_CP na [_IP may [_NP isda] sa bahay
said.PF GEN Pedro that have fish LOC house
[_CP na niluto] ang guro]] kay Fred.
LNK cooked.PF NOM teacher DAT Fred
'Pedro told Fred that the teacher has at home fish that was cooked.'

c. *sinabi ni Pedro [_CP na [_IP may [_NP isda] sa bahay
said.PF GEN Pedro that have fish LOC house
ang guro]] kay Fred [_CP na [_IP niluto]]
NOM teacher DAT Fred LNK cooked.PF
'Pedro told Fred that the teacher has at home fish that was cooked.'

In the a and b examples in (57) and (58), the relative clause CP is in the clause of which the NP that it modifies is an argument. In (57c) and (58c), the relative clause CP appears in the matrix clause after the matrix argument *kay Fred* 'to Fred' violating the Right-roof Constraint.

The examples in (59) are of special interest. One might think that (59b) is derived from (59a) by moving the trigger argument in the RC to the right of the possessor argument:

(59) a. may [NP [CP [IP niluto-ng   isda]]] ang guro.
         have   cooked.PF-LNK fish   NOM teacher
         'The teacher has fish that was cooked.'

    b. may [NP [CP [IP niluto t_i]]] ang guro [na isda]$_i$
        have   cooked.PF   NOM teacher LNK fish
        'The teacher has fish that was cooked.'

    c. may [NP Ø$_N$ [CP [IP niluto]]] ang guro [CP na isda].
        have   cooked.PF   NOM teacher LNK fish
        'The teacher has what was cooked that was fish.'

But such a derivation is impossible, as general constraints on extraction bar movement out of an RC (see the discussion of (12a), Section 2.1). However, there is an alternative analysis for (59b) that is in principle possible, namely, the analysis in (59c). The structure in (59c) suggests that the sentence in (59b) is a case of stacking RCs that we see in (22b). The RC modifies an empty head noun, giving rise to the literal interpretation given in the translation.

4.6   Three properties of the EC and the PC

The IC indeed has the three properties of the EC and the PC that other constructions do not share (see Section 3.2).

First, the predicate *may* or *mayroon* at the beginning of the IC is formally invariant. It is used whether the sentence as a whole is interpreted as present as in (60a), past as in (60b) or future as in (60c). This is most evident with a temporal adverbial:

(60) a. ngayon may/mayroong [NP [CP [IP nagluto-ng   **guro**   GEN fish
         now   exist   cooked.AF-LNK teacher ng   isda]]]
         'Right now, there is a teacher who cooked fish.'

    b. kahapon may/mayroong [NP [CP [IP nagluto-ng   **guro**   ng isda]]]
        yesterday exist   cooked.AF-LNK teacher GEN fish
        'Yesterday, there was a teacher who cooked fish.'

    c. bukas   may/mayroong [NP [CP [IP nagluto-ng   **guro** ng isda]]]
        tomorrow exist   cooked.AF-LNK teacher GEN fish
        'Tomorrow, there will be a teacher who cooked fish.'

Second, in the IC, the NP argument immediately following the predicate *may* cannot be preceded by *ang* (see (36a)) or *ng*, in sharp contrast with other predicates:

(61) a. may (*ang) [NP [CP [IP nagluto-ng   **guro** ng isda]]]
         have NOM   cooked.AF-LNK teacher GEN fish
         'There is a teacher who cooked fish.'

b. may (*ng) [$_{NP}$ [$_{CP}$ [$_{IP}$ niluto-ng   isda]]] ang guro.
   have GEN   cooked.PF-LNK fish   NOM teacher
   'The teacher has fish that was cooked.'

Third, like the EC and the PC, the IC allows extraction of the Theme argument (only with the predicate *mayroon*), the possessor argument or an adverbial (with either *may* and *mayroon*):

(62) a. [ilang [$_{NP}$ Ø$_{N}$ [$_{CP}$ [$_{IP}$ nagluto   ng isda]]]]$_i$ mayroon/*may t_i?
        how.many.LNK   cooked.AF GEN fish   exist
        'How many who cooked fish are there?'

   b. [ilang [$_{NP}$ Ø$_{N}$ [$_{CP}$ [$_{IP}$ niluto]]]]$_i$ mayroon/*may t_i ang guro?
        how.many.LNK   cooked.PF   have   NOM teacher
        'How many things that were cooked does the teacher have?'

(63) a. ang guro$_i$ ay mayroong/may [$_{NP}$ [$_{CP}$ [$_{IP}$ niluto-ng   isda]]] t_i
        NOM teacher AY have   cooked.PF-LNK fish
        'The teacher has fish that was cooked.'

   b. saan$_i$ mayroong/may [$_{NP}$ Ø$_{N}$ [$_{CP}$ [$_{IP}$ nagluto   ng isda]]] t_i?
        where exist   cooked.AF GEN fish
        'Where are there people who cooked fish?'

   c. saan$_i$ mayroong/may [$_{NP}$ [$_{CP}$ [$_{IP}$ niluto-ng   isda]]] t_i ang guro?
        where have   cooked.PF-LNK fish   NOM teacher
        'Where does the teacher have fish that was cooked?'

If the IC were not an EC or PC, then it would be a coincidence that the IC shares with the EC and the PC these same three properties.

5. Conclusion

In sum, it is quite clear that the IC is just an instance of the EC or the PC. The similarities among them are just too many for them to be treated differently. A range of facts follow straightforwardly from the IC having the structure of an EC or a PC. These include the interpretation of the phrase following the predicate *may/mayroon*, word order, argument-marking, pluralization, interpretation and multiple occurrence of adverbs, extraction as well as non-contiguous RCs. In fact, the IC also has the three properties of the EC and the PC that other constructions do not share.

The conclusion that the IC is structurally an EC or PC is hardly surprising. Given the independently possible forms of the RC and structures of the EC and the PC, the syntactic structure of the IC is simply an instance of the EC or PC in which the argument immediately after the formally invariant predicate *may/mayoong* is an internally headed or headless RC.

References

Adams, K.L. & Manaster-Ramer, A. 1988. Some questions of topic/focus choice in Tagalog. *Oceanic Linguistics* 27: 79–101.
Aldridge, E. 2003. Remnant movement in Tagalog relative clauses formation. *Linguistic Inquiry* 34: 631–640.
Aldridge, E. 2004. Ergativity and Word order in Austronesian Languages. PhD dissertation, Cornell University.
Huang, J., Cheng-Teh. 1982. Logical Relations in Chinese and Theory of Grammar. PhD dissertation, MIT.
Kayne, R. 1994. *The Antisymmetry of Syntax*. Cambridge MA: The MIT Press.
Keenan, E. & Comrie, B. 1977. Noun phrase accessibility and Universal Grammar. *Linguistic Inquiry* 8: 63–99.
Kroeger, P. 1993. *Phrase Structure and Grammatical Relations in Tagalog*. Stanford CA: CSLI.
Law, P. 2006. Argument-marking and the distribution of *wh*-phrases in Malagasy, Tagalog and Tsou. *Oceanic Linguistics* 45: 153–190.
Nakamura, M. 1998. Reference set, minimal link condition, and parameterization. In *Is the Best Good Enough? Optimality and Competition in Syntax*, P. Barbosa, D. Fox, P. Hagstrom & M. McGinnis (eds), 292–313, Cambridge MA: The MIT Press.
Rackowski, A. & Richards, N. 2005. Phase edge and extraction: A Tagalog case study. *Linguistic Inquiry* 36: 565–599.
Ramos, T. 1971. *Tagalog Structures*. Honolulu HI: University of Hawaii Press.
Ross, J.R. 1967. Constraints on Variables in Syntax. PhD dissertation. MIT.
Sabbagh, J. 2005. Non-verbal Argument Structure: Evidence from Tagalog. PhD dissertation, MIT.
Schachter, P. 1987. Tagalog. In *The World's Major Languages*, B. Comrie (ed.), 936–958. Oxford: OUP.
Schachter, P. 1996. *The Subject in Tagalog: Still None of the Above* [UCLA Occasional Papers in Linguistics 15]. Los Angeles CA: UCLA, Department of Linguistics.
Schachter, P. & Otanes, F. 1972. *Tagalog Reference Grammar*. Berkeley CA: University of California Press.
Vergnaud, J.-R. 1974. French Relative Clauses. PhD dissertation, MIT.

Anaphora in traditional Jambi Malay*

Peter Cole, Gabriella Hermon and Yanti
University of Delaware, Max Planck Institute for Evolutionary Anthropology and Atma Jaya Catholic University

The traditional Malay spoken in the villages across the Batanghari River from Jambi City in Sumatra, Indonesia displays an anaphoric system in which all anaphoric forms can be used in both "pronominal" and "reflexive" environments. Some forms, however, show a *preference* for a local ("reflexive") interpretation, while other forms prefer a non-local ("pronominal") interpretation. In contrast, in Standard Malay/Indonesian these forms are categorially either pronominal or reflexive. In this paper, we examine in detail the distribution of the anaphoric forms in the village dialects, and argue that this distribution is pragmatically based rather than determined by the Binding Theory. We conclude that it is plausible to view the distribution in the standard language as a grammaticalization of the system found in the villages, and not as a direct reflection of UG principles.

1. Introduction

It is widely held, despite apparent counter examples, that the distribution of anaphora in natural language (binding) is determined by principles of Universal Grammar (the Binding Theory). For instance, Cole, et al. (2006: 22) state:

---

* The research reported on here was undertaken as part of a study of the traditional Malay dialects spoken near Jambi City, Sumatra. The project is supported by the National Science Foundation (BCS-0444649) and the Max Planck Institute of Evolutionary Anthropology. Without their help this work could not have been carried out.
This chapter grows out of presentations at ISMIL 9 (Maninjau, Sumatra Barat, 2005), AFLA 14 (McGill, 2007) and the Max Planck Institute of Evolutionary Anthropology (Leipzig, 2007). We would like to thank our audiences for their comments and suggestions. Special thanks are due to Bernard Comrie, Bill Davies, David Gil, Martin Haspelmath and Uri Tadmor for their help in thinking through the interpretation of the data we report on here. We also thank the anonymous reviewers who provided us with extensive comments on this chapter.

The fact that so many genetically unrelated, areally separated and typologically dissimilar languages have anaphoric elements that conform to the same distributional restrictions constitutes convincing support for the view that Binding is determined by principles of Universal Grammar.

With respect to apparent counter examples to a universal Binding Theory, the mainstream approaches to anaphora aim at showing that divergences among binding systems that appear to be inconsistent with traditional Binding Theory can in fact be reconciled with some modified version of a universal theory of binding. For instance, as illustrated in Table 2 the anaphoric devices available in Mandarin appear to be divided into three classes of anaphora: pronouns, local reflexives and long distance reflexives, in contradiction to the expectations of the classical Binding Theory of Chomsky (1981), which predicts the existence of only two classes of anaphora: pronouns and local reflexives (as shown in Table 1).

While the existence of long distance reflexives appears to suggest that Mandarin has an anaphoric system fundamentally different from that of English and other "binding theoretic" languages, it has been argued by a variety of authors starting with Battistella (1989) that the seemingly divergent anaphoric system of Mandarin can be reduced to the familiar binding system of English once the application of movement rules has been taken into account. Tree (1) illustrates schematically how the movement of *ziji* to the main clause reduces the problem presented by Chinese long distance reflexives to an issue of traditional Binding Theory plus movement (see Cole, et al. (2001 and 2006)).[1]

(1)

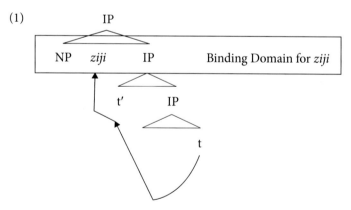

Despite a number of difficulties, some as yet to be overcome, the movement approach to long distance reflexives provides a plausible means of reducing the aberrant properties of long distance reflexives to the less troublesome, Binding Theory compatible, properties of European-type local reflexives. Anaphora in Standard Malay/

---

1. Cole, et al. (2001 and 2006) provide a detailed examination of the advantages and disadvantages of movement approaches to long distance reflexives.

Table 1. Binding theoretic anaphoric system

Reflexive	– Must have antecedent
	– Local antecedent only
	– C-commanding antecedent
	– Sloppy reference
Pronoun	– Optional antecedent
	– Antecedent obligatorily non-local
	– C-command *not* required
	– Strict or sloppy reference[2]

Table 2. The anaphoric system of Mandarin[3]

Local reflexive (*ta ziji*)	– Must have antecedent
	– Local antecedent only
	– C-commanding antecedent
	– Sloppy reference
Long distance reflexive (*ziji*)	– Must have antecedent
	– Local or long distance, but not discourse antecedent
	– C-commanding antecedent
	– Sloppy reference
Pronoun (*ta*)	– Optional antecedent
	– Antecedent obligatorily non-local
	– C-command *not* required
	– Strict or sloppy reference

Indonesian, (SMI), however, puts a different sort of strain on the claim that the Binding Theory is part of Universal Grammar. As we discussed in earlier work (Cole & Hermon 1998 and 2005), three types of anaphors are found in SMI: pronouns and local reflexives, both of which show the distribution predicted by the Binding Theory, and underspecified anaphors, which appear in the union of the environments in which pronouns and reflexives occur. A similar distribution occurs in the Peranakan Javanese of Semarang, which is examined in detail in Cole, et al. (2007).

---

2. As noted by a referee, the relationship between strict/sloppy readings and reflexives may be less straight-forward than other properties of anaphors.

3. We ignore the complications to the system created by logophoric uses of both pronouns and reflexives. See Cole, et al. (2001 and 2006) for description and discussion of how logophoricity relates to the distribution of long distance anaphors.

Table 3. The anaphoric system of Standard Malay/Indonesian (3rd person singular)

True reflexive *dirinya sendiri* (*diri* + 3 *sendiri*)	– Must have antecedent – Local antecedent only – C-commanding antecedent – Sloppy reference
Underspecified anaphor *dirinya* (*diri* + 3)	– Antecedent optional – Local, long distance or discourse antecedent – C-command *not* required – Strict or sloppy reference
Pronoun *dia* (3)	– Optional antecedent – Obligatorily non-local antecedent – C-command *not* required – Strict or sloppy reference

As is shown in Table 3, there are three types of anaphors in SMI. Two are unproblematic from the perspective of the Binding Theory: pronouns and true reflexives. The third type, unspecified anaphors, displays the union of the properties expected of reflexives and pronouns. The antecedents for unspecified anaphors may occur within the sentence or be understood from the discourse. They can be local or long distance:

(2) *Ahmad$_i$ tahu Salmah$_j$ akan membeli baju untuk dirinya$_{i/j/k}$.*
    Ahmad know Salmah will MENG-buy clothes for self-3
    'Ahmad knows Salmah will buy clothes for him/herself.'

C-command is possible but it is not required:

(3) [$_{NP}$ *Bapak$_i$ Siti$_j$*]$_l$ *tidak suka dirinya$_{i/j/k}$.*[4]
    father Siti not like self-3
    'Siti's father does not like her/himself/him.'

When VP ellipsis occurs, both strict and sloppy readings are available:

(4) *John nampak dirinya di dalam cermin; Frank pun.*
    John see self-3 in inside mirror Frank also
    'John saw himself/him in the mirror and Frank did too.'

(4′) Both Strict and Sloppy Readings are Well-formed
   a. Strict Reading
      [John saw x$_1$ in the mirror ∧ Frank saw x$_1$ in the mirror]$^{x_1 \rightarrow John}$
   b. Sloppy Reading
      λx[x saw x in the mirror] (John) ∧ λx[x saw x in the mirror] (Frank)

---

4. The index *k* on *dirinya* indicates that *dirinya* can refer to someone in the discourse other than Siti or Siti's father.

An implicit assumption of many syntacticians is that Binding Theory provides an exhaustive description of the anaphoric devices available in human language; hence, the properties of pronouns and bound anaphors constitute the definition of possible natural language anaphor. The anaphoric system of SMI is problematic for this view because it points to the existence of anaphors that are outside the system defined by Binding Theory. The facts of SMI suggest that the properties of pronouns and reflexives cannot provide an independent definition of a natural language anaphor. Rather, these facts appear to demand a different approach, that there are two categories of anaphors: those that are (classical) Binding Theory compatible and those that are not. As was discussed by a variety of authors going back at least to Burzio (1989, 1991), and discussed more recently by Haspelmath (2005), such a situation would not be fatal for the notion that there is a UG basis for binding if there are independent, universal definitions for pronoun and anaphor. These, however, do not exist. As Haspelmath notes, the claims of Binding Theory cannot be tested empirically. Apparent counter examples to the predictions of Binding Theory could always be claimed to be instances of non-Binding Theory compatible anaphors rather than true counter examples to the Binding Theory.

We have seen that the binding facts of SMI undercut the universality of the classical Binding Theory because there exists a form in SMI that appears to be exempt from binding. Despite the existence of this form, SMI provides a sort of back door support for the universality of Binding Theory as well. This is because SMI also contains forms that appear to be garden variety pronouns and reflexives which are in conformity with binding. Thus, it can be claimed on the basis of SMI and similar languages that even the very languages containing forms incompatible with classical Binding Theory are subject to the Binding Theory in some area of the grammar, a seeming confirmation of the universality of Binding Theory in human language. Any such support, however, will be seen to be illusory. We shall turn next to a variety of Malay in which there are no forms that conform to the requirements of Binding.

2. Village Jambi Malay

We shall now turn to a variety of Malay that appears not to contain any forms that are compatible with the Binding Theory. Although most theoretically-oriented studies of Malay/Indonesian have been based on SMI, in reality SMI is problematic as an object of study. Even though SMI is a major world language with about 250 million speakers in Indonesia, Malaysia, Brunei Darussalam and Singapore, and, is taught in schools and employed for official purposes, SMI has very few native speakers. Almost no children learn SMI as their first language. Instead, they acquire one of the many local languages spoken in the region, or a colloquial variety of Malay/Indonesian. Unlike the colloquial varieties, the grammar of SMI has been determined to a large extent by the fiat of the language planners in Malaysia and Indonesia. Indeed, it could be argued that SMI, as described by the language planners, is an artificial creation rather than a natural language. The artificiality of SMI is moderated by the existence of a "near standard Malay/Indonesian", which a number of authors (including the authors of this chapter) have argued is an appropriate subject for linguistic investigation since speakers of near standard have strong and consistent intuitions about grammaticality. These intuitions often contradict both the fiat of the language planners and the grammars of the colloquial varieties of Malay/Indonesian spoken by these same individuals in other contexts. Thus, near standard is an appropriate object of study for linguists. Still, despite the legitimacy of examining the characteristics of the near standard, it is of even greater importance to study local varieties of Malay/Indonesian so as to learn the properties of the language as acquired in an unselfconscious fashion by native speakers.

The current study of anaphora in Jambi Malay is part of an investigation of the Malay spoken in the villages around the city of Jambi in Sumatra. Village Jambi Malay is a "traditional" Malay language, spoken in the Malay heartland of Central Sumatra, the region where Malay is widely believed to have originated. Although there has been extensive contact with other languages (especially Javanese) and with other dialects of Malay, the village dialects around Jambi City have been transmitted in an uninterrupted fashion from generation to generation, as far as we know, back to the earliest speakers of Malay. This is to be contrasted with "contact" varieties of Malay/Indonesian, like Jakarta Indonesian. According to Tjung (2006), Wouk (1999), Sneddon (2006) and many others, Jakarta Indonesian developed through a process of accommodation among a highly restricted dialect (Standard Indonesian) and a number of other sources. The most significant sources were Betawi Malay, Chinese Malay, Javanese, and Sundanese, which were the languages/dialects spoken by the major population groups living in the city at the time Jakarta Indonesian came into existence. Such an origin cannot be posited for the village dialects of Jambi. Rather, the village dialects instantiate slow divergence among neighboring speech communities, similar to what has been observed for dialects of Romance, Germanic etc. Thus, it is unsurprising if village Jambi Malay displays grammatical characteristics that are distinct from those found in contact varieties of colloquial Malay.

3. Anaphora in traditional Jambi Malay

The data presented in this paper are drawn from two dialects of Jambi Malay: Tanjung Raden and Mudung Darat (named after the villages in which the dialects are spoken). All varieties of Jambi Malay are mutually comprehensible, but the grammars of the dialects exhibit differences that are noted and, sometimes, discussed by native speakers. (As a whole Jambi Malay is not mutually comprehensible with Standard Indonesian, Jakarta Indonesian and other dialects not native to the area around Jambi City, but speakers of Jambi Malay typically have at least a passive knowledge of SMI and Jakarta

Indonesian from school and the media.) We employ a combination of naturalistic data drawn from texts and elicited data.

Unlike SMI, Mudung Darat and Tanjung Raden (henceforth MD and TR respectively) 'pronouns' (i.e. the form cognate with pronouns in Standard Malay/Indonesian) can corefer with local and LD antecedents. (Preferred interpretations are *italicized*. *Dio* and *ɲo* are alternative forms of the third person pronoun, related to *dia* and *-nya* in SMI. Unlike SMI *-nya*, Jambi *ɲo* is an independent pronoun rather than a clitic.)

(5) a. *dio cinto dio* (MD)
       3   love 3
       'He loves himself/*him*.'

    b. *dio cinto samo ɲo-la* (MD)
       3   love with 3-EMPH
       'He loves *himself*/him.'

(6) a. *yanti neŋo? dio di tipi* (MD/TR)
       Yanti N-see 3 LOC television
       'Yanti saw herself on TV.'/ '*Yanti saw him on TV.*'

    b. *yanti neŋo? dio-la di tipi* (MD/TR)
       Yanti N-see 3-EMPH LOC television
       '*Yanti saw herself on TV.*'/ 'Yanti saw him on TV.'

(The choice of *dio* versus *ɲo* in (5)-(6) is accidental and does not affect the interpretation.)

As is seen in (5)-(6), the addition of the emphatic focus marker *-la* changes the preferred interpretation for the pronouns. When *-la* is present ((5b) and (6b)), the preferred interpretation is that the antecedent for *dio/ɲo* is local. In contrast, when *-la* is absent, the preferred antecedent is non-local, i.e., a discourse antecedent. A similar effect is observed when the intensifier *dewe?* follows the pronoun:

(7) *arna cinto dŋan dio? dewe?* (TR)
    Arna love with 3 INT
    'Arna loves *herself*/ (only) him.'

(8) *mama? nik cinto dio dewe?* (MD)
    mother Nick love 3 INT
    'Nick's mother loves *herself*/ (only) him.'

As we will see below, the primary use of *dewe?* is to signal contrast. Like SMI *sendiri*, *dewe?* is often translated as 'only' or 'alone'. In examples like (7)-(8), the effect of *dewe?* is similar to that of *-la* in that it changes the preference for the interpretation of *dio* from 'him' to 'himself'. *-La*, unlike *dewe?*, is purely an emphatic or focal marker, and does not carry an interpretation as 'only' or 'alone'.

Dewe? and *-la* can also be used in combination:

(9) *kami cinto kami dewe?-la* (MD)
    1   love 1   INT-EMPH
    'I love only myself.'

The presence of *dewe?* and *-la* together both emphasizes the pronoun *kami* and increases the likelihood that the pronoun is coreferential with its antecedent. (In the case of first person pronouns, as in (9), no other interpretation is possible.)

Despite the fact that *dewe?* and *-la* make a local coreferential interpretation likely, long distance and discourse interpretations are not ruled out:

(10) *yanti pikir [arna cinto dio dewe?/dio-la]* (MD/TR)
     Yanti think Arna love 3   INT/ 3-EMPH
     'Yanti thinks Arna loves *Arna/Yanti*/him.'

Furthermore, the absence of *dewe?* and *-la* does not block the possibility of a reflexive interpretation:

(11) *yanti pikir [arna cinto dio]* (MD)
     Yanti think Arna love 3
     'Yanti thinks Arna loves Arna/*Yanti*/him/her.'

While, in isolation, the most likely interpretation for *dio* in (11) is 'Yanti' or a discourse antecedent, the sentence is well formed to mean 'Yanti thinks that Arna loves herself.' Furthermore, *dio dewe?* does not display subject orientation nor does it require a c-commanding antecedent. So, it does not display the constellation of properties typical of a "long distance reflexive":

(12) *yanti bacakap samo arna tntaŋ dio dewe?* (MD)
     Yanti INTR-talk with Arna about 3   INT
     'Yanti talked to Arna about *Arna/Yanti*/him/her.'

Dio dewe? in (12) can refer to the object of the preposition *samo* 'with' as well as to the c-commanding subject (*Yanti*).

We have shown that both the bare pronouns (*dio/dio?*) and pronoun +-*la* and pronoun + *dewe?* can be used for local, long distance and discourse reference. In addition, these forms can be used regardless of whether or not the antecedent c-commands the anaphoric form, as was shown in (8) (repeated) for *dio dewe?* and as shown for *dio-la/ɲo-la* in (13).

(8) *mama? nik cinto dio dewe?* (MD)
    mother Nick love 3   INT
    'Nick's mother loves herself/ (only) him.'

(13) *mama? nik cinto ana?-e, laki-e,*
     mother Nick love child-3 husband-3

> *jugo dɲan dio-la/   ɲo-la* (MD)
> also with 3-EMPH/3-EMPH
> 'Nick's mother loves her child, her husband and also herself/him.'

In both (8) and (13), the antecedent for the anaphoric form can be the c-commanding nominal (*mamaʔ nik*) or the non-commanding possessor (*nik*).

To summarize, both the bare pronouns (*dio/dioʔ*) and pronoun + *-la* and pronoun + *deweʔ* are underspecified anaphoric forms, which are vague in their referential possibilities and which can be used for local, long distance and discourse coreference whenever the context is right. None of the forms requires a c-commanding antecedent. That is, Mudung Darat and Tanjung Raden do not divide anaphora into two types (pronouns and reflexives), as does English; three types (pronouns, reflexives and "long distance reflexives"), as does Chinese; or three different types (pronouns, reflexives and underspecified anaphors), as does Standard Malay/Indonesian. Rather, *all* anaphors are unspecified with respect to local/long distance, c-command etc.

4. The absence of dedicated reflexives in other Austronesian languages

The first question we would like to examine is whether the distribution we have just described is typologically attested in Austronesian languages. From the perspective of contemporary European languages, the absence of a division between reflexives and pronouns may seem aberrant, but this state of affairs is far from unusual among Austronesian languages. The lack of specification as a reflexive or a pronoun is reported in Besnier (2000) for Tuvaluan: there are no special forms for reflexive pronouns. Reflexivity is expressed by pronouns or by a pronoun plus an intensifying adverb *(ei)loa*.

> (14) *Nee taa   (eiloa) nee Lusi a   ia* (Besnier, 1070)
>   Pst strike indeed Erg Lusi contrastive he
>   'Lusi killed himself/him.'

The addition of an emphatic marker *eiloa* does not force a coreferential interpretation in (14). The likelihood of a reflexive interpretation can be increased by adding *loa* in more than one position:

> (15) *Nee taa   nee Lusi **loa**   a   ia **loa*** (Besnier, 1074)
>   Pst strike Erg Lusi indeed contrastive he indeed
>   'Lusi killed himself.'

That is, the presence of the intensifier increases the likelihood of a coreferential interpretation, but does not make it obligatory. Multiple instances of the intensifier increase the likelihood to the point that the interpretation is virtually assured.

Davies (2008) reports similar facts for Madurese. In Madurese, *aba'na dibi'* occurs in environments typical of a reflexive:

(16) *Dwita ngennal-lagi* **aba'na dibi'** *ka Bambang.* (Madurese, Davies, 1)
Dwita av-know-caus 3(-self) to Bambang
'Dwita introduced him/her/herself to Bambang.'

However, *aba'na dibi'* can also occur in environments in which reflexives would not be expected (non-c-commanding antecedent in (17) and discourse antecedent in (18)):

(17) *Bakto-na Ali nyetir motor,* **aba'na dibi'** *senneng.*
time-def Ali av-drive car 3(-self) happy
'When Ali$_i$ drives the car, he$_i$ is happy.'

(18) *Oreng rowa se a-careta ka sengko' ja' maleng rowa*
person that rel av-story to me comp thief that
ngeco' sapedha. Saongguna **aba'na dibi'** *ngeco'.*
av-steal bicycle actually 3(-self) av.steal
'That guy$_i$ told me that the thief$_j$ stole the bicycle. Actually he$_i$ stole it.'

To date, no broad typological study has been conducted that examines the distribution of anaphoric systems across the range of Austronesian languages. We can, however, say that the employment of a single form for both local and long distance anaphora and the use of an intensifier or emphatic to increase the likelihood of a reflexive interpretation is not limited to traditional dialects of Jambi Malay and seems to be common within Austronesian.

5. Non-reflexive uses of intensifiers and emphatics in traditional Jambi Malay

Thus far, we have seen that intensifiers and emphatics play a critical role in obtaining a reflexive interpretation in both Traditional Jambi Malay and SMI. We would therefore like to examine the broader role of intensifiers and emphatics in the grammar of the language. While our discussion is incomplete, it provides a general picture of how these forms are employed.

Dewe? is cognate with and perhaps borrowed from Javanese *dhewe*. *Dewe?* is used as an intensifier akin to Javanese *dhewe* and Madurese *dibi'*, and it expresses many of the same meanings described for *sendiri* by Sneddon (1996) (Standard Indonesian) and Gil (2001) (Riau Indonesian).

(19) Riau Indonesian 'deagentive' (Gil, 15)
Bisa di-buka **sendiri** *pintu-nya.*
can PAT-open sendiri door-ASSOC
'Its doors can open by themselves.'

(20) Riau Indonesian 'dealiative' (Gil, 16)
Aku **sendiri** tak ada rumah.
1:SG sendiri NEG EXIST house
'Only I don't have a house.'

(21) Riau Indonesian 'intensive' (Gil, 22)
Mister **sendiri** yang kasi.
white.person sendiri REL give
'You yourself gave them to me.'

5.1 Uses of *Dewe?(-la)* as a general exclusivity marker or intensifier in TR and MD

In the examples that follow, *dewe?* modifies a referring expression (rather than an anaphor) or has an adverbial function (modifying a predicate):

(22) dulu aku da?do me? jeliya dewe?-la
sibling 1SG NEG.exist aunt Jeliya INT-EMPH
'I don't have sisters or brothers, it's only aunt Jeliya.'
['I don't have sisters or brothers except for aunt Jeliya.']

(23) sila makın dewe? makın maɲa? umo-e
Sila more INT more a.lot paddy-3
'The more Sila works alone, the more paddy fields she has.'

(24) motoŋ sayo dewe?-la
N-cut 1SG INT-EMPH
'I myself cut it.'

In (22), *dewe?* modifies *me? jeliya* and indicates exclusivity ('only X', 'Aunt Jeliya and no other'). In contrast, in (23), *dewe?* modifies *makın*, i.e., the predicate and indicates 'alone'. In (24), *dewe?* can be understood as predicate modification, 'I cut it alone.' or as modifying *sayo* 'I myself', 'I and no other'. In all the examples, *dewe?* indicates exclusivity or contrast, either with respect to the arguments or with respect to the predicate. Thus, the general effect of *dewe?* appears to be contrastive focus, 'X as distinct from/in contrast with Y', where X can be an argument or a predicate.

It might be hypothesized that, while *dewe?* and *-la* have a general function of contrastive focus (*dewe?*) or emphasis/focus in general (*-la*), when combined with a pronoun, they constitute a distinct "construction", and take on a new interpretation as part of a dedicated reflexive. We have already seen elicited sentences that are counter examples to this claim. This hypothesis is also contradicted by examples taken from our corpus of naturalistic narratives. These examples show that pronoun + *dewe?* and pronoun + *-la* do not need an antecedent in the sentence, and are not necessarily associated with a reflexive predicate. Indeed, we often find both *dewe?* and *-la* (doubly emphatic) in the same sentence, but no reflexive interpretation is necessary:

(25) *suharto-tu militer dioʔ-la*
Soeharto-DEM.DIST military 3-EMPH
'[Soekarno_i] Soeharto was his_i soldier.' [Speaker is explaining how Soeharto succeeded Soekarno as President of Indonesia.]

(26) *mntla-e, dioʔ-la, kan?*
before-3 3-EMPH Q
'He used to do it by himself. ['*Dio*' refers to the father of the individual under discussion who used to work on his paddy fields himself.]⁵

(27) *biaʔ dioʔ makan papon*
although 3 eat thing
dioʔ makan dioʔ deweʔ-la k-dalam
3 eat 3 INT-EMPH to-inside
'Even though he ate many things he ate by himself inside.'

(28) *teŋoʔ dioʔ deweʔ ɲan makan papoan daʔ oaŋ bakuŋ ɲbʊt*
look 3 INT very eat thing NEG person Bakung N-mention
'See, he himself doesn't eat many things, said Bakung people.
[Bakung people said that he himself just eats whatever he finds.]

None of the uses of pronoun + *deweʔ* or *deweʔ-la* in (25)-(28) have a reflexive interpretation. It is clear from the context that the reference of *dioʔ-la* in (25) is to Soekarno rather than to Soeharto. The consultant is saying that Soeharto was Soekarno's soldier, not that Soeharto was his own soldier. Similarly, in (26)-(28), no reflexive predicate occurs. In (26), *dioʔ-la* refers to the father of the subject of the sentence rather than to the subject himself. No act of self-cannibalism is described in (27)-(28). In summary, naturalistic data confirms the results of elicitation. A non-reflexive interpretation for pronoun + *deweʔ* or *deweʔ-la* is well-formed. The uses of pronoun + *deweʔ* or *deweʔ-la* appear to be the same as those for *deweʔ* or *deweʔ-la* plus a non-pronominal constituent.

5.2 Other potential dedicated reflexives

We have shown that neither pronoun + *deweʔ* nor pronoun + *deweʔ-la* is a dedicated reflexive. There is an additional possible source for a dedicated reflexive which should be considered. This is *diri* + pronoun. As was discussed earlier with respect to Table 3, in SMI *diri* + pronoun + *sendiri* is a dedicated reflexive and *diri* + pronoun is an indeterminate anaphor that can be used as either a pronoun or a reflexive.

A reflexive interpretation for *diri* + pronoun is indeed possible in village Jambi Malay:

---

5. This highly elliptic example is included as typical of Jambi Malay discourse. The interpretation is less clear than other naturalistic examples.

(29) *cuman awaʔ jago diri awaʔ, jaŋan sampe... anu* (MD)
only 1/2/3 keep self 1/2/3 do.not reach whachamacallit
'But you have to take care of yourselves, don't make... whachamacallit.'

(30) *rsi trʊs diri awaʔ* (MD)
clean continue self 1/2/3
'We keep ourselves clean.'

(31) *aku mrkam-la diri aku deweʔ* (TR)
1SG N-record-EMPH self 1SG INT
'So, I recorded myself.'
[Eko (one of our assistants in Tanjung Raden) telling how he took the Hi-MD recorder to the kitchen to complete the recording of a story, after he forgot to do his work earlier.]

(32) *edi nʊlʊŋ diri dioʔ deweʔ-la* (TR)
Edi N-help self 3 INT-EMPH
'Edi helps himself.'

In all these examples, *diri* + pronoun + *deweʔ* indicates a reflexive predicate.

However, not all instances of *diri* + pronoun or *diri* + pronoun + *deweʔ* indicate reflexives:

(33) *apo yaŋ tar-jadi bakal di diri kito, kito trimo* (TR)
what REL PFCT.PASS-become future LOC self 1PL 1PL accept
'Whatever happens to us, we accept it.'

(34) *h-m, uji-an diri awaʔ* (TR)
uh-uh test-NMLZ self 1/2/3
'Yeah, it's a test for us.'

(35) *la ɲlamat-i diri awaʔ* (TR)
PFCT N-safe-APPL self 1/2/3
'He saved me.'

Thus, we conclude that *diri* + pronoun is not a dedicated reflexive in the traditional Jambi dialects.

There is one form which does appear to be a dedicated reflexive, but it is not used productively. As in SMI and Riau Indonesian, the use of *diri* alone (without a pronominal form) is restricted to reflexive predicates, but, just as in SMI and Riau Indonesian, this use of *diri* is not productive and occurs with only a few lexicalized forms like 'commit suicide' and 'retire':[6]

---

6. See the discussion of the restrictions on *diri* alone in Riau Indonesian, as presented in Gil (2001).

(36) ha, tu   dapat bibi crito-e-tu,   ŋantuŋ diri   (TR)
     EXCL that get   aunt story-3-DEM.DIST   N-hang self
     'I got info that he hung himself.'

(37) munu   diri dewe?   (TR)
     N-kill self INT
     '[They] are killing themselves.' [meant to say 'their act is just the same as killing themselves.']

(38) ŋun^dur-kan   diri   (TR)
     N-withdraw-APPL self
     'Retire.'

Thus, we conclude that *diri* alone does not constitute a productive, dedicated reflexive.[7]

Table 4 summarizes the distribution of anaphora in Traditional Jambi Malay:

We conclude that Traditional Jambi Malay is a representative language in which none of the productive anaphoric forms constitutes a clear instance of a dedicated reflexive or a dedicated pronoun.

Table 4. Summary of anaphoric forms for Traditional Jambi Malay dialects (TR, MD)

	TR/MD traditional dialects (Third Person)
Underspecified anaphoric forms (pseudo reflexives)	*dio(ʔ)*
	dio(ʔ)la
	dio(ʔ) dewe?
	diri dio(ʔ) (dewe?)
	diriɲo (dewe?)

---

7. While the reflexive use of *diri* is restricted to only a few predicates, at least for some speakers, *diri + dewe?* appears to have a broader use.

(i) dioʔ-tu   mɪkɪr   diri dewe?   (TR, Elic)
     3-DEM.DIST   N-think self INT
     'He cares about himself.' [*him]

(ii) abaŋ   yanti pɪkɪr   arna nuluŋ   diri dewe?-la   (TR, Elic)
     older.brother   Yanti think   Arna N-help self INT-EMPH
     'Yanti's brother thinks Arna helped herself.' [only refers to Arna]

Gil (2001) notes that *diri sendiri*, the Riau Indonesian functional equivalent of Jambi *diri dewe?*, can, in Riau Indonesian, be used with an open class of predicates despite the fact that *diri* alone is restricted to a small, closed class of predicates. In the case of our Jambi data, the use of *diri dewe?* as an apparent dedicated reflexive appears only in elicited examples. This may indicate that this usage is in reality a borrowing from SMI. This possibility can only be excluded if the form is found to occur in a larger natural corpus. Thus, we shall withhold judgment as to whether *diri dewe?* constitutes a genuine instance of a productive, dedicated reflexive in a Traditional Jambi dialect until our corpus is large enough to allow us to evaluate the claim.

6. The universality of Binding

Traditional Jambi Malay is an example of a language for which the Binding Theory arguably plays no role in determining the properties of anaphors. All clearly productive anaphoric forms can be used as local, long distance or discourse anaphors. Thus, at the very least, one must conclude that there exist human languages in which Binding Theory plays no role. Furthermore, this conclusion would hold regardless of whether one assumes the classical Binding Theory of Chomsky or some more recent version of Binding like that of Reinhart & Reuland (1991 and/or 1993). Still, Jambi Malay has a productive system of anaphora, one in which the *same* grammatical devices used to unambiguously indicate reflexivity in SMI play a critical role in signaling the *probability* of a reflexive interpretation. On the assumption that principles of Universal Grammar define the parameters within which human language is possible, a UG-based Binding Theory could not predict interpretive probabilities. Rather, UG would define what is possible, and probability would be determined by some aspect of the theory of language use (pragmatics, discourse etc.). The fact that the theory of language use predicts *probabilistically* in one dialect the same distribution predicted *exceptionlessly* by the Binding Theory in another raises the question of whether the distribution should not have a unitary explanation in both dialects. If a unitary explanation is assumed, that explanation *could not* be UG-based, since UG, by assumption, can not make probabilistic predictions. Thus, the distribution would necessarily be derived from the theory of language use, i.e. discourse and pragmatics. Thus, the distribution of anaphora in Malay at least suggests that anaphoric binding in Malay should not be explained in terms of UG but rather in terms of discourse and pragmatics.

A full solution to this conundrum is beyond the scope of this paper, but we would like to allude to how the problem might be approached. A possible answer to the apparent contradiction is to take the approach that there are two sources for our knowledge of the grammar of specific languages, the principles of Universal Grammar and language specific grammatical rules derived from the grammaticalization of various functional aspects of language use. As speakers, we are aware of our grammatical judgments, but we do not know whether a particular judgment is based directly on UG or whether it is systematic grammatical knowledge that is due to grammaticalization. In order to provide a unitary, cross-dialectal analysis of anaphoric forms in SMI and Jambi, we interpret the distribution of pronouns and intensifiers in SMI as the result of the grammaticalization of the effects of language use (pragmatics and discourse) rather than as the direct application of UG principles. That is, the state of affairs found in Jambi is analyzed as a pre-grammaticalization stage and that in SMI as the result of grammaticalization.

In employing grammaticalization as a solution to the analytic problems of SMI/Jambi anaphora, we made the claim that there are systematic aspects of grammar that are the result of grammaticalization and not directly due to UG. While such a position may be commonplace for many linguists, it contradicts the assumption currently made by some Minimalist syntacticians that apparent language specific "grammar" is an epiphenomenon. In current Minimalist approaches, grammatical principles are universal (or universal but subject to very limited parameterization) and language specific "grammar" is no more than the interaction of UG principles with the idiosyncratic properties of individual lexical items. Speakers do not know language specific "grammatical rules" that are separate from both UG and the featural content of lexical items. That is, from this perspective, knowledge of a language does not involve systematic grammatical generalizations that are not associated with specific lexical items or specific functional heads. In opposition to this perspective, we are arguing in favor of a more traditional approach to language in which part of our knowledge of language is knowledge of a grammatical system that is separate from particular lexical items.

In applying this approach to Malay/Indonesian, it is, therefore, incumbent on us to show that there is a functional explanation for the fact that intensifiers and markers of focus increase the likelihood of a reflexive interpretation. While this has not been attempted for any Malayic language, the general outlines of the analysis are available from the study of reflexives in other languages. Faltz (1985) and a variety of later authors (prominent among them, König & Siemund (2000 inter alia), Keenan (2002 inter alia)) have applied this approach to the historical development of reflexives in English and other European languages. We would argue that Old English and Modern English reflexives display historically the same contrast Jambi and SMI display synchronically. Specifically, in Old English pronouns could be used to express reflexive predicates, and *-self* forms were used emphatically. The use of emphasis increased the likelihood of a reflexive interpretation. The increased likelihood was later grammaticalized.

Assume that this approach to reflexives and pronouns is on the right track, not just for English and Malay, but for a wide variety of languages. Then, it suggests that treating Binding Theory as a component of Universal Grammar should not be the explanation for the unexpectedly frequent occurrence of the particular set of grammatical restrictions found cross-linguistically in Binding Theoretically compatible anaphoric systems. Rather, the pattern should be ascribed to a natural, and, therefore, frequently observed, grammaticalization path.

References

Battistella, E. 1989. Chinese reflexivization: A movement to INFL approach. *Linguistics* 27: 987–1012.
Besnier, N. 2000. *Tuvaluan: A Polynesian Language of the Central Pacific*. London: Routledge.
Burzio, L. 1989. On the non-existence of disjoint reference principles. *Rivista di Grammatica Generativa* 14: 3–27.
Burzio, L. 1991. The morphological basis of anaphora. *Journal of Linguistics* 27(1): 1–60.
Chomsky, N. 1981. *Lectures on Government and Binding*. Dordrecht: Foris.

Cole, P. & Hermon, G. 1998. Long distance reflexives in Singapore Malay: An apparent typological anomaly. *Linguistic Typology* 2(1): 57–98.

Cole, P. & Hermon, G. 2005. The typology of Malay reflexives. *Lingua* 115(5): 627–644.

Cole, P., Hermon, G. & Huang, C.-T.J. 2001. Long distance reflexives: The states of the art. In *Syntax and Semantics: Long Distance Reflexive*, P. Cole, G. Hermon & C.-T. J. Huang (eds), xiii-xlvii. New York NY: Academic Press.

Cole, P., Hermon, G. & Huang, C.-T.J. 2006. Long-distance binding in Asian languages. In *The Blackwell Companion to Syntax*, Vol. 3, Ch. 39, M. Everaert & H.C. van Riemsdijk (eds), 21–84. Malden MA: Blackwell.

Cole, P., Hermon G., Tjung Y., Sim, C.-Y. & Kim, C. 2007. *Anaphoric Expressions in the Peranakan Javanese of Semarang*. Munich: Lincom.

Davies, W.D. 2008. Madurese reflexives with reference to Malay/Indonesian. *Lingua* 18(10): 1603–1616.

Faltz, L.M. 1985. *Reflexivization: A Study in Universal Syntax*. New York NY: Garland. (published version of 1977 UCLA dissertation).

Gil, D. 2001. Reflexive anaphor or conjunctive operator: Riau Indonesian *Sendiri*. In *Syntax and Semantics: Long Distance Reflexives*, P. Cole, G. Hermon & C.-T. J. Huang (eds), 83–118. New York NY: Academic Press.

Haspelmath, M. 2005. A frequentist explanation of some universals of reflexive marking. Ms. <http://www.eva.mpg.de/~haspelmt/ReflexiveMarking.pdf>.

Keenan, E.L. 2002. Explaining the creation of reflexive pronouns in English. In *Studies in the History of English: A Millennial Perspective*, D. Minkova & R. Stockwell (eds), 325–355. Berlin: Mouton de Gruyter.

König, E. & Siemund, P. 2000. The development of complex reflexives and intensifiers in English. *Diachronica* 17(1): 39–84.

Reinhart, T. & Reuland, E. 1991. Anaphors and logophors: An argument Structure perspective. In *Long Distance Anaphors*, J. Koster & E. Reuland (eds), 283–321. Cambridge: CUP.

Reinhart, T. & Reuland, E. 1993. Reflexivity. *Linguistic Inquiry* 24: 657–720.

Sneddon, J.N. 1996. *Indonesian: A Comprehensive Grammar*. London: Routledge.

Tjung, Y. 2006. The Formation of Relative Clauses in Jakarta Indonesian: A Subject-Object Asymmetry. PhD dissertation, Universal of Delaware.

Wouk, F. 1999. Dialect contact and koineization in Jakarta, Indonesia. *Language Sciences* 21: 61–86.

On parameters of agreement in Austronesian languages*

Mark C. Baker
Rutgers University

Baker 2008 claims that two parameters account for observed crosslinguistic variation in the syntax of agreement. One concerns the direction of agreement: whether or not an agreed-with NP must c-command the agreeing head. The other concerns the relationship of agreement to case: whether or not a head can agree with something it does not share a case feature with. In this article, I consider how these two parameters apply to Austronesian languages, concentrating on three representative case studies: Fijian, Tukang Besi, and Kapampangan. All three languages require upward agreement, but agreement is case-dependent only in Kapampangan. The agreement parameters also interact with certain differences in clause structure and movement, giving somewhat different agreement patterns in different languages.

---

* For help with the Kinande data reported in this paper, I thank Philip Mutaka. For fascinating and helpful discussion of the grammar of Austronesian languages, I thank Paul Kroeger, Mark Donohue, and the many other inspiring attendees of AFLA XIV. Mark Donohue was especially generous in helping me to understand the Tukang Besi data, in filling in some gaps in that data with new fieldwork, and in calling to my attention other Austronesian languages that have interesting agreement systems. I thank Lisa Travis for providing the occasion for me to work out how my views on agreement apply to Austronesian languages in more detail. Finally, I thank Lisa Travis and an anonymous reviewer for comments on the written version. All mistakes are my own responsibility.

Abbreviations used in the glosses of examples include the following: ABS, absolutive case; ACC, accusative case; AF, agent focus; AFF, affirmative; ALL, allative; APPL, applicative; ASP, aspect; ART, article; C, complementizer; DAT, dative case; DEF, definite; DIR, directional; DISJ, disjunct marker; EMP, emphatic; ERG, ergative case; FUT, future tense; FV, final vowel; GF, goal focus; I, irrealis; IF, instrument focus; LOC, locative; MASC, masculine; NEG, negation; NOM, nominative case; OBL, oblique case; OM, object marker; PASS, passive; PAST, past tense; PCPL, participle; PERF, perfective aspect; PL, plural; POSS, possessive; PRES, present tense; R, realis mood; REC, recent past; SG, singular; T, tense marker; TF, theme focus; TR, transitivity marker.

1. Two agreement parameters

Agreement has long been seen as one of the principal devices (along with case marking and word order) that natural languages employ to indicate grammatical functions – which noun phrase is the subject of the clause, which is the object, what adjective goes with what noun, and so on. Building on this, in the recent generative literature, Chomsky (2000, 2001) has picked out agreement as one of the primary linguistic relationships: it is fundamental to the syntax of human language, and provides a precondition for both movement and case marking. Moreover, Chomsky's theory of the Agree relation is a universalist one, intended to hold for all languages. One central feature of this Agree relation is that the head that bears agreement must be higher in the structure than (i.e., must c-command) the NP that it agrees with. A second putatively universal feature of agreement concerns its relationship to Case assignment: the agreed-with NP must not already have Case at the time that agreement happens, and this NP may end up receiving Case from the agreeing head as a side effect of the agreement. For example, in a sentence like *She is writing a letter*, the present tense associated with *be* agrees downward with the third person singular NP *she* before *she* moves to the Spec, TP position, thereby showing up as a third person singular form (*is*, rather than *are* or *am*) and fixing the case of the subject pronoun as nominative (*she* rather than *her*).

A possible concern with this universalist approach is that agreement is certainly not one of the more universal-looking features of language. The particular affixes that indicate agreement vary greatly from language to language, as one would expect. But languages also vary greatly in how much agreement they have: languages like Chinese have no overt agreement at all, whereas in languages like Swahili and Mohawk, agreement shows up on practically every word, sometimes more than once. Languages also vary as to which categories are involved in agreement: some have object agreement and others do not; some have agreement on adpositons or complementizers and others do not; some have agreement between an NP and its modifiers and others do not. Interactions between word order and agreement are found in some languages and not others. In some languages, agreement seems to work on a nominative-accusative basis, whereas in others it seems to work on an ergative-absolutive basis. Given all this, agreement is a domain in which we might expect to see a good deal of random and idiosyncratic morphosyntactic variation. Standard generative theory tends to downplay such variation, assuming at least as a starting point that the same syntactic agreement relationships are present in all languages, the primary difference being which of these relationships are spelled out overtly in a given language. But one might wonder whether there are interesting subregularities that are missed by simply assuming complete syntactic uniformity even in the face of significant morphological diversity.

In Baker 2008, I argued that something important is missed by this approach. Sitting between the universal aspects of agreement and the language particular morphological details, there is a level of description at which one can observe patterned crosslinguistic variation in the syntax of agreement. More specifically, I claimed that the theory of agreement allows for two parameters in how agreement happens. Whereas Chomsky says that functional heads always probe downward in the phrase structure tree for something to agree with, I claim that this is parameterized: some languages allow a functional head to look downward for something to agree with, but others insist that functional heads look upward. This is expressed in the Direction of Agreement Parameter, stated in (1).

(1) *The Direction of Agreement Parameter (DAP):*
F agrees with DP/NP only if DP/NP asymmetrically c-commands F (Yes or No).

Furthermore, whereas Chomsky claims that a functional head assigns abstract Case to an NP it agrees with (under some conditions), I claim that this too is parameterized, happening in some languages but not others. This is expressed in the Case Dependence of Agreement Parameter:

(2) *The Case Dependence of Agreement Parameter (CDAP)*
F agrees with DP/NP only if F values the Case feature of DP/NP or vice versa (Yes or No).

These two parameters were originally motivated by comparing Niger-Congo (NC) languages with Indo-Europoean (IE) languages. Most NC languages have the "yes" setting of the DAP and the "no" setting for the CDAP, whereas most IE languages have the opposite settings. It is thus a mistake to take (implicitly or explicitly) the IE settings as principles of Universal Grammar. I further claimed that the DAP and the CDAP are parameters in the classical sense of Chomsky (1981): they are variations in the syntactic principles that define a language and are not reducible to the feature specifications of individual items in the lexicon. Thus, in general, all of the functional heads in a given language show the same syntactic behavior with respect to (1) and (2), if they agree at all.

The Austronesian languages are generally not as rich in agreement as (say) the Bantu languages are. Nevertheless, if it is right to think of the differences between NC and IE languages in terms of parameters embedded within a theory of Universal Grammar, then those parameters should in principle be applicable to any language family – including Austronesian. With this in mind, Baker 2008: ch.5 tested the validity of the DAP and the CDAP on a sample of 108 languages from around the world, based on the core sample of the *World Atlas of Language Structures* (*WALS*) (Haspelmath et al. 2005). The purpose of this article is to discuss more specifically how these parameters apply to the Austronesian languages in that sample, going into more detail than was possible in Baker 2008. I also extend the discussion by discussing for the first time an interesting pattern of agreement found in some languages of the Philippines, brought to my attention by Paul Kroeger and Mark Donohue.

The *WALS* core languages sample includes eight Austronesian languages: Chamorro, Tukang Besi, Fijian, Paiwan, Indonesian, Malagasy, Rapanui, and Tagalog. Of these, the last five do not have much in the way of agreement phenomena (according to *WALS*), and agreement in Chamorro has already been studied thoroughly from a generative perspective by Chung (1998). Fijian and Tukang Besi, however, provide interesting new fields for study. In Section 2, I show that Fijian has the same less familiar settings of the DAP and the CDAP that are used in Bantu languages. This is an important replication of one of the more novel parts of this overall approach to agreement. I then consider Tukang Besi (Section 3), which shows some of the same behavior as Fijian, but which also has overt case marking on its noun phrases. The interaction of case and agreement is thus much richer in Tukang Besi. While some of these interactions support the CDAP, others look problematic – until one integrates in a view of how Case is assigned in Tukang Besi. Finally, I consider Kapampangan, which is like Tukang Besi in some respects, but strikingly different in others (Section 4). I show that the difference between these two Austronesian languages is not only in the agreement parameters, but also involves differences in the movement processes that create the configurations over which agreement is defined. These three case studies serve to illustrate how a small number of agreement parameters can interact with other aspects of grammar to characterize the rather rich diversity of agreement systems that we observe. I hope that they also illustrate the value of having meaningful interaction between general theorists/typologists and linguists who are cognizant of the intricate details of a particular language family.

2. The Bantu parameter settings in Austronesian: Fijian

I begin, then, with Fijian. Fijian is superficially rather like Kinande and the other Bantu languages that originally motivated the DAP and the CDAP in that it has no overt case marking and no Philippines-style voice system. Hence, it provides a relatively straightforward opportunity to see how these two agreement parameters are supposed to work.

2.1 The direction of agreement parameter

Consider first the DAP, stated in (1). Perhaps the most obvious effect of this parameter being set positively in the Bantu language Kinande is that finite T always agrees with the phrase that has moved to Spec, TP, a position from which it c-commands T. In the most common sentences in this SVO language, the moved NP is the agentive subject, which results in normal subject agreement ((3a)). But Kinande also allows PPs to move to Spec, TP, in locative inversion sentences like (3b). When this happens, T agrees with the locative PP. Kinande also allows the object to move to Spec, TP when there is contrastive focus on the subject. When this happens, T agrees with the fronted object ((3c)). Finally, it is possible for no NP to move to Spec, TP, as in (3d). Then T does not agree with any NP in the clause, and the agreement slot is filled by an expletive element *ha*.

(3) a. *Abakali ba-*[a]*-gul-a eritunda.*
 woman.2 2s-T-buy-FV fruit.5
 'The woman bought a fruit.'

 b. *Oko-mesa kw-a-hir-aw-a ehilanga.*
 LOC.17-table 17s-T-put-PASS-FV peanuts.19
 'On the table were put peanuts.' (Baker 2003)

 c. *Olukwi si-lu-li-seny-a bakali* (*omo-mbasa*).
 wood.11 NEG-11s-PRES-chop-FV women.2 LOC.18-axe.9
 'WOMEN do not chop wood (with an axe).'

 d. *Mo-ha-teta-sat-a mukali* (*omo-soko*).
 AFF-there-NEG/PAST-dance-FV woman.1 LOC.18-market
 'No woman danced (in the market).

In none of these sentence types can T agree with anything that has not moved to Spec, TP. In this respect, Kinande differs markedly from English and other IE languages, in which T can agree with the nominative subject even when Spec, TP is occupied by something else. (4a) shows this for locative inversion in English, (4b) shows it for adverb fronting in Yiddish (assuming, for the sake of argument, the analysis of Diesing 1990); example from Lisa Travis, personal communication), and (4c) shows it for expletive constructions in English.

(4) a. On the table *were* put *peanuts*, (Locative inversion)

 b. Der tate zogt az haynt esn di kinder broyt.
 The father says that today.SG eat.3pS the.PL child.PL bread
 'The father says that today the children eat bread.' (Yiddish)

 c. There *are*/**is some peanuts* on the table.

These differences follow if one says that DP must c-command T for T to agree with DP in Kinande but not in the IE languages, as per the DAP.[1]

---

1. A more traditional way of accounting for the difference between (3) and (4) is to say that a head can only agree with a phrase in its specifier position in Bantu languages (see, for example, Kinyalolo 1991). The main advantage of (1) over this alternative is that it allows predicate adjectives to agree with their subjects in Bantu languages, even though the subject is never in Spec, AP; see Baker (2008) for discussion. The Austronesian languages considered here do not have adjectival agreement, however, so the difference between the these formulations is not very crucial here.

Consider now Fijian. Finite verbs generally agree with their subjects in Fijian – with the notable exception of existential constructions. Thus, there is third person plural agreement on the intransitive verb in (5b), but not on the existential verb in (5a).

(5) a. e sō na vūlagi (Schütz 1985: 329)
    3sS be.some DEF villagers
    'There were some villagers.'

  b. era yaco māī e sō na vūlagi
    3pS arrive DIR 3s some DEF villagers
    'Some villagers arrived.'

This contrast would follow from the DAP being set positively in Fijian, plus the assumption that the Spec, TP position can be filled by a null expletive comparable to English *there* in existential sentences only.[2] The phrase 'some villagers' must thus raise to Spec, TP where it can trigger agreement on the c-commanded head T in (5b), but not in (5a). The same contrast is seen in Chamorro, and is analyzed by Chung (1998: 68–69, 182–183). Inasmuch as there is no agreement in (5a), Fijian is more like Kinande ((3d)) than like English ((4c)) in this respect.

There is also evidence that v can agree with the object in Bantu languages only if the object c-commands v. In some of these languages, including Kinande, object agreement appears on the verb only if the object is dislocated to the edge of the clause:

(6) a. N-a-(*ri)-gul-a eritunda. (Baker 2003)
    1sS-T-OM5-buy-FV fruit.5
    'I bought a fruit.'

  b. Eritunda, n-a-ri-gul-a.
    fruit.5   1sS-T-OM5-buy-FV
    'The fruit, I bought it.'

In other Bantu languages, like Zulu and Swahili, the evidence is more subtle. There is no obvious difference in word order between (7a), which does not have object agreement on the verb, and (7b), which does have it.

---

2. A complicating factor is whether the expletive pronoun in the Spec, TP of an expletive construction in a given language has phi-features of its own or not: English *there* does not, but French *il* and German *es* do (they are third person singular). If the expletive has phi-features, then the verb agrees with it in both DAP = yes and DAP = no languages; the parametric difference is apparent only in languages in which the expletive does not have phi-features, where T might have the chance to look elsewhere for something to agree with. Given this, an alternative explanation of (5a) in Fijian could be that its null expletive has third person singular phi-features, like French *il*. I tentatively assume that this analysis is ruled out because null expletives have no lexical entry of their own (they are not "lexical items"), hence there is no possibility of them having phi-features specified in their entry. But the matter deserves more study.

(7) a. Ngi-leth-el-a   umfundisi incwadi   (Zulu)
       1sS-bring-APPL-FV teacher.1   book   (Doke 1963: 299)
       'I am bringing a teacher a book.'
    b. Ngi-ya-*m*-lethela   *umfundisi* incwadi
       1sS-DISJ-OM1-bring-APPL-FV teacher.1 book
       'I am bringing the teacher a book.'

There is a difference in interpretation however: the agreed-with object in (7b) is understood as being "definite" (or some related notion – the semantic details have not been studied carefully), whereas the unagreed-with object in (7a) is not. Following the general idea of Diesing 1992, I take the strong/definite reading in (7b) to be a sign that the object has moved out of VP, the domain of existential closure, and into Spec, vP in (7b), whereas there is no such movement in (7a). This movement has no effect on surface word order in Zulu, because the verb moves past v to T:

(8) a. $[_{TP}$ T + bring$_k$ $[_{vP}$ (*AGR$_i$+)v $[\exists$ $[_{VP}$ teacher$_i$ t$_k$ book]]]   (=(7a))
    b. $[_{TP}$ T + bring$_k$ $[_{vP}$ teacher$_i$ AGR$_i$ + v $[\exists$ $[_{VP}$ t$_i$ t$_k$ book]]]   (=(7b))

The object shift does affect agreement, however. In (8b), the shifted object c-commands v and v can agree with it, given the "yes" setting of the DAP. In contrast, v cannot agree downward with the unshifted object in (8a). There is no similar restriction that agreement be upward in IE languages. Ormazabal and Romero (2006: 18) argue that *les* in a sentence like (9) from a *leista* dialect of Spanish counts as an object agreement. If so, then it is agreement with an undislocated, indefinite NP inside VP – the kind of agreement that is not allowed in (6a) and (7a) in the Bantu languages.

(9) (Yo) *les*-llevé   a   unos jóvenes   al   pueblo.
    I   3pO-carry ACC   a.PL youngsters to.the town
    'I gave some young people a ride to the town.'

The fact that v can agree downward into VP in IE but not in NC is parallel to the fact that T can agree downward into vP in IE but not Bantu, as shown in (3) versus (4) – a testimony to the generality of the DAP.

Consider now Fijian. Dixon (1988) shows that transitive verbs in Fijian normally bear a special "transitivity suffix" that varies depending on whether the object is singular or plural; the singular version is seen in (10b). This is a relatively impoverished kind of object agreement, presumably associated with v. However, the agreement-bearing transitivity suffix is absent in (10a), which has an indefinite object, in what is traditionally analyzed as a noun incorporation construction.

(10) a. [E'au.i vola mai]   a   cauravou.   (Dixon 1988: 49)
        deliver letter to.here the youth
        'The youth is delivering letters.'

b. [E'au-*ta* – mai] *a-i-vola yai* a cauravou.
    deliver-TR.3sO to.here the-letter this the youth
    'The youth is delivering the letter.'

I assume that Massam's (2001) analysis of pseudo-noun incorporation in Niuean also applies to the alternation between (10a) and (10b) in Fijian. According to this view, the bracketed constituent in (10a) is not a word-like unit, but a full VP, its right edge marked by the adverbial particle *mai*. An indefinite object stays inside VP, just as in Zulu, whereas a definite object moves out of VP to a higher position. This accounts for both the morpheme order difference between (10a) and (10b) and the difference in the interpretation of the object, given Diesing's Mapping Hypothesis.[3] Taken together with the idea that the DAP is set "yes" in Fijian, it also explains the fact that the agreement-bearing transitivity marker is present in (10b) but not in (10a): the object moves to a position that c-commands v only in (10b). The contrast between (10a) and (10b) in Fijian is thus very similar to the contrast between (7a) and (7b) in Zulu.

Finally, consider the possibility of agreement on prepositions. Kinyalolo (1991: 111) shows that in Kilega P does not agree with its object when the object remains *in situ*. The object of the P can however undergo focus movement, and can move to the subject position in a passive. When it does, then the P does agree with the moved object. (11) replicates this observation in Kinande.

(11) a. Kambale a-ka-kanay-a na-(*bo) abasyakulu
         Kambale 3sS-PRES-speak-FV with-2 2.old.people
         'Kambale is speaking with the old people.'
     b. *Abasyakulu* si-ba-li-kan-ibaw-a na-*bo*.
         2.old.people NEG-2S-PRES-speak-PASS-FV with-2
         'Old people are not spoken with.'

This contrast can also be attributed to the "yes" setting of the DAP in Kinande and Kilega. The unmoved NP in (11a) does not asymmetrically c-command P (rather, there is mutual c-command), so P cannot agree with it. In its final position in a sentence like (11b) (or more likely in some intermediate position), however, NP does asymmetrically c-command P; hence agreement is possible in this structure. In contrast, Ps can agree with their complements even when the complement has not been moved in Welsh, showing that the DAP is not set positively in this IE language.[4]

---

3. I leave open whether predicate fronting – VP movement to a Spec position at the left edge of the clause – happens in Fijian the way that it does in Niuean or not. The fact that basic word order is VSO in Niuean but it is VOS in Fijian might suggest that specifiers are on the right in Fijian but not Niuean. Also, since I assume that the agreed-with subject in Fijian is in Spec, TP in sentences like (5b), the VP cannot move to Spec, TP in Fijian. Either predicate fronting targets the specifier of some functional head higher than T, or it does not take place in Fijian at all.

4. There is agreement on P only with pronominal objects in Welsh, a restriction that I have no explanation for. However, agreement does co-occur with overt pronouns *in situ*, suggesting that it is true agreement, not simply a case of a pronoun cliticizing/incorporating into the preposition.

(12) Soniais I amdan-*o*   *ef.*   (Harlow 1981: 220)
    talked I about-3sMASC him
    'I talked about him.'

Once again, Fijian may be like a Bantu language and not like an IE language in this respect. Dixon (1988: 42, 248) shows that there is a third singular agreement of sorts on P in Fijian if and only if its NP complement is extracted (by topicalization, in this case).[5]

(13) a. 'Eimami saa qaaqaa   a   'ai-Boumaa [i-na   drano].
        we   ASP victorious ART native-place about-ART lake
        'We, natives of Boumaa, were victorious concerning the lake.'

    b. A   drano 'eimami saa qaaqaa   ['i-na –]   a   'ai-Boumaa.
       ART lake we   ASP victorious about+3.SG ART native-place
       'The lake, we Boumaa people were victorious concerning it.'

Agreement does not appear on as wide a range of functional heads in Fijian as in Kinande. In Kinande, agreement appears on some quantifiers, on complementizers, on the focus particle, and on a VP-internal particle, as well as on T, v, and P. For all of these heads, it can be shown that agreement depends on the agreed with NP asymmetrically c-commanding the agreeing head. In Fijian, however, quantifiers and complementizers do not undergo agreement at all, so the setting of the DAP is moot for those categories.[6]

2.2 The case dependence of agreement parameter

Next I review the kinds of data that motivate the CDAP in (2), and consider how it applies in Fijian.

In many IE languages, it is transparently true that T agrees with an NP only if that NP is assigned nominative case (Bobaljik 2008). For example, the finite verb

---

5. An alternative interpretation, suggested by Lisa Travis and an anonymous reviewer, is that '*ina* in (13b) is the fusion of a preposition and a resumptive pronoun left by topicalization. As in most languages, it is tricky in Fijian to discern whether an inflected form is the manifestation of a weak pronoun cliticizing to a head or of an agreeing head licensing a null pronoun, and the task is not made easier by the suppletive nature of *(k)ina*. I was not able to find evidence in Dixon 1988 or Schütz 1985 that resolves the question to my satisfaction. If the resumptive pronoun analysis is correct, my overall analysis would not change, but there would be less evidence for it; then Ps are simply not agreement-bearers in Fijian, and the DAP is irrelevant to them.

6. See Chung 1998 for evidence that there is a kind of upward-probing agreement between C and the NP in Spec, CP in Chamorro. This is not phi-feature agreement, however, so it is not clear whether my theory of agreement can and should be extended to cover it as well.

agrees with a nominative subject in Icelandic, but not with a dative subject; if anything, the finite verb agrees with the nominative object in dative subject constructions in this language:

(14) Henni   leidd*ust*   *þeir*.   (Icelandic)
      She-DAT was.bored.by-3p they.NOM
      'She was bored with them.'

Similarly, in Hindi the finite verb agrees with a nominative subject (15a), but not with a subject marked with ergative case (15b).

(15) a. *Niina*   baalak-ko   ut^{h}aa-eg-*ii*.   (Hindi)
         Nina.F.NOM boy.M-ACC lift-FUT-F.SG
         'Nina will lift up the boy.'

     b. Niinaa-ne   baalak-ko   ut^{h}aa-y-*aa*.   (*uthaa-y-ii)
         Nina.F-ERG boy.M-ACC lift-PERF-M.SG lift-PERF-F.SG
         'Nina lifted up the boy.'

There is arguably no such requirement in Bantu languages. Claims about Case assignment in the Bantu languages are necessarily somewhat abstract, since there is no morphological case marking in these languages. In general, I assume that the CDAP in (2) refers to the assignment of abstract Case – the kind of Case that satisfies Case Filter requirements. This abstract case is presumably not too radically divorced from visible morphological case, but there is always the possibility of neutralizations or syncretisms arising at the morphological level, with the result that some Case distinctions present in the syntax are lost on the surface (Legate 2008). Bantu languages are a limiting case of this: all Cases are spelled out with the same (null) affix at PF, making it hard to observe what is what.

One can, however, make some progress by indirect reasoning. Recall that in locative inversion and object fronting structures, T agrees with the fronted XP in the Bantu languages, as shown again in (16).

(16) a. *Oko-mesa*   *kw*-a-hir-aw-a   ehilanga.   (Kinande)
         LOC.17-table 17s-T-put-PASS-FV peanuts.19
         'On the table were put peanuts.'

     b. *Olukwi*   si-*lu*-li-seny-a   bakali   (omo-mbasa).
         wood.11 NEG-11s-PRES-chop-FV women.2 LOC.18-axe.9
         'WOMEN do not chop wood (with an axe).'

Why is this kind of agreement possible in Bantu languages, but not in IE languages, from the point of view of Case theory? The IE side of the question is straightforward: T cannot agree with the fronted phrase because it does not assign it nominative Case; rather, the object has accusative case in (4b) from Yiddish, and the PP has no case at all in (4a) from English. Now how does Case work in Bantu? The most conservative possibility is that Case in Bantu works the same way that it does in IE languages: the postverbal NPs in (16a,b) have nominative Case (what other case could they have?), the preverbal NP in (16b) has accusative Case, and the locative expression in (16a) has no Case at all. If so, it is clear that T agreeing with a phrase does not depend on T giving that phrase nominative Case in Kinande. There are other conceivable approaches to this issue, which try to maintain a tight relationship between Case and agreement even in Bantu, but they all lead to reasonably well-known difficulties (see Ndayiragije 1999 for some discussion).[7]

Next consider v. It is widely assumed that similar considerations apply to v, such that v can only agree with the NP that it assigns accusative case to in IE languages. This is certainly true for the Spanish example in (9), where the verb agrees with the plural direct object in accusative case, not with the singular dative expression. However, true object agreement is rare enough in IE languages that it is hard to show compelling evidence for this assumption. As for NC languages, given that (2) is set "no", we might expect that v could agree with an argument in oblique case rather than an accusative object in Bantu. This certainly can happen in some other languages (see (27) below), but for Bantu the issue is again moot because there is no accusative/oblique case distinction.

Given that Bantu languages don't have overt case marking, the clearest consequence of the CDAP being set "no" is the possibility of having multiple full agreement in auxiliary constructions. Only one finite verb can agree with a given argument in IE languages. Thus, complex tenses can be built out of a finite auxiliary and an uninflected participle, but they cannot be built out of two agreeing verbs, as shown in (17).[8]

(17) a. Chris is coming.
     b. *Chris is comes.

Why are all examples like (17b) ruled out? Their ungrammaticality can be derived from the CDAP. The lower functional head (Participle or Tense) agrees with the thematic subject, by hypothesis. Given a positive setting of the CDAP, this is only possible if the lower head values the Case of the agreed-with NP as (say) nominative. Now Case assignment is unique; the Case feature of an NP can only be valued once. Once the

---

7. A more radical possibility worth considering is that Case assignment does not take place at all in Bantu languages. This would require one to seriously rethink the Case filter and related principles, but it may have advantages. Even so, it follows that the CDAP must be set "no" in Bantu, since then T agrees with subjects without Case-marking any of them.

8. I do not necessarily intend (17b) to be doubly marked for present tense; my point is about double *agreement* being banned, not about double tense marking. However, the two are of course deeply intertwined in English.

Some qualifications to the generalization in the text are needed to take into account the fact that participles show reduced, number-gender agreement with the subject in some IE languages. This is possible because these participles also agree with the subject in Case (see Baker 2008: 211).

lower head values the Case feature of the subject NP, the higher head (T) cannot do so. The positive setting of the CDAP then implies that the higher head cannot agree with the subject NP. Either the higher head could agree, or the lower one, but not both, given the positive setting of the CDAP and the uniqueness of Case assignment. But structures like (17b) are entirely possible in many Bantu languages; (18) gives two Kinande examples.

(18) a. *Abakali ba*-bya *ba*-ka-gul-a amatunda.
women.2 2S-were 2S-PCPL-buy-FV fruits.6
'The women were buying fruits.'

b. *Tú*-lwé *tú*-ká-ly-a.
1pS-leave 1pS-PCPL-eat-FV
'We were eating.'

I thus conclude that the CDAP is set negatively in these Bantu languages.

Consider now Fijian. Like Kinande, Fijian does not have overt morphological case. It does not even have inversion constructions comparable to (16), as far as I know. We thus cannot expect there to be a wide range of evidence as to how the CDAP is set. However, Fijian does have auxiliary-plus-main verb constructions, and in some of these there is agreement on both verbs, much as there is in Kinande:

(19) *Era* dodunu me+*ra* la'o (Dixon 1988: 280)
3pS must C-3pS go
'They must go.' (similarly with *bese* 'not want')

This suggests that Case assignment is not a requirement for agreement in Fijian, any more than it is in Bantu.[9]

I conclude that Fijian has the same parameter settings as Kinande, and the kinds of data that motivate those settings are similar, apart from a few obvious surface differences (like the fact that Fijian has VOS word order and Kinande SVO). Fijian thus provides an important replication of the parameters in (1) and (2), confirming that they have value in the analysis of languages outside the IE and NC families – as one would hope if they are truly parameters embedded in a theory of Universal Grammar. The evidence for these parameters is admittedly not as rich in Fijian as it is in Kinande, simply because Fijian does not have as many inversion constructions as Kinande, not as many functional heads bear agreement in Fijian as in Kinande, and there is no case marking in Fijian. Nevertheless, the evidence for these parameter settings in Fijian is

---

9. In contrast, double agreement with the subject apparently never happens in auxiliary constructions in Chamorro (Topping 1973). I thus tentatively assume that the CDAP and the DAP are both set positively in Chamorro. If so, then Chamorro (like Kapampangan) illustrates a different combination of parameter settings than either English or Kinande. One cannot get much converging evidence for this though, given that T is the only robustly agreeing head, and Chamorro has little overt case marking.

far from trivial, especially for the DAP. The three categories that (arguably) bear agreement in Fijian – T, v, and P – all behave in a consistent way: each kind of agreement is contingent on some kind of movement taking the agreed-with NP to a high position (NP raising to Spec, TP; object shift out of VP; topicalization out of PP). The functional heads thus have uniform behavior in Fijian, as in Kinande. This supports my claim that (1) and (2) are true parameters in the syntax of agreement, not simply the result of stipulations in the lexical entries of the functional heads, which could differ from one functional head to the next within the same language.

3. Challenge of Tukang Besi

Having shown that the agreement parameters apply in a fairly straightforward way to Fijian, I turn now to the more complex case of Tukang Besi, as described by Mark Donohue (1999). Unlike Fijian, Tukang Besi has a system of morphological case marking on NPs, which includes the markers *na* "nominative", *te* "core" (default structural case), *i/di* "oblique", and *nu* "genitive" (the labels are Donohue's). The potential for case marking interacting with agreement is thus richer. Tukang Besi also has a Philippines-style topic/voice system, so there are more kinds of movement that can affect agreement. The question, then, is whether the two agreement parameters apply in a consistent way in this language, as well.

3.1 The direction of agreement parameter

Consider first the DAP. Donohue's analysis makes it plain that object agreement appears on the verb in Tukang Besi if and only if the object moves out of the VP. This is shown by the comparison in (20).

(20) a. [$_{VP}$ No-'ita+te kene-no]   na   ana.
         3R-see+CORE friend-3POSS NOM child
         'The child saw its friend.'   (Donohue 1999: 70)

     b. [$_{VP}$ No-'ita-'e] te   ana   na   kene-no.
         3R-see-3O CORE child NOM friend-3POSS
         'The child saw its friend.'   (Donohue 1999: 70)
         (*No-'ita-'e + te ana na kene-no)

In (20a), the thematic object is next to the verb, closer to it than the agentive subject, and its case particle encliticizes to the verb, showing that the two are in the same phonological phrase. In this sentence, the verb does not agree with the object. In (20b), the object is outside of the VP: it can follow the subject, and even when it is linearly adjacent to the verb its case particle cannot cliticize to the verb, showing that there is a phonological phrase boundary between them.[10] Furthermore, in this sentence there is a suffix on the verb that agrees with the object. This is similar to what we saw in Kinande and Fijian, suggesting that the DAP is set "yes" in Tukang Besi as well, allowing v to agree only with NPs that have moved out of VP. Indeed, Donohue himself observes the similarity between object agreement in Tukang Besi and object agreement in Bantu languages (see Bresnan & Mchombo 1987) – an insightful comparison, I believe.

Next consider agreement on T in Tukang Besi. Most verbs in Tukang Besi bear a prefix that agrees with the subject:

(21) *No*-tinti/*no*-buti na ana. (Donohue 1999: 51)
3R-run/3R-fall NOM child
'The child is running/the child fell.'

This prefix varies with the mood of the clause (realis or irrealis), suggesting that it is agreement on T, in accordance with normal generative assumptions. (In contrast, the object agreement suffixes are invariant, showing no dependence on the mood or tense of the clause, consistent with the idea that they are realizations of agreement on v, not T.) The interesting point for us is that this type of subject agreement is not found in existential clauses such as the ones shown in (22) (Donohue 1999: 58).

(22) a. Ane i Tindoi na po'o koruo.
exist OBL Tindoi NOM mango many
'There are many mangoes in Tindoi.'

b. Mbea'e-mo na po'o koruo i Tindoi.
Not.exist.PERF NOM mango many OBL Tindoi
'There aren't many mangoes in Tindoi anymore.'

Moreover, subject agreement is not required in passive clauses:

(23) a. 'U-to-'ita na iko'o. (Donohue 1999: 158, 275)
2sS.R-PASS-see NOM you
'You were seen.'

b. *No*-to-'ita na iko'o.
3R-PASS-see NOM you
'You were visible.'

We may assume that subjects normally move to Spec, TP (at the right edge of TP) in Tukang Besi to satisfy an EPP feature of T. In existential sentences, however, that

---

10. Note that the case markers on the subject and the object are different in (20a) and (20b). This shows that (20b) is not simply derived by right dislocation of the object, since right dislocation does not affect case marking inside the clause. Rather, the object in (20b) has undergone some sort of focus-like movement that feeds the case marking rules of Tukang Besi; see below for more discussion.

property is satisfied by a null expletive, whereas in passive sentences we may suppose that it can be satisfied by the passive morpheme itself (see Alexiadou & Anagnostopoulou 1998 on the possibility of morphemes on the verb satisfying the EPP in some languages). Thus the NP does not (need to) move to Spec, TP in these sentence types. When it does not, T cannot agree with NP by the DAP, in contrast to English (see (4a,c)). In fact, Donohue (1999: 479) provides other evidence that the "subjects" in (22) and (23b) do not occupy the same structural position as other subjects do: for example, the "subjects" in (22) and (23) do not count as discourse topics, and they cannot be co-construed with floated quantifiers the way that other subjects can be in Tukang Besi. These data are thus reminiscent of what we saw in Kinande and Fijian, where subject agreement depends on word order (Kinande) or on the lexical properties of the predicate (Fijian). This confirms that the DAP is also set positively in Tukang Besi.

T and v are the only agreement-bearing heads in Tukang Besi; there is no agreement on D, C, or P in this language. But the evidence from T and v is consistent, just as it is in Fijian and Kinande. Again, this supports the idea that the DAP is a unified syntactic parameter.

3.2 The case dependence of agreement parameter

The evidence for the setting of the CDAP in (2) seems at first glance to be somewhat more mixed. I will claim that this parameter is set negatively in Tukang Besi, making Tukang Besi less like an IE language and more like Burushaski or Georgian – languages with overt case marking that have the CDAP set negatively, as discussed in Baker (2008).

Subject agreement does not depend on the case of the subject in Burushaski the way it does in Hindi or Icelandic. The same first person singular agreement is found on the verb in both (24a), where the subject is nominative, and (24b), where the subject is ergative (contrast Hindi (15)).

(24) a. Jɛ   uːn̩ɛ xidmʌt ɛč-a   b-a.   (Lorimer 1935: 317)
       I.NOM your service do-1sS be-1sS
       '(For these many years) I have been at your service.'

   b. Ja   be.ʌdʌpi.ɛn ɛt-a   b-a.   (Lorimer 1935: 321)
       I.ERG discourtesy do-1sS be-1sS
       'I have committed a discourtesy.'

Subject agreement does not depend on the case of the subject in Tukang Besi either (Donohue 1999: 53). In (25a), the agentive subject is marked with nominative case and in (25b) (in which the object has moved out of VP, as in (20b)) it is marked with core/default case; nevertheless it triggers the same subject agreement on the verb in both examples.

(25) a. *Ko*-hu'u te ika *na* iko'o te iaku.
    2s.I-give CORE fish NOM you CORE me
    'You will give me some fish.' (Donohue 1999: 55)

   b. *Ko*-hu'u-aku te ika na iaku *te* iko'o.
    2s.I-give-1sO CORE fish NOM me CORE you
    'You will give me some fish.'

This shows that T does not have to assign a particular case to an NP in order to agree with it in Tukang Besi, the way it does in Icelandic and Hindi. In other words, the CDAP is set negatively.

A second consequence of the CDAP being set negatively in Burushaski is the fact that multiple heads can agree with the same NP, as in Kinande ((18)) but not English ((17)). This can also be seen in (24), where the main verb and the auxiliary both bear the first person singular marker *a* (contrast εč-*u* b-*o* 'she is doing it', εč-*i* b-*i* 'it is doing it', etc.). Double agreement is also found in some auxiliary constructions in Tukang Besi – the kind Donohue (1999) calls "ambient serialization":[11]

(26) a. Te tukatutu *no*-agori *no*-tode...
    CORE blacksmith 3R-immediate 3R-flee
    'The blacksmith fled without delay...'

   b. '*U*-po'oli-mo '*u*-po-'awa ke iai-su?
    2sS.R-finish-PERF 2sS.R-REC-obtain with young.sib-1sPOSS
    'Have you met my younger sister already?'

   c. *Ku*-hematuu-mo *ku*-henahenai te pogau Wanse.
    1sS-begin-PERF 1sS-learn CORE language Wansi
    'I have begun to learn Wansi.'

Tukang Besi is also like Fijian in this respect (see (19)).

---

11. Certain other auxiliary-like verbs in Tukang Besi always bear default third person agreement, while full agreement shows up on the main verb. These could be analyzed as verbs that take clausal complements but do not trigger raising to subject (like *probable* as opposed *likely* in English). If the subject doesn't raise to the Spec, TP position above the higher verb, then the higher T cannot agree with it, given that the DAP is set positively.

An anonymous reviewer asks how it would affect the analysis if the examples in (26) were analyzed as restructuring constructions, rather than auxiliary constructions. The answer depends on what analysis of restructuring is assumed; on some analyses, restructuring verbs simply are verbs that can (perhaps optionally) be analyzed as auxiliaries that take a VP complement. The crucial question is whether there is a single argument chain that counts as the subject of both verbs or not: if there is, and the two verbs agree with that single argument, then the CDAP must be set "no", regardless of the exact details of the structure. If, however, the examples in (26) are really a species of control structure, then they might tell us nothing about the setting of the CDAP: then one verb could agree with the overt NP and the other with PRO, a distinct nominal. (Questions would then arise about the case and agreement properties of PRO itself.)

The complication comes with object agreement. In canonical languages with the CDAP set "no", like Burushaski, object agreement happens regardless of the case of the object. Thus, the same agreement *gu-* is found in both (27a) and (27b), even though the agreed-with pronoun is in absolutive case in (27a) and in dative case in (27b) (Lorimer 1935).

(27) a. (U:ṇ) *gu*-yɛtsʌ-m.
        you-ABS 2sO-see-1sS
        'I saw you.'

   b. U:ṇər hik trʌṇ *gu*-čičʌ-m.
        you-DAT one half   2sS-give-1sS
        'I shall give a half to you.'

No such contrast can be found in Tukang Besi. Object agreement in Tukang Besi only happens when the agreed-with object bears nominative case, not when it has the "core" case, as shown by the contrast in (28).

(28) a. *No-kiki'i-*ko te*   iko'o na beka.
        3R-bite-2sO   CORE you   NOM cat
        'The cat bit you.'
        (OK is: *No-kiki'i te iko'o na beka*, without object agreement)

   b. No-kiki'i-*ko na*   iko'o te beka.
        3R-see-2sO   NOM you   CORE cat
        'The cat bit you.'

The question, then, is why is (28a) ruled out.

The interpretation of this fact that would be most threatening to the general approach of Baker (2008) would be to say that Tukang Besi is inconsistent with respect to the CDAP: T does not need to assign a particular case to an NP in order to agree with it, but v does. This would imply that different functional categories within the same language can show different behaviors with respect to the syntax of agreement. That would refute my claim that (1) and (2) are unified syntactic parameters, not reducible to the specification of features on individual lexical items.

This pessimistic interpretation is unwarranted. Rather, I claim that the badness of (28a) as opposed to (28b) follows from the positive setting of the Direction of Agreement Parameter, plus independently motivated properties of how *na* (NOM) case is assigned in Tukang Besi.

First, notice that allowing the CDAP to be set positively for some functional heads but not others within a single language would only explain (28) at a cost. The CDAP can only explain why agreement is possible in (28b) but not (28a) if one says that v (the bearer of object agreement) is the head that assigns nominative case to 'you' in (28b). This is not very plausible as a general principle of case assignment in Tukang Besi; nominative case is normally assigned by T, not by v. If we took this path, there would be no unified explanation for the assignment of nominative case in (28b) and its assignment in intransitive sentences like (21), or in passive sentences like (23). Therefore, one cannot simply retreat from the claim that parameters apply to languages as a whole to account for these facts; rather, some different conception of case and its relationship to agreement is needed for Tukang Besi.

In this light, I propose that nominative case in Tukang Besi is not assigned by *any* functional head. Rather, it is assigned by the simple configurational rule in (29).[12]

(29) a. Assign *na* (NOM) to NP1 if NP1 is the highest NP in its clause (if there is no other NP, NP2, such that NP2 is in the same clause as NP1 and NP2 c-commands NP1).

b. Assign *te* (CORE) to all other nonoblique NPs in the clause.

The rules in (29) capture several properties of case marking in Tukang Besi in a very straightforward way. First, they are consistent with the fact that the nominative NP does not need to agree with any particular functional head: it can agree with T ((21), (23a), (25a)), or with v ((25b), (28b)), or with no functional head ((22), (23b)). Second, they are consistent with the fact that the nominative NP need not occupy a particular syntactic position: it can be in Spec, TP ((21)), but it can also be VP-internal, as long as there is no higher NP ((22), (23b)). Third, they fit with the fact that there can only be one nominative-marked NP per clause in Tukang Besi. For example, in clauses that contain a triadic verb, there can be two or more NPs marked with the "core" case marker *te*, but there can only be one NP that is marked with nominative *na* (see (25)). This follows from (29) together with the fact that there can be at most one NP that is not c-commanded by any other NP in a clause, under normal assumptions about clause structure. Finally, (29) is consistent with the fact that nominative case can appear even in nonfinite control clauses, which do not have the sort of T that one would expect to assign nominative case. Thus, both (30a) and (30b) are possible in Tukang Besi.

(30) a. Ku-nde'u   manga te   senga
1sS-not.want eat   CORE fried.food
'I don't want to eat the senga.'   (Donohue 1999: 468)

b. Ku-nde'u   manga-'e na   *senga*.
1sS-not.want eat-3O   NOM fried.food
'I don't want to eat the senga.'   (Donohue, p.c.)

The embedded verb *manga* 'eat' in these examples has no subject agreement and no marking for realis/irrealis mood, and its subject is controlled by the subject of the matrix verb. Hence, it has no finite T. Nevertheless, the object can still be marked nominative, as shown in (30b). This is problematic for the normal generative assumption that

---

12. Compare Marantz 1991, who proposes an approach to morphological case in which case is never assigned by functional heads, but by checking what domain an NP is in and what other NPs are inside the same domain.

nominative is assigned by finite T, but perfectly explainable in terms of (29). We can simply assume that the object can move to a specifier position above the position of the controlled PRO subject in (30b) without disrupting the mechanisms of control. This, then, is strong evidence that nominative case is assigned in a different way in Tukang Besi than it is in English and other more familiar languages.[13]

What are the implications of this understanding of nominative case assignment for the problem of object agreement in Tukang Besi? We already know that v can only agree with the object in Tukang Besi if the object moves out of VP; this follows from the positive setting of the DAP. Now we can add the following assumption about clause structure:

(31) Spec, vP is not possible as a final landing site in Tukang Besi; it can only be passed through on the way to a higher position.

Reasonably closely related languages are known to differ in this respect. For example, NPs can stay in Spec, vP in Icelandic ("object shift") but not in English or French, where they only pass through Spec, vP on their way to Spec, CP (Chomsky 2001). Similarly, NPs can stay in Spec, vP in Zulu, but can only move through it to the right periphery in Kinande ((6) vs. (7)). In the same spirit, I propose that NPs can stay in Spec, vP in Fijian, but can only move through it in Tukang Besi. This implies that NP cannot get out of VP by moving only a short distance in Tukang Besi; if it moves at all, it has to move to the periphery of the clause. If it doesn't move, v cannot agree with it, by the DAP. If it does move, it becomes the highest NP in the clause, in which case it gets nominative case by (29). If "short movement" of the object, such that it did not cross the subject, were allowed in Tukang Besi, then the object could be agreed with and bear the "core" (default) case marking, but (31) says that this is impossible.[14]

This analysis is committed to the view that the surface position of the agreed-with object is higher than the normal position of the subject; otherwise (29) would assign nominative case to the subject rather than the object in (say) (28b). There is

---

13. Additional evidence for (29) might be gleaned from relative clauses in which the subject is extracted. The verb in such clauses is marked with -*um*- and does not bear subject agreement. It is plausible to analyze this as an active participle, hence as a clause with nonfinite T. Nevertheless, *na* can be assigned to the thematic object in these relative clauses, as in (ib).

(i) a. Ku-sepa-'e   na   mia   t-um-opa te   La Udi
       1sS-kick-3O   NOM   person   UM-slap   CORE   Udi
       'I kicked the person who was slapping Udi.'

    b. Ku-sepa-'e   na   mia   t-um-opa-'e   na   La Udi
       1sS-kick-3O   NOM   person   UM-slap-3O   NOM   Udi
       'I kicked the person who had been slapping Udi.'

14. Lisa Travis (personal communication) points out that, for this reasoning to go through, it must also be the case that no other functional head higher than vP and lower than TP can provide a final resting place for the object in Tukang Besi; either there are no other functional heads in this language, or (perhaps more likely) (31) must be generalized to apply to all of them.

some evidence that this is true. Donohue (1999: 79–80) shows that objects bearing nominative case can appear after time adverbs, whereas subjects bearing nominative case cannot:

(32) a. No-manga-'e-mo te   ana-no   dinggawi *na bae*.
         3R-eat-3O-PERF CORE child-3POSS yesterday NOM rice
         'Their children ate the rice yesterday.'

   b. [3R-eat *te* rice] (*yesterday) na + child-their (yesterday)

This makes sense if time adverbs are right-adjoined to TP. As such, they are higher than the normal position of the subject (Spec, TP, on the right of TP), but lower than the position of the moved object – perhaps Spec, FocusP, on the right of FocusP, or some similar peripheral discourse-related position. (The nominative object also *tends* to follow the subject in core case (Donohue 1990: 80), but the opposite order is also possible, perhaps due to stylistically driven reordering within the same phase at PF.)

In conclusion, once we adopt a plausible, independently motivated view of nominative case assignment in Tukang Besi, a natural solution to the problem of object agreement emerges. In the end, then, the agreement parameters in Tukang Besi have the same consistent settings as they do in Fijian and Kinande.[15] In particular, neither v nor T needs to assign case to the NP it agrees with. As a result, both can agree with the nominative NP, even though it is not case-marked by any functional head. The differences between Tukang Besi and Fijian reduce to the fact that there is overt case marking in Tukang Besi (as in (29)), plus the fact that the two languages allow different kinds of object movement (as in (31)).

4. An extension to Kapampangan

As my last investigation into agreement in Austronesian languages, I consider Kapampangan, a language not considered in Baker 2008 but drawn to my attention by Paul Kroeger and Mark Donohue.[16] It is interesting to compare Kapampangan with

---

15. Rackowski and Richards (2005) argue that the so-called voice morphology in Tagalog is really a reflection of v agreeing in case with the NP that has moved to Spec, vP. If they are correct, then Tagalog has the same parameter settings as Fijian and Tukang Besi. That v agrees only with an NP in Spec, vP, not with one inside VP, suggests that the DAP is set "yes". That v agrees with this NP in any of a variety of cases shows that the case of the NP does not come from v itself, so the CDAP is set "no". These Austronesian languages thus have the same parameter settings, even though the type of agreement that they display is different.

16. Paul Kroeger actually recommended that I look at Ilocano, but Ilocano seems to be very much like Kapampangan in the relevant respects, based on information in Rubino (2000). In particular, agreement on T and v and its interaction with the focus/voice system seems to be syntactically identical. The one notable difference is that v and T in Ilocano assign

Tukang Besi because it has a more prototypical Philippines-style voice system, very similar to Tagalog. It also has a case and agreement system organized along more or less ergative lines (Mirikitani 1972). I claim that while agreement must be upward in Kapampangan as in other Austronesian languages, agreement is case-dependent in Kapampangan. There is also another difference in the landing sites available for objects, which results in a more ergative syntax.

A basic description of the key facts is as follows. Agreement with the agentive subject is encliticized to the verb in both intransitive sentences and transitive "agent focus" constructions (Mirikitani 1972):

(33) a. Makasulat *ka* ngeni. (p. 62)
can-write 2sA now
'You can write now.'

b. Migaral *ya* ng Inglis *i* Nena. (p. 166)
AF.studied 3sA ACC English NOM Nena
'Nena studied English.'

c. Sumulat *ya* ng poesia *ing lalaki* king mestra para king babai.
AF.write 3sA ACC-poem NOM-boy OBL-teacher for OBL girl
'The boy wrote the poem to the teacher for the girl.'

In theme or oblique focus constructions, this same kind of agreement appears, reflecting the phi-features of the focalized argument. There is also a second agreement morpheme, morphologically distinct, that expresses the phi-features of the nonfocused agent argument:

(34) a. Asulat me (**mu**+*ya*) *ing istorya* ngeni
can-write 2sE+3sA the story now
'Can you write the story now?' (Mirikitani 1972: 62)

b. Saupan *na*-**ka** *ning lalaki*
TF.help 3sE+2sA the boy
'The boy will help you.' (p. 175)

c. Pigaralan ne (*na*-**ya**) ng Nena **ing Ingles**
TF.Studied 3sE+3sA ERG Nena NOM English
'English was studied by Nena.' (p. 167)

A focused argument headed by a common noun always appears with the case marker *ing*, as in (33b), (34a), and (34c) (for proper nouns, the form is *i*, as in (33b)). If the agent argument is not focused, it appears with the case marker *ning*, as in (34b) (*ng* with a proper noun, as in (34c)). All other arguments are marked with *ng* or *king*. (35) illustrates this by giving two other voice forms of the sentence in (33c). Notice

---

identical-looking cases (both realized as *ti*) in Ilocano, whereas the two structural cases are morphologically distinct in Kapampangan.

that in each version the NP marked with the *ing* particle is different (Mirikitani 1972: 117).

(35) a. Isulat ne ing poesia ning lalaki king mestra para king babai.
TF-write 3sE+3sA NOM-poem ERG-boy OBL-teacher for OBL girl
'The poem will be written by the boy to the teacher for the girl.'

b. Sulatanan ne ng poesia ning lalaki ing mestra para king babai.
GF-write 3sE+3sA ACC-poem ERG-boy NOM-teacher for OBL girl
'The teacher will be written a poem by the boy for the girl.'

Since agreement is not transparently aligned with subjects and objects, it is not immediately obvious which kind of agreement goes with which functional head in Kapampangan. I assume that the agreement with the focused argument – the one realized as 2s *ka* in (33a) and (34b) and as 3s *ya* in (33b) and many other examples – is agreement on T. Evidence for this is the fact that Kapampangan has one tense/aspect category, the recent past, in which there is no absolutive agreement, as shown in (36). Note that the second kind of agreement – the kind realized as 2s *mu* in (34a) and as 3s *na* in (34b,c) and (35), reflecting the phi-features of the agent – is still present in this tense (Mirikitani 1972: 134, 65).

(36) a. Kapuputut *na ning* babai ng manuk.
just-cut 3sE ERG woman ACC chicken
'The woman just cut a chicken.'

b. Kararatang *na ning* mestra.
just-came 3sE ERG teacher
'The teacher just came.'

Thus, whether *ka/ya* agreement is present or not depends on the particular tense-aspect inflection that is used, whereas *mu/na* is possible in all verbal clause types. Conversely, *ka/ya*-type agreement is found on nonverbal predicates, but *mu/na*-type agreement is not (Mirikitani 1972: 44, 57):

(37) a. Mestro *ya ing* lalaki.
teacher 3sA NOM boy
'The boy is a teacher.'

b. Masanting *ya ing* lalaki; mangasanting *la reng* lalaki.
handsome 3sA NOM boy handsome 3p NOM.pl boy
'The boy is handsome; the boys are handsome.'

These are presumably sentences that have a T head (present tense) but no v head. This distribution follows if the *ka/ya*-type agreement manifests agreement on T and the *mu/na*-type manifests agreement on v.

The next thing to take into account is that there is a perfect correlation between agreement and case marking in Kapampangan. An NP headed by a common noun that triggers agreement on T always bears *ing* case. An NP that triggers agreement on v always bears *ning* case.[17] In the sentences in (36), there is no agreement-bearing T, and there is also no nominal that has *ing* case. In the sentences in (37), there is no agreement-bearing v, and there is also no nominal that has *ning* case. Kapampangan is quite different from Tukang Besi in this respect; in Tukang Besi, T can agree with either a *te*-marked NP or with a *na*-marked NP. Moreover, in Tukang Besi clauses that have no "subject" agreement, such as (22) and (23b), it is still possible to have an NP that bears nominative case, unlike what we see in (36). I conclude from this that Kapampangan is a language in which the CDAP is set "yes": T agrees with an NP if and only if it assigns nominative case (*ing*) to that NP; v agrees with an NP if and only if it assigns ergative case (*ning*) to that NP. This contrast between Kapampangan and Tukang Besi provides us with our first example of parametric variation in agreement within the Austronesian languages.

If the CDAP is set "yes" in Kapampangan, then I predict that Kapampangan should not have auxiliary constructions with double agreement, the way Tukang Besi and Fijian do. This seems to be correct, according to my limited data: no such construction is mentioned in Mirikitani 1972. The following examples are comparable to the Tukang Besi examples in (26), but agreement occurs only on the highest verb:

(38) a. Kailangan-*ku* ng sumulat istorya king Inglis. (p. 226)
        have.to-1sA C write   story   OBL English
        'I have to write a story in English.'

   b. Susubukan *ke*-ng   bubuklat ing   awang.   (p. 221)
        try   1sE+3sA-C open   NOM window
        'I am trying to open the window.'

(Constructions with 'try' have double agreement in Tukang Besi, according to Donohue 1999: 191.)

Now what is the setting of the DAP? If I have identified the agreements correctly, then it is clear that T agrees with an NP only if the NP has been focused. Assuming that "focusing" in Kapampangan involves movement to a functional specifier high in the clause, as many people have argued for Tagalog (Guilfoyle et al. 1992), this suggests that T can only agree upward. (This conclusion follows regardless of the much-debated question of whether "focusing" is an A or A-bar movement; cf. Pearson 2005.) Meanwhile, v agrees only with the agent phrase, never with a theme or other internal argument. This suggests that v also only agrees upward, with an NP in Spec, vP, never downward with an NP inside VP. We thus have converging evidence that the DAP is set "yes" in Kapampangan, just as it is in Tukang Besi and Fijian. Kapampangan is

---

17. *Ning* also appears on the possessor in possessed nominals, and the possessed nominal bears a *mu/na*-type morpheme that agrees with the possessor. The correlation between the type of agreement triggered and the type of case marking borne thus extends even to the nominal domain.

therefore a new example of a language in which both parameters are set positively – the rarest type in Baker's (2008) typological survey.

This similarity in the setting of the DAP, however, belies an important difference between Tukang Besi and Kapampangan – one that is not explained purely by the settings of the agreement parameters. This concerns Kapampangan being more or less ergative in its case-and-agreement system in a way that Tukang Besi is not. The difference does not show up in intransitive clauses, or in clauses where the agent is focused, but it does show up in transitive clauses in which the object is focused (moved out of VP). In such clauses, T continues to agree with the thematic subject in Tukang Besi, while v agrees with the moved object. In contrast, T agrees with the moved object in Kapampangan, while v agrees with the thematic subject. As a result, T consistently agrees with the thematic subject in Tukang Besi, whereas it agrees with the thematic object in the most common type of transitive clause in Kapampangan. Agreement thus follows a (split) absolutive pattern in Kapampangan. Meanwhile, v is involved in object agreement in Tukang Besi, whereas it agrees with ergative thematic subjects in Kapampangan. This difference cannot be attributed to the DAP, because the two languages have the same setting for that parameter. Nor can it be attributed to the CDAP: since this parameter is set "no" in Tukang Besi, it does not constrain agreement in that language. In Kapampangan, the agreement pattern is semi-ergative because the case pattern is semi-ergative and agreement depends on case assignment, but this does not determine which NP each functional head must both agree with and case mark.

Instead, I believe that this difference between the two languages comes down to a difference in clause structure. More specifically, I suggest that the difference is in the landing site that is targeted by object movement in the "object focus" construction. Consider first Tukang Besi. Why does T agree with the agent in this language, and not with the focused object? We know that agreement must be upward in this language. This pattern then follows if the agent is always the first NP that T finds when it probes upward. In other words, the agentive subject is in Spec, TP. Indeed, Donohue shows that even when it is not topicalized, the agent phrase is outside the verb phrase in Tukang Besi. For example, the case marker associated with the subject never encliticizes onto the verb in Tukang Besi, the way that the case marker associated with an *in situ* object does (see (20)). This suggests that the thematic subject always moves to Spec, TP (except in existential sentences and some passives), and thus is not part of the vP phase. It then follows that the focused object must be even higher – say in Spec, FocP – given that it gets nominative case and often appears farther from the verb than the subject in Spec, TP (see (32) and related discussion). As a result, T always agrees with the thematic subject, never with the focused object, by the locality conditions on agreement.

Now consider agreement on v in Tukang Besi in a construction with a moved object. This is c-commanded by both the trace of the moved object and by the base position of the subject. It is not clear which is closer to v if both are specifiers (or adjuncts) of vP; this depends on controversial assumptions about the fine structure of vP. Suppose that in principle v can agree with either one. T, however, can only agree with the agent, as we have seen. If v also agreed with the agent, that agreement would be redundant, whereas if v agreed with the theme, it would be doing something new. It is plausible to think that languages favor the second situation. Kinyalolo (1991) and Carstens (2005) argue that a condition like the following holds in KiLega and certain other Bantu languages:

(39) *Kinyalolo's Constraint:* * Agreement on a lower head with NP X if there is a higher head that also agrees with X and the two functional heads are part of the same word at PF.

(39) is motivated in KiLega by the fact that agreement between T and the subject, which is normally obligatory, is suppressed when the subject raises to Spec, CP and the verb raises to C, because then ordinary subject agreement is redundant with the agreement between C and its specifier.

Kinyalolo's Constraint is not universal. There are a few languages in which v and T both seem able to agree with the same NP. One is the Austronesian language Nuaula, brought my attention by Mark Donohue (another is Burushaski; see Baker 2008: 215). Nuaulu is an SVO language that seems to have the same parameter settings as Tukang Besi. Like Tukang Besi, it uses prefixes to agree with subjects in Spec, TP and suffixes to agree with objects which have moved out of VP (or are null pronouns). However, unlike Tukang Besi, both T and v agree with the sole argument of some intransitive verbs, resulting in double agreement:

(40) a. *Ina-i   na ama-i   o-mata-so.*
        Mother-3sP and father-3sP 3pS-die-3pO
        'His mother and father died.'

   b. *Ami a-eu-ma   nau   nuae.*
        We   1pS-go-1pO seaward   sea
        'We went toward the sea.'

In one sense, it is not surprising that this sort of double agreement would arise. The subject in Spec, TP is the closest NP that c-commands both T and v in these intransitive sentences, hence both T and v can in principle agree with it given the positive setting of the DAP. Moreover, no multiple case assignment is implied by the double agreement in (40), given that the CDAP is set negatively in these languages. Thus, it is actually expected that v and T could both agree with the same NP in languages like this. What needs to be explained is why the same sort of double agreement is not found in Tukang Besi, as shown in (41).

(41) a. To-manga-do.   (*to-manga-kita)
        1p.R-eat-EMP   1p.R-eat-1pO
        'Let's eat first.'   (Donohue 1999: 130)

b. No-wila na ana kua daoa (*no-wila-'e)
   3s.R-go NOM child ALL market 3s.R-go-3O
   'The child went to the market.' (Donohue 1999: 118)

Kinyalolo's Constraint in (39) fills this need, ruling out intransitive verb forms that have both object agreement and subject agreement.

The same principle then can determine what v agrees with in transitive clauses with focused objects. T necessarily agrees with the subject in Spec, TP, and (39) forbids v from also agreeing with this argument. This pushes v to agree with the trace of the moved object adjoined to vP instead. On this analysis, then, the structure of a transitive sentence like (20b) with a focused object in Tukang Besi is (42).

(42) a. No-'ita-'e te ana na kene-no. (=(20b))
       3R-see-3O CORE child NOM friend-3POSS
       'The child saw its friend.'

   b. [$_{FocP}$ [$_{TP}$ Realis [[$_{vP}$ v [$_{VP}$ see t_i] t_k] t_i] te + child$_k$] na + friend$_i$]

Now let us see how a slight change in the assumptions about clause structure and movement can give us the more ergative agreement pattern in Kapampangan. In this language, T always agrees with the focused phrase, whatever the thematic role of that phrase might be. T never agrees with the agent unless the agent is the focused phrase. The easiest way to get this result would be to say that the landing site of focus object movement in Kapampangan is Spec, TP, not a distinct focus/topic position. This implies that when the object (or other internal argument) undergoes focus movement, the subject must stay in its thematic position, Spec, vP, lower than T. It follows from this that T can only agree with the focused argument in Kapampangan, not with the unfocused subject.

The question then arises as to why v in Kapampangan agrees with the unmoved subject in Spec, vP rather than with a trace of the object adjoined to vP. In principle, v could agree with either, but Kinyalolo's Constraint cuts the opposite way in Kapampangan than it does in Tukang Besi. In Kapampangan, T agrees with the focused object; hence v must agree with the *in situ* subject; otherwise it would agree with the same NP that T does. The same anti-redundancy principle thus favors v agreeing with the thematic subject in Kapampangan, but with the thematic object in Tukang Besi. The more ergative agreement pattern in Kapampangan, then, is a reflection of a different structure of the TP-CP space, such that the landing site for object focus is distinct from the Spec, TP position in Tukang Besi but not in Kapampangan. The structure for a simple transitive sentence with object focus in Kapampangan is (43).

(43) a. Pigaralan ne (*na-ya*) ng Nena **ing Ingles** (=(34c))
       studied 3sE+3sA ERG Nena NOM English
       'English was studied by Nena.'

b.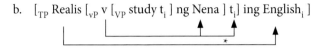

This difference in clause structure is by no means unprecedented in the literature. On the contrary, there have been several proposals that say that A-bar movement of the topic or focus type targets Spec, TP in some languages and a distinct position of its own in others: Icelandic and Yiddish are supposed to differ from other Germanic languages in this respect, for example (Diesing 1990); see also Goodall 2001 on *wh*-movement targeting Spec, TP and bleeding subject raising in Spanish (but not English). When this relatively familiar point of variation interacts with the less familiar settings of the agreement parameters, the different agreement systems of Tukang Besi and Kapampangan pop out. Austronesianists have also begun to explore the idea that object movement has different kinds of landing sites in different Austronesian languages (Rackowski & Richards 2005; Pearson 2005), so there is a degree of convergence between this line of inquiry and my approach to agreement.

Ideally, one would want to find a cluster of observable differences that follow from this basic difference in clause structure. Unfortunately, exploring this seriously goes beyond my expertise and the data available to me. I can mention only one other suggestive fact here. We saw above that subject control in Tukang Besi is possible and is independent of whether the object in the embedded clause is focused or not. Thus, the version with object focus and the version without it are both grammatical:

(44) a. Ku-nde'u manga te senga. (=(30))
  1sS-not.want eat CORE fried.food
  'I don't want to eat the senga.'

 b. Ku-nde'u manga-'e na senga.
  1sS-not.want eat-3O NOM fried.food
  'I don't want to eat the senga.'

In contrast, subject control and focalization do not seem to be independent of each other in Kapampangan. In all of the examples of subject control given in Mirikitani 1972, the embedded verb is always in the actor focus form, never in the theme focus form. The examples in (45) are typical in this respect. Note also that the object is always in unmarked/default case, and apparently cannot bear the nominative case marker *ing*.

(45) a. Sumaup ku-ng maglinis bale keka.
  help 1sA-C AF.clean house you.OBL
  'I will help you clean the house.'

 b. Kailangan-ku ng sumulat istorya king Inglis (p. 226)
  have.to-1sA C AF.write story OBL English
  'I have to write a story in English.'

This difference between the two languages is not unexpected given the difference in clause structure shown in (42) and (43). Suppose that subject control in both languages happens when the agent of the embedded clause is a PRO that occupies the Spec, TP position of a nonfinite TP. Object focus in Kapampangan crucially targets the Spec, TP position; therefore object focus and subject control are incompatible in Kapampangan. However, object focus in Tukang Besi targets a position distinct from (higher than) Spec, TP; hence it is in principle independent of subject control, and may occur in a nonfinite control clause. If data like this bears up under further scrutiny – or other better data can be found that supports the same conclusion – then the difference in clause structure that I have suggested is not merely a kludge to explain the differences in agreement in these two languages, but an important feature of their syntax more generally.[18]

5. Conclusion

In this article, I have shown that two parameters that concern the syntax of agreement, which were originally discovered by comparing NC languages and IE languages, also apply in interesting ways to various Austronesian languages. In particular, Fijian is demonstrably similar to the Bantu language Kinande, and its agreement system is characterized by the same parameter settings. Those parameter settings also apply to Tukang Besi; moreover, they account for the interaction between agreement and overt case marking, an issue that does not arise in Kinande and Fijian. Finally, Kapampangan shares the same positive setting of the Direction of Agreement Parameter as its Austronesian kin, but it differs from them in also having a positive setting of the Case Dependency of Agreement Parameter. As such, it provides a new example of the rarest kind of language in my typology.

We have also seen that the two parameters in (1) and (2) are not the only factors that determine the character of agreement that a language will have. Parameters that concern clause structure and the landing sites of movement also play an important role. Of particular importance is the question of where objects can move to. In Fijian,

---

18. here seems to be a related difference between Tukang Besi and Kapampangan in the syntax of nonfinite (participial) relative clauses. Nonfinite relative clauses marked by the infix -um- in Tukang Besi are always understood as having the subject argument of the nonfinite verb as the head of the relative, and it is possible to focalize the object inside such a relative clause (see note 13). In contrast, when the head of the relative clause is the agent in Kapampangan, the verb must be in agent-focus form, and it is not possible to focalize the object inside such a relative clause. This difference could follow if the head of this sort of relative clause must always move from the Spec, TP position. Then this sort of relativization will interfere with object movement in Kapampangan (which also crucially involves the Spec, TP position), but not in Tukang Besi. But the data are complex, and there are other sorts of relative clauses that must be included in a complete analysis.

the object can stop in Spec, vP, whereas in Tukang Besi and Kapampangan it can only transit through that position on its way to a clause peripheral position. Moreover, in Kapampangan, object movement targets the same Spec, TP position that the subject could otherwise occupy, whereas in Tukang Besi it targets a distinct A-bar position. All these various kinds of object movement are known to exist in well-studied IE languages. When they interact with the non-IE-like settings of the agreement parameters found in Austronesian languages, however, the result is some unfamiliar patterns of agreement.

A more general moral of this study is that it is valuable to have deep and meaningful interaction between general theorists and typologists on the one hand and experts on particular Austronesian languages on the other hand. With the exception of Chung 1998, agreement has not gotten much attention from Austronesianists interested in formal linguistics. Perhaps it takes an outsider like me, eager to replicate my Bantu results in some other language family, to show what a rich and interesting domain this could be, full of potential insights into clause structure, movement processes, and other topics of general interest. I am, however, very aware of how much I have depended on the detailed and insightful discussions of the specialists on these languages to pursue this topic as far as I have here, and how much more collaboration would be needed to take the matter farther. My naive study of agreement has led me to the deepest waters of Austronesian linguistics, including the nature of the topic/focalization structures, and the crucially different notions of "subject" that are at work. The experts will have to judge whether what I have conjectured about these matters for the sake of agreement is viable on other grounds. More generally, I think that this is the kind of healthy and constructive interplay between the concerns of the generalists and those of the specialists that we should work for throughout the field of linguistics.

References

Alexiadou, A., & Anagnostopoulou, E. 1998. Parametrizing AGR: Word order, V-movement and EPP-checking. *Natural Language and Linguistic Theory* 16: 491–539.
Baker, M. 2003. Agreement, dislocation, and partial configurationality. In *Formal Approaches to Function in Grammar*, A. Carnie, H. Harley & M. Willie (eds), 107–134. Amsterdam: John Benjamins.
Baker, M. 2008. *The Syntax of Agreement and Concord*. Cambridge: CUP.
Bobaljik, J. 2008. Where's Phi? Agreement as a post-syntactic operation. In *Phi Theory: Phi Features Across Interfaces and Modules*, D. Adger, D. Harbour & S. Béjar (eds), 295–328. Oxford: OUP.
Bresnan, J. & Mchombo, S. 1987. Topic, pronoun, and agreement in Chichewa. *Language* 63: 741–782.
Carstens, V. 2005. Agree and EPP in Bantu. *Natural Language and Linguistic Theory* 23: 219–279.
Chomsky, N. 1981. *Lectures on Government and Binding*. Dordrecht: Foris.

Chomsky, N. 2000. Minimalist inquiries: the framework. In *Step by Step*, R. Martin, D. Michaels & J. Uriagereka (eds), 89–155. Cambridge MA: The MIT Press.

Chomsky, N. 2001. Derivation by phase. In *Ken Hale: A life in language*, M. Kenstowicz (ed.), 1–52. Cambridge MA: The MIT Press.

Chung, S. 1998. *The Design of Agreement*. Chicago IL: University of Chicago Press.

Diesing, M. 1990. Verb movement and the subject position in Yiddish. *Natural Language and Linguistic Theory* 8: 41–80.

Diesing, M. 1992. *Indefinites*. Cambridge MA: The MIT Press.

Dixon, R.M.W. 1988. *A Grammar of Boumaa Fijian*. Chicago IL: University of Chicago Press.

Doke, Clement. 1963. *Textbook of Zulu Grammar*. London: Longmans.

Donohue, M. 1999. *A Grammar of Tukang Besi*. Berlin: Mouton de Gruyter.

Goodall, G. 2001. The EPP in Spanish. In *Objects and Other Subjects*, W. Davies & S. Dubinsky (eds), 193–224. Dordrecht: Kluwer.

Guilfoyle, E., Hung, H. & Travis, L. 1992. Spec of IP and Spec of VP: Two subjects in Austronesian languages. *Natural Language and Linguistic Theory* 10: 375–414.

Harlow, S. 1981. Government and relativization in Celtic. In *Binding and Filtering*, F. Heny (ed), 213–254. Cambridge MA: The MIT Press.

Haspelmath, M., Dryer, M., Gil, D. & Comrie, B. (eds.) 2005. *The World Atlas of Language Structures*. Oxford: OUP.

Kinyalolo, K. 1991. Syntactic Dependencies and the SPEC-head Agreement Hypothesis in KiLega. PhD dissertation, UCLA.

Legate, J. 2008. Morphological and abstract case. *Linguisitic Inquiry* 39: 55–102.

Lorimer, D.L.R. 1935. *The Burushaski language: Introduction and Grammar*, Vol. 1. Cambridge MA: Harvard University Press.

Marantz, Alec. 1991. Case and licensing. Paper presented at the 8th Eastern States Conference on Linguistics, University of Maryland, Baltimore.

Massam, D. 2001. Pseudo noun incorporation in Niuean. *Natural Language and Linguistic Theory* 19: 153–197.

Mirikitani, L. 1972. *Kapampangan Syntax*. Honolulu HI: University Press of Hawaii.

Ndayiragije, J. 1999. Checking economy. *Linguistic Inquiry* 30: 399–444.

Ormazabal, J. & Romero, J. 2006. Object clitics and agreement. Ms, University of the Basque Country and University of Alcalá.

Pearson, M. 2005. The Malagasy subject/topic as an A'-element. *Natural Language and Linguistic Theory* 23: 381–457.

Rackowski, A. & Richards, N. 2005. Phase edge and extraction: A Tagalog case study. *Linguisitic Inquiry* 36: 565–599.

Rubino, C. 2000. *Ilocano Dictionary and Grammar*. Honolulu HI: University of Hawai'i Press.

Schütz, A. 1985. *The Fijian Language*. Honolulu HI: University of Hawaii Press.

Topping, D. 1973. *Chamorro Reference Grammar*. Honolulu HI: University of Hawaii Press.

Index

A
A-bar movement *See movement, A-bar movement*
adjective 27, 47, 65, 68–72, 74, 76, 78, 145, 153–156, 159, 284, 346
adjunction 183, 184, 187, 191, 199, 207, 271
adverbials 27, 92, 163–181, 183, 184, 197–200, 206, 207, 220–233 passim, 238, 239, 271–273, 275–281, 283, 285, 291–292, 297, 300, 305, 309–324 passim, 335, 349, 352, 364
   adverbial verb 163–175, 177–181, 183–186, 189–191, 193–195, 197–207
   cardinal frequency adverbial 197
   frequency adverbial 165, 176, 197, 207
   long-distance construal 316, 318, 321
   multiple occurrence 297, 300, 309, 311, 316, 318, 324
AF-only Restriction 165, 166, 185–190, 192, 201, 202, 206
Agree 90, 93–95, 99, 291, 346
agreement 2, 105, 108–110, 115, 142, 172, 173, 175, 218, 241, 345–373
   subject agreement 175, 348, 354, 358, 359, 362, 363f, 367, 369, 370
   object agreement 346, 349, 350, 351, 354, 355, 357, 358, 361, 363, 364, 368, 370
alienable *See possession, alienable*
alignment 48, 57
Amis 181, 185, 187, 188, 196, 199, 200
anaphora 215, 327–332, 334–338, 340–342
   Underspecified anaphor 329, 330, 335

applicative 207, 250, 251, 255–258, 262, 263, 267–269, 272, 277–284 passim, 286, 287, 290, 292, 345
Appl 207, 255, 272f, 276, 279, 286, 292, 339, 340, 345, 351
applicative head 207
applied object *See object, applied object*
Arabic 66, 171
   Classical Arabic 171f
argument composition 2, 249, 262, 263
argument-marking 253, 254, 297–301, 303, 316, 317, 324
Atayal 184, 185, 200, 201, 203
   Squliq Atayal 184, 200
   Mayrinax Atayal 185, 201, 203
Atayalic language 163, 166f
Austro-Asiatic 45, 55, 61, 172
auxiliary 165, 166, 168, 178, 262, 355, 356, 360, 367
Avava 143f

B
Bantu language 173f, 347–351, 353, 354–356, 358, 369, 372, 373
Betawi *Malay See Malay, Betawi Malay*
binding 2–4, 262, 289
   Binding Theory 327–331, 341, 342
Boni 124f,
Bunun 169, 181, 186
   Takbanuaz Bunun 169
Burushaski 359–361, 369

C
Car Nicobarese 4, 172
case 103–115, 122, 123, 130, 134, 196, 207, 221f, 241, 249–252, 254, 256, 259– 269 passim, 273–275, 296, 301f, 312, 345–348, 353–372

case assignment 346, 354–356, 361, 363, 364, 368, 369
case filter 354, 355f
c-command 125, 134, 289, 329, 330, 334–336, 345–352, 362, 368, 369
Celtic 171
Chamorro 348, 350, 353, 356
Chinese 122, 328, 335, 346
Choapan Zapotec 4, 172
clause structure 232, 236, 245, 275, 345, 362, 363, 368, 370–373
Clause Union 263
cleft 96–99, 170, 171
clitic 4, 65–76 passim, 80, 92, 108, 109, 122, 128, 163, 164, 170, 173f, 176–179 passim, 189, 192, 194, 203, 207, 255, 282, 283, 298f, 301f, 312, 333, 352f, 353f, 357, 365, 368
   definite clitic 66, 68
complementation 183, 184, 187, 191, 193, 206, 207
complementizer 142f, 177, 273, 345, 346, 353
compound 2, 3, 65–72, 74–80, 143, 144, 280
connectivity 218
constraint conjunction 63
constraint disjunction 56f, 60
contiguity 49, 58, 69, 160, 321
control 137, 149, 163, 183, 184, 187, 188, 192, 194, 198, 360, 362, 363, 371, 372
   semantic control 137, 138
   pragmatic control 3
correspondence 1, 45–47, 49–53, 57, 59, 60, 63

D
definite 66–68, 85, 118f, 174, 214–216, 223–225, 227, 235, 236, 239, 311, 345, 351, 352
definiteness 214, 215, 223, 227

Distributed Morphology 65, 282
definite clitic *See clitic, definite clitic*
ditransitive 86–88, 90, 105f, 113, 114, 234, 237, 256
Dutch 236, 245

E
edge 1, 45–61, 83f, 90–94, 96, 99, 127, 238, 251, 285, 288, 350, 352, 358
edge feature 71
emergence of the unmarked (TETU) 48, 54, 63
English 3, 4, 66, 74, 122, 148–150, 153, 166, 169–171, 173–180 passim, 206, 207, 217–219, 222, 226, 229, 237, 241, 243–245, 255, 280, 297f, 305, 328, 335, 342, 349–356 passim, 359, 360, 363, 371
EPP 81, 93, 99, 127, 274, 275, 358, 359
ergative 104, 106, 112–114, 118f, 122, 127, 133f, 164f, 249f, 252–257, 265–268 passim, 272f, 274, 345f, 346, 354, 359, 365–370 passim
Estonian 4, 173
existentials 2, 297, 300, 309, 350, 351, 358, 368
existential clause 358
existential construction 2, 297, 300, 309, 350
expletive 349, 350, 359
extended EPP 81, 93, 99
extraction 128, 135, 159f, 160, 188–191 passim, 220f, 265–269, 290, 296, 300, 302, 309–314 passim, 319–324 passim, 353, 363f

F
faithfulness 46, 49, 52, 53, 60, 61,
Fijian 228f, 345, 348, 350–353, 356–360, 363, 364, 367, 372
Finnish 4, 173, 175, 199
focus 81–84, 88, 89, 92–99, 142f, 163–167, 184–186, 190, 191, 196, 208, 217, 220f, 221, 225f, 228, 232f, 272f, 289, 297f, 333, 337, 342, 345f, 349, 352, 353, 358f, 364–372

Broad Focus (BF) 82–93, 95, 99
Narrow Focus (NF) 82, 83, 92–99
Focus Harmony Restriction 185f, 186, 190, 191, 196
force 90, 91, 94, 95, 98–99
Formosan 1–3, 163, 165, 167f, 169, 170, 172, 173, 175, 180, 181, 183–187, 189–193, 196, 198, 200, 202, 206, 207
French 53, 206, 262, 350f, 363
Quebec French 53, 63f
Parisian French 53
functional head 2, 72, 91, 99, 142, 156, 183, 184, 198–207, 226, 227, 264, 271, 272, 281, 285, 286, 290–292, 342, 347, 352–357 passim, 361–369

G
Gaelic
Irish Gaelic 226f
Scottish Gaelic 4, 171, 226f
Generalized "Doubly Filled Comp Filter" 156
genitive 2, 69, 103, 105–110, 114–115, 117–122, 126–129 passim, 131–139, 149, 150, 164f, 208, 221f, 272f, 289, 297f, 357
genitive relative construction *Seee relative clause, genitive relative construction*
Georgian 4, 359
Germanic languages 274, 332, 371
Greek 243, 244

H
Haitian 194
Hawaiian 118, 119, 121
head 2, 69–73, 78, 90–98 passim, 117–119, 126, 127, 134–139 passim, 141–152 passim, 156–160, 165, 166, 172, 175–181 passim, 183, 202, 207, 223, 226–228, 251, 255, 260–263, 267, 273, 281–287, 290–292, 301–309, 312, 315–318, 321, 323, 345–372 passim
functional head *See functional head*
head movement *See movement, head movement*

headless relative construction *See relative clause, headless relative*
high argument merge 288, 291
Hindi 4, 354, 359, 360
HPSG 2–4, 251, 258–263, 265, 266

I
Ibibio 173f
Icelandic 4, 354, 359, 360, 363, 371
identity 39, 215, 219f, 226–228
Ilocano 364f, 365f
imperative 2, 3, 78, 166f, 178, 179f, 189, 192, 202, 203, 208, 231–237, 239–246
inalienable *See possession, inalienable*
incorporation 117, 124, 125, 127, 135, 139, 172, 258, 283, 284, 351, 352
object incorporation 124
indefinite (non-definite), 85f, 125, 131, 132, 135, 214, 216f, 223
indirect possession *See possession, indirect possession*
indirect possession noun (IPN) *See possession, indirect possession*
Indo-European (IE) languages 2, 4, 347, 349, 351–356, 359, 372, 373
Indonesian 25, 26, 37, 42, 66, 107, 108, 110, 327, 329–333, 335–337, 339, 340f, 342, 348
Jakarta Indonesian 332
Standard Indonesian 25, 26, 37, 42, 327, 328, 330, 332, 333, 335, 336
Riau Indonesian 25, 26, 37, 42, 336, 337, 339, 340
information structure 81, 235
innovation 19, 26, 37–40, 42
intensifier 27, 333, 335–337, 341, 342
interface 1, 4, 65, 76, 78, 81–84, 87, 90, 92, 93, 95, 98, 99, 262f
intonation 2, 4, 81–84, 86, 87, 89–91, 94f, 95f, 97, 98, 241
Inuktitut 283
inverse order *See word order, inverse order*
inverse VO languages 4, 81, 82, 84, 90

inversion 2, 213, 214, 220f,
    226–229, 285, 314, 348, 349,
    354, 356
  prosodic inversion 282, 283
Irish Gaelic *See Gaelic, Irish Gaelic*
Italian 4, 82, 83, 86, 90, 91, 99, 124f

J

Jakarta Indonesian *See Indonesian, Jakarta Indonesian*
Jambi Malay *See Malay, Jambi Malay*
Japanese 75, 122, 137, 236f
Javanese 1–3, 7–11, 18–21, 23, 65, 66, 68–70, 73–79, 154f, 329, 332, 336
  Peranakan Javanese 329

K

Kanakanavu 186, 201, 202
Kapampangan 345, 348, 356f, 364–368, 370–373
Kavalan 183–185, 187, 189, 192–196, 198–203, 206
Kilega 4, 352, 369
Kinande 4, 345, 348–350, 352–360, 363, 364, 372
Korean 262

L

language change 3, 26, 38, 39, 67
laryngoscopy 12, 13
larynx height 7–11, 13, 14, 18, 19, 21
lax stops 1, 7–12, 15–18, 20, 21, 23
Lexical Decomposition Grammar (LDG) 4, 104, 111, 114, 115
lexical phonology 74, 78
Linear Correspondence Axiom (LCA) 141, 142, 153, 160
linear precedence constraint (LPC) 261–263
linker 143–146, 150, 185–187, 190, 192, 193, 206, 208, 226–229, 272f, 297– 304 passim, 312f
locality 285, 287, 289, 291, 297, 301, 316, 368
  local antecedent 329, 330
locative inversion 348, 349, 354
long distance relations 137, 194, 196, 207, 289, 335
  anaphora 329f, 330, 336, 341

long distance antecedent 331
long distance construal of adverbs, *See adverb, long distance construal*
long distance coreference 134, 139, 334, 335
long distance passive *See passive, long distance passive*
long distance reflexive 328, 329, 334, 335
long-distance dependency (LDD) 249–251, 258, 260, 264–266, 268, 269

M

Madurese 4, 19, 336
Mainland Southeast Asian languages 7, 9, 18, 19, 21
main prominence (prosody) 82, 90–92, 94, 96–98
Malagasy 1–4, 81, 82, 89–91, 93, 95–99, 213–215, 217–222, 225–229, 231–233, 236f, 239, 241, 242, 244, 245, 278, 348
Malayalam 74
Malay
  Betawi Malay 332
  Chinese Malay 332
  Jambi Malay 2–4, 327, 331, 332, 336, 338, 340–342
  Tanjung Raden Malay 1, 25, 27, 31, 37, 332, 333, 335, 339
Malayo-Polynesian 11, 46
Mandarin 328, 329
Maori 118, 119, 121, 137, 149, 228f, 245f, 282, 283, 290
Marantz's Generalization 46f, 52, 57
may 297–300, 309–324, 307–324
Mayali 124f
Mayrinax Atayal *See Atayal, Mayrinax Atayal*
mayroon 297–300, 309–320, 323, 324
medial clusters 52
mirror-image 141, 142, 152–154, 157, 159
  Unua mirror-image ordering 152
modal (voice quality) 9
modal 175, 189, 192, 208, 220, 222, 273, 276, 279, 280
Mohawk 346

Mon-Khmer 18
morphology 4, 31, 72f, 84, 107, 109, 112, 114, 130, 142, 149, 163–180, 187, 197, 198, 206, 207, 214, 218, 219, 241–244 passim, 282, 283, 297, 364f
movement 2, 4, 71, 81, 91, 92, 126–128, 139, 142, 153, 175, 181, 194–198 passim, 207, 224f, 235f, 236, 251, 266, 271–276 passim, 281–292, 302f, 310, 314, 320–323 passim, 328, 345–352 passim, 357, 358f, 363, 364, 367–372
  A-bar movement 367, 371
  head movement 2, 175, 255, 281–283, 286
  phrasal movement 2, 127, 141, 142, 153, 159, 160
  remnant movement 81, 91, 248, 274, 287, 291, 292, 325
  roll-up movement 2, 156, 282, 284–292 *See also phrasal roll-up*
  V-movement 4, 91
  vP movement 91, 92, 99, 285, 352
  wh-movement, 128, 218, 371
  See also extraction, predicate fronting, and raising
Mudung Darat 332, 333, 335

N

Nakanai 57f
Naman 143f
Nese 143f
Neve'ei 143f
Nias 106, 110, 113, 114
Niger-Congo languages (NC) 2, 4, 347, 351, 355, 356, 372
Nilotic language 19
Niuean 1, 3, 91, 110, 117, 120, 121, 138, 228, 249–252, 254, 256–261, 263, 264, 266f, 268, 269, 271–286, 289–292, 352
nominal predicate 172, 214–216, 223, 228, 275
non-contiguous relative clause *See relative clause, non-contiguous relative clause*
nonfinite 202, 207, 362, 363, 372
Nootka 4, 172, 173f
Nuaula 369

O

object 83f, 87, 88, 94, 95, 103–107, 109, 115, 118, 120, 124, 136, c142f, 151, 174, 194, 196, 207, 220f, 233–237 passim, 240, 249–259, 262–268 passim, 271, 273–275, 285–292 passim, 306, 334, 345–373 passim
  applied object 207, 255–258, 262–264, 286, 287
  object agreement, *See agreement, object agreement*
  object incorporation *See incorpiration, object incorporation*
  object relative *See relative clause, object relative*
  object shift 291, 351, 357, 363
Oceanic 124, 141–143, 160, 249f, 288
Optimality Theory (OT) 45–50, 54, 55, 57, 63, 64

P

Paiwan 167f, 185, 187, 190, 193, 198, 199, 201, 206, 348
Palu'e 109, 110
paradigm uniformity 75
parameter 2, 3, 4, 232, 262, 341, 342, 345–348, 353, 356, 357, 359, 361, 362, 364, 368, 369, 371–373
particles 120f, 134, 156, 173f, 176, 213–217 passim, 220, 223, 227, 228, 249, 262, 271–279, 282–284, 288, 291, 292, 352, 353, 357, 366
passive 108, 122, 137, 168, 194, 207, 218, 232f, 239, 240, 297f, 302, 308, 316, 345f, 352, 358, 359, 362, 368
  long distance 194f, 207
Peranakan Javanese *See Javanese, Peranakan Javanese*
phase 4, 70–72, 78, 82, 87, 88, 90, 91, 93, 95f, 127, 137, 289, 364, 368
phonological word (p-word) 68, 72–77
phrasal roll-up 2, 156, 282, 284–292 *See also movement, roll-up movement*
pitch 7–10, 18–20, 82–84, 92–96, 98, 99

Polynesian 3, 46, 117–119, 137–139, 149, 228f, 249, 251, 255, 264, 271, 273, 281
possession 2, 105, 106f, 141–145, 151, 158, 160
  alienable 143
  direct possession 142
  direct possession noun (DPN) 142, 142–147, 150–153, 157–160
  inalienable 143, 145, 146
  indirect possession 2, 141–144
  indirect possession noun (IPN) 143–147, 150–160
  possessed nominal 107, 367f
possessive construction 2, 3, 107, 119, 143, 149, 151, 152, 297, 300
possessor argument 2, 3, 103–111 passim, 114, 115, 119–123 passim, 126, 130–138 passim, 141–160, 300, 306, 312–315 passim, 319–322, 324, 335, 367f
possessor roles in Unua 150
pragmatic coreference 125, 134–137
Precedence Based Phonology (PBP) 1, 25, 26, 31, 37, 43
predicate fronting 4, 81, 82, 90–93, 99, 181, 236f, 271, 272, 274, 275, 281, 282, 286, 291, 292, 352f
predicate-internal subject *See subject, predicate-internal subject*
prefix harmony 186, 187
preposition 87, 88, 119, 121, 130, 134, 151, 152, 249–254, 256, 259, 260–262, 266–268, 275–280 passim, 285, 286, 306, 334, 352, 353
presentatives 215
probe 90, 94, 347, 368
prominence 45, 52, 57, 59, 61, 82, 83f, 90–92, 94, 96–98
pronoun 83f, 94f, 117–135, 138, 139, 142, 143, 158, 159, 170, 178, 184, 189, 192, 203, 205, 208, 215, 221, 222, 235, 239, 241–243, 249f, 252, 264–266, 272f, 274, 277, 279, 314f, 327–335, 337–342, 346, 350f, 352f, 353f, 361, 369
  resumptive pronoun 128, 129, 264–266, 272f, 277, 279, 353f

prosodic structure 75, 76
prosodic word 48, 65, 75, 76
Proto-Austronesian 7, 8
Proto-Malayo-Polynesian 11
pseudoclefts 217
pseudo-noun incorporation 273, 284, 352
Puyuma 184, 202

Q

quantifier 169–172, 174, 254, 255, 272, 277, 289, 353
  floating quantifier 84f, 254, 256, 258, 268, 277, 359

R

raising 70–74, 77, 78, 84f, 94, 96, 117, 124–127 passim, 137, 153, 156–159 passim, 168, 169, 181, 183, 184, 192, 207, 223, 236, 257, 258, 268, 289, 350, 357, 360f, 370, 371
Rapanui 348
reduplication 1, 3, 4, 25–43, 45–47, 49, 50, 52, 54, 55, 57–59, 61, 77, 80, 208, 283
  C[aʔ] reduplication 30, 37
  full reduplication 25–28, 32–35, 37–39, 41, 42, 54, 55, 58
  reduplication with glottal stop 28, 34, 35, 41, 42
  reduplication without consonant 33, 38
reflexive 32, 232f, 235, 327–331, 334–342
  true reflexive 330
register 7, 8, 16, 18–21, 66, 143f, 156
relative clause (RC) 2, 96, 97, 108, 109, 117–122, 126–128, 131–139 passim, 142f, 144, 154, 268, 284, 300–324, 363f, 372f
  externally headed relative clause 301, 302
  free relative clause 96, 218, 301, 307
  genitive relative construction (GRC) 3, 117, 118, 120–122, 126–129, 131, 132, 134, 135–139, 289
  headless relative 97, 214, 216, 221, 223, 225–227, 235, 301, 306, 307, 313, 324

internally headed relative clause 301–303, 306, 307, 315, 324
non-contiguous relative clause 304, 321, 322, 324
object relative 118f, 136
stacked relative clause 304, 321
relativization 84, 105f, 117, 120, 126, 128, 134, 135, 174, 178, 208, 264, 289, 372f
restructuring 72f, 168, 169, 174, 175, 178–180, 207, 360f
restructuring verb *See* verbs, restructuring verb
Riau Indonesian *See* Indonesian, Riau Indonesian
Right-roof constraint 305, 306, 322
Romance 332

S
Saaroa 186
Saisiyat 201
Scottish Gaelic *See* Gaelic, Scottish Gaelic
scrambling 91, 93, 95, 99, 137, 231, 233–236, 238, 240
Seediq 2, 163–170, 173–178, 180, 184, 198, 199, 201, 203
Truku Seediq 201
Semai 55f, 61f
Semitic 171
serial verb constructions 184, 193
Shona 53
Sino-Tibetan 18
Siraya 186, 187, 193
Spanish 4, 180, 351, 355, 371
specificational 2, 3, 213–215, 217–219, 225–229
specificational sentence 213–215, 219, 225–229
Spec, TP 93, 223, 224, 346, 348–350, 352f, 357–360, 362, 364, 368–373
spell-out 1, 4, 31, 65, 70–74, 77, 78, 81f, 90, 91, 99, 159, 226–228, 354
structural position 122, 137, 148, 238, 273, 310f, 359
subject 2, 84f, 93, 96, 103–111 passim, 115, 117–129 passim, 134–137, 139, 142, 168–175, 181, 194, 196, 213–217, 220–229, 231–246, 252, 262f, 271, 274, 275, 285–290 passim, 316f, 334, 338, 346–373 passim

dative subject 354
predicate-internal subject 231, 233, 236, 237
subject agreement *See* agreement, subject agreement
subordination 108, 165, 176, 185, 193, 208
Sundanese 332
Swahili 4, 346, 350
syncretism 103–105, 107–111, 114, 115, 354

T
Tagalog 1–4, 81, 82, 84–93, 95–99, 106, 107, 110, 114, 167f, 213, 228, 229, 286, 297, 300–302, 304, 305, 311, 313f, 314f, 320, 348, 364f, 365, 367
tense stops 7–9, 16–18, 20
theta-feature 136, 137, 139, 289, 291
theta-role 124, 135, 136, 139, 227, 271, 289–291
theta-role assignment 271
Tinrin 105, 110, 113
Tongan 2, 3, 110, 117, 120–124, 126–130, 132, 137–139, 249f
topic 81f, 114, 122, 123, 127, 128, 132, 134, 213–224, 227–229, 231, 239, 289, 357, 359, 370, 371, 373
topicalized 213, 215–217, 220, 223–228, 264, 353, 357, 368
trigger 83–92, 96, 97, 99, 157, 186, 214, 231f, 241, 283, 298–304, 306, 307, 311–318, 320, 322, 350, 359, 360, 367
Tsou 165, 167f, 170f, 183f, 185–187, 190, 191, 193, 196–200, 202, 204–206
Tukang Besi 108, 110, 172, 249f, 345, 348, 357–365, 367–373
Tuvaluan 4, 228f, 335

U
Ulu Muar Malay 1, 3, 45–50, 52, 54, 55, 57, 58, 61
Unua 2, 3, 141–143, 148–153, 158, 160
possessor roles in Unua *See* possessor argument, possessor roles in Unua
Unua mirror-image ordering *See* mirror-image, Unua mirror-image ordering
Unua-Pangkumu 2, 3, 141

V
Vanuatu 141, 142
verbs 2, 4, 76, 77, 84–97, 105–114 passim, 117, 120, 126, 127, 133–139, 142, 150–152, 163–181, 183–207, 214, 220, 222, 231, 233, 236–240, 249–269, 271–291 passim, 297–308 passim, 314–318, 350–372 passim
V-initial 2, 81, 82, 91, 95f, 124, 163, 170–173, 181, 191, 271, 272f
adverbial verb *See* adverbial, adverbial verb
restructuring verb 168, 174, 175, 178–180, 360f
vocative 2, 231, 232, 240–246
voice (syntax) 78, 84, 105f, 106, 109f, 114, 147, 164–168, 175, 184–187, 198–208 passim, 214, 218, 290, 348, 357, 364f, 365
voice system 214, 348, 357, 364f, 365
voice (phonology)
voice onset time (VOT) 7–10
voice quality 7–10, 18, 20
voicing 7, 11, 16, 18, 19, 66f
vowel harmony 67, 77

W
Welsh 4, 352
word order 2, 4, 71, 81, 82, 84, 163, 170, 181, 191, 217, 222, 228, 229, 231–240, 242, 245f, 271, 272, 275, 278, 281, 286, 289–292 passim, 297–304 passim, 316–318, 324, 346, 350–352, 356, 359
VOS word order 89, 172, 181, 214, 231–233, 236f, 240, 352f, 356
VSO word order 124, 171f, 181, 231–233, 236, 239–242, 245, 271, 272, 282, 289, 352f
inverse order 271, 272, 278, 279, 281–285, 292

Y
Yiddish 349, 354, 371

Z
Zulu 4, 350, 351, 352, 363

Linguistik Aktuell/Linguistics Today

A complete list of titles in this series can be found on the publishers' website, *www.benjamins.com*

174 **LOMASHVILI, Leila:** Complex Predicates. The syntax-morphology interface. *Expected March 2011*
173 **SAPP, Christopher D.:** The Verbal Complex in Subordinate Clauses from Medieval to Modern German. x, 230 pp. + index. *Expected February 2011*
172 **JUNG, Hakyung:** The Syntax of the BE-Possessive. Parametric variation and surface diversities. ca. 275 pp. *Expected March 2011*
171 **SLEEMAN, Petra and Harry PERRIDON (eds.):** The Noun Phrase in Romance and Germanic. Structure, variation, and change. vii, 280 pp. + index. *Expected February 2011*
170 **HUNTER, Tim:** Syntactic Effects of Conjunctivist Semantics. Unifying movement and adjunction. ca. 200 pp. *Expected February 2011*
169 **SÁNCHEZ, Liliana:** The Morphology and Syntax of Topic and Focus. Minimalist inquiries in the Quechua periphery. 2010. xiii, 242 pp.
168 **FELDHAUSEN, Ingo:** Sentential Form and Prosodic Structure of Catalan. 2010. xiii, 285 pp.
167 **MERCADO, Raphael, Eric POTSDAM and Lisa deMena TRAVIS (eds.):** Austronesian and Theoretical Linguistics. 2010. vii, 379 pp.
166 **BRANDT, Patrick and Marco GARCÍA GARCÍA (eds.):** Transitivity. Form, Meaning, Acquisition, and Processing. 2010. vii, 308 pp.
165 **BREUL, Carsten and Edward GÖBBEL (eds.):** Comparative and Contrastive Studies of Information Structure. 2010. xii, 306 pp.
164 **ZWART, Jan-Wouter and Mark de VRIES (eds.):** Structure Preserved. Studies in syntax for Jan Koster. 2010. xxiii, 395 pp.
163 **KIZIAK, Tanja:** Extraction Asymmetries. Experimental evidence from German. 2010. xvi, 273 pp.
162 **BOTT, Oliver:** The Processing of Events. 2010. xvii, 383 pp.
161 **HAAN, Germen J. de:** Studies in West Frisian Grammar. Edited by Jarich Hoekstra, Willem Visser and Goffe Jensma. 2010. x, 384 pp.
160 **MAVROGIORGOS, Marios:** Clitics in Greek. A minimalist account of proclisis and enclisis. 2010. x, 294 pp.
159 **BREITBARTH, Anne, Christopher LUCAS, Sheila WATTS and David WILLIS (eds.):** Continuity and Change in Grammar. 2010. viii, 359 pp.
158 **DUGUINE, Maia, Susana HUIDOBRO and Nerea MADARIAGA (eds.):** Argument Structure and Syntactic Relations. A cross-linguistic perspective. 2010. vi, 348 pp.
157 **FISCHER, Susann:** Word-Order Change as a Source of Grammaticalisation. 2010. ix, 200 pp.
156 **DI SCIULLO, Anna Maria and Virginia HILL (eds.):** Edges, Heads, and Projections. Interface properties. 2010. vii, 265 pp.
155 **SATO, Yosuke:** Minimalist Interfaces. Evidence from Indonesian and Javanese. 2010. xiii, 159 pp.
154 **HORNSTEIN, Norbert and Maria POLINSKY (eds.):** Movement Theory of Control. 2010. vii, 330 pp.
153 **CABREDO HOFHERR, Patricia and Ora MATUSHANSKY (eds.):** Adjectives. Formal analyses in syntax and semantics. 2010. vii, 335 pp.
152 **GALLEGO, Ángel J.:** Phase Theory. 2010. xii, 365 pp.
151 **SUDHOFF, Stefan:** Focus Particles in German. Syntax, prosody, and information structure. 2010. xiii, 335 pp.
150 **EVERAERT, Martin, Tom LENTZ, Hannah de MULDER, Øystein NILSEN and Arjen ZONDERVAN (eds.):** The Linguistics Enterprise. From knowledge of language to knowledge in linguistics. 2010. ix, 379 pp.
149 **AELBRECHT, Lobke:** The Syntactic Licensing of Ellipsis. 2010. xii, 230 pp.
148 **HOGEWEG, Lotte, Helen de HOOP and Andrej MALCHUKOV (eds.):** Cross-linguistic Semantics of Tense, Aspect, and Modality. 2009. vii, 406 pp.
147 **GHOMESHI, Jila, Ileana PAUL and Martina WILTSCHKO (eds.):** Determiners. Universals and variation. 2009. vii, 247 pp.
146 **GELDEREN, Elly van (ed.):** Cyclical Change. 2009. viii, 329 pp.
145 **WESTERGAARD, Marit:** The Acquisition of Word Order. Micro-cues, information structure, and economy. 2009. xii, 245 pp.
144 **PUTNAM, Michael T. (ed.):** Towards a Derivational Syntax. Survive-minimalism. 2009. x, 269 pp.

143 **ROTHMAYR, Antonia:** The Structure of Stative Verbs. 2009. xv, 216 pp.
142 **NUNES, Jairo (ed.):** Minimalist Essays on Brazilian Portuguese Syntax. 2009. vi, 243 pp.
141 **ALEXIADOU, Artemis, Jorge HANKAMER, Thomas McFADDEN, Justin NUGER and Florian SCHÄFER (eds.):** Advances in Comparative Germanic Syntax. 2009. xv, 395 pp.
140 **ROEHRS, Dorian:** Demonstratives and Definite Articles as Nominal Auxiliaries. 2009. xii, 196 pp.
139 **HICKS, Glyn:** The Derivation of Anaphoric Relations. 2009. xii, 309 pp.
138 **SIDDIQI, Daniel:** Syntax within the Word. Economy, allomorphy, and argument selection in Distributed Morphology. 2009. xii, 138 pp.
137 **PFAU, Roland:** Grammar as Processor. A Distributed Morphology account of spontaneous speech errors. 2009. xiii, 372 pp.
136 **KANDYBOWICZ, Jason:** The Grammar of Repetition. Nupe grammar at the syntax–phonology interface. 2008. xiii, 168 pp.
135 **LEWIS, William D., Simin KARIMI, Heidi HARLEY and Scott O. FARRAR (eds.):** Time and Again. Theoretical perspectives on formal linguistics. In honor of D. Terence Langendoen. 2009. xiv, 265 pp.
134 **ARMON-LOTEM, Sharon, Gabi DANON and Susan D. ROTHSTEIN (eds.):** Current Issues in Generative Hebrew Linguistics. 2008. vii, 393 pp.
133 **MACDONALD, Jonathan E.:** The Syntactic Nature of Inner Aspect. A minimalist perspective. 2008. xv, 241 pp.
132 **BIBERAUER, Theresa (ed.):** The Limits of Syntactic Variation. 2008. vii, 521 pp.
131 **DE CAT, Cécile and Katherine DEMUTH (eds.):** The Bantu–Romance Connection. A comparative investigation of verbal agreement, DPs, and information structure. 2008. xix, 355 pp.
130 **KALLULLI, Dalina and Liliane TASMOWSKI (eds.):** Clitic Doubling in the Balkan Languages. 2008. ix, 442 pp.
129 **STURGEON, Anne:** The Left Periphery. The interaction of syntax, pragmatics and prosody in Czech. 2008. xi, 143 pp.
128 **TALEGHANI, Azita H.:** Modality, Aspect and Negation in Persian. 2008. ix, 183 pp.
127 **DURRLEMAN-TAME, Stephanie:** The Syntax of Jamaican Creole. A cartographic perspective. 2008. xii, 190 pp.
126 **SCHÄFER, Florian:** The Syntax of (Anti-)Causatives. External arguments in change-of-state contexts. 2008. xi, 324 pp.
125 **ROTHSTEIN, Björn:** The Perfect Time Span. On the present perfect in German, Swedish and English. 2008. xi, 171 pp.
124 **IHSANE, Tabea:** The Layered DP. Form and meaning of French indefinites. 2008. ix, 260 pp.
123 **STOYANOVA, Marina:** Unique Focus. Languages without multiple wh-questions. 2008. xi, 184 pp.
122 **OOSTERHOF, Albert M.:** The Semantics of Generics in Dutch and Related Languages. 2008. xviii, 286 pp.
121 **TUNGSETH, Mai Ellin:** Verbal Prepositions and Argument Structure. Path, place and possession in Norwegian. 2008. ix, 187 pp.
120 **ASBURY, Anna, Jakub DOTLAČIL, Berit GEHRKE and Rick NOUWEN (eds.):** Syntax and Semantics of Spatial P. 2008. vi, 416 pp.
119 **FORTUNY, Jordi:** The Emergence of Order in Syntax. 2008. viii, 211 pp.
118 **JÄGER, Agnes:** History of German Negation. 2008. ix, 350 pp.
117 **HAUGEN, Jason D.:** Morphology at the Interfaces. Reduplication and Noun Incorporation in Uto-Aztecan. 2008. xv, 257 pp.
116 **ENDO, Yoshio:** Locality and Information Structure. A cartographic approach to Japanese. 2007. x, 235 pp.
115 **PUTNAM, Michael T.:** Scrambling and the Survive Principle. 2007. x, 216 pp.
114 **LEE-SCHOENFELD, Vera:** Beyond Coherence. The syntax of opacity in German. 2007. viii, 206 pp.
113 **EYTHÓRSSON, Thórhallur (ed.):** Grammatical Change and Linguistic Theory. The Rosendal papers. 2008. vi, 441 pp.
112 **AXEL, Katrin:** Studies on Old High German Syntax. Left sentence periphery, verb placement and verb-second. 2007. xii, 364 pp.
111 **EGUREN, Luis and Olga FERNÁNDEZ-SORIANO (eds.):** Coreference, Modality, and Focus. Studies on the syntax–semantics interface. 2007. xii, 239 pp.
110 **ROTHSTEIN, Susan D. (ed.):** Theoretical and Crosslinguistic Approaches to the Semantics of Aspect. 2008. viii, 453 pp.

109 **CHOCANO, Gema:** Narrow Syntax and Phonological Form. Scrambling in the Germanic languages. 2007. x, 333 pp.

108 **REULAND, Eric, Tanmoy BHATTACHARYA and Giorgos SPATHAS (eds.):** Argument Structure. 2007. xviii, 243 pp.

107 **CORVER, Norbert and Jairo NUNES (eds.):** The Copy Theory of Movement. 2007. vi, 388 pp.

106 **DEHÉ, Nicole and Yordanka KAVALOVA (eds.):** Parentheticals. 2007. xii, 314 pp.

105 **HAUMANN, Dagmar:** Adverb Licensing and Clause Structure in English. 2007. ix, 438 pp.

104 **JEONG, Youngmi:** Applicatives. Structure and interpretation from a minimalist perspective. 2007. vii, 144 pp.

103 **WURFF, Wim van der (ed.):** Imperative Clauses in Generative Grammar. Studies in honour of Frits Beukema. 2007. viii, 352 pp.

102 **BAYER, Josef, Tanmoy BHATTACHARYA and M.T. Hany BABU (eds.):** Linguistic Theory and South Asian Languages. Essays in honour of K. A. Jayaseelan. 2007. x, 282 pp.

101 **KARIMI, Simin, Vida SAMIIAN and Wendy K. WILKINS (eds.):** Phrasal and Clausal Architecture. Syntactic derivation and interpretation. In honor of Joseph E. Emonds. 2007. vi, 424 pp.

100 **SCHWABE, Kerstin and Susanne WINKLER (eds.):** On Information Structure, Meaning and Form. Generalizations across languages. 2007. vii, 570 pp.

99 **MARTÍNEZ-GIL, Fernando and Sonia COLINA (eds.):** Optimality-Theoretic Studies in Spanish Phonology. 2007. viii, 564 pp.

98 **PIRES, Acrisio:** The Minimalist Syntax of Defective Domains. Gerunds and infinitives. 2006. xiv, 188 pp.

97 **HARTMANN, Jutta M. and László MOLNÁRFI (eds.):** Comparative Studies in Germanic Syntax. From Afrikaans to Zurich German. 2006. vi, 332 pp.

96 **LYNGFELT, Benjamin and Torgrim SOLSTAD (eds.):** Demoting the Agent. Passive, middle and other voice phenomena. 2006. x, 333 pp.

95 **VOGELEER, Svetlana and Liliane TASMOWSKI (eds.):** Non-definiteness and Plurality. 2006. vi, 358 pp.

94 **ARCHE, María J.:** Individuals in Time. Tense, aspect and the individual/stage distinction. 2006. xiv, 281 pp.

93 **PROGOVAC, Ljiljana, Kate PAESANI, Eugenia CASIELLES and Ellen BARTON (eds.):** The Syntax of Nonsententials. Multidisciplinary perspectives. 2006. x, 372 pp.

92 **BOECKX, Cedric (ed.):** Agreement Systems. 2006. ix, 346 pp.

91 **BOECKX, Cedric (ed.):** Minimalist Essays. 2006. xvi, 399 pp.

90 **DALMI, Gréte:** The Role of Agreement in Non-Finite Predication. 2005. xvi, 222 pp.

89 **VELDE, John R. te:** Deriving Coordinate Symmetries. A phase-based approach integrating Select, Merge, Copy and Match. 2006. x, 385 pp.

88 **MOHR, Sabine:** Clausal Architecture and Subject Positions. Impersonal constructions in the Germanic languages. 2005. viii, 207 pp.

87 **JULIEN, Marit:** Nominal Phrases from a Scandinavian Perspective. 2005. xvi, 348 pp.

86 **COSTA, João and Maria Cristina FIGUEIREDO SILVA (eds.):** Studies on Agreement. 2006. vi, 285 pp.

85 **MIKKELSEN, Line:** Copular Clauses. Specification, predication and equation. 2005. viii, 210 pp.

84 **PAFEL, Jürgen:** Quantifier Scope in German. 2006. xvi, 312 pp.

83 **SCHWEIKERT, Walter:** The Order of Prepositional Phrases in the Structure of the Clause. 2005. xii, 338 pp.

82 **QUINN, Heidi:** The Distribution of Pronoun Case Forms in English. 2005. xii, 409 pp.

81 **FUSS, Eric:** The Rise of Agreement. A formal approach to the syntax and grammaticalization of verbal inflection. 2005. xii, 336 pp.

80 **BURKHARDT SCHUMACHER, Petra:** The Syntax–Discourse Interface. Representing and interpreting dependency. 2005. xii, 259 pp.

79 **SCHMID, Tanja:** Infinitival Syntax. Infinitivus Pro Participio as a repair strategy. 2005. xiv, 251 pp.

78 **DIKKEN, Marcel den and Christina TORTORA (eds.):** The Function of Function Words and Functional Categories. 2005. vii, 292 pp.

77 **ÖZTÜRK, Balkız:** Case, Referentiality and Phrase Structure. 2005. x, 268 pp.

76 **STAVROU, Melita and Arhonto TERZI (eds.):** Advances in Greek Generative Syntax. In honor of Dimitra Theophanopoulou-Kontou. 2005. viii, 366 pp.

75 **DI SCIULLO, Anna Maria (ed.):** UG and External Systems. Language, brain and computation. 2005. xviii, 398 pp.

74 HEGGIE, Lorie and Francisco ORDÓÑEZ (eds.): Clitic and Affix Combinations. Theoretical perspectives. 2005. viii, 390 pp.

73 CARNIE, Andrew, Heidi HARLEY and Sheila Ann DOOLEY (eds.): Verb First. On the syntax of verb-initial languages. 2005. xiv, 434 pp.

72 FUSS, Eric and Carola TRIPS (eds.): Diachronic Clues to Synchronic Grammar. 2004. viii, 228 pp.

71 GELDEREN, Elly van: Grammaticalization as Economy. 2004. xvi, 320 pp.

70 AUSTIN, Jennifer R., Stefan ENGELBERG and Gisa RAUH (eds.): Adverbials. The interplay between meaning, context, and syntactic structure. 2004. x, 346 pp.

69 KISS, Katalin É. and Henk van RIEMSDIJK (eds.): Verb Clusters. A study of Hungarian, German and Dutch. 2004. vi, 514 pp.

68 BREUL, Carsten: Focus Structure in Generative Grammar. An integrated syntactic, semantic and intonational approach. 2004. x, 432 pp.

67 MIŠESKA TOMIĆ, Olga (ed.): Balkan Syntax and Semantics. 2004. xvi, 499 pp.

66 GROHMANN, Kleanthes K.: Prolific Domains. On the Anti-Locality of movement dependencies. 2003. xvi, 372 pp.

65 MANNINEN, Satu Helena: Small Phrase Layers. A study of Finnish Manner Adverbials. 2003. xii, 275 pp.

64 BOECKX, Cedric and Kleanthes K. GROHMANN (eds.): Multiple Wh-Fronting. 2003. x, 292 pp.

63 BOECKX, Cedric: Islands and Chains. Resumption as stranding. 2003. xii, 224 pp.

62 CARNIE, Andrew, Heidi HARLEY and MaryAnn WILLIE (eds.): Formal Approaches to Function in Grammar. In honor of Eloise Jelinek. 2003. xii, 378 pp.

61 SCHWABE, Kerstin and Susanne WINKLER (eds.): The Interfaces. Deriving and interpreting omitted structures. 2003. vi, 403 pp.

60 TRIPS, Carola: From OV to VO in Early Middle English. 2002. xiv, 359 pp.

59 DEHÉ, Nicole: Particle Verbs in English. Syntax, information structure and intonation. 2002. xii, 305 pp.

58 DI SCIULLO, Anna Maria (ed.): Asymmetry in Grammar. Volume 2: Morphology, phonology, acquisition. 2003. vi, 309 pp.

57 DI SCIULLO, Anna Maria (ed.): Asymmetry in Grammar. Volume 1: Syntax and semantics. 2003. vi, 405 pp.

56 COENE, Martine and Yves D'HULST (eds.): From NP to DP. Volume 2: The expression of possession in noun phrases. 2003. x, 295 pp.

55 COENE, Martine and Yves D'HULST (eds.): From NP to DP. Volume 1: The syntax and semantics of noun phrases. 2003. vi, 362 pp.

54 BAPTISTA, Marlyse: The Syntax of Cape Verdean Creole. The Sotavento varieties. 2003. xxii, 294 pp. (incl. CD-rom).

53 ZWART, Jan-Wouter and Werner ABRAHAM (eds.): Studies in Comparative Germanic Syntax. Proceedings from the 15th Workshop on Comparative Germanic Syntax (Groningen, May 26–27, 2000). 2002. xiv, 407 pp.

52 SIMON, Horst J. and Heike WIESE (eds.): Pronouns – Grammar and Representation. 2002. xii, 294 pp.

51 GERLACH, Birgit: Clitics between Syntax and Lexicon. 2002. xii, 282 pp.

50 STEINBACH, Markus: Middle Voice. A comparative study in the syntax-semantics interface of German. 2002. xii, 340 pp.

49 ALEXIADOU, Artemis (ed.): Theoretical Approaches to Universals. 2002. viii, 319 pp.

48 ALEXIADOU, Artemis, Elena ANAGNOSTOPOULOU, Sjef BARBIERS and Hans-Martin GÄRTNER (eds.): Dimensions of Movement. From features to remnants. 2002. vi, 345 pp.

47 BARBIERS, Sjef, Frits BEUKEMA and Wim van der WURFF (eds.): Modality and its Interaction with the Verbal System. 2002. x, 290 pp.

46 PANAGIOTIDIS, E. Phoevos: Pronouns, Clitics and Empty Nouns. 'Pronominality' and licensing in syntax. 2002. x, 214 pp.

45 ABRAHAM, Werner and Jan-Wouter ZWART (eds.): Issues in Formal German(ic) Typology. 2002. xviii, 336 pp.

44 TAYLAN, Eser Erguvanlı (ed.): The Verb in Turkish. 2002. xviii, 267 pp.

43 FEATHERSTON, Sam: Empty Categories in Sentence Processing. 2001. xvi, 279 pp.

42 ALEXIADOU, Artemis: Functional Structure in Nominals. Nominalization and ergativity. 2001. x, 233 pp.

41 ZELLER, Jochen: Particle Verbs and Local Domains. 2001. xii, 325 pp.